JACK &LEM

JOHN F. KENNEDY AND LEM BILLINGS
THE UNTOLD STORY OF AN EXTRAORDINARY FRIENDSHIP

David Pitts

CARROLL & GRAF PUBLISHERS
NEW YORK

JACK AND LEM
John F. Kennedy and Lem Billings: The Untold Story of an Extraordinary Friendship

Carroll & Graf Publishers
An Imprint of Avalon Publishing Group, Inc.
245 West 17th Street, 11th Floor
New York, NY 10011

AVALON
publishing group incorporated

ISBN-13: 978-0-78671-989-1
ISBN-10: 0-7867-1989-3

9 8 7 6 5 4 3 2 1

Interior design by *Ivelisse Robles Marrero*

Printed in the United States of America
Distributed by Publishers Group West

For more information, and to hear a short phone call between Jack and Lem, please visit www.jackandlem.com.

For my mother, Rachel (1921–2005)
Who believed in JFK and me

Contents

Preface

༄

On the morning of January 21, 1961, I was in the living room of my parents' home in Manchester, England. There was little daytime television in the country then. But I noticed in the newspaper that one of the two networks was showing a videotape of the inaugural address of President John F. Kennedy. Americans had been able to watch it live the day before, but in those days before satellite transmissions, videotape arrived by airplane much delayed. At thirteen, I was interested, but not very interested, in the events across the pond. Probably because I had nothing better to do that day, I switched on the television to watch the new American president.

I recall that as John Kennedy began talking, I was almost instantly riveted by the man and his message. My mother was in the room at the time. Not being similarly persuaded, she switched on the vacuum cleaner, drowning out a section of the president's speech. Fortunately, I was able to convince her to switch it off, so I was able to hear most of it. I remember saying to her, "This guy sounds different, Mom" (or maybe it was, "This bloke sounds different"). In a very real sense, the seed for this book was planted on that day forty-five years ago. In the ensuing four and a half decades, I devoured all the information I could get my hands on about John Kennedy, which included the many television documentaries as well as books and newspaper articles. I was not always impressed with what I eventually learned about him, particularly after a U.S. Senate committee during the mid-1970s detailed the existence of largescale covert operations against Cuba, including sabotage, long after the Bay of Pigs invasion early in his administration ended in failure. Nevertheless, I remained fascinated by the man and his legacy and generally approving of his presidency, particularly in light of the caliber of leaders who followed him.

In fact, Camelot was part of the reason I emigrated right after college. It was the thing to do then, although most Brits who left went to Canada or Australia, not the United States. The British government charitably referred to us as "the brain drain." I arrived in the United States in 1969 and have been writing about America in America ever since. When I left full-time journalism in 2003, I knew I would write a John Kennedy book. When I told friends of my intention, however, the general reaction was: not *another* JFK book? What is to be written that has not already been written? It was a good question, especially since I wanted to write a book about JFK's political legacy, a territory well traveled by scores of other authors. At a minimum, I thought I should tell a story about JFK that had never been told before.

In reading JFK books over the years, I had become aware of a man named Lem Billings, who was identified as John Kennedy's best friend from his days at prep school. The two men remained close until JFK was killed in Dallas. A few authors interviewed Lem before his death in 1981, seeking out additional information about JFK. But there was little about Lem himself in the various books, probably because he was not a member of the Kennedy administration. The role he played in John Kennedy's life seemed important but was obscure. I was curious. *Here's my book,* I told myself. Why not explore the friendship between the two men and no doubt uncover Lem's hitherto unknown influence on JFK's political philosophy? I was sure Lem was a key player, since I could not conceive of JFK maintaining a close friendship with any man who was not political.

It was not to be. As I began research for the book and started interviewing people who'd known them both, I quickly learned that politics—in the conventional sense of that word—played only an indirect role in the friendship between John Kennedy and Lem Billings. I discovered that their attachment was much deeper and was rooted not in politics but in fundamental human needs. It flourished despite their differing interests and temperaments, as friendships often do. Everyone close to them witnessed their mysterious bond, although few claim to have fully understood it. For most of JFK's inner political circle, Lem was an enigma.

That is not to say, however, that Lem had no political function in JFK's life. Although he had little interest in policy or the workings of government, Lem played a crucial role in listening to JFK vent during the great events of his presidency, most critically during the 1962 Cuban Missile Crisis. During those thirteen days, Lem encouraged JFK to have confidence in his own instincts rather than to follow the near-unanimous advice he received to mount an invasion of Cuba, an action that we now know would almost assuredly have led to nuclear war. John Kennedy's absolute trust in Lem and comfort level in discussing matters with him freely and candidly—in a way he could not do with aides and advisors—helped reassure the president at a time of maximum danger. No one, I learned, could stiffen JFK's resolve and improve his mood, political or otherwise, quite like Lem Billings.

Lem's role behind the scenes at the White House in soothing the president and nurturing his self-confidence, which has not been known until now, was not inconsequential for someone close to a leader with his finger on the nuclear button. And it should not be unimportant to historians, even though Lem clearly was not someone to whom JFK routinely turned for detailed advice on politics in the way he did, for example, with Ted Sorensen. Lem Billings played a much larger and more complex role in John Kennedy's life than that of political advisor. He was JFK's oldest and best friend. Inevitably, politics was part of their friendship, especially in the later years, but it was far from being the glue that held them together.

So this turned out to be, not just another political book about JFK after all, but rather the story of a profoundly close friendship between two men, one of whom happened to become "the most charismatic leader in our nation's history," in the words of author Seymour Hersh. It is, in effect, a love story that is unknown to most Americans. In a way, I'm glad the book turned out to be different than I intended. I already knew a great deal about the public record of John Kennedy the politician and president. I knew much less about John Kennedy the man. Through following the story and exploring his friendship with Lem, I think I have come to know him better. After reading the book, I hope the reader will feel that way, too.

Introduction

◠

"The courage of life is often a less dramatic spectacle than the courage of a final moment, but it is no less a magnificent mixture of triumph and tragedy."
—John F. Kennedy, *Profiles in Courage*

As the motorcade carrying President John F. Kennedy and his wife crawled through central Dallas, welcomed by huge crowds, fifteen hundred miles away in New York City, the president's best and closest friend for more than thirty years was getting ready to take lunch away from his job as an executive at the Manhattan advertising firm of Lennen & Newell.

Not long before two, eastern standard time, on the afternoon of November 22, 1963, Lem returned to his office on Madison Avenue. There appeared to be some confusion on the streets. As he walked through the lobby doors of the building, he witnessed total chaos. Something had happened. People were streaming out of the building and onto the streets. Some looked stunned and shocked, exhibiting blank stares. Others were visibly upset, with tears streaming down their cheeks.

A familiar face appeared in front of Lem and said, "I'm so sorry about the president." And then he knew. He knew that something very bad had happened.

Not knowing what to do, Lem, oblivious to everything around him, went back out onto the streets and began walking north along Madison Avenue. Eventually, he found himself on Fifth Avenue at Fifty-first Street in front of St. Patrick's Cathedral. He went inside and quietly prayed for Jack, sensing but not really knowing that from this point on his life would never be the same again. Despite the enormity of the event, however, he did not fall apart. He knew he would have to hold himself together. For him and for the Kennedy family, a terrible personal tragedy had occurred. But it also was a national calamity of enormous proportions. He knew he would have to be strong for the Kennedy family as the eyes of the world became riveted on them.

Even though he was bewildered, unable to fully process what had happened, Lem was thinking of what Jackie, who could so easily have been killed as well, and the rest of Jack's family must be going through—Jack's sisters and brothers, whom Lem had known since they were kids, and of course Jack's mother and father, Joe and Rose. Lem talked on the phone with Jack's sister Eunice, who happened to be at the White House when the shooting occurred. They didn't need to say much. Eunice and Lem had adored each other since they first met in the early 1930s when Jack brought Lem home to the Kennedy estate in Palm Beach. They both knew only too well what each was feeling. Instead, they concentrated on what needed to be done. Despite his state of shock, Lem offered to fly to Santa Monica to accompany Jack's sister, Pat, and her husband, movie actor Peter Lawford, back to Washington. But Eunice told him that it wasn't necessary, that Bobby had already arranged a flight. Lem and Eunice ended their phone call knowing that unbearable days in the nation's capital lay ahead.

In Lem's datebook for November 22, 1963, there is the following: "2-30-S. Smith 3021 Park," after which is added one word: "canceled." As the reality of what had happened sank in, Lem finally began to shed tears. During these terrible moments, his mind must have reeled back through the decades to a happy and carefree time when a friendship formed that would become the central relationship in his life. No one knows precisely what went through his mind on this, the worst day of his life, but it's probably safe to assume he thought about the first time he met John Kennedy—at Choate Preparatory School for Boys.

This is the story of John F. Kennedy and his best friend, Kirk LeMoyne Billings. It is largely unknown to the public and yet crucial to understanding who Jack Kennedy was. Jack and Lem met at Choate in 1933 when they were both teenagers. They became friends almost immediately, drawn to each other by their mutual distaste for their school and its headmaster. Not long after they met, Jack learned that Lem was what today we would call a gay man. Despite his own heterosexuality, Jack didn't reject Lem. Their friendship lasted thirty more years—until the gunfire in Dallas.

During school vacations, Jack would invite Lem to his parents' home either in Palm Beach or Hyannis Port. They took a summerlong vacation together in Europe in 1937 as the continent drifted toward war. They also went to the same college for a while. They were together—driving in Washington, D.C.—when they heard the news on the car radio that Pearl Harbor had been attacked. Though they followed different paths during World War II, they remained in regular contact during the conflict.

"It's hard to describe it as just friendship; it was a complete liberation of the spirit," said Eunice Kennedy Shriver. "I think that's what Lem did for President Kennedy. President Kennedy was a completely liberated man when he was with Lem."

Their friendship emerged from their wartime experiences stronger than ever, and Lem was by Jack's side as he began his rapid political ascent from election to the House of Representatives in 1946, through his time in the Senate beginning in 1953, and finally during his years at the pinnacle of power in the White House in the early 1960s. Jack married Jacqueline Bouvier in 1953 at the age of thirty-six, but Lem remained a lifelong bachelor, devoted to John F. Kennedy till the day he died.

Lem often stayed with President Kennedy and Jackie at the White House—he had his own room there—and was a regular guest at the Kennedys' country home in Glen Ora in nearby Virginia. He also traveled with Jack during the White House years. He accompanied the president on his first European trip, when he met Russian leader Nikita Khrushchev in Vienna, and also on the last trip to Europe, during the summer of 1963, when Jack gave his famous "Ich bin ein Berliner" speech.

When they were apart, especially during their formative years, Jack and Lem exchanged hundreds of letters and telegrams, which are extraordinarily candid and indicative of their closeness. Some are teasing and playful. Others are serious and reflective. Amazingly, they kept most of the letters. These letters provide a remarkable record of the depth and scope of their friendship at this time and so are quoted from extensively in the earlier chapters of the book. (It should also be noted, however, that both men were prolific letter writers and corresponded with many other people in addition to each other.)

Jack and Lem's friendship was accepted by Jacqueline Kennedy and the Kennedy family, as well as by others who were close to John Kennedy. Jack's parents and brothers and sisters, in particular, adored Lem. Jackie, too, remained fond of him, although she was sometimes frustrated by his omnipresence. However, not everyone outside the Kennedy family liked Lem. He had a high-pitched voice, which could be irritating to some. Jack's political advisors, especially, considered him to be a lightweight. But everyone knew he was Jack's best friend and that was that. They accepted Lem even if they didn't always approve of him.

Kirk LeMoyne Billings was born in Pittsburgh, Pennsylvania, in 1916, the second son of Josh, a prominent physician, and Romaine. The family had strong roots in the United States, going back to the arrival of the *Mayflower*. There were links on one side of the family to George Washington. It was a Protestant family proud of its ancestral and religious heritage. They were well-to-do, but not rich.

John Fitzgerald Kennedy was born in 1917 in Brookline, Massachusetts, the second son of Rose and Joseph Kennedy. The family was Irish American; their ancestors had fled to the United States in the 1840s during the potato famine. It was a Catholic family that had suffered discrimination in a city then dominated by prominent Protestant Yankee families. In contrast to the Billingses, the Kennedys were superrich.

Nevertheless, both families could afford to send their children to private schools. Jack and Lem's worlds came together in the depths of the Great Depression at one of the most prestigious preparatory schools in the nation—Choate, in Wallingford, Connecticut. It was there, the evidence indicates, that Jack first learned that Lem was gay.

Despite their closeness, little attention has been paid to the role that Lem Billings played in the life of a president who lingers in the American imagination. He is a shadowy figure who appears only briefly in books published about President Kennedy's life, most likely because he played no formal role in the Kennedy administration. Before his death—in 1981 at the age of sixty-five—he was mostly asked questions about JFK, not about his own life.

In some publications, Lem is portrayed as a kind of court jester. Gore Vidal referred to him in his memoir as "Jack's slave" and "chief faggot at Camelot." Still others have suggested that the friendship was one-sided, with Lem always in pursuit of time with Jack. Many of Jack's political friends confess to having been mystified by his friendship with Lem. In reality, it was far more complicated than many people who were close to them realized. After all, Jack and Lem were best friends for twenty-seven years before Jack was elected president.

Their friendship, far from being one-sided, was deeply mutual and important to both men. "Lem was President Kennedy's best friend and it was my opinion the feeling was mutual," said Eunice Kennedy Shriver. That is why no profile of John F. Kennedy—and his place in history—can be complete without a full understanding of the role Lem Billings played in his life.

For some, the fact that John Kennedy's best friend for three decades was gay will be shocking and will be yet another reason to debunk the Kennedy legend. But for most people, those who subscribe to contemporary values and standards, I believe it will raise their estimation of the thirty-fifth president. That John Kennedy maintained a deep friendship with a man whom he knew to be gay and did so in an age of homophobia—at great potential risk to his political career and reputation—is an extraordinary demonstration of loyalty and commitment.

As far as Lem is concerned, it would have been inappropriate to cite his sexual orientation while he was alive, given his decision to keep it private. But it has now been more than twenty-five years since his death. Many Americans, hopefully most, now view a person's sexual preference as nothing to be either ashamed or proud of, but merely as a fact of life that says something about a person, but by no means everything. Now the time has come to tell his story and his love for a president in all its richness, without the stereotypes, caricatures, and innuendo, before it is lost to history.

Although Lem was his best friend, John Kennedy nurtured many other friendships over the years, not dealt with in detail in this book—including with Ted Sorensen, Ben Bradlee, Chuck Spalding, Bill Walton, Torby Macdonald, Rip Horton, Dave Powers, Paul ("Red") Fay, Charlie Bartlett, David Ormsby-Gore, Kenny O'Donnell, Larry O'Brien, and many others. These people were close to him as well and their roles in his life were significant. John Kennedy wanted and needed people around him who appealed to different parts of his personality. He had an enormous gift for friendship with a wide range of individuals. In telling the story of Jack and Lem's friendship, there is no intention to diminish the importance of the other people in John Kennedy's life.

Had he lived, John F. Kennedy would have been ninety in May 2007, a sobering thought for a generation that came of age during his "New Frontier" and now is beyond middle age. It is a generation that cannot forget him even though more than four decades have passed since his death. He was just forty-six years old, forever fixed in our memories as a symbol of youth and vitality, and representative of a special time in the history of this nation when everything seemed possible and hope was boundless.

Television came of age during the Kennedy presidency. For the first time, the nation saw its chief executive up close—in moments both formal and informal—captured for all time mostly on grainy black-and-white film and videotape. Who can forget the scenes of John Kennedy in Berlin and Ireland, of he and Jackie sailing off the coast of Cape Cod with their picture-perfect children, John and Caroline, or their dazzling appearances at the White House on state occasions? Inevitably, the video images make the memories of John Kennedy more vivid; the events of his life seem so much more real.

But the sense of loss on hearing the news of his death went deeper than that. John Kennedy's appeal was much more substantive than the creation of an image through a television camera, went beyond glamour and style, was largely unconnected to our sadness at the tragedy of an administration cut short by assassination. After all, no one today much remembers McKinley or Garfield.

John Kennedy seemed to touch something deep within us all. He represented a new form of leadership, a break with the pomposity and piety of the past, an embrace of a more vital form of idealism. He aimed so high. The disappointments he faced, both in public and in private, seemed to mirror the frustration we all feel when we try to stretch our capabilities and enlarge our concern.

Simply put, people identified, or wanted to identify, with John Kennedy—and not just people of his generation. In part because of the television images, young people, too, are curious about him and his legacy. So great was his impact in the very different world of the early 1960s, that the legend, the mystique, of his one thousand days as president of the United States has been passed down through the generations. Even though more than half of all Americans alive today were born after his death, and even though his presidency was one of the shortest in American history, he remains a vivid presence in our national psyche.

In poll after poll, he is rated among the top three presidents ever elected, even though historians consider his accomplishments to be relatively modest. Despite the brevity of his time in office, his name is identified with an entire era, remembered by many as a more glamorous and even gallant age. It was, we now know, the last decade in which liberalism dominated American life—a far cry from the conservative, some would say reactionary, political climate prevalent today. And that may be a major reason why John Kennedy remains vivid in our imagination—because we have lost what we were and are uncomfortable with what we have become.

The passage of time has inevitably resulted in a reevaluation of his accomplishments. We have learned to separate his rhetoric from his actions, his vision from his policies, his private behavior from his public record. He made grave mistakes, some of which would not become fully apparent until years after his death. But it is also true that Kennedy faced unprecedented challenges in the postwar world at home and abroad. Despite his misjudgments and missteps, his policies generated a new spirit of hope across the land and beyond our shores.

Kennedy set high standards and lofty objectives that were not always attained. But it is neither the achievements nor the failures of the Kennedy political record that we remember, or even the contradictions in this most complicated of men. What we remember is that John

Kennedy made us feel we could remake the world, that we could create our own destiny on this planet, that mankind is not doomed, that "on earth," as he said, "God's work must truly be our own." That is no mean accomplishment—despite falling short of his promise, as we all do.

We forget today that Kennedy mania was an international as well as a national phenomenon. He was as popular overseas as he was in his own country, and for two years and ten months America's reputation glowed more brightly around the world than at any time before or since. To Europeans, he seemed the quintessential American ideal—youthful, witty, successful, energetic, optimistic, informal, yet possessing great style. With JFK, it all seemed to come together. When he visited the continent during his final summer of life, Europeans went wild, especially in Ireland, his ancestral birthplace. Yet, it was as much John Kennedy the man they loved as John Kennedy the president.

In the years since he was murdered, scores of books and films have tried to explain John Kennedy, with varying degrees of success. And yet there remains a thirst for more, testimony to the fact that we still are not fully satisfied that we know who he was and how he came to dominate his age so completely and to set a standard for leadership still emulated—but unmatched—today.

This book is not another exhaustive history of the Kennedy political record—from the disastrous Bay of Pigs invasion of Cuba early in his administration to the triumph of the Nuclear Test Ban Treaty just prior to its end. Nor is it yet another attempt to tell the full story of the Kennedy family and John Kennedy's place in it, replete with every revelation about his personal life that has been detailed over and over again in recent years. Rather, this book focuses on the central friendship in John Kennedy's life—with Kirk LeMoyne Billings.

Since Jack and Lem's friendship formed early in life—decades before John Kennedy became president—this book necessarily emphasizes the earlier period. But it also covers John F. Kennedy's rise to power and ultimately to the presidency. Lem continued to be an essential part of Jack's life after his victory in the 1960 election despite having no formal position in the Kennedy administration. President Kennedy got together with Lem often during the White House years in much the same way he always had. Lem remained as devoted as ever. In later years, he admitted that he had loved John Kennedy all his life. According to people who knew him, he never got over the assassination and became a much-diminished man in the years after Dallas.

Jack and Lem fills in one of the few chapters still unexplored in the life of John F. Kennedy. Most of all, it is a great human story of a friendship that grew and survived—against the odds—during a period of unparalleled glamour and idealism but also of rampant prejudice. That a friendship between a major public figure, eventually a president, and a gay man flourished during this era is an astonishing demonstration of the courage and strength of both men. It was apparent from my interviews for the book that Jack and Lem also had an enormous capacity for friendship with others as well as each other, inspiring a degree of affection and loyalty decades after their deaths that is remarkable and rare. It is clear that John Kennedy was no ordinary president, and Lem Billings no ordinary man.

President Kennedy was an avid and fast reader who devoured books of all kinds. He once complained, however, that he was "reading more and enjoying it less." At the risk of being presumptuous, I believe this might be one of the books he would enjoy were he alive today. It is a story that could not be told in his time but that can only add to our understanding of him as a man, and as a president, in our time.

PART ONE

❧

The Earlier Period

1

THE TIES THAT BIND
(CHOATE, 1933–35)

"Oh God, the sea is so great and my boat is so small."
—John F. Kennedy, May 23, 1963, quoting an old Breton prayer

It was a friendship that took off from the start. Within days of first meeting each other, Jack Kennedy and Lem Billings were inseparable, the beginning of a lifelong bond that deepened over the following three decades.

At some point, however, probably not long after they met, Lem's feelings for Jack went beyond friendship. Lem fell in love with Jack and sought to have sexual relations with him. Jack rejected the sexual overture, but not the friendship. Unlike many teen friendships, which fade over the years, theirs endured despite the difference in how they felt about each other.

The year was 1933, a time of pivotal change both in the United States and in Europe. But worldly concerns were not foremost in the minds of young Jack and Lem in the spring of that year. Doing well in their studies—enough to satisfy their families, anyway—and having a good time were their top priorities, as is typical of most young people at this stage of life.

Lem was sixteen, and Jack was fifteen, when they met while working on the school yearbook at Choate School for Boys, the prestigious New England preparatory school located in Wallingford, Connecticut. It was founded in 1896 by Mary Atwater Choate and her husband, Judge William G. Choate. Jack had just been elected to the business board of "The Brief," as the school yearbook was called. Lem had joined the previous year.

From all accounts, it was instant friendship. They were bound together by a love of fun and practical jokes, resentment of Choate, and envy of their higher-achieving elder siblings—Joe, Jack's brother, and Josh, Lem's brother. Both older brothers were also at Choate, an elite institution patterned on spartan, forbidding private schools in England, such as Eton and Harrow.

Lem and Jack, winter term, Choate, 1934.

Jack and Lem, however, were anything but forbidding. They were full of life, fun loving, and disrespectful of empty tradition and meaningless ceremony. Their high spirits contrasted with the dour ambience of the school and they frequently got in trouble, incidents galore that only served to bring them closer together. These harmless pranks cemented the friendship. Lem's "lifelong friendship with Jack grew out of carefree early escapades at Choate," said Edward (Teddy) Kennedy, Jack's youngest brother.

For Jack, Lem became the first close friend he had outside of his large, active family. He loved Lem's spontaneity, joie de vivre, and huge, raucous laugh. He also liked Lem's genuineness. There was nothing pretentious about Lem, according to Ethel Kennedy, who got to know him later. "Forgoing cynicism, he saw the ridiculousness of the human condition and parodied it until tears ran down his cheeks (and yours) and an asthmatic coughing fit ended his glee," she said. Lem's rebellious, devil-may-care attitude seemed to mesh perfectly with Jack's view of life. In Jack's opinion, most people took themselves much too seriously. Lem was one human being who clearly did not.

For Lem, Jack was funny and mischievous—a risk taker like himself—who liked nothing more than to flout rules for which he saw no useful purpose and to rebel against authority of any kind. Jack's sense of humor was more cerebral than his own, but they both loved to laugh and often found the same things funny, especially pomposity and arrogance. "Jack had the best sense of humor of anybody I've known in my life," said Lem. "And I don't think I've known anybody who was as much fun." They soon developed a fierce loyalty to each other, a bond of trust that no one—certainly not the headmaster of Choate at the time, the austere George St. John—could break.

And try to break it he did, since schools like Choate at that time did not readily tolerate spontaneous, outspoken students of the likes of Jack and Lem. Choate prized discipline instead of a free spirit, rigorous attention to academics instead of originality of thought, group loyalty instead of individual initiative, and stoicism rather than anything that might resemble emotion. Some boys thrived under this kind of regime, but Jack and Lem thought it was stultifying and ridiculous and were determined to resist St. John and his band of uptight schoolmasters.

In later life, however, it would become evident that Choate had left its mark on Jack and Lem. Both men were highly self-disciplined and loathed the expression of emotion in public. They exhibited a shyness and reserve, which they masked with humor—more typical of Europeans than Americans. This was the product, to a large degree, of their years at Choate. But the last thing that Jack and Lem wanted was to become cookie-cutter Choate men, and they resisted anything that would place them in that mold, no matter how hard the school tried. "Jack couldn't or wouldn't conform," remembered Rose Kennedy. "He did pretty much what he wanted, rather than what the school wanted of him."

It was different at Choate for Jack and Lem's older brothers, Joe and Josh. F. Tremaine "Josh" Billings Jr., class of '29, was captain of the varsity football team, a letterman in three sports, president of his class, and editor in chief of *The Brief.* He retains fond memories of his Choate days into his nineties and views his brother's academic achievements—to some degree blaming Lem's friendship with Jack—as less than stellar. Lem's father also thought that Lem was not up to standard, certainly compared with Josh. "My father did try very hard to have me line up as well as my brother in every area and was rather disappointed that I didn't. I tried very hard," Lem remembered.

John Seigenthaler, a reporter for the *Tennessean* who later worked for Bobby Kennedy at the Justice Department and who knew both Josh and Lem, said, "Josh was nothing like Lem. They were totally different personalities and I think Lem got on Josh's nerves a bit although he did love him, from a distance." Lem was less serious; he was full of fun and had a great sense of humor, he added. During Jack's presidency, Jack and Bobby would tell Seigenthaler dozens of stories about Lem. "Often, the stories revolved around a funny quip that Lem had made."

Joseph P. Kennedy Jr., '33, was vice president of a school charity organization and a letterman on the undefeated football team of 1933. Like Josh, Joe, too, viewed his kid brother as insufficiently serious. For a while, especially during the Choate years, Jack and Joe did not get along and rarely saw much of each other in school. In fact, they became closer after they left Choate. Jack seemed to revel in his reputation for being less attentive to his studies than his brother. In December 1934, he wrote to his father, "LeMoyne and I have been talking about how poorly we have done this quarter. I really feel, now that I think it over, that I have been bluffing myself about how much real work I have been doing."

On one occasion, Jack gleefully reported back home that Joe had been paddled, a not unusual punishment in a school of this kind at the time. "He was roughhousing in the hall; a sixth former caught him," Jack said. "He led him in and all the sixth formers had a swat or two. Did the sixth formers lick him? Oh man, he was all blisters. They paddled the life out of him. What I wouldn't have given to be a sixth former." Jack might have gotten a kick out of Joe being on the receiving end of corporal punishment, but years later when he was president, he declined an invitation by a reporter to endorse corporal punishment in schools.

Jack and Lem knew that their elder brothers were more highly prized at Choate by the headmaster, among others, and were considered distinctly better students. And both knew that their fathers held their eldest sons in greater esteem; they frequently praised them for their accomplishments while neglecting Jack and Lem. In point of fact, Jack and Lem's academic records were not markedly different from those of their elder brothers. Choate's records reveal, for example, that Jack had a grade point average of 73, compared to 75 for Joe. But it is certainly true that they projected a lack of interest in formal study and disrespect for the school's regimen.

In fact, however, both Jack and Lem were intellectually curious and shared an interest in all manner of subjects, especially history. This was another characteristic the boys had in common. Almost everyone who met Jack remarked on his curiosity and his constant interest in asking questions rather than giving answers. Lem, too, "burned with curiosity about everything and everyone," even in later life, said Robert F. Kennedy Jr. Both boys developed a particular interest in biography, especially historical biography, which they consumed in large quantities. But they never could endorse Choate's regimented, authoritarian approach to education and hated the school's archaic rules and regulations. They were committed to flouting them at every opportunity.

Fortunately, the school did not succeed, as some schools do, in turning off Jack and Lem from learning and study. Jack was the only boy Lem knew at Choate, for example, to have a subscription to the *New York Times*. He read it assiduously every day, even though he was only in his early teens. Lem remembers Jack reading as much as he could whenever he got the chance. He was sick and confined to bed so much as a child that there were many such opportunities. Books became his consolation, fueling his legendary curiosity. "All my life, sometimes when I wanted to talk with him, he would be reading," recalled Lem, a decade after Jack's death. "My picture of him still is seeing him reading."

Jack's bookishness was encouraged by both Rose and Joe. They thought it was important for their children to be aware of the world around them. Lem's parents, too, pressed their children to succeed, although perhaps not quite as relentlessly as the Kennedy family. Feeling the pressures from school and family, Jack and Lem put their faith in each other, developing an impenetrable defense against the outside world and drawing energy and support from the time they spent in each other's company. "Together, they really had everything," said Robert F. Kennedy Jr. "They loved each other and they got satisfaction out of the successes that each of them enjoyed."

According to Lem's niece, Sally Carpenter, one series of boys' books that interested them both when they were younger was Billy Whiskers, the name of a playful goat that is always getting into mischief. Probably because Lem reminded Jack of Billy Whiskers, Jack's favorite nickname for his friend, one of many, was Billy Billings. Other names Jack used were Lemmer, Leem, or Moynie, and even Delemma, and LeMoan. Lem's names for Jack included Ken or Kenadosus, and, when he was feeling less charitable, Ratface. He also frequently called him Johnny.

In some ways, Jack and Lem were unlikely comrades. Lem was two inches taller at six feet two inches, and much stockier, 175 pounds to Jack's 155 pounds. Lem was also gawkier and more awkward looking. He had a high forehead, wore thick glasses necessitated by his terrible eyesight, and had a high-pitched voice. Jack was leaner and better looking, with the killer smile that would later seduce millions. But in these early years he often looked painfully thin and gaunt and often weighed even less than his standard 155 pounds.

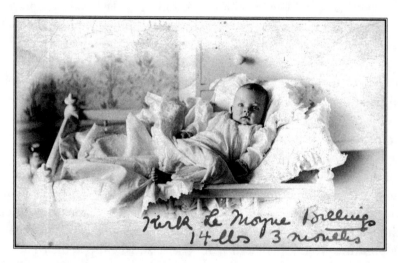

Lem, age three months, 1916.

The two boys came from different backgrounds, as well. Jack was Catholic. Lem was Protestant. Jack's American Irish ancestry went back only to the nineteenth century, whereas Lem's ancestors dated back to the early years of the Republic and before. Jack's family was subjected to rampant discrimination in Boston at a time when No Irish Need Apply signs were commonplace. Lem's family suffered no prejudice of any kind, although they were active in opposing discrimination against others, particularly African Americans.

There were other differences. The Kennedys eventually prospered in the United States. By the time Jack was born, in 1917, his father was on his way to making his fortune. During the 1920s, especially, Joe Kennedy accumulated vast wealth, mostly in the movie, banking, and liquor businesses. He also speculated in stocks but was wise, or lucky, enough to relinquish many of them before Wall Street crashed in 1929. Even after the Kennedys became wealthy, however, they were by no means fully accepted by the Yankees, the upper-crust New England Protestant families.

Lem's ancestors were professionals, pioneers in the field of medicine. Consequently, they were well-to-do, but not superrich like the Kennedys. Lem's mother, Romaine, was a direct descendant of John LeMoyne, a French physician whose son, Dr. Francis LeMoyne, became a noted abolitionist who established LeMoyne College for African Americans in Memphis, Tennessee. His home was also part of the Underground Railroad, a network of hiding places for runaway slaves from the South. Unlike the Kennedys, the Billingses suffered from the stock market crash. More significantly, Lem's father, Josh Sr., a prominent doctor in Pittsburgh, died in 1933, the year Lem met Jack, placing additional strain on the family's finances.

The death of Lem's father had a profound effect on him, coming as it did when he was a teenager away at school, according to surviving relatives and friends. "He talked a good deal about his father. He was rather proud of him," said Francis McAdoo, a friend of Lem's at Princeton. "He was affected by his father's death and it took him a while to get over it. Then there was the effect on the family finances," said Lem's niece, Sally Carpenter. Jack provided an important distraction for Lem during this difficult first year of their friendship after Josh died.

Romaine, Lem's mother, did what she could to manage the family finances and keep Lem at Choate, but times were difficult. Lem was also very close to her and remained so all his life. He always remembered what she tried to do for him and his sister and brother during the difficult Depression years. Fortunately, she didn't have to worry about tuition costs. Lem obtained a full scholarship at Choate during his later years there, although he was often short of spending money.

Jack would help him out—when he remembered to carry money, that is. But the young Kennedy was notoriously careless about a dollar and would often borrow cash from friends and forget to pay them back, even when he was president. Money just never seemed important to him. Those who knew Jack and Lem said they both were a bit tight with a buck, although if there was one person Jack was generous with, it was Lem.

Perhaps because he had lost his father while still a teenager, Lem gradually became close to the entire Kennedy family, not just Jack. Joe became somewhat of a substitute father to him over the years, especially after Jack began to take Lem home during school vacations. Joe also helped Lem out in various other ways. But it was Jack who was the center of Lem's world. At Choate, Lem increasingly became the center of Jack's world, as well. At this point in his life, Jack needed someone who accepted him uncritically and unconditionally, and just as important, who believed in him. Joe and Rose, for all their virtues, were remote figures once he was enrolled at Choate. They also made demands on Jack academically and in other ways, whereas Lem always accepted Jack, no questions asked.

Rose, particularly, was concerned with imposing discipline as well as offering affection. She was also far more religious than Jack. He was never that comfortable with her religious piety. Sometimes she held herself at arm's length from him and sometimes he did the same with her, a pattern that may have affected his relations with women as he grew older. But the most important fact of his life at this time was that he was away from home in a boys-only boarding school. It is not unusual in schools of this kind, especially those patterned on the overly strict British model, for a boy to form a close friendship with another boy. In that sense, Jack's friendship with Lem was nothing unusual. For Jack, Lem provided the affection and adulation he needed in that kind of environment.

Asked to explain the bond between Jack and Lem, author Gore Vidal, who knew them both and who also went to a boys-only prep school, said, "Jack was charismatic from the age of fourteen on. Everyone wanted to be his buddy. Jack and Lem got to be roommates I think by accident at Choate, and suddenly Lem was his slave. And active, glittering boys like to have slaves around to pick up the pieces. Lem started out doing that and went on doing it to the end of his life, transferring his loyalty after Jack died to other members of the Kennedy family." Others, however, dispute Gore's characterization and portray the friendship more as one of equals. That was certainly the view of Eunice Kennedy Shriver, who met Lem when he was at Choate with Jack. "Lem was always an equal to Jack," she said. "In friendship, you must have an equal amount of affection and respect for one another, and they had that."

The bond between Jack and Lem grew to be so tight that they really had little need for friendships with any of the other boys, although Jack eventually became close to fellow Choater Rip Horton and later developed meaningful friendships with a wide variety of people. On one occasion, Lem spoke about Jack's capacity for friendship. "I certainly don't think he was cold in any way. He had a very warm personality. I think he cared a great deal about people and his feelings of loyalty were far above average. I'd go even further. I never knew anyone with stronger feelings of loyalty." He added: "I think that anytime that he really established in his own mind that a man was his

"To Lem. A neat guy and a swell gent. You're aces with me. Best of luck now and always you horse's 'arse.'"—Jack, Choate, circa 1933.

friend, he never deserted him. His feeling of loyalty to that person never lessened. This was true even when his loyalty was sorely tried."

In a 1985 article, Seymour St. John, who succeeded his father George St. John as headmaster of Choate and who knew Jack and Lem when they were boys at the school, wrote that "their schoolboy banter was humorously critical, devil-may-care, which gave them a protective veneer and a sense of security." He added: "At school, Lem, like Jack, needed a friend. In order to have one, he was ready to follow and applaud Jack in every escapade." The notorious J. J. Maher, Jack and Lem's house-master while they were rooming together at the school, however, was much more critical of the friendship, referring to their "silly, giggling, inseparable companionship." Jack and Lem loathed Maher, a bachelor wedded to discipline, and they were always searching for ways to annoy him. Lem remembered one time when Maher yelled at Jack for taking his trunk down to the cellar after a vacation. There was a great deal of noise as it clunked down the stairs, disturbing the temperamental Maher. He boomed at Jack, telling him that that kind of thing should be done in the morning. So Jack finished moving the trunk the next morning— according to Lem, before sunrise! "Of course, this infuriated the teacher, much to Jack's amusement," Lem said.

The formation of the Muckers Club, which occurred in 1935 during Jack's senior year, was the most serious incident at Choate involving Jack and Lem and nearly resulted in their expulsion. It occurred when they were rooming together in the West Wing dormitory: the case of the "Muckers" versus George St. John, headmaster—nay, absolute dictator of Choate since 1908. It was Jack who persuaded Lem to help him form the Muckers Club at the school. The members were them-selves, Rip Horton, and ten other boys. The name derived from the headmaster's term for any boy who incurred his displeasure, for what-ever reason.

The secret society met nightly in Jack and Lem's room. A prime perk of membership was being able to listen to all the latest records on Jack's old Victrola, which was nevertheless in mint condition. The rebels would gather in his room usually before chapel. By today's stan-dards, the club was harmless and didn't seriously violate any of Choate's important rules. But merely forming it without approval was sufficient to incur St. John's wrath. He would not tolerate nonconformity or rebellion of any kind.

The Choate "Muckers." Rip Horton, Lem, Butch Schrieber, and Jack, 1934.

Unfortunately, St. John learned of the Muckers' existence when one boy squealed on the group's plan to dump a pile of horse manure in the school gym. St. John was furious. He was determined to stamp out the Muckers and set an example. Jack and Lem were particularly vulnerable. They had already earned the school nicknames Public Enemy Number One and Public Enemy Number Two. Jack was Public Enemy Number One. St. John had been fed up with the two boys ever since they started rooming together in the fall semester. Housemaster Maher recommended to St. John that they be separated. St. John considered it, but, perhaps unwisely from his point of view, decided to leave them together. He scribbled a note to himself—"not feasible." But now Jack and Lem had done the unthinkable. They were Muckers, the ringleaders of the most notorious club on campus.

In St. John's bizarre world, this was a capital crime. The thirteen offenders, including Lem and Jack, who made things worse by being late, were summoned to his study and lined up in front of him to await the inevitable sentence. As the ringleaders, Jack and Lem both were singled out. Incredibly, St. John expelled them on the spot for forming an illegal club. Fortunately, however, on reflection he was persuaded to commute their sentence. A sympathetic assistant headmaster persuaded St. John to reduce their punishment to strict probation.

Joe Kennedy learned about the matter, and even though he had just been made chairman of President Franklin Roosevelt's new Securities and Exchange Commission and was busy in Washington, he traveled to Choate to discuss the crisis with St. John. Lem's mother, Romaine, also came from Pittsburgh. It's possible that the critical factor in St. John's change of mind about expelling Jack and Lem was Joe's usefulness to the school. St. John was well aware that Joe Kennedy was a rich man. In a letter to Joe, just a few weeks after Jack enrolled at Choate, St. John, who also knew about Joe's connection to the movie business, lamented the school's lack of a movie projector, coyly asking his advice about what might be done to rectify the situation. Joe got the message. A few weeks later, he sent St. John a brand-new movie projector. It cost $3,500, a princely sum in those days. Needless to say, the movie showings at the school were one of the most popular events with the boys.

Joe's earlier generosity may have saved Jack and Lem from expulsion, but it didn't take the edge off St. John's concern about Jack and Lem's behavior. Years later, he still recalled the Muckers incident with some apparent anger. Jack, he said, "was the chief mover in the group. . . . They weren't wicked kids, but they were a nuisance. At one time, it came to the point where I was saying to myself, 'Well, I have two things to do, one to run the school, another to run Jack Kennedy and his friends.' And they weren't that bad, you know, but they had to be looked after."

For Jack and Lem, it was all much ado about nothing. Commenting on the incident decades later, Lem said of St. John, "He lacked the proper qualities to head up a boys' school. Although he had the ability to raise money and to favorably impress parents, he had absolutely no understanding of young boys in their most important, developing years. He took a very serious and dim view of the way Jack and I behaved. . . . Mr. Kennedy, wise as he was, saw that the headmaster was making too much of little things. Although he wasn't at all pleased with Jack's immature behavior, he never had any interest in the school again after Jack graduated." But Joe never regretted sending Jack to Choate. He "felt strongly that the boys should have a wider knowledge of other people aside from Catholics," remembered Lem. "He felt that the Catholic schools offered too narrowing an education for the boys and that they should go to nonsectarian schools."

"If the Muckers Club would have been mine, you can be sure it would not have started with an *m*," Joe told Jack. But Rose, who took life much more seriously than Joe, was not amused. Three decades later, she recalled the Muckers caper in a television interview with CBS newsman Harry Reasoner. "Jack had to have a good talking-to," she said, "and was told to become more serious about his studies. He did pull up his grades a bit," she said.

In the aftermath of the Muckers incident, St. John arranged for Jack to talk to a psychologist, who reported "that Jack has established a reputation in the family for thoughtlessness, sloppiness, and inefficiency, and he feels entirely at home in the role." He added: "A good deal of his trouble is due to comparison with his older brother." It didn't matter what the psychologist said, however; Jack wasn't going to change. While he was at Choate, he continued to rebel and enlisted Lem in all his schemes. At one point, Jack and Lem sent off letters applying to enlist in the French foreign legion. But St. John intercepted their correspondence and told them that he would put them on a foreign legion diet if such foolishness didn't stop.

Of course, it didn't. May at Choate meant Festivities Weekend. Attendance at the school musical—in 1935, a Gilbert and Sullivan production called *Patience*—was mandatory. But Jack and Lem didn't want to take their dates, Pussy Brooks (Pussy was Lem's date) and Olive Cawley, to what they felt would be an excruciatingly boring event. So they decided to go off campus with a friend in his car, even though this was a severe infringement of yet another Choate rule, and even though both boys were only three weeks away from graduation. They intended to come back and sneak back into the school before the festivities were concluded. It almost proved to be their undoing.

While they were driving around, they noticed a car following them. It turned out to be driven by the school proctors. Jack and Lem and their two dates crouched down in their car while the friend put his foot to the floor in an attempt to elude their pursuers. When they felt they had lost the pursuing car, Jack, Lem, and Olive jumped out and hid in what turned out to be a barnyard. Lem's date, Pussy, stayed in the car with the driver, Pete. Eventually, when they felt the coast was clear, Lem and Olive returned to the vehicle. "Olive rushed out to the car and lay on the floor at Pussy's feet with a coat thrown over her," recalled Lem. "I dashed to the back—Pete opened the trunk—and I jumped in. He closed me in. We didn't dare yell for Jack—so we left him behind." All of them, except Jack, were safely whisked back to school by the driver.

Jack remained hidden in the barn. He eventually walked back to school through two miles of woodland. Fortunately, he was able to sneak back into school unnoticed as well. Both Public Enemy Number One and Public Enemy Number Two survived the ordeal without alerting St. John to a caper that, if discovered, would surely have resulted in their being tossed out of school just before graduation. Their Choate careers would have been dismal failures had they not emerged unscathed from this prank.

Even though Jack met Olive while he was at school and the affair never really became serious, she was one girl with whom he kept in contact till the end of his life, according to Lem. For the most part, however, Jack played the field. "Whenever he was home, there was always a girl around—usually it was a different girl each time," Lem said. "He was very successful in his relationship with girls and, I felt, more successful than I was." He added: "All his life, Jack Kennedy was a ladies' man and he was very interested in anything that had to do with the ladies.

"Almost, without exception, every girl he showed any interest in became very fond of him. I think the reason for this was that he was not only attractive but also he had tremendous interest in girls. They really liked him," said Lem. But Jack never got very involved. He was "primarily interested in dating them at night and didn't want them particularly as friends or pals."

On another occasion, Jack and Lem were driving well over the speed limit. Jack was at the wheel of the car. All his life, he was a notoriously bad driver. Even at Choate as a teenager, he received so many traffic tickets that he was close to having his license revoked. Suddenly, a cop came up behind their speeding car. Sensing trouble and a threat to his license, Jack persuaded Lem to change seats while the car was still moving so that it would be Lem who was at the wheel, and not Jack, when the cop finally pulled them over. The subterfuge, which could have resulted in a horrendous accident, worked. Once again, they barely escaped major trouble.

Some of Jack's pranks had a serious edge, Lem remembered. On one occasion, Jack and Lem were driving with a fellow Choater named Jack

Shinkle, who came from a very wealthy family and harbored deeply racist views, although Lem said he later embraced integration. "I remember we were driving along in the rain one day in Jack's station wagon. I was in the front seat next to Jack, and Shinkle was in the seat immediately behind us. As we drove along, Kennedy saw about six very large Negro laborers who were obviously looking for a ride. It was raining hard and they were dirty and wet, having been sweating all day in a construction gang. Kennedy offered them a lift, asking them to get in the back with Shinkle. They were terribly polite and tried very hard not to crowd Shinkle. . . . They all tried to crowd in the middle seat [in front of Shinkle and behind Jack and Lem]. Kennedy noticed this and said, 'I'm having a little trouble steering, men. There's too much weight in the front. Would you mind, all of you, sitting in the back seat with my friend [Shinkle].' So they all crowded all over Shinkle, sat on him, sat around him and everything else. Shinkle almost died, and we had a very good laugh." Boys like Shinkle soon learned to be more wary of Jack and Lem's penchant for pranks and mischief-making.

Both Rose and Joe knew that Jack and Lem's friendship was part of the problem at Choate. Jack and Lem together spelled much more trouble than Jack and Lem apart. But both parents also knew that the friendship was important to Jack and therefore they accepted it. Even Rose, much more the disciplinarian than Joe, instinctively realized the importance of Lem to Jack even though she didn't necessarily approve of the friendship in the early days. Later on, however, she grew to appreciate Lem, as did all the Kennedy family. Lem "remained Jack's lifelong close friend, confidant, sharer in old memories and new experiences," she wrote.

The two boys also bonded because they were not that popular with most of the other kids in school. Even the charismatic Jack was not so attractive a figure to some of his other school chums at first, especially those who had the misfortune of being on the receiving end of Jack's barbs. "I wouldn't say that Jack was widely respected by his contemporaries at Choate," remembered Lem. "I know he never gave this much thought. He really had no desire, at that time, to be respected or even to be popular."

Jack may have been carefree and mischievous at Choate, but his health was not nearly as good as Lem's. In fact, it was a major problem. During their years at the school, Jack was often ill, suffering from a variety of ailments that could not always be easily diagnosed. Even before he went to Choate, he caught just about every childhood disease, and nearly died from scarlet fever as an infant, one of many brushes with death that would help form the stalwart character of the future president. At Choate, he was frequently in the school infirmary with colds, allergies, and stomach upsets.

"Almost all his life, it seemed, he had to battle against the misfortunes of health," recalled Rose Kennedy. "Perhaps this gave him another source of strength that helped him to become the great man he became." Jack was also born with one leg shorter than the other, triggering the back problem that plagued him throughout his life and that was made worse by injuries he incurred while playing football at Harvard, and later in combat during World War II.

But Jack rarely complained about any of his medical problems and developed a level of stoicism and resilience that served him well in the years ahead. He had an air of detachment, a sense of the essential absurdity and randomness of the human condition. It fortified his spirit and became an indelible part of his character. Although he didn't complain, Jack did need reassurance and comfort during the periods of illness. His family provided that, to some extent. "I know that there are few simple answers to anything," said Rose Kennedy. "In our family, in sickness and in health, we were all involved with one another, all in the same life, a continuum, a seamless fabric, a flow of time," she said.

But after he met Lem at Choate, Jack increasingly turned to his friend for more consistent support. "He was one of the few people with whom Jack shared his physical suffering," said Chris Lawford, who knew Lem later in life. "Jack was in acute physical pain most of the days of his life from his back and stomach. He spoke about it to almost no one except Lem." In fact, Rose never visited Jack while he was at Choate, even when he contracted a serious, mysterious illness early in 1934. "Actually, he came very close to dying," Lem said later. "It was diagnosed one time as leukemia. Obviously, it couldn't have been leukemia. It was some very serious blood condition." A lot of people were praying for him at that time, Lem added.

The full extent of Jack's health problems from childhood onward has only been fully documented in recent years, particularly in books by Robert Dallek and Richard Reeves. What has not been known until now is the role Lem played in helping Jack navigate the minefield of illnesses, many of which would have destroyed a less determined individual. Gore Vidal thinks that Lem's early devotion to Jack, especially when he was ill, helps explain the unbreakable bond between them. "He needed a Lem Billings to get around," he said. Not only did Lem assist Jack physically, more importantly perhaps, he helped lift Jack's spirits during the many times when he could easily have sunk into despair. Not only did Lem love Jack, he believed in him and was always ready to help him whenever he could, especially when he wasn't feeling good, which was often.

"I seldom ever heard him complain," Lem recalled. "I knew his different maladies, and they were many. We used to joke about the fact that if I ever wrote his biography, I would call it *John F. Kennedy, A Medical History*. At one time or another, he really did have almost every medical problem—take any illness, Jack Kennedy had it. Many of them were very, very painful."

While Lem agonized over Jack's condition, Jack masked his concern with humor, his way of dealing with anything serious in life. As always seemed to happen, Jack eventually recovered from the illness. Much has been made of Rose's failure to visit Jack at Choate when he was very ill. But she was concerned about his condition and wrote scores of letters to the headmaster's wife, Clara St. John, inquiring about his health and making suggestions about what might help. In one letter, she expressed alarm about Jack's weight, which, at one point, dipped to 115 pounds. It is not clear why she didn't go to Choate when he was very ill, but her letters indicate she was concerned.

While Lem's health was infinitely better than Jack's, he was not completely free of problems. He developed asthma, a condition that would flare up often for the rest of his life. "Sometimes he found it hard to breathe," said Francis McAdoo. Even in later years, he was hospitalized on more than one occasion because of his asthma. He also had very bad eyesight that was only moderately improved with eyeglasses. His brother, Josh, said that Lem was among the first to try out contact lenses when they were developed in World War II in an attempt to pass the navy's eye examination. Nevertheless, Lem was a comparatively healthy individual compared to Jack.

No matter how he was feeling, however, Jack made sure it didn't dampen his emerging sexual appetite. He engaged in a number of sexual escapades while at school, the most elaborate of which involved he and Lem going to a prostitute in Harlem to lose their virginity. They made the trip there in January 1934, while they were still enrolled at Choate. Jack's idea, according to his friend Rip Horton, was that he and Lem should both lose their virginity to the same prostitute. It is not clear, however, that both boys did in fact lose their virginity, since they each went into the prostitute's room separately. It is likely that Jack succeeded in doing so, but whether Lem did is doubtful. In later years, he told his friend, author Larry Quirk, "I closed my eyes and masturbated at the whorehouse."

Whatever went down, however, it must have been quite an adventure for the two teenage boys. Following the experience, Jack and Lem anxiously looked for the nearest hospital to get supplies of creams and lotions to combat any venereal disease they thought they might have contracted. Whether all the medicinal potions worked, no one knows. It was a precautionary measure, though, since they knew VD is always a risk when the services of a prostitute are engaged. In fact, historian Robert Dallek, in his book *An Unfinished Life*, revealed that Jack did in fact contract a bad case of gonorrhea that plagued him for years. Whether he got infected on this occasion is not clear.

In addition to the high jinks in school, it was these kinds of escapades—the trip to Harlem being the most risky—that further solidified Jack and Lem's friendship. Its parameters were becoming increasingly apparent. Pranks and their dislike of Choate were the glue that held the friendship together—plus their mutual determination not to take life too seriously. "They had a similar sense of humor in most respects," Sally Carpenter said. "But Uncle Moyne's was more off-the-wall." As they got to know each other better, they eventually became intimates, sharing their private thoughts and feelings about family, school, and other matters.

Their friendship wasn't free of tensions, however. Lem tended to be oversensitive and quick to perceive an insult and wasn't shy about telling Jack how he felt. He also constantly sought time with Jack. On the other hand, Jack sought ways of keeping Lem alternately at arm's length and then close, a somewhat contradictory pattern that Jack tried to finesse with his sharp wit and occasional sarcasm.

The letters that Jack and Lem exchanged, beginning during the Choate years and lasting until 1946, offer remarkable insight into their friendship at this time. They reveal a connection that is close and affectionate but also sometimes contentious. Jack enjoyed teasing and needling his friend. "Dear Pithecanthropus Erectus" (the walking ape man), he addressed one letter to Lem, a not-so-muted reference to Lem's high forehead and awkward appearance.

In these early days, before Jack realized that Lem wasn't really interested in women, he would also poke fun at Lem's lack of success with the opposite sex. Writing Lem about Olive Cawley, Jack said, "You know she and K [person unknown] think your sex appeal is a joke." On another occasion, Jack wrote, "If I hadn't just come from talking to girls who think that the words Billings and wacky are synonymous, I would be impressed."

Lem could take most of Jack's taunts but was sometimes offended by perceived slights. On one occasion, Lem got upset over a snafu concerning an invitation to the Kennedy home in Palm Beach. Jack responded angrily. "Of all the cheap shit I have ever gotten this is about the cheapest," he wrote. "You were invited down on Thanksgiving when the family was not coming. But then you were too busy and you and Rip [Horton] were going to St. Lawrence. Then you decide to come down as Rip was going to. But by that time, the family had decided to come down. Then you get hot in the arse because there may not be room enough, not forgetting that there was room enough at Thanksgiving but you didn't want to come until Rip decided he wanted to come. . . . Then I heard from dad saying it was okay. That was the situation: as regards the cheap shit you are pulling, you can do what you want. . . . If you look at this thing you will see you are not so fucking abused."

It is clear from this letter that Jack could get offended, too, and was sensitive to allegations that he was abusing Lem or treating him unfairly. Like many close attachments, their friendship was complicated, and neither boy likely fully understood its nature or limitations at this time in their lives. Lem was clearly the more emotionally involved. He needed Jack and Jack knew it. But it also was apparent that Jack needed Lem, too. In the early years, they tested each other, as boys are prone to do, each seeking dominance.

During his various hospitalizations, Jack would often tantalize Lem with long, lurid descriptions of what the doctors were doing to him, some of it no doubt teenage bravado. "Yesterday, I went through the most harassing experience of my life," he wrote to Lem in one letter. "First they gave me 5 enemas until I was white as snow inside." He also bragged about his appeal to the nurses. Lem probably took Jack's boasts with a grain of salt, but he likely would have enjoyed reading every one of Jack's letters—even if they had been recitations of Webster's dictionary.

For Lem, at some point at Choate, this had become more than just a friendship. The blunt fact is that he was sexually attracted to Jack. As Lem's attraction to Jack grew more powerful, he found it difficult to restrain himself. He felt pretty sure that the feelings weren't reciprocal, but he wasn't sure. At first, Lem was satisfied with just friendship and pretended that his interest was purely platonic. For his part, all Jack knew for sure was that Lem was a great friend, albeit a bit weird sometimes.

Lem's desire for physical intimacy with Jack was so overpowering that he couldn't keep it hidden. He had to find some way of letting Jack know. But Lem didn't want to talk to Jack directly and discuss the matter with him openly. He didn't want to risk admitting to Jack that he was the object of his sexual desires and emotions, because he was afraid it would end their friendship.

So, he decided to drop a hint. There was an unspoken tradition at Choate that was not unusual in an all-boys school of this kind. Boys who wanted sexual activity with other boys—it was not referred to as "gay" or "homosexual"—exchanged notes written on toilet paper to indicate their interest. Toilet paper was used because it could easily be swallowed or discarded to eliminate any paper trail. It was an inherited tradition from the English private school system. The giveaway was the use of toilet paper for the communication. After much thought, and no doubt going backward and forward in his mind as to whether to do it, Lem finally took the plunge and sent such a note to Jack. There is no record of what he wrote on the note, but he no doubt sent it after much trepidation and uncertainty. Whatever he wrote, however, it backfired.

When Jack received it, he was angry and upset. There is a record of his response to Lem in a letter he sent. On June 27, 1934, while he was hospitalized at St. Mary's Hospital in Rochester, Jack wrote, "Please don't write to me on toilet paper anymore. I'm not that kind of boy." Curiously, most of the letter was about his medical condition, providing Lem with extensive descriptions of the procedures he had undergone. "My virility is slowly being sapped," he said. "I'm just a shell of the former man." The

"I'm not that kind of boy" comment was separated from the rest of the letter with parentheses, almost as if it were an incidental remark.

Nevertheless, it was a clear indication to Lem that Jack did not share his preference, did not want to experiment, and wanted nothing to do with homosexual behavior. Lem wisely backed off. But unlike most straight men confronted with this situation, certainly at that time, Jack didn't break off the friendship with Lem. Jack liked Lem, enjoyed good times with him, and was determined that the friendship would continue, despite Lem's apparent sexual desires. From then on, the subject likely was off-limits.

The emphasis for Jack was on friendship, not the kind of love that Lem felt. It is not clear precisely at what moment it dawned on Jack that Lem was interested in him and uninterested in girls. Certainly one incident of this kind at an all-boys prep school does not a gay man make. Some boys, no doubt, experimented with same-sex sexual activity in that restricted environment and went on to become 100 percent heterosexuals. The evidence in Lem's case, however, is that he did not. Undoubtedly, though, it would have taken Jack some time to put two and two together and realize that Lem was a gay man.

In the very first letter from Jack to Lem, dated June 23, 1933— before the "I'm not that kind of boy" letter—it is clear that Jack felt Lem might be a ladies' man, too. "Dear Le Moines," he wrote. "If you should want me to do anything during the summer, I will be at the above address during the next three months [in Hyannis Port]. Please give my best to Pussy [Brooks] and take it easy on the women."

But soon he was making light of Lem's apparent lack of interest in girls and seemingly perplexed as to why. "You're certainly not ugly looking exactly. I guess you are just not cut out to be a ladies' man. Frankly my son, I'm stumped," he wrote. But being as sophisticated and perceptive as he was, later Jack must have sensed that Lem's number-one interest was him. We have no record of what he thought about it or how he reacted to it, other than his sharp rebuke to Lem in his letter back to him and his clear indication, after he received the toilet paper note, that he wasn't interested in sexual activity with Lem.

Asked in later years why they had become so close, Lem gave different answers depending on whom he was talking to. On one occasion, he said, "I don't know. Jack had the best sense of humor of anybody I have known in my life. And I don't think I've known anybody who was so much fun. I think our sense of humors must have jibed. We had a hell of a good time together and I think that's what makes two people like each other. I've always thought a good sense of humor was as important as hell. And then your common interests enter into it, and the longer you know somebody the more interests you have in common. I think it's the ability of two people to enjoy each other. And we did." That, of course, was true, as far as it went. But it wasn't the whole story.

On another occasion, Lem came close to admitting his love for Jack. "Jack made a big difference in my life," he said. "Because of him, I was never lonely. He may have been the reason I never got married. I mean, I could have had a wife and a family, but what the hell—do you think I would have had a better life having been Jack Kennedy's best friend, having been with him during so many moments of his presidency, having had my own room at the White House, having had the best friend anybody ever had—or having been married, and settled down, and living somewhere?"

Even in later life, when he said this, it is clear that Lem found it tough to express his feelings. It is not difficult to understand why, in the world of the 1930s, Lem would have been even more reticent. Homosexuality was a gigantic taboo in the United States, and much of the rest of the world at that time, and for decades beyond that. The word was not even mentioned in polite company, and most gays stayed firmly in the closet, fearing rejection, discrimination, or worse. In the 1930s, it is no exaggeration to say that many people thought of gays, if they thought about them at all, as almost subhuman—certainly sinful and degenerate.

Lem was a man of his time and it is not in the least surprising that he would decide to try to pass, to not be an openly gay man. Almost everyone who was gay in those days made the same decision. It was virtually a requirement, not only to avoid being ostracized, but also to be able to make a living in almost any line of work. But this is not to say that Jack, and his other friends, did not eventually sense that Lem was different. They did.

Rip Horton, who was with Jack and Lem at Choate and later roomed with them during a semester at Princeton, said he'd always assumed Lem was gay but had never discussed it with either Jack or Lem.

Rip said that for those of Jack's friends who had disdain for homosexuality, which was virtually all of them, Lem complicated their relationship with Jack because Lem was so often with him. Jack didn't seem to care whether Lem was gay or not, Rip said. "Jack was a hell of a forgiving guy. He was terribly understanding," Horton added. Newspaperman Charlie Bartlett, who became a friend of Jack and Lem's after World War II, said the same thing, although he was unaware that Lem was gay. "I liked Lem and saw that he was a good friend of Jack's," he said. "Jack was not a judgmental type of guy. He accepted his friends without passing judgment on them."

In a 1989 interview with author Nigel Hamilton, then Choate headmaster Seymour St. John seemed mystified by Lem and his closeness to Jack at the school. "He was a tragedy," St. John said, "a tragedy in himself and really for Jack and Jack's children. He was a strange man and Josh Billings, LeMoyne's brother, was a very good friend of mine. He had nothing really to hold onto and when he found Jack Kennedy, he just thought this was his, this was for him. And he would do anything for Jack Kennedy. And anything Jack did, he would follow right along with him and be the stooge. He roomed with him for those last two years, which was not good for Jack. Jack liked him. He liked very much having somebody at his beck and call and would always go along with his jokes, or whatever."

But St. John also saw a good side to the friendship. "It was Billings's loyalty that helped him [Jack] to emerge from his adolescent trials with his confidence in himself strengthened rather than broken," he said. "If a boy like Billings could follow him through the proverbial thick and thin and still believe in him, then life, his life, must be important and worthwhile." In the case of Jack and Lem, each party felt that at least some fundamental needs were being met, even though their needs were different.

Jack came from a large family and had to battle, along with his siblings, for the attention of Joe and Rose, both of whom were more focused on the higher-achieving Joe Jr. during the Choate years. When Jack met Lem, he found someone who idolized him, who was always there when he needed him, and, most important, who cared about him in a profound way. Lem offered Jack unconditional love and continued to do so for all the years of their friendship. Lem boosted Jack's confidence and self-esteem at a time when it counted. A bond so deeply forged at an early age does not easily come asunder. In the case of Jack and Lem, it never did.

Despite the mutuality of the friendship, however, it clearly was more difficult for Lem because, to a degree, it was unrequited. Lem also likely felt that he loved Jack more than Jack loved him—even in a platonic sense. So, on a number of levels, the friendship made Lem feel insecure. He always needed more time and more reassurance, as their letters indicate. Frequently, for example, Lem complains that Jack hasn't written often enough. Unrequited love always leads to a kind of unreasoning desperation. In Lem's case, this was muted by the fact that he knew that he and Jack would always be friends, that the friendship would always be there. But he also knew that the price he had to pay was restraint as well as discretion.

As the years went by, Lem's inability to be open about his sexuality—a requirement in the early 1930s—would have serious consequences for him. He became self-destructive, particularly as public attitudes changed and he no longer felt as comfortable with the decision he'd made as a teenager, decades before. But all that was in the future—after Jack was killed. In the Depression years, there was only one thing on his mind, and that was how to remain as close as possible to Jack Kennedy without scaring him off.

The two boys graduated from Choate in June 1935. Jack was voted "Most Likely to Succeed," Lem "Best Natured." They exchanged copies of their senior photographs. Jack signed his, "To Lemmer, the gayest [gay did not necessarily mean homosexual in the 1930s] soul I know, in memory of two tense years and in hopes of many more. Your old pal and supporter, Ken." Lem was actually one year older but from this point on subtracted a year from his age. The reason was that in 1934, at the end of Lem's first senior year, he decided that he wanted to spend another year at Choate so he could be with Jack, according to Peter W. Kaplan, one of Lem's closest friends. It was remarkable that Lem was allowed to do this, since he was on scholarship because of his father's death.

Lem undertook the subterfuge even though he hated Choate, because being with Jack Kennedy was more important to him. Lem Billings knew he had found the person to whom he would be devoted all his life. He was determined that the friendship not slip away after school, as so many friendships do. Fortunately for Lem, Jack wanted the friendship to continue, as well. It would grow in myriad different ways over the next three decades. But it was their time together at Choate that Jack and Lem would always treasure. "I was at Choate two years before I really knew him," recalled Lem many years later. "But, as I think back, it was those two years with Jack which I really enjoyed. He was largely responsible for the pleasant feeling I have about Choate, because he just made those wonderful years for me." As for the school itself, however, neither Jack nor Lem ever had much good to say about it. "I think I might say here that Jack Kennedy didn't like Choate when he graduated and neither did I," said Lem. That's one reason, he added, that Bobby went to an entirely different school—Milton.

Over time, however, their attitude toward the school mellowed—somewhat. "After Jack entered Congress, he became one of Choate's star alumni and was asked every year to come back and make a speech at graduation, etc.," remembered Lem. "He didn't really want to because of his negative feeling about Choate. But, I remember, he agreed to go back if I went with him. I agreed to go if he'd put some of the teachers in their place—those teachers whom we felt had behaved very badly toward us. I thought this would be rather fun. So he agreed, and we went back and he was the major speaker. I remember the speech he made. It was an excellent one. It expressed Jack's view that those who had the privilege of an elite private school education owe society something in return, and that there could be no more important contribution than to enter public life." Even as adults, it seems, Jack and Lem were still getting back at Choate and deriving great pleasure from annoying their old teachers. This time, of course, Jack and Lem were in the driving seat.

Almost thirty years later, on May 5, 1963, President Kennedy asked Lem to represent him in a ceremony at Choate to unveil a portrait of him as president. It showed Jack in the white rocking chair that was such a fixture during his time in the White House. Lem eagerly accepted the assignment. In his speech to the school, Lem said, "Since those days at Choate many years ago, my roommate and I have taken different paths. He went his way and I went mine. He wanted to be with us today, but his duties have kept him elsewhere." Then Lem politely referenced the rebellious reputations of the two former students. "Thirty years ago when I came to Choate as a new boy in the usual mood of bafflement and hope, in due course, I acquired a roommate and we spent our senior year together, endeavoring in our own manner to sustain and amplify the traditions of the school. It cannot be said that our manner was always the Choate manner or that our efforts won the unqualified admiration of the headmaster."

Lem then read a message from President Kennedy to the school. Although he was respectful, it was clear that Jack still harbored some resentment of Choate, as well. But the president's doubts were expressed in political terms. "These schools will not survive," he said, "if they become the exclusive preserve of a single class, or creed, or color. They will enlarge their influence only as they incorporate within themselves the variety which accounts for so much of the drive and the creativity of the American tradition."

Jack no doubt derived a certain amount of amusement from sending Lem to Choate to read that message. The president of the country, who had once been the leader of the Muckers, finally got his chance to put Choate on the carpet instead of the other way around. Choate, apparently, did get the message. By the early years of the twenty-first century, the school, now named Choate Rosemary Hall, was coeducational and almost 30 percent of the students were persons of color. More than $5.5 million was awarded in financial aid to ensure that the student body was much more diverse, in terms of economic as well as social background, than it was during Jack and Lem's time.

After Jack's death, some published reports indicated that Rip Horton also roomed with Jack and Lem at the school, an inaccuracy that annoyed Lem exceedingly since Rip roomed with them in college, not at Choate. In a letter to the development director at Choate dated June 9, 1965, Lem attempted to set the record straight. "As you know, I roomed alone with Jack during my Sixth Form year although I have seen it published somewhere that Rip roomed with us at Choate. Actually, he never did room with Jack until we all three roomed together at 9 South Reunion the early part of our freshman year at Princeton." Lem always conceded that Jack had other friends at Choate, including Rip. But he also wanted everyone to know that, "although he had many friends, I was his closest friend at Choate."

Jack, Rip Horton, and Lem, Princeton University, 1935.

During their time at Choate, Jack often invited Lem to stay with him during vacation time and continued to do so even after the incident involving the toilet paper. If Jack had reservations about Lem's sexual orientation, it didn't stop him from introducing Lem to his family and routinely inviting him to stay at the Kennedy vacation homes, usually Hyannis Port in the summer and Palm Beach in the winter.

The Kennedys had no problem maintaining the two vacation estates. There was no Great Depression for them. As a consequence of Joe's shrewd investments, the family survived the catastrophe on Wall Street with their wealth mostly intact. The Kennedys got used to luxurious living. But they never became the idle rich. Joe Kennedy wanted his sons, especially, to get a good education, to work hard, to be somebody, and to work for the greater good. Joe had made the family's money, now it was up to his children to give something back to the country.

Achieving economic security was never enough to satisfy the ambitions of Joe Kennedy, even for himself. He wanted political power, as well, and wisely placed his bets on the election of Franklin Delano Roosevelt in 1933. He hitched his star to FDR hoping that it would result in a political payoff even though he didn't share FDR's liberal views. Despite his economic success, Joe continually pushed himself and his children to do better and always to win. "He made it clear that he wanted to see them win at everything they did," Lem said. He was a perpetual Rodney Dangerfield, always seeking respect, and feeling, no matter how rich or powerful he became, that he never quite got as much as he deserved. He was determined that that would not be the case for the next generation of Kennedys.

Lem's first real exposure to the drive and energy of the Kennedy family came in 1933, when Jack first took Lem home. Instead of the stuffed shirt atmosphere so commonplace in upper-class WASP residences at the time, the Kennedy home was a madhouse of activity—with eight children in addition to Jack and a mix of governesses, maids, visiting relatives, and dogs and cats—all under the loose control of Joe and Rose. "For me, the beginning with Lem came extremely early, during Christmas vacation in 1933. I was ten months old and Jack was sixteen when he brought his roommate down from Choate to see us in Palm Beach," Teddy Kennedy said, obviously not quite remembering that particular first visit. "Actually, I was three years old before it dawned on me that Lem wasn't one more older brother," he added. So often did Lem come home with Jack that he kept more clothes in the closet than Jack did, Teddy added.

A visit with Jack to the Kennedy home in Hyannis Port in the summer of 1934, however, was almost his undoing. After a day of exercise, which included touch football, a game the Kennedys revered, Lem decided to take a shower. He stepped into the stall and turned on the cold-water faucet. What he didn't know was that plumbers had recently worked on the bathroom and had inadvertently reversed the faucets indicating hot and cold. Lem was hit by a jet of scalding hot water. Momentarily stunned, he slipped and fell on his back with the boiling water cascading over him. He couldn't get up and started yelling for help. Finally, Rose responded to his screams and got him out of the shower. He was taken to Cape Cod Hospital in Hyannis, where he stayed for three weeks.

All three of the Billings kids were in the hospital that summer. Lem's older brother, Josh, contracted polio while in England on a Rhodes scholarship. His older sister, Lucretia, was suffering complications from the birth of her daughter, Sally. And now Lem was hospitalized with

Lem, Cape Cod Hospital, 1934.

third-degree burns. Despite all three of her children being in distress, Lem's mother, Romaine, made sure she made it up to the Cape to see Lem. "They called it Mother's terrible summer," said Sally. All the Kennedys who were in Hyannis Port at the time, including Rose and Bobby, also visited Lem. "All the kids came over to see me," remembered Lem. "I really got to know them well. . . . I really watched them grow up and I saw their unusual relationship develop—their closeness and competitive spirit." It was in the hospital that summer that Lem got to know Bobby, who was very young and shy then—not yet ten years old. It was the beginning of a bond with him, too, that grew stronger as the years went by, especially after Jack's death in 1963.

But while Jack was alive, everyone knew that Jack was number one with Lem. Unfortunately, Jack was the one person who couldn't visit Lem in the hospital. Because of an intestinal problem, Jack was in the Mayo Clinic in Rochester, Minnesota. They corresponded regularly, however, from their respective hospital beds. As usual, Jack made light of the situation. "Tough about your burns," he wrote, "but to get back to a much more interesting subject . . . my bowels have utterly ceased to be of service and so the only way that I am able to unload is for someone to blow me out from the top down or from the bottom up."

From 1934 on, it is no exaggeration to say that Lem was accepted as a member of the Kennedy family. He was a regular guest for all the summers at Hyannis Port, and many of the winters at Palm Beach, until the war broke out in Europe in 1939. Rose Kennedy remembered Lem's frequent visits. "After a while, though, it was no surprise to see LeMoyne Billings, who became Jack's best friend and finally his roommate. They had great rapport," she said. Lem was Jack's "best friend" for the rest of his life after they met at Choate, said Eunice Kennedy Shriver.

Rose Kennedy and Lem, Palm Beach, 1939.

On Lem's part, he not only treasured Jack as his best friend, he also adopted the rest of the family, as well. They, in turn, adopted him. He grew close to Eunice, Rose, and Joe, and to all the other Kennedy children, and especially to Bobby. Eunice remembers one Christmas when Rose put her foot down about having visitors. Jack sent her a wire saying that he had a wonderful surprise Christmas present for her. When he arrived on the twenty-fourth, said Eunice, the Christmas surprise turned out to be Lem. "We were always thinking of ways to make sure he came," she said.

Lem participated in birthdays and other family events and was even a vocal participant in the famed family debates that took place around the dinner table. Often as not, the discussions centered on politics. "I can hardly remember a mealtime," Bobby Kennedy said, "when the conversation was not dominated by what Franklin Roosevelt was doing or what was happening in the world." Lem felt these political discussions, moderated by Joe, were an important factor in fostering Jack's consuming interest in politics. "The father kept the level of conversation at a very high level such as current affairs and what was going on in the world," Lem recalled. "If you weren't able to discuss this, you didn't talk."

Evelyn Lincoln, later Jack's personal secretary, agreed. The family dinner debates helped Jack, as well as his brothers and sisters, to develop curious and inquiring minds, she said. "His father would always assign a subject—Algeria, for example—to one child and instruct him to find out all he could on the subject. Then he would tell the other children to do the same so they could question the first one who made his report and see how much he really knew. Both father and mother tried to develop alert minds in their children by giving them mental exercise."

Lem also had a positive view of Joe's insistence on serious conversations at mealtime and didn't view it as onerous, although he said he felt compelled to brush up on current events before visiting. Joe "encouraged them to form their own ideas and opinions," he said. "He encouraged them to thoroughly discuss why they felt certain ways, and he encouraged them to disagree with him. This is an example of Mr. Kennedy's careful raising of his children." He added: "Mr. Kennedy had as much love for his children as any man could have. They were his real interest in life." Lem said the reason that Joe gave each of the children a million-dollar trust fund "was because he wanted them to be independent [so that they] could thumb their nose at him when they came into their money." None, of course, ever did, and they remained devoted to their father even when his reputation among his fellow citizens crashed after the attack on Pearl Harbor.

Although Lem was not as interested in politics as Jack, "he was very bright. He had a great sense of history, he absorbed the world in all its dimensions, and he made everybody else look amusing," remembered Eunice. The family trusted him, and he trusted them. "He has continued to be to this day for all our family, a wonderful friend to all of us, in all weathers, at all times," wrote Rose. "Lem is always there whenever he feels that help may be needed. He has really been part of our family since that first time he showed up at our house as one of 'Jack's surprises.'"

Lem was just as entranced with the Kennedys. "With them, life speeded up," he wrote. The enormous energy of the Kennedys, as well as their open-mindedness and insatiable curiosity, held enormous appeal for Lem, who was raised in a more restrained and controlled atmosphere. He loved their informality, their humor, and especially their teasing. Jack was the worst teaser, of course. One of the main ways he liked to embarrass Lem was by goading him into singing, often in front of other family members or visitors. He particularly liked to have Lem sing a Mae West song called "I'm No Angel," which contained some very saucy lyrics: "Make that low-down music trickle up your spine, baby, I can warm you with this love of mine, I'm no angel."

On one occasion, when Lem was visiting the Kennedys' Palm Beach home, Jack decided to goad Lem more than usual. He offered Lem a hundred dollars to surprise his father. This was a lot of money for Lem, who, since the death of his own father in 1933, was often low on cash. But Jack's proposition would take courage.

It seems that Joe often worked in the nude in the "bullpen," a small space that he used as his office. Anyone who disturbed him there while he was working did so at his or her peril. Jack said to Lem, "I'll give you a hundred dollars right now if you'll take off all your clothes and walk into my father's bullpen. All you have to do," said Jack, "is say, 'Hi, Dad. I know you've always wanted me to call you "Dad," and these are words I've always wanted to tell you.'" Then Lem was supposed to burst out singing "I'm No Angel," the opening line of which is, "Aw, come on, let me cling to you like a vine." It would be Lem in the altogether singing to Joe in the altogether. Some deal!

Lem just couldn't do it, of course, not even for a much-needed hundred dollars. But decades later, when Jack was in the White House, he told Joe Kennedy the story. And Joe said, "Sing it now. I want to hear it now. Sing it." So, Lem finally sang "I'm No Angel"—but with his clothes on. Joe said Jack should have offered him five hundred dollars instead of one hundred.

On most occasions, however, Jack didn't need to bribe Lem into singing. Lem was ready to sing anywhere, anytime. One of his favorite songs was "Lucky Lindy," about the ace aviator Charles Lindbergh. Lem knew the words not only to that song but also to a slew of others, including "Frankie and Johnny," "Over There," "Old Kentucky Home," and "Old Man River," according to Robert F. Kennedy Jr.

Jack liked to sing, too, but he usually sang more meaningful songs, such as "The Wearing of the Green," about the fight for Irish independence— "They're hanging men and women for the wearing of the green"—and "September Song," about love and the fleeting nature of life—"I haven't got time for the waiting game . . . these few precious days I'll spend with you." According to Kenny O'Donnell, Jack sang that haunting song to a group of people after dinner on his last weekend as president before he left for Dallas.

When Jack wasn't trying to get Lem to sing on family occasions, he was cajoling him into playing sports—usually touch football, a game Lem came to loathe. Lem felt that the physical regimen at the Kennedy vacation homes was even more exacting than at Choate. They were especially fanatical about touch football. Jacqueline Bouvier would have the same problem, using every possible excuse to avoid the game, after she and Jack were married in 1953.

Lem and Jack, Hyannis Port, 1955.

Lem, Bobby, and Jack, Hyannis Port, 1955.

Being a guest of the Kennedys required vigor, a word that would become an indispensable part of JFK's vocabulary three decades later when, as president, he reinvigorated the Council on Youth Fitness and urged young Americans especially to become more active. They enjoyed the mix of intellectual and physical pursuits, believing that both were necessary for a full life. Unfortunately, Jack had to be careful while playing sports because of his perpetual problems with his back. This was one reason he developed a love for swimming; not only was it good exercise, but it soothed his back pain. Jack had problems with his back even at this time—before he injured it playing football at Harvard and before he further damaged it during the war. "It was basically a weak back from the beginning," Lem said.

Joe Sr., who didn't miss much that went on around him, got to know Lem pretty well during his many visits to Hyannis Port and Palm Beach. He liked the way Lem supported Jack. A few years after his first visit to Hyannis Port, Lem received a letter from Joe. "This is as good a time to tell you that the Kennedy children from young Joe down should be very proud to be your friends because year in and year out you have given them what few people really enjoy. True friendship. I'm glad we all know you," Joe wrote. For Joe, this was an unusual endorsement, full of affection and regard. It was Joe's way of telling Lem that he was accepted. Lem always treasured the letter and had it framed. In a later letter, Joe referred to Lem as "a second son."

Still, Joe was surprised at how often Jack brought Lem home. Once, on one of Lem's visits, Joe quipped, "That boy arrives with his suitcase and never leaves." As a shrewd and worldly man who met many gays in Hollywood, Joe likely knew that Lem was gay and also probably sensed his attraction to Jack. But Joe was just as certain that Jack was heterosexual and shared his own prodigious appetite for women. Joe felt that Lem was a good friend to Jack, was totally loyal to him, and would help keep his son out of trouble. Whatever else he was, Joe Kennedy was not a moralist and did not share the prevalent view of the time that homosexuality was an abomination.

Jack was not a moralist, either. But it is likely that for Jack, Lem's homosexuality was not something to which he gave much thought, especially after the initial shock of the toilet paper incident wore off. Lem was his friend, his sidekick, and that was all that mattered. In terms of tolerance and acceptance of gays, Jack was decades ahead of his time. But it's almost certain that this was not because Jack had any conception of gay rights (the term and the concept were beyond the imagination of almost everyone then, including most gays and including Lem) but rather because he accepted individuals, especially people he liked, for who they were. Despite his Catholicism, he was not a moralist, and he certainly was no prude.

After they graduated from Choate, it was time to have some fun before the college grind began. In the summer of 1935, Jack spent a lot of time sailing, often with his brother Joe. During the Edgartown Regatta that season, Jack and Joe threw a party that got out of hand. The police were called, and Joe and Jack spent a night in jail. Lem was not there on that occasion. But he did spend much of the summer with Jack. One of the events they attended was a costume party at the Wianno Yacht Club. Jack went dressed as Mahatma Gandhi, the Indian apostle of nonviolence who would eventually force the British out of India. Four girls accompanied him, dressed up as Jack's wives. Lem turned up at the party wrapped in a sheet he thought would pass as a sari. "Who are you supposed to be?" people there asked. "Oh, me, I'm wife number five," he responded. Unfortunately for Lem, as he got close to the platform at the event, the sheet he had wrapped around himself flew off, his glasses fell to the ground, and he stood there naked but for his underwear.

As the friendship between Jack and Lem deepened amid the relative calm and serenity of New England, the march toward barbarity had already begun in Europe. The month they met, March 1933, the first concentration camp was established at Dachau. The following month, a nationwide boycott of Jewish-owned businesses began, and Jews were excluded from government employment in Germany, a harbinger of things to come. In addition to Jews, homosexuals, gypsies, socialists and communists, labor leaders, and many others whom the Nazis deemed to be degenerate also were eventually targeted. During 1934 and 1935, the situation only worsened.

Both men were keenly interested in events overseas. But as Jack and Lem prepared to go to college in the fall of 1935, neither they nor their fellow citizens could foresee just how much the world would spin out of control during the last half of the decade. It was also impossible to predict that Jack's father, FDR's first chairman of the Securities and Exchange Commission, would be an active participant in events in Europe as U.S. ambassador to England, supporting policies and voicing views that ultimately destroyed his political career and earned him the enmity of millions.

In the summer of 1935, however, Joe's thoughts were on domestic matters and his role in promoting FDR's New Deal. He was also thinking about Jack's college career. Joe wanted Jack to enroll at Harvard, the college he had attended. But Jack had other ideas. This was one of those times, rare in the early years, when Jack defied his father. Jack and Lem had become so close by this time that they were determined to go to the same college—Princeton.

2

REBELS WITH A CAUSE
(COLLEGE, 1935–37)

"'There are few earthly things more beautiful than a university,' wrote John Masefield in his tribute to English universities—and his words are equally true today."
—John F. Kennedy, June 10, 1963

A
s his time at Choate drew to a close in the summer of 1935, Lem worried that he and Jack might now go their separate ways. He knew that Jack valued his friendship and that they would remain friends. But he wanted to continue to see Jack every day, the way he had at Choate. That issue was resolved when they both applied to Princeton for the fall semester.

Jack had also applied to Harvard in case he was turned down for his first choice, and to placate his father, who really wanted him to go to his alma mater. But Jack wanted to go to Princeton with Lem. "I believe Ambassador Kennedy was very intent on Jack going to Harvard, but Jack wanted to go to Princeton," recalled Rip Horton, a fellow Choater, who also went to Princeton and roomed with Jack and Lem there.

After Jack wired him saying he was admitted to Princeton while

Lem's application was still pending, Lem spent some anxious days at his mother's home in Baltimore before his own acceptance finally arrived in the mail. Lem was elated. He and Jack would soon be going to college together. But his joy soon turned to disappointment when Jack next told him that he was going to Europe, his first trip overseas, instead of to Princeton. After failing to push Jack into attending Harvard, Jack's father wanted to broaden his education by enrolling him at the London School of Economics under famed socialist professor Harold Laski.

It seemed an odd choice for the right-winger and unrelenting capitalist to want his son to study under Laski, an extreme left-winger. But Joe always wanted his sons to see as many aspects of life as possible, and he wanted them in particular to understand what the have-nots experienced. "These boys are going to have a little money when they get older, and they should know what the 'have-nots' are thinking and planning," he said. "I disagreed with everything he [Laski] wrote . . . but I never taught the boys to disapprove of someone just because I didn't accept his ideas. They heard enough from me, and I decided they should be exposed to someone of intelligence and vitality on the other side."

Although reluctant, Jack ultimately decided to abide by his father's wishes. He and Joe Sr. set sail for England in September 1935. Even before arriving in England to study under Laski, Jack wrote Lem from his cabin aboard the SS *Normandie*. "Dear Lemmie," he wrote, "Had quite a farewell at the dock. Thanks for the telegram. Probably the strangest sight at the pier was Ann Amory with a crew cut in a green tweed suit. It was probably the strangest sight I've seen since I saw Rip in the rumble carrying on a conversation with Nancy Jaeger. There are not many young people aboard except a French guy who is rather nice and a terrific girl. Tonight is the captain's ball. Don't be dirty Kirk. I am not discussing his vital organs . . . I wish the Ripper were here as you would be very much a bore since you don't drink.

"This is the fourth day out and it is getting pretty god dammed rough," Jack continued. "Have had a pretty fair time so far and have worked out 1hr a day in the gym boxing. The food here is very pimp laden and my face is causing much comment from the old man, and it is getting damned embarrassing. He really rang the bell when, after helping myself to the dessert that was oozing with potential pimps, he said my face was getting to look like yours."

Then Jack told Lem a strange story about "a fat Frenchie aboard who is a 'homo.' He had me to his cabin more than once and is trying to bed me." There is no explanation as to why Jack would visit his cabin more than once in view of the Frenchman's apparent sexual orientation. But Jack enjoyed getting attention from everyone, and it is likely that he was teasing the French guy—and Lem. "How is everything going?" Jack concluded his letter. "I suppose you people are having quite a time in Portland. Write to me at the Claridge [hotel]. My next letter on my foreign experience will be to Rip from London. Remember me to him."

"Dear Unattractive," Jack wrote Lem when he reached London. "Got your exciting letter. Have had quite some time since I last wrote you. We were to get off at Plymouth at 3.00 Sunday night—we ran into a storm and we were blown to a place in France after staying up all night." Jack and Joe then took the ferryboat to Dover on the English coast. "I was on deck singing to one of the women in the party. I was singing 'The Man on the Flying Trapeze' and when I came to the part where you break into the chorus with ooooh, etc., a woman behind me retched all over me with 'oh my god that's the finish'—you can imagine me covered from tip to toe with hot vomit."

Once he arrived in the British capital, Jack lost no time having fun in the swinging London of that day, the city not yet ravaged by the wartime shortages that soon would make life there difficult. The aristocracy was still living high on the hog, although the same could not be said of the British working classes. Jack mixed easily in all social settings, however, and had the time of his life. But he didn't enjoy studying under the humorless Laski, whose cardboard socialism struck him as impractical and unrealistic. Jack was more attuned to politics than his older brother Joe, but he thought that Laski took himself way too seriously. He was determined to get away from the London School of Economics as quickly as possible. As so often happened, he was bailed out by falling ill. At first, it appeared quite serious. Once again, it was a mystery illness that the doctors couldn't seem to diagnose, although Jack seemed to feel that the terrible English weather somehow contributed to it.

In mid-October, Jack wrote to Lem from the hospital. "They are doing a number of strange things to me, not the least of which is to shove a tremendous needle up my cheeks. Today was most embarrassing as one doctor came in just after I had woken up and was reclining with a semi [erection] on due to the cold weather. His plan was to stick his finger under my pickle and have me cough. His plan quickly changed however when he drew back the covers and there was 'JJ Maher' quivering with life." [Jack named his penis JJ Maher after Jack and Lem's housemaster at Choate, whom they both despised. Sometimes he would refer to it as Jack Maher, or simply JJ.]

"This would certainly be no place for you," Jack wrote Lem, claiming he had met "a cousin of yours in this hospital, Prince Surloff, who is supposed to be the next Czar, or some such shit. He ran at Oxford and knew 'Charlie' Stanwood. The prince stated that Charlie was certainly a prince among men and I heartily agreed that he certainly was. I have met a number of earls + lords here and I am getting rather royal myself." Jack also talked about Lem's activities at Princeton. "You will no doubt get kicked out of Princeton if you continue to try and hook the Nassau Bell Clapper [the Princeton college bell that was so noisy that Lem swore he would put it out of action]. If I were you, I would worry more about my own clapper and the pimple on it than I would about the clapper on Nassau Hall."

Jack and Lem's friendship had now developed to the point that they felt they could confide in each other. But this was probably more true of Jack than of Lem, who still held back for fear of scaring Jack off with the intensity of his attachment. Lem told an interviewer years later, however, that they both told each other their secrets. "He had never been secretive with me. We grew up together and we shared secrets," Lem said. "Why were we so close? Maybe it was because he could really tell me everything. Things that were certainly not for the family. I knew more about his personal life than his family did." But did Jack know more about Lem than his family did? The answer was probably yes, even though Lem felt he could not level with Jack about his personal feelings to the extent that Jack did.

In an early example of his business acumen, Lem made some much-needed money while at Princeton by handing out free samples of the newly-introduced Juicy Fruit gum around campus as part of the company's promotion campaign. But it was not enough to get by. Worried about Lem's money troubles, Jack, despite being notorious for always borrowing cash himself, offered to help Lem out, one of many occasions on which he did so, always being careful not to injure Lem's fragile self-esteem. "Your financial worries have upset me, as Princeton would not be awfully jolly without your sif [syphilis] covered face." Offering Lem $500, he added, "I won't need it. You can pay me after you get out of college. You then would not have to borrow from that old prick Uncle Ike [Lem's uncle]. Let me know about this, and whether you need it, because I won't be needing it. How is Olive? Let me know how she is doing and don't screw her. Dad says I can go home if I want to."

It was the green light Jack needed to leave England. Although he liked London, Jack was determined to jettison the London School of Economics and return to the States as quickly as possible to attend Princeton with Lem. On October 21, he wired Lem with the surprising and welcome news, "Arriving Princeton Thursday afternoon. Hope you can arrange rooming—Ken." Lem was ecstatic. He wired Jack back, "Nothing could possibly sound better. So hurry home." Lem soon realized he had a problem, however. He couldn't afford the sort of accommodation to which Jack was accustomed. Lem had already rented a two-bedroom apartment with a living room in Nassau Hall with Rip Horton. It was the cheapest accommodation on campus. The bathroom was down in the cellar, well away from the fourth-floor apartment. They had to walk up and down seventy-two steps to reach it. But it was affordable, and it suited Lem and Rip. Lem worried, however, that Jack might want a better place. He needn't have been concerned. Jack didn't mind roughing it with Lem and Rip in the least.

But Joe did. He arrived to visit one day in a chauffeured Cadillac wearing a heavy topcoat even though it was a warm day and was not amused when he saw the section of campus in which Jack was staying. He was even less amused when he discovered he had to climb the seventy-two steps to reach the boys' less-than-luxurious apartment. Joe let Jack know in no uncertain terms that this was not the kind of accommodation befitting the son of Joe Kennedy. But it was often Joe's way to jump up and down about something and then eventually settle down and become reasonable, even indulgent. Despite his overbearing nature, he was genuinely concerned about Jack's future and wanted the best for his second son. In this instance, Joe acquiesced, and Jack stayed in the apartment with Lem and Rip.

Joe knew Jack was intelligent, but he worried that he was too much of a wise guy whose number-one goal in life was having a good time. Joe felt that Jack was not applying himself to the maximum of his ability, which was true. Jack's grades during the fall semester at Princeton were less than stellar. Joe was even more concerned about Jack's health, which still was not good. He was six feet tall and weighed only 135 pounds. He was sick most of the time he was at Princeton, according to Lem. In particular, his skin had a tendency to turn inexplicably yellow. But the doctors always failed to diagnose what was wrong. During his visit, Joe took the time to visit the university doctor to discuss what might be done.

Joe was worried, but Jack wasn't. He took his health problems in stride. He, Lem, and Rip had a ball during that fall semester at Princeton, frequently taking trips to New York on the weekend. All three would look back on it as a golden time in their lives. At the close of the semester, they sent out a joint Christmas card featuring a photograph of each of them in pajamas. "We're puttin' on our top hats, tyin' up our white tie, brushin' off our tails," the greeting read—adopting the lyrics of Irving Berlin's 1935 hit "Top Hat." The card was addressed from Rip, Lem, and Ken (the nickname Jack sometimes used). But by December, Jack's illness, which was finally diagnosed as jaundice, had worsened, forcing him to withdraw from the university.

Years later, Lem doubted it was in fact jaundice. "It had the appearance of jaundice. Actually, it was probably hepatitis," he said. Even though he was ill most of the semester and had to leave the university, however, Jack wrote, "I will always have a very tender spot in my heart for Old Nassau." Jack and Lem were apart once again, but they stayed in close contact through their continuing exchange of letters and telegrams.

Jack spent Christmas 1935 in Palm Beach trying to regain his strength and asked Lem to join him there during the college vacation. He knew Lem still was short of money. His original plan was to book a compartment on the train going down and sneak Lem into it without paying for him. But Rose put her foot down, saying there was no need for a compartment, which cost thirty dollars more. Jack still wanted Lem to come down, however, and offered to kick in half the cost of taking the bus. "Will pay half of bus ticket," Jack wired. "My share thus amounting to fifteen smackeroos. Let me know when you arrive. Hello Mrs. Warren. Sweet essence of buttermilk mercy." The two boys had sent so many wires back and forth by this time that they were well known to Mrs. Warren, the telegraph manager at Princeton. It was all that Lem needed.

He was on his way, having first checked with his mother to see if it was okay to spend Christmas in Palm Beach with Jack instead of with her in Baltimore. It was. On December 15, Lem wired Jack with his plans and thanked him for a gift. "Are you sure dad wants me there and are you sure you want to give me so large a present. Lemule."

Jack was happy to see Lem in Palm Beach, but he also was glad to be away from Princeton. Although he loved being with Lem and Rip and desperately wanted to rejoin them there, he hated what he saw as the snobbery and provincialism of the college. Like Choate, it was a Protestant school that, during these years, didn't readily tolerate Catholics and Jews. Moreover, Jack didn't like his classes or his teachers. He was glad to move on.

But despite the rest and recuperation with Lem in Palm Beach over Christmas, he still felt terrible. After the holidays, he found himself at the Peter Bent Brigham Hospital in Boston for further tests. If he was worried about his condition, he didn't give any indication of it to Lem in his letters. "Here I sit for the next two months at least that is how it looks," he wrote Lem in Princeton. "My tan is completely gone and I am now as white as you are . . . I don't know why you and Rip are so unpopular with girls. You're not ugly looking exactly. I guess there's just something about you that makes girls dislike you on sight."

Exhibiting more teenage bravado, he also told Lem about the tests he was enduring. "They were doing this to test my acidosis. Soon I felt myself getting high. I had this thing up my nose for 2 hours and they just took it out (don't be dirty Kirk) and now I have a 'head-on' and a 'hard-on' as when they had finished a beautiful nurse came in and rubbed my whole body. Took a look at my chart and discovered I do not have sif [syphilis]."

Despite Jack's joking, the situation was serious, and he was told once again that he could have leukemia. But he had learned to take these kinds of dire warnings in stride, and he continued with an active social life in between the various tests at the hospital. He was still dating Olive Cawley, the girl he'd met while he was at Choate, and in one letter to Lem asked his advice about how to deal with her. "Am coming to you for advice on the Cawley situation—should I ask her after this deliberate slight [she had not answered a letter]. It's your roomie who is asking you and he's also asking you to leave my writing paper alone. That writing paper was a present from one of my feminine admirers, a woman who worships the very air I breathe [the writing paper was a gift to Jack from Lem's mother, Romaine] but who unfortunately has a son with bad breath."

Fortunately, the doctors had misdiagnosed his situation again, and the possible leukemia diagnosis was rescinded. Nevertheless, Joe wasn't taking any chances. He encouraged his son to take a long recuperation in the Southwest. In the spring of 1936, Jack headed to the Jay Six Cattle Ranch in Arizona. On April 29, he wrote Lem, teasing him as usual. "Of all the old ladies I have been lucky enough to meet, you take the first prize as being the biggest; in fact, LeMoyne, you are in a class by yourself." Amazingly, free of the worries of school and enjoying himself on the ranch, Jack's health improved and he regained his strength. While in the West, he also visited Mexico and Los Angeles.

Jack and Lem relaxing, Palm Beach, 1937.

After the Christmas vacation at the Kennedy home in Palm Beach, Lem reluctantly returned to Princeton without Jack, eventually majoring in art and archaeology. Art, sculpture, and architecture would remain major interests throughout his life. Although life on campus was not as exciting for Lem without Jack there, he nevertheless enjoyed his time at Princeton. In later life, he often recalled that Albert Einstein wandered the campus wearing no socks, and he would talk about the time he headed for the hills after hearing Orson Welles announce on the radio that the Martians were torching Nassau Hall.

Lem still saw Jack whenever he could, however. In fact, they got together prior to Jack's trip out West. A wire from Lem to Jack dated February 9, 1936, warns him of traffic problems. "Bus driver says roads treacherous beyond Meriden, so wire on arrival." Lem also saw Jack again at Easter when he went down to Palm Beach at Jack's invitation.

But without Jack at Princeton, Lem did not do well academically. When Lem failed his midyear exams and lost his scholarship, Jack wrote to him, "Dear Out-On-Your-Ass." Despite the humor, Jack was genuinely concerned that Lem might not make it through college. He knew Lem would listen to him, so for once he got serious with his sidekick. "If you decide to go on vacation, you can come here since we have plenty of room," he wrote. "However, you have been a terrific ass, and unless you come around, you haven't a chance. If you do good work now, maybe you can get the scholarship back." Lem listened to Jack, as he always did, and did do better, eventually regaining his scholarship.

Meanwhile, Joe was pushing Jack to enroll in Harvard rather than return to Princeton. And this time Jack was more receptive, having experienced what Princeton was like. Despite Jack's desire to be reunited with his best friend, he enrolled at Harvard in the fall of 1936, eventually majoring in economics, political science, and history. Unfortunately, while there, Jack further injured his back playing football. According to Rose Kennedy, this was "the beginning of troubles with his back that were to haunt him for the rest of his life." But, in fact, he had suffered back problems even at Choate.

To compensate for the fact that they were now attending different colleges, Jack and Lem met in New York City almost every weekend. "I saw him an awful lot," Lem recalled, despite the fact that it was tough to get down to New York so often. They regularly sent telegrams to each other—sometimes as many as seven in one day—making arrangements for their get-togethers. Typical is this one from Jack. "Will be in town around 9-45 dressed. Wire me in Bronxville address to meet you. Will have Rolls or Chrysler. Have you got me a date? Best. Ken."

In another communication, Jack berated Lem for taking his hat. "You certainly are a large size prick to keep my hat as I can't find my other one and consequently am hatless. Please send it as I am sending yours—I don't know what the idea was in walking off with it in the first place. Harvard has not made me grasping but you are getting a certain carefree communistic attitude and a share of the wealth attitude that is rather worrying to we who are wealthy. Therefore, I am going to crack down. Inadvertently, you are certainly lacking in your possessions as well as mine. . . . Anyway; I take the train after the game—arriving in NY around 8:00. Will meet you when you want at what time you say. Let me know." It was typical of Jack to rib Lem in the wires. "Billings, if you had a brain, you would have one [a hat], Jack."

It was Jack who suggested most of the get-togethers. But he always had to be careful not to hurt Lem's feelings. According to those who knew him, Lem's self-esteem was a problem throughout his life. He could easily feel slighted or offended. In one telegram, Jack wrote, "Sorry you were not able to get to NY—If you would stop feeling injured, you would realize that you have missed plenty of weekends such as two weeks ago when you scurried off to Pittsburgh." When they did meet in New York, Lem would most often hitchhike from Princeton while Jack took the train from Boston, not far from the Harvard campus. One of their favorite haunts in New York was the Stork Club on Fifty-third Street, considered very fashionable during the 1930s. "We went there a lot," remembered Lem. Since they were at different colleges now, "Our relationship at this time was based pretty much on weekends and summer vacations," he added.

Jack drank very little because he knew that Lem couldn't afford the drink prices at the Stork. Sometimes they would sneak out to a bar where they could get a few cheap beers and then return to the Stork. Even though Jack was rolling in money compared to Lem, he often had even less money on him than Lem did. Jack was notorious for being forgetful about cash and frequently had to borrow some—even as president—not only from Lem but from anybody else who might be around. Most often, he wouldn't pay the money back, either, because he was absent-minded about it, as the rich can afford to be. Even so, with Lem, most of the time, he was conscious of money issues and tried to help out in such a way as not to damage his best friend's pride.

During their college years, both men went out with women and had steady dates for a while. Lem dated Katharine Duncan Hart from Stamford,

Connecticut, and Jack continued to date Olive Cawley, although Olive was by no means the only woman Jack went out with during his college years— far from it. It is likely that at this stage in his life Lem was dating women because he wanted to be straight, or perhaps because he wanted to pass as straight, but also because he wanted to please Jack. Lem knew that Jack liked double-dating, and so Lem went along with the program. All along, however, Lem would likely have preferred just being with Jack.

Though Jack was more conscientious at Harvard than he had been at Princeton or Choate, he always reserved sufficient time for his burgeoning sexual appetite. He wrote to Lem frequently about his sexual trysts with women even though he knew Lem would not write similar letters to him. When they were together, sometimes Jack's dates would be managed by Lem. One date, Charlotte McDonnell, said that if Jack wanted to cancel a date, or change it, it was Lem who usually did the calling. She would get a call from Lem saying, "'Well, Jack's tied up. He's having a massage.' Then Lem would come over to get me and bring me to Jack."

On one occasion, Jack wrote to Lem saying he would like to come to Princeton for a change instead of meeting Lem in New York. "Get me a room away from all others, and especially from your girl, as I don't want you coming in for a chat in the middle, as usual, and discussing how sore my cock is." Jack apparently had so much sex during his college years that it led to problems with his penis, and he had to be circumcised at the Mayo Clinic. He wrote Lem: "As for your rather unnatural interest in my becoming circumcised, JJ has never been in better shape or doing better service."

As he had at Choate, Jack often invited Lem during vacation time to Hyannis Port and Palm Beach during the years he was at Harvard. In a letter to Lem from Florida, Jack wrote, "You're sort of a prick as I sent you a wire asking you down for a couple of weeks and got no answer. You're getting pretty fucking social Billings with these weddings, etc. But as I always say, you better get your belly full of them as an usher because with a head like yours, that's as close as you'll get."

During Jack and Lem's college years, FDR's New Deal was in full swing. Jack, in particular, was strongly influenced by FDR's progressive politics and his ability to project optimism even at a time of great suffering.

"There is a mysterious cycle to human events," FDR said. "To some generations, much is given. Of other generations, much is expected. This generation of Americans has a rendezvous with destiny." Jack noted the impact of the president's words, as well as his actions, on the American people. He would learn that lesson well—taking equal care with his own presidential speeches, which would inspire a different generation of Americans almost three decades later.

Unlike Jack, Joe was suspicious of FDR's New Deal but nevertheless fully supported his reelection campaign in 1936. He even wrote a campaign volume in praise of FDR with the help of *New York Times* columnist Arthur Krock. His dedication to FDR, titled "I'm for Roosevelt," was widely read around the country. FDR expected no less but remained skeptical of Joe and his ambitions. He didn't have much regard for Arthur Krock, either, referring to him privately as "the Krockpot."

Lem was a Republican at this time and not nearly as enamored as Jack of FDR, who was regarded as a "traitor to his class" by the well-to-do. Lem wasn't well-off, but his family had been Republicans dating back to the Civil War period, when the Republican Party was much more liberal than it is now. It was antislavery before the War between the States and then pro-Reconstruction after it. Lem's ancestors were ardent abolitionists who championed the education of free blacks after the South was defeated. During the 1930s, the Republican Party was not yet dominated by its conservative wing. Lem's Republicanism didn't mean he was a conservative; far from it.

FDR gave his "Rendezvous with destiny" speech in the summer of 1936. Abroad, Hitler and Mussolini had a very different fate in mind for their peoples. In March, Hitler invaded the Rhineland in violation of the Treaty of Versailles and the Locarno Pact. Mussolini annexed Abyssinia (today Ethiopia), the only African country never to have been colonized. Most ominously, Germany and Italy formed an alliance—the Rome-Berlin Axis—that threatened neighboring countries as well as Britain and France. And the Spanish Civil War, Europe's dress rehearsal for World War II, also erupted that year. Germany and Italy aided Franco's rebellion against the democratically elected Republican government, while the Americans, British, and French stood by and let the Republican government fend for itself.

For most Americans, the troubles in Europe were far away and of little interest. Even after the outbreak of full-scale war in Europe in September 1939, most Americans wanted no part of it. They were much more concerned with daunting problems at home. With most of the country dead set against involvement in Europe's troubles, FDR felt compelled to sign a series of neutrality acts, even though he knew that Hitler and Mussolini would ultimately threaten the United States as well. But for the moment, at least, America would not intervene in Europe's internecine conflicts, and U.S. diplomats in Europe were instructed to be on their best diplomatic behavior.

Jack and Lem watched events in Europe from the comfort of college in the United States with a mixture of alarm and fascination. In search of youthful adventure, they were determined to see Europe for themselves. Their chance would come during their college vacation in the summer of 1937. Of course, they wanted to see as many places as possible and have as much fun as they could, but they also wanted to observe what was going on politically, particularly in Germany and Italy, but also in Spain, where the civil war was raging. In July, they set sail on the adventure of a lifetime aboard the SS *George Washington*. They were energetic, self-confident, free of attachments and responsibilities, and determined to take Europe by storm. Jack's sister Kathleen gave her brother a leather-bound diary labeled "My Trip Abroad" to record his impressions, which he dutifully did.

3

TRIP OF A LIFETIME
(1937)

"Goethe tells us in his greatest poem that Faust lost the liberty of his soul when he said to the passing moment, 'Stay, thou art so fair.'"
— John F. Kennedy, June 25, 1963

In May 1937, a small item appeared in a Pittsburgh newspaper. "Though all American passports legibly state, 'not good in Spain,' ex-Pittsburgher K. LeMoyne Billings, son of Mrs. Frederic T. Billings who moved to Baltimore last year, and John Kennedy, son of Joseph P. Kennedy of Washington, will visit that war-torn country this summer for three weeks. They sail on June 30 on the *George Washington,* and will attempt to study war conditions."

Jack and Lem were eager to get into Spain, where the brutal civil war was raging. They longed to see what was happening for themselves. But they also wanted to do a grand European tour, and for a lot longer than three weeks. It wasn't just war that was on their minds, but fun and excitement, too. Joe was all in favor of the venture and wrote to Lem's uncle Ike (since Lem's father was deceased) to solicit his support, albeit laying it on a bit thick. "I really feel that this trip would be a fine opportunity for the boys, not only because of the conditions in Europe today, which would be unusually interesting to observe, but because of the fact that I have a number of friends in the diplomatic service, and a number of friends who are members of the big newspaper syndicates in the capitals of Europe, all of whom I know would open to them an entirely new and interesting aspect of conditions there." Uncle Ike succumbed to Joe's entreaty.

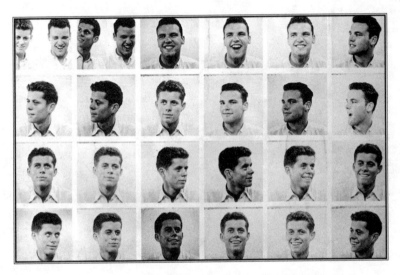

Jack and Lem in a Palm Beach photo booth just before their European tour, 1937.

Jack and Lem's summer in Europe began on July 1, 1937. Joe generously paid for half the cost of Lem's ticket on the way over, saying Lem could pay at least part of it back when he graduated from Princeton. "I borrowed the other half from an inheritance I was about to receive from my grandmother after I graduated from college," remembered Lem. Both boys kept diaries on the trip, though Lem's was more of a scrapbook. It contained scores of photographs of himself and Jack in Europe, as well as a handwritten narrative. It would go on to become one of his most prized possessions.

"Very smooth crossing. Looked pretty dull the first couple of days, but investigation disclosed some girls—chiefly Ann Reid," Jack wrote in his diary. "Stayed up all night to see Ireland—found it was not worth it as it necessitated sleeping the entire next day," wrote Lem. Jack's Ford convertible was sent to Le Havre so that the two young Americans could tour Europe in style. (Convertibles were a rare sight then in European cities. In fact, most Europeans did not yet own cars of any kind.)

Lem in Cannes, France, during the trip to Europe with Jack, 1937.

Although they moved about Europe in style in their flashy car, looking every inch the two young wealthy Americans, their accommodations were decidedly spartan. As the son of a multi-millionaire, Jack could afford to stay in the finest hotels, but Lem could not. "I went over with very little money because my father had recently died," Lem said. "This is another side of Jack's character. He was perfectly happy to live at places for forty cents a night, and we ate frightful food . . . but he did it [because] that was the only way I could go with him."

"We went on a really educational tour of Europe and I don't think either of us ever again toured museums and castles and châteaus and historical sights so extensively as we did that year," remembered Lem. Lem exhibited an avid interest in all the great cathedrals and other impressive architecture in France, trying to make Jack aware of an area of life in which he had hitherto shown little interest. It seems to have worked, judging by Jack's diary entries. "July 7. The cathedral at Rouen most impressive. We reached it only after turning around from our route to Mt. St. [Michel]." Lem's diary entry was more personal. "Extremely impressed . . . I was glad to see the building that made me practically flunk my final sub exam."

"After lunching at Rouen, we proceeded to Beauvais where we were greatly impressed by the height and size of the cathedral," wrote Jack.

"Stayed at a little inn where we ran into our first Fr[ench] breaths [he complained during the trip that many people in France had bad breath, not to mention other hygiene problems]—went to a fair that night and then to bed." Even then, however, the Kennedy wit was in evidence. "July 8—Rheims. Where we looked at the cathedral and then to the Hotel Majesty. My French improving a bit and Billings' breath getting French." Lem's breath notwithstanding, his curiosity about Europe's old cathedrals and castles and other historic buildings rubbed off on Jack even more as the trip progressed.

"He did enjoy seeing the cultural side of Europe," remembered Lem. "Having been a sophomore at Princeton, I had taken my first architectural course there and my interests were in that direction anyway. I enjoyed seeing the Gothic cathedrals and other architectural treasures, which I had actually studied in college. I felt very much at home seeing them and was very excited about it. He hadn't taken an architectural course at that time, and yet he was just as interested as I was. He never complained when I asked to go to all the different cathedrals around Paris."

In addition to his growing appreciation for art and architecture, Jack's diary entries also reflected his burgeoning interest in politics, even though his comments at this time in his life were simplistic. "July 9—Rheims, Château-Thierry, and Paris. The general impression seems to be that Roosevelt—his type of government—would not succeed in a country like France, which seems to lack the ability of seeing a problem as a whole. They don't like Blum [Léon Blum, French prime minister at the time in the Popular Front government] as he takes away their money and gives it to someone else. That to a Frenchman is *tres mauvais*. The general impression also seems to be that there will not be a war in the near future and that France is much too well prepared for Germany. The permanence of the alliance of Germany and Italy is also questionable. From there [Rheims] we went to Château-Thierry picking up two French officers on the way. Arrived in Paris around eight. By mistake in French, invited one of the officers to dinner but succeeded in making him pay for it. Looked around and got a fairly cheap room for the night."

Although it is obvious from his scrapbook that Lem was much more interested in the art and architecture of Europe than he was in the politics of the continent, he did show some political interest. "France seems to be pretty well prepared as far as an active army is concerned," he wrote. But otherwise he found France to be "still a pretty primitive nation" in terms of the modern conveniences to which even Depression-era Americans had become accustomed. In addition to keeping a diary, Jack wrote letters to his father back home describing his political impressions. He reported, for example, that the French were confident that the Maginot Line would be an effective bulwark against any Nazi invasion. Lem dispatched long letters to his mother, occasionally mentioning politics but mostly describing the art and architecture, especially the châteaus.

Jack and Lem were overjoyed when they reached Paris, a place they had heard so much about, especially from Rose, who visited the City of Light frequently. "July 10—Paris. Awoke at 1-00. Found a new place to stay for 70 francs," wrote Jack. "Have now acquired the habit of leaving the car around the block to keep the price from going up [at the hotel]. Had the lights fixed and got another screwing. These French will try and rob at every turn. Went to Notre Dame, then looked around Paris. That night, went out to Moulin Rouge and Café of Artists and met some of the well-known French artists. Billings wanted to come home early, but didn't."

While in Paris, Jack and Lem also hooked up with old friends from the States. "July 15—Paris. Had lunch with Billings' friend from Princeton, which was rather interesting though expensive," wrote Jack. "In the afternoon, made a flying visit thru the Louvre. That evening, took in a movie and went to bed. Have picked up quite a bit although my knowledge is quite vague. Have decided to read *Inside Europe*, by John Gunther." Although impressed with Europe's history, Jack noted that the lives of ordinary people were far from prosperous in the Europe of this time. "July 20—[location unreadable]. Americans do not seem to realize how fortunate they are. These people are satisfied with very little and they have very little so it is really a very conservative country, at least outside of Paris." As a rich kid, however, Jack may not have known that many Americans had very little at this time, either. There was still massive unemployment in the United States eight years into the Depression. But that, of course, had not impacted the Kennedy family.

"While we were in France, Jack spent a great deal of time talking to the French as to how they felt about Germany, and whether there was going to be a war, and if so, could Germany invade France again," Lem recalled. "The French were very confident in those days that the Germans couldn't do anything to them—they felt that they were very strong and that the Maginot Line was their protection." While they spent much of the daytime sightseeing and talking with the locals, Jack and Lem hit the nightclubs at night—the ones that they could find that were cheap enough, anyway. "Wherever the girls were, we went," said Lem.

On July 26, Jack and Lem went to a bullfight in Saint-Jean-de-Luz on the Côte Basque in southwestern France not far from the Spanish border. "Very interesting, but very cruel," Jack wrote in his diary, "especially when the bull gored the horse. Believe all the atrocity stories now as the southerners such as these French and Spanish are happiest at scenes of cruelty." Lem, too, thought the sport was very brutal. "We felt the bull didn't have a prayer. Of course, maybe we didn't understand the finer points of the sport. I remember Jack's drawing my attention to a French woman and her child, a little boy, sitting beside us. When one of the horses was badly gored with his guts spilled out over the arena, and they led him out with his guts dragging behind, the mother made a great issue out of making sure her child saw this very exciting episode. Of course, we didn't understand this temperament at all and we were disgusted by it."

The next day, for a change, Lem, and not Jack, became ill. It wasn't quite clear what the problem was, but his temperature reached 103. The boys took it easy for a few days while Lem recovered. Then they traveled to the French–Spanish border. They hoped to cross into Spain. But when they reached the border area, they were turned back by the police. Nevertheless, they were shocked at what they saw—even on the border.

World War II was still two years away, but the Spanish Civil War was a harbinger of what was to come. Jack and Lem met Spaniards who were streaming into France with horrifying stories about the brutality of aerial bombardment. Many were broken in mind and spirit, some unable to come to terms with what they had endured. It was Jack and Lem's first direct experience of the reality of war. They talked to Spanish refugees who were being cared for in Saint-Jean-de-Luz and other towns near the border, listening to their heartbreaking stories of destruction and carnage. "Jack Kennedy was intensely interested in the whole revolution," recalled Lem. "That was the reason we stayed there as long as we did. He was very anxious to get into Spain, but there was absolutely no way we could do this since our passports were clearly marked, 'Not Good for Travel in Spain.'

"Jack spent a great deal of time talking to the refugees, making notes, and writing a good deal," Lem continued. "He kept records of his thinking, and he wrote rather extensively to his father. As I remember, those we met at Saint-Jean-de-Luz were probably upper-class refugees of the non-Franco group. So we heard some pretty blood-curdling tales of what the Francos were doing in Spain. At the time we were very shocked."

In 1937, massive aerial bombardment was a new experience for Europeans, although it soon would become all too familiar across the continent. "Story of father starved, kept in prison for a week without food for a week," Jack noted in his diary, "[he was] brought a piece of meat, ate it—then saw his son's body with piece of meat cut out of it."

The civil war had begun the year earlier, after fascist forces, under the control of General Francisco Franco, attacked the elected Republican government. Franco's methods included indiscriminate bombing of civilians and other acts of brutality, a dress rehearsal for the terror that would soon envelop all of Europe. The reports from Spain terrified a generation that had not yet witnessed warfare of this kind, but whose memories of the great slaughter of World War I, which had ended only eighteen years earlier, were still vivid.

The town of Guernica, which suffered more than most from Franco's bombing, became a metaphor for aerial mass murder after it was immortalized in Picasso's painting. Fascist Germany and Italy provided important aid to Franco. But Britain, France, and the United States maintained a hands-off policy, effectively sealing the fate of the Republican government in Madrid.

Thousands of European and American volunteers, however, flocked to Spain to fight against the fascists, an astonishing display of idealism that is hard to imagine being duplicated today. But they could not save Spanish democracy. Franco won the civil war in 1939 at a cost of 350,000 lives. The country was devastated, one reason he—wisely—kept his country out of World War II. Consequently, he did not suffer the same fate as his fellow dictators Mussolini and Hitler. Franco was still the supreme leader of Spain when Jack entered the White House in 1961.

The most famous war correspondent in Spain was Ernest Hemingway, whose novels Jack eagerly devoured. Hemingway's most ambitious and famous work, *For Whom the Bell Tolls*, published in 1940, was inspired by events in Spain. Hemingway, who was an ardent antifascist, sympathized with the Republican cause and lionized Americans who went to Spain to fight for it. "Our dead live in the hearts and minds of the Spanish peasants, of the Spanish workers, of all the good, simple honest people who believed in, and fought for, the Spanish Republic," he wrote.

At twenty, Jack's views on the conflict were less clear than those of the accomplished, older Hemingway, but his interest in politics was growing all the time. Although his opinions were not fully formed at this stage, he had already come to the judgment that fascism was bad news, though he did see a few redeeming qualities in the ideology. In the unfolding conflict in Spain, his sympathies were clearly on the Republican side. His diary entries, however, reflect his interest in analysis and observation, a journalist's instinct that would serve him well in the years ahead. "The important thing in the question of victory [in the Spanish Civil War] is how far Germany, Italy, and Russia [will] go in trying to secure victory for their side." Germany and Italy were backing Franco, while the Russians were supporting the nonfascist cause.

Lem, never as political as Jack, was particularly uninterested in abstract ideological issues, but he had an instinctive liberal sensibility and was deeply affected by what he saw on the French–Spanish border. Lem was more interested in the humanitarian disaster that the war had created, the effects of which he and Jack had seen up close. "These southern French and Spaniards are very cruel," he wrote.

After their disturbing visit to southwestern France, Jack and Lem drove on to Italy, then under the control of dictator Benito Mussolini. "August 2—Milan. Pictures of Mussolini everywhere. How long can he last without money, and is he liable to fight when he goes broke. If not, I don't see how there can be a war until 1945 or 50," Jack wrote. Jack and Lem attended a Mussolini rally, witnessing firsthand Il Duce's strutting pronouncements about the country's destiny—nothing less, in his demented vision, than the establishment of a new Roman empire. Lem, who was good at impersonations, regularly amused Jack with his renditions of the pompous Mussolini style.

"He [Jack] was tremendously inquisitive about everything in Europe at that time," recalled Lem. "We went into Italy and he was inquisitive about Benito Mussolini—what Mussolini was doing in Italy and how the people felt about him." Lem felt "that Mussolini had done a lot of good for Italy—that there was much less poverty under the Mussolini regime and that the general public were not too unhappy. Of course, later on most Italians say they were unhappy, but at that time [before the war] we felt he was seemingly doing a good job for the people. At least, that's the way I felt," said Lem. "Italy was cleaner and the people looked more prosperous than we had anticipated."

On their way to Pisa, Jack and Lem gave a ride to a German boy. "Rather interesting as he was anti–National Socialist [anti-Nazi]. He told us many of the abuses they suffer," Jack wrote. "Told us how the Germans hated the Russians. Looks as if the next war could come from that direction especially as England and the rest of Europe seems to be drawing away from Russia." There were also some lighthearted entries in Jack's diary about his, and particularly Lem's, misadventures. "August 4—Pisa. Had great difficulty escaping due to Billings being accused of tearing Madame's towel, leaving one half on the writing table and the other in the toilet. Big crowd and much cursing in Italian."

On August 5, Jack and Lem arrived in the Italian capital. "Arrived in Rome around five-thirty and went to the American Express where I got a wire from Dad and heard that Mother and Joe were on their way to Europe with Kick [Jack's sister Kathleen]. That night snuck into the Coliseum and found it filled with people. Very impressive by moonlight," Jack wrote. But his opinion of the Italians as people was only marginally better than his view of the French. "Have decided that the Italians are the nosiest race in existence. They have to be in on everything even if it is only Billings blowing his nose," he wrote.

While in Rome, the boys also had a private audience with Cardinal Eugenio Pacelli (who later became Pope Pius XII) at the Vatican, an event arranged by Joe, who knew the church official. Jack and Lem also saw Pope Pius XI speak to an audience of about five thousand people. "He looked very sick but made a long speech," wrote Jack.

Lem (left) and Jack (right), looking serious with a group of tourists at the Vatican, 1937. That's a Swiss Guard in the middle of the back row.

"After that we went to Tivoli to see the beautiful fountains which are amazing. The most unusual is the one that played music by means of the water rushing through it. We then returned to Rome and had dinner at Gabazzi's. He gave me quite a talk about the virtues of fascism and it really seemed to have some points—especially the corporate system—which seems quite an interesting step forward."

In mid-August, Jack and Lem left Rome and drove to Florence "after much battling with the cross-eyed proprietor [of the hotel] who turned out to be a terrific crook despite being an Italian and a gentleman," wrote Jack. "Managed to save about 50 lira but left Rome amidst the usual cursing porters. Reached Florence and stayed in our best hotel of the trip." However, the two friends, unlike most tourists, found Florence to be less than enthralling. Jack wrote, "Looked around Florence in the morning and rather disappointed, although quite impressed with Michelangelo's *David.* Left in the afternoon for Venice and quite impressed by the canals which were much more numerous than we expected. Once again, we got our 25-lira room while the Germans got theirs for 8. We will have to get some shorts." Lem was more effusive about Michelangelo's *David,* which he described as "the most beautiful statue I've ever seen or hope to see."

While in Venice, Jack and Lem again met up with friends from back home. One of them was Al Lerner, who was at Choate when Jack and Lem were there. Lerner also knew Jack at Harvard. In 1943, Alan Jay Lerner, as he later became known, teamed up with Frederick Loewe and together they wrote some of the most beloved Broadway musicals, including *Brigadoon, My Fair Lady,* and *Camelot.* The latter was a favorite of Jack's. He often played the soundtrack during his years in the White House. In an interview with journalist Teddy White shortly after Jack's death, Jackie used the word *Camelot* to describe Jack's time in office. The name stuck.

Francis McAdoo, Lem's friend from Princeton and later his boss at the Emerson Drug Company in Baltimore, also happened to be in Venice, with his wife-to-be Cynthia. Mac and Cynthia spent a memorable few hours with the two friends, talking about the situation in Europe and what might happen there. Almost seven decades later, McAdoo still vividly remembered the occasion. "We ran into them on the beach and just talked and had fun. They seemed to be having a great time there. Lem always seemed happiest when he was with Jack. Gosh, we were all so young," he said. "Some evenings later, we met them on the canal for some moonlight gondoliering and troubadoring afloat. LeMoyne asked Cynthia to join him in a gondola. Unaware of this personal invitation, I tagged along."

On August 15, the two boys spent more time with Al Lerner and then went to the American Bar. "And Billings finally had his picture with the pigeons," Jack wrote. There is a similar shot of Jack with the pigeons. The photographs of both of them on that day have survived. There is

Lem feeding the pigeons, St. Mark's Square, Venice, Italy, 1937.

Jack feeding the pigeons.

also a curious reference in his diary on August 15 to Jack's apparent date with a girl and he, she, and Lem taking a trip on a gondola. "Billings managed to make a gay threesome," Jack wrote. "Billings objects to this most unjust statement."

After Venice, the next stop was Austria (which had not yet been absorbed by Germany), where the weather was distinctly colder than in Italy. "Bad driving and by the time we got to the Brenner Pass it was pretty cold. The Austrian people impressed us very much as they were certainly different than the Italians. Stayed at a youth hostel in Innsbruck, which caused 'her ladyship' [presumably Lem] much discomfiture. It was none too good as there were about 40 in a closet and it is considered a disgrace to take a bath." August 17—Tuesday, Innsbruck, Munich. "Up early though not from choice. Her ladyship [Lem] stated that her night had been far from pleasant. Started over the Alps to Germany. . . . Arrived in Munich around nightfall. Hitler seems as popular here as Mussolini was in Italy, although propaganda seems to be his strongest weapon." Once they reached Germany, Lem recalled that Jack "was absolutely overcome with interest in the Hitler movement."

The next day, August 18, was the boys' first full day in the city where Hitler got his start. "Got up late and none too spry. Had a talk with proprietor who is quite a Hitler fan. There is no doubt that these dictators are more popular in the country than outside due to their effective propaganda," wrote Jack. "That night went to see, *Swing High, Swing Low,* [starring Carole Lombard and Fred MacMurray—American movies remained popular in Hitler's Germany] and enjoyed it more than the first [time] probably because we haven't seen a picture lately."

If Jack and Lem had reservations about the Italians, they found the Germans positively scary. Mussolini may have been absolute ruler of Italy, but as far as brutality is concerned, his regime was no match for the Nazis. The two American boys had little idea about what was really happening in Germany but nevertheless developed a sense of foreboding. In Munich, they quickly tired of the arrogant, beer-guzzling brownshirts they ran into at the Hofbräuhaus, a favorite watering hole for Nazis as well as foreign tourists. It was here—in 1923—that Hitler planned his failed putsch against the democratic Weimar Republic. "We just had awful experiences there," recalled Lem. The brownshirts "were just so haughty and sure of themselves."

The brownshirts had reason to be self-confident, however. Two years before, Germany had marched into the Rhineland. It was the first major abrogation of the Treaty of Versailles, but England and France didn't lift a finger. It didn't take Jack and Lem much time to become aware of the pervasiveness of virulent nationalism and anti-Americanism, especially in Munich. After they took as much as they could stand of the southern German city, they drove to Nuremberg, the location of legendary Nazi rallies. Unfortunately, they missed seeing Hitler speak by just a few days. "We always wished afterwards that we had just stayed three days longer there, because we missed Hitler by that length of time," said Lem.

Jack and Lem failed to make any friends in Germany, unlike in the other countries they visited, except one—Dunker, a lovable dachshund that they ran into on their way to Nuremberg. "August 19—Stopped on the way and bought Dunker, a dachshund of great beauty for 8.00 as a present for Olive [Cawley]. Immediately got hay fever etc. so it looks like the odds are 8-1 towards Dunker getting to America," Jack wrote.

Both Jack and Lem were crazy about dogs and soon fell totally in love with little Dunker. They always remembered him as the nicest German they ever met. Jack had to keep his distance from dogs, however, because of his allergies. As the boys moved around Germany, his allergic reaction to Dunker unfortunately got worse. But he tried to make do as best he could. "August 20—Friday—Nuremberg, Wurtenberg. Started out as usual only this time we had the added attraction of being spit on. Due to the cold, stopped short of Frankfurt. Dunker is quite a problem because when he's got to go, he goes," Jack wrote.

On August 21, Jack, Lem, and Dunker set out for Cologne. Dunker loved strutting his stuff on the road and apparently regarded himself as quite the stud where other dogs were concerned, as the boys discovered whenever they stopped the car. The Germans they met en route also warmed up to Dunker, although not necessarily to his masters. "They weren't very appreciative of Americans having heard all the propaganda about the United States on the radio, but for Dunker they had a soft spot," Lem remembered.

Jack and Lem were amazed at how good the roads were in Germany, especially the autobahns, the world's first interstate highways. (Dunker didn't care.) But they were also suspicious about Hitler's real purpose in building them. "From Cologne we headed for Utrecht on one of the autostradas, which are said to be the finest roads in the world," Lem said. "They seem, however, absolutely unnecessary as there is very little traffic. However, perhaps Hitler, in building them, has something up his sleeve and is planning to use them for military purposes."

The two boys' diary entries reflected their concern—even in 1937— that Germany was heading in a direction that could lead to war. Lem wrote in his scrapbook: "It looks like the next war will come from that direction especially as England seems to be drawing away from Russia." He said later, "We disliked the whole setup. We left there with a very bad taste in our mouths."

The whole experience in Germany impacted Jack enormously. "There was a noticeable change in Jack Kennedy," said Lem. "In the summer of 1937, he had just completed his freshman year at Harvard and he was beginning to show more interest and more of a desire to think out the problems of the world and to record his ideas than he did two years before at Choate. He insisted, for instance, that we pick up every German hitchhiker. This worked out very well because a high percentage of them were students and could speak English. In that way, we learned a great deal about Germany. I remember picking up two German soldiers who were on leave. . . . They were with us for a week and we gathered that their general attitude was pro-Hitler. We picked up another German student who was very anti-Hitler. He is probably dead now."

Next stop after Utrecht was The Hague, where Jack and Lem decided—sadly—that they would have to leave Dunker behind. Jack's allergies were out of control. He had a test done to see if it was Dunker that was giving him the hay fever, and the result showed that it was. In the American Express office there, they ran into someone who was interested in buying Dunker. So they sold him for five guilders. They were both heartbroken about leaving him behind, but there was no other choice. But the little dachshund, immortalized in some of the photographs they took, would always be a symbol for them of their great trip to Europe in the prewar days.

Jack and Lem visited Belgium before embarking for London from Calais on August 25. There was a mix-up with their departure, however, and Lem stayed behind with the car for a short time before joining Jack later in London. Kick, Joe, and Rose were in England at the time, so the two boys were able to hook up with them and catch up on all of the news from the States. This was before Joe had become U.S. ambassador to Britain, so if the two boys, having roughed it in continental Europe, thought they were going to live it up in England, they were mistaken. Kick found them a cheap boardinghouse on Talbot Square off Hyde Park where they stayed during their time in the British capital. "I remembered we listened to the Joe Louis–Tommy Farr fight over the radio at that boardinghouse," said Lem.

On August 27, however, Jack got sick. While seeing his mother on the south coast, he helped himself to "a liberal dose of chocolates and tomato juice," he wrote. "When I arrived back in London found myself with the Hives. Went home and was damn sick. August 28—Still sick— had very tough night. Billings got a Kent doctor who wondered if I mixed my chocolates and tomato juice in a big glass. Finally convinced him I hadn't. Got another doctor." Lem remembered that "it was very worrying because we didn't know anybody, and we didn't have a clue about what kind of doctor to get. Somebody at the boardinghouse recommended a doctor who wasn't very good. We had a lot of trouble. I bring up sickness because Jack Kennedy all during his life had few days when he wasn't in pain or sick in some way." Jack went to four doctors in all before the hives mysteriously disappeared.

The last stop on the boy's trip was Scotland and a visit to the country estate of Sir James Calder, a business acquaintance of Joe's who owned Haig & Haig Whiskey. Joe owned the Haig & Haig concession in the United States, a deal he had made with Sir James before he became ambassador. Despite his wealth, aristocratic lineage, and huge estate, Sir James was an eccentric who switched off all the lights in the mansion at ten each evening—a real problem since the house was huge, with thirty rooms and only one bathroom, which was difficult to find in the dark. "September 3—very good meals here—the best hour is 10:00 and from then on it is perilous to move about as Sir James is very cautious on the electricity," wrote Jack. Moreover, the place was cold and damp, typical of most British homes, large or small, at the time. For the youthful vacationers, however, it was all part of the adventure, which included a hunting trip on the Scottish moors.

After Scotland, it was time to return to London and then head home in time for the fall college semester. On the voyage back, Jack met a huge—about 280 pounds—Dutch wrestling champion who complained that he had no one to wrestle with. Naturally, Jack suggested Lem. As usual, Lem went along with Jack's crazy idea, although he had serious doubts about wrestling an experienced pro that he knew could make mincemeat out of him. "Unbeknownst to me, Jack gave him a greatly exaggerated account of my wrestling career, and arranged to have me wrestle him," recalled Lem. "When I went to the gym the next day I had no choice but to wrestle him. From then on, I wrestled this guy every day, and thank God, the crossing wasn't that long." The bouts continued off and on throughout the trip, with Jack enthusiastically assuming the role of referee. Lem was the worse for wear when the voyage finally ended, having been tossed and thrown, and sat on, by someone who weighed 100 pounds more than he did.

On September 16, the boys' ship arrived back in the United States. "Mother, Uncle Ike, Rip, Kick, and Olive were there to meet us," Lem wrote. "It was a wonderful trip. I'm sorry that it's over."

4

THE RESTLESS YEARS
(1938–41)

"Dante once said that the hottest places in hell are reserved for those who, in a period of moral crisis, maintain their neutrality."

—John F. Kennedy, June 24, 1963

Upon returning to the States after their European vacation, Lem resumed his studies at Princeton while Jack went back to Harvard. In February 1938, Joe Kennedy realized his dream of becoming the first Irish American ambassador to Great Britain. It was a satisfying moment for the man who had seen No Irish Need Apply signs as a kid in Boston. Joe, like many Irish Americans, resented the continued British rule in part of Ireland. (The thirty-two counties of southern Ireland became independent in 1922, but six counties in the north were part of the United Kingdom when Joe was ambassador and remain so.) He relished the fact that the British now had to deal with him, a proud Irish American.

The month after he became ambassador, Joe moved most of his family to the ambassadorial residence in London. But Jack remained at

Harvard working on his degree. The reserved British were bowled over by the extroverted Kennedys, with their joie de vivre and million-dollar smiles, and welcomed them like they were Hollywood stars, despite Joe's views on Ireland. To some extent, however, the welcome was self-serving. The situation in Europe was deteriorating. The British knew that their survival might easily depend on an American lifeline and were determined to keep good relations with the giant across the Atlantic.

"It was a period during which any ambassador would have been popular in London because they obviously needed our help during this period and knew they were going to need it more," remembered Lem. "Mr. Kennedy, although being probably the first American of Irish descent who had been ambassador to the Court of St. James's, was exceedingly popular in the beginning and he became a very close friend, for instance, of the king [George V] and queen [Elizabeth]. He was a great admirer of Queen Elizabeth [the late Queen Mother] and thought she was one of the most capable, charming women whom he'd ever met. I heard him say this time and time again. I know that until the time he had the differences with Roosevelt, he was a very popular ambassador." Later on, his views "were not popular with the English," who, unlike Joe, wanted the United States fighting on their side in the war.

For better or worse, Joe was FDR's representative, so the British treated Joe and his family like they were royalty during the early part of his ambassadorship. Although the United States was a neutral country, it was clearly more sympathetic to Britain and France than to Germany and Italy. Just how much good relations with the United States counted became evident only weeks after Joe became ambassador. Hitler seized Austria—the Anschluss—without a shot being fired. Later in 1938, the Germans also gained control of the Sudetenland, part of Czechoslovakia. The British knew they were under threat. Joe, as well as British prime minister Neville Chamberlain, was in favor of letting Hitler have his way to preserve the peace. So, it must be said, were most Britons at the time. Throughout 1938, Joe remained surprisingly popular.

Jack's younger sister Kathleen was particularly well liked and exhibited the same witty and self-deprecating humor as Jack. Lem had become especially close to Kathleen during these years. They wrote to each other as well, especially after she moved to England with Joe and Rose. There was speculation that Lem was courting Kathleen. But Kick wisely put off a proposal from Lem, saying to him, "Come on Lem, you know you're not the marrying kind." Kick likely sensed that Lem's main attachment was to Jack.

There is no doubt, however, that Lem's affection for Kick, who was one of the few people he knew who was as outgoing as he was, was genuine. They had the same fun-loving ways, as well as similar interests and temperaments. Lem's niece, Sally Carpenter, said that Lem often talked about Kick, even years after she had died. It was her impression that the relationship between them was very close. As far as Jack and the rest of the Kennedy family was concerned, it seemed natural that Lem and Kick would be good friends, especially since Jack and Kick were close as well. But it is very unlikely that the relationship was ever intimate. For his part, Lem never told anyone close to him whether it was or wasn't, preferring to leave the issue open to doubt.

Kick was not the only woman in Lem's early life, although she clearly was the most important to him. There was of course Pussy Brooks, whom he'd met at Choate. Later, he even tried to compete with Jack in dating glamorous movie stars, including Universal pinup Ella Raines. But the overwhelming evidence says that for Lem, these were platonic involvements. Lem was close to many women all his life. He enjoyed their company, but he didn't want marriage, even an arranged marriage, which many gays did then for cover—or sometimes because they were genuinely trying to overcome their true natures.

In the summer of 1938, Jack once again returned to Europe, spending most of it in London with the ambassador, as he would be known henceforth, and the rest of the family. Lem was disappointed that he would

Movie star Ella Raines, 1954. She and Lem were friends.

not be able to join Jack in Europe on this trip. It was just too expensive, and he couldn't afford to take the time away from college. "Of course, I continued to see Jack throughout the year until he went over to Europe in the summer," he recalled. At the end of the summer, when Jack returned to the United States, Lem was there to meet him as he descended from the gangplank of the ship. They caught up on all the news and talked about completing college as soon as possible. As was his custom, Jack spent Christmas at his family's Palm Beach estate. "He was the only member of the family there [since Joe and the rest of the family were in England], so he had the house to himself," remembered Lem. "He asked me down."

As 1939 began, most Europeans and Americans desperately hoped that peace would prevail in Europe. The British and French had made concession after concession to appease the German führer, but it would all be to no avail. Before the year was out, the continent would be engulfed by another war, only eighteen years after the previous one—billed as the war to end all wars—had ended.

Lem was still in college as the year began. He graduated in the fall and took a job at Continental Can for a while, working on an assembly line for twenty-five dollars a week. He later found a job in Baltimore, where his mother, Romaine, lived. It wasn't a great position—selling Coca-Cola dispensers to drugstores. But during these years, people felt lucky to get any job. Lem was delighted to be back in the same town as his mother. Jack congratulated him on the good news, "Very good about your job. Big J. P. [his dad, Joe Kennedy] is very pleased."

Two months before he graduated from Princeton, in the spring of 1939, Lem wrote to Kick about his view of the job market in Depression-era America. Even though the war in Europe had not yet begun, it's clear that Lem sensed the peace

Lem and his mother, Romaine, in the early days.

would not last, even for the United States. "None of us are worrying too much about jobs," he wrote. "This country is getting more and more war-conscious and we all expect to be over there at least by fall. Last night at the movies, they showed the newsreel pictures of our Air Force and Army maneuvers and everyone hysterically got up and cheered—even brother Jack's flat feet and bad stomach won't keep him out of this one."

Jack, by contrast, did not graduate, in 1939. Unlike Lem, who had to work, he felt no urgency to do so. Jack didn't get his degree from Harvard until the following year, because he again spent so much of the year in Europe. On February 24, he boarded the *Queen Mary* with his father, now Ambassador Joseph Kennedy. Lem wanted to go to Europe with Jack but again felt he had to stay at home, finish college, and then go to work.

When he arrived in London, Jack wrote Lem, "Been having a great time. Had a plenty rough trip over but not sick. Been working every day and going to dinner with dad. Met the King this morning at court here. It takes place in the morning and you wear tails. The King stands as you go up and bow. Met Queen Mary and was [had] a tea with Princess Elizabeth with whom I made a great deal of time. . . . Friday I leave for Rome as JP has been appointed to represent Roosevelt at the Pope's coronation."

Jack was elated, not only at being in Europe again at a time when so much history was being made, but also at the chance to make his mark representing his dad. Still, he missed having Lem in Europe with him this time around. "If you come over this summer," he wrote, "contemplating driving to Greece and Constantinople so you can explain art to me."

Jack found the situation in Europe to be much grimmer than when he and Lem had traveled there two years earlier. Talk of war was every-where. During his stay in England, Jack followed events closely. Being the U.S. ambassador's son gave him access to the thinking of prominent and powerful Brits. But he also talked extensively with ordinary people about the worsening European situation and their views about what Britain should do. Jack being Jack, he also found time for an active social life, which included plenty of parties and dates.

While overseas, Jack also visited other European countries, including France, Austria, Germany, Russia, Hungary, Czechoslovakia, Poland, and the Baltic republics—plus Turkey, Egypt, and Palestine. The latter was ruled by the British under a mandate from the League of Nations. Jack favored partition as a way of appeasing both sides. "It seems to me that the only thing to do will be to break the country up into two autonomous districts giving them both self government to the extent that they do not interfere with each other," he wrote. "Jerusalem, having the background that it has, should be an independent unit. Though this is a difficult solution, yet it is the only one that I think can work."

In Paris, he stayed with Ambassador William C. Bullitt and had lunch with Charles and Anne Morrow Lindbergh. The Lindberghs had lived in Europe for years. They'd fled there after their baby was kidnapped and murdered in the United States but more recently were famous, or really infamous, for their antipathy to democracy. Jack wrote to Lem in Baltimore about meeting the Lindberghs, attending the coronation of the pope in Rome, and about Choate. "I got an especially sickening letter from Choate wanting me to recommend a boy who will carry on the traditions of the present Sixth. So far I have not been able to think of a big enough prick but am giving it a lot of thought. . . . Was at lunch today with the Lindberghs and they are the most attractive couple I've seen. She takes a rotten picture and is really as pretty as hell, and very nice. . . . Am living it up in the embassy and living like a king. Offie [Carmel Offie], Ambassador Bullitt's chief aide and I are now the greatest of pals and he is really a pretty good guy though I suppose it will make you a bit ill to hear it. . . . The pope didn't actually mention you by name but he gave me the impression that he was thinking of you. Offie has just rang for me so I guess I have to get the old paper ready and go in and wipe his arse."

Jack's time in Europe in 1939 was not a vacation. He was there to do political errands for his father, mostly fact-finding both in England and on the continent. Still, he allowed plenty of time for fun and adventure, which included lots of girls. Jack was accompanied some of the time by Torby Macdonald, his friend from Harvard, but he also traveled alone and got himself into a little trouble here and there. His visit to Germany, in particular, set off a diplomatic row. With war only weeks away, Jack traveled to Berlin by way of Nazi-occupied Prague, a city so much on edge that the State Department had declared it off-limits to U.S. tourists.

U.S. foreign service officer George Kennan, who was saddled with the responsibility of making sure Jack's travels were trouble free, thought he was "an upstart and an ignoramus." But although Jack had no official status and was an obvious pain to the State Department, he was no ignoramus, as his letters to Lem back in the States indicate. In one letter from Danzig, an area the Germans desperately wanted to reclaim from Poland, Jack wrote: "Was up in Danzig for a couple of days. Danzig is completely Nazified, much heiling of Hitler, etc. Talked with the Nazi heads and all the consuls up there. The situation there is complicated, but roughly here it is. The question of Danzig and the corridor are inseparable. The Germans feel that both must be returned. If this is done, then Poland is cut off from the sea."

Jack continued: "Poland is determined not to give up Danzig and you can take it as official that Poland will not give up Danzig, and second, that she will not give Germany extra-territoriality rights in the corridor for the highways. She will offer compromises, but never give up. What Germany will decide to do if she decides to go to war—will be to try to put Poland in the position of being the aggressor—and then go to work. Poland has an army of 4,000,000 who are damn good—but poorly equipped." Jack included a hand-drawn map of the area to give Lem a better idea of the situation there.

Jack also suggested that Lem read Buell's *Poland—Key to Europe*. He then wrote, "Remember, however, that Poles are not Czechs & they will fight." That prediction was soon put to the test. The outlook changed dramatically for the Poles on August 21, 1939, when Hitler and Stalin signed their infamous Nazi–Soviet nonaggression pact. The alliance between Germany and Russia meant that Poland now faced a threat from the east as well as the west.

Jack was in Berlin on the very day the pact was signed and witnessed the joy in the streets of Berlin after state-controlled radio announced the new agreement with Russia. It contained a secret provision that allowed Stalin to seize part of Poland after the Germans invaded from the west. With the start of World War II less than a month away, the communists and the fascists, historically ideological foes, were now unlikely allies busily dividing up Poland between them.

While he was in Germany, Jack bought a movie camera and projector and took some film of prewar Berlin before the massive wartime air raids that would decimate the city. Jack teased Lem, telling him that he bought the camera "so we could spend a lot of time getting close-ups of you in color." He also commented on his own face in color. "Incidentally, my face in color would be quite a sensation after one week of these

German meals. I still don't think there will be a war, but I think the Germans have gone so far internally with their propaganda stories on Danzig + the Corridor that it is hard to see them backing down. England seems firm this time, but that is not completely understood here [in Berlin], the big danger here lies in the German counting on another Munich + finding themselves in a war when Chamberlain refuses to give in."

Jack was right. This time, the Germans miscalculated. With his eastern flank secured, on September 1, 1939, Hitler's armies blitzkrieged their way into Poland. Against the odds, just as Jack predicted, the Poles, unlike the Czechs and the Austrians, fought back. Britain and France found themselves in a box, having already assured the Poles that they would come to their aid if they were attacked. British prime minister Neville Chamberlain issued an ultimatum for the Germans to withdraw. With Hitler's refusal to respond, the die was cast.

On September 3, Chamberlain announced that Britain was at war with Germany. Britons, many of whom vividly remembered the last war, which had cost one million lives out of a total population of forty million, dreaded what lay ahead, especially since the Spanish Civil War had already demonstrated that civilian populations could now be subject to massive aerial attack to a degree that had been unthinkable in World War I.

Jack, Joe Jr., and Kick, as well as their mother, Rose, were present in the visitors' gallery of the House of Commons and heard Chamberlain's forlorn lament. "Everything that I have worked for, everything that I have hoped for, everything that I have believed in during my public life has crashed in ruins."

Rose Kennedy, who, like her husband, admired and respected Chamberlain, recalled that "when we were on our way home from the House of Commons the air-raid sirens began to howl, and we ran for refuge into the nearest shelter we could find." As it turned out, it was a false alarm. The Battle of Britain was months away.

Lem, like most Americans, followed the depressing news on the radio. Edward R. Murrow's shortwave broadcasts from London, in particular, vividly evoked the atmosphere of a continent about to fall apart. Lem worried about Jack, and the rest of the Kennedy family, who were still in London. But there was little he could do in Baltimore except hope for the best, listen to the news, and eagerly await Jack's letters.

The outbreak of war obliterated Chamberlain's appeasement policy.

The British government's agreement to the dismemberment of Czecho-slovakia at Munich in 1938, in a futile attempt to head off the conflict, was now viewed by the public in a totally different light. Most important to Jack, the onset of war also devastated his father, who had backed the appeasement policy unequivocally.

With Hitler's march into Poland (Germany gobbled up the rest of Czechoslovakia in March 1939), it was clear that German aggression had no limit and that the very future of Britain and Europe, and ultimately even North America and the rest of the world, was at stake. Churchill had been proven right. Appeasement as a policy was dead. For Britain and France, at least, the war both nations had sought so strenuously to avoid was about to begin.

But it wasn't just the British policy that was dead. Neville Chamber-lain and Joe Kennedy, who were two peas in a pod in their embrace of appeasement, also suffered mortal political wounds, although they both lingered on in their jobs for months. Joe's job was safe for the time being because FDR was up for reelection in 1940 and didn't want to give the boot to his Irish American ambassador before the American people, and large numbers of Irish Americans, voted. So he craftily encouraged Joe to speak out on his behalf throughout the months leading up to the presi-dential election in November. In the crucial period just before the elec-tion, Joe gave a radio address supporting FDR.

Lem heard the broadcast and wrote Jack, "Listened to your pappy's speech tonight. It was the clearest and most sensible one I've heard in the whole [1940 presidential] campaign. I was a Willkie [Republican presi-dential nominee Wendell Willkie] worker but I could never argue too effectively with Big JP." Joe Kennedy's endorsement of FDR was effective especially with Irish American and Catholic voters. But there was no love lost between him and FDR.

A month after the U.S. election—on December 2, 1940—with Win-ston Churchill now leading Great Britain and FDR safely reelected, Joe Kennedy resigned his post and returned to the United States. FDR didn't need old Joe anymore. But he didn't need to fire him. Joe was only too ready to get out of Britain, which he thought was going down the tubes anyway. Before he resigned, Joe sent hysterical cables back to Washington indicating that Britain was finished. At one point, he predicted that Hitler would be in Buckingham Palace within two weeks of the outbreak of war.

Joe made his most incriminating statement, incredibly, to a journalist. Believing he was talking off the record, Joe said, "Democracy is
finished in Britain, and maybe America, too." But after his comments
were published, it was Joe who was finished.

In Jack's case, it was not a question of "like father, like son." He
would eventually, but not immediately, disagree with his father's support
of Chamberlain's appeasement policy. "It's my feeling," said Lem later,
"and I am sure I am right, that Jack absolutely disagreed with his father
a hundred percent." Jack's thesis at Harvard was devoted to an explanation of why Britain failed to anticipate, and plan, for the grave threat to
its national security posed by the fascist dictators. He titled it "Appeasement in Munich."

In July 1940, shortly after he graduated from Harvard, it was turned
into a book about Britain's wrongheaded policies during the 1930s,
although with major changes, since Churchill had now become prime
minister. It was titled *Why England Slept*. One Harvard wit suggested a
better title might have been *Why Daddy Slept*.

However, in the book, Jack is careful not to stroll too far from his
father's viewpoint. He is much more critical of Britain's failure to rearm
than he is of the Munich Agreement, which Joe had applauded. The revi-
sionist take on Chamberlain's pact with Hitler was that it gave the British
valuable time to build up their military.

In a radio interview just after the book was published, Jack said,
"This book is an attempt to analyze the reasons for Britain's failure to
rearm." He criticized the U.S. press for focusing on the Munich Agreement itself rather than on the need for rearmament. Asked what his
father thought of the book, Jack said that Joe hadn't read it at that point
so he didn't know "if he agrees with me or not."

Typically, Joe did his best to make the book a success, which
included buying thousands of copies himself, despite his son's criticism.
Lem was thrilled that Jack was now an author and busily promoted the
book, too. With Joe and Lem behind him, no wonder Jack's book sold
well. Lem didn't really care about Jack's point of view, although he leaned
toward his friend's opinion of appeasement. His backing for Jack was
always unconditional.

John Kennedy was just twenty-three years old and already regarded
as something of an authority on British political history, not only because

of the book, but also because of the extensive time he had spent in the country while his father was ambassador. Although he mostly associated with members of the British upper class, whose elegance and lifestyle he admired, he was also well aware of the vastly inferior condition of the British working class during his stays in Britain. He felt that, sooner or later, this would lead to radical change there.

John Kennedy's views about the cold war, Vietnam, and other crises he confronted as president can clearly be traced to the opinions he formed during the pre–World War II period in Britain. He was determined that if he ever gained political power, he would not make the same mistakes the British had made between the two world wars. He could not ensure, of course, that he would not make new mistakes, and he made more than a few of those. But maintaining a military second to none was not one of them. It is not so well remembered today that while urging negotiations with the Soviet Union, he also initiated a sizable increase in U.S. military spending.

In the fall of 1940, with his Harvard degree under his belt and his book, *Why England Slept,* a success, Jack was back on the West Coast while Lem continued working for Coca-Cola in Baltimore. Jack enrolled in Stanford University's business school, but his main interest while in California was girls and Hollywood. "I know why he went to Stanford," remembered Lem. "It was because he was trying to fill in his time until he went into the service because he knew, as we all knew, that it was only a matter of time before we got into the war. . . . There was no question in our minds in 1940 that we were going to be in the war, and we were just the age to go."

On October 4, 1940, Jack wrote Lem, "Well very well settled here. Have my own cottage on the campus and living very well. Have met a lot of people and they are very friendly—quite a change from the East. Still can't get used to the co-eds but am taking them in my stride. Expect to cut one out of the herd and brand one shortly but am taking it very slow as do not want to be known as the beast from the East." Lem wrote back warning Jack about the California sun and making fun of his desire for a perpetual suntan. "My advice is to keep out of the sun because as far as you're concerned it will be far more stylish to be yellow this year," an apparent reference to Japan's rise as a great power.

While at Stanford, Jack ran into an old Choate boy that he and Lem had known there. Jack wrote Lem, "Do you remember a fat blond boy named Jim Filer at Choate? Well, he's out here—and quite the man about campus. He has quite a hero notion of me from Choate and from what I can gather most of the younger boys at school thought of me as sort of a god-like Casanova, if you know what I mean, and thought you were a big shit, as near as I can tell. Anyway, Jim is launching me on the campus. I am glad I was nice to the younger fellows back at Choate as it only shows. The next time I see him I will go into more detail about why nobody at Choate liked you, although to tell the truth, he was rather vague about you—just thinks you're a shit. Best Jack."

Being in California also gave Jack the opportunity to brush up against Hollywood royalty. At one party, he chatted with screen legends Clark Gable and Spencer Tracy. As a boy, Jack had been excited whenever Joe returned from Hollywood with the latest movies, especially if they were cowboy films. Joe even brought back Tom Mix (a Western hero of the time) cowboy suits. Joe's stories about Hollywood entranced young Jack and stimulated an interest in the movie colony that never waned, even after he became president. In later years, Jack would often remark on the similarities between politics and the movies. Both professions were concerned with image as well as substance and, as far as the public was concerned, the former was likely to count much more than the latter.

Later, when he got to know movie star Peter Lawford, who married his sister Pat, Jack would ask Peter for tips about how to look and act the part. Jack wanted to woo voters the way movie stars seduced audiences. Peter was always smooth and perfectly tailored in public, no matter how disheveled his private life might be, and Jack felt he could learn a lot from him. In this first early visit to Tinseltown, however, Jack was just happy to be among the stars.

His friend Chuck Spalding was working for Gary Cooper at the time. The tall, handsome actor, who epitomized American macho, was box office gold. Jack talked to Chuck for hours about how Cooper had achieved and maintained his stardom. Jack wasn't interested in being an actor, but if he went into politics, he certainly wanted to be a star.

In November, he wrote Lem: "I regret that I haven't communicated with you earlier. As you may have heard, went down to Hollywood and took it by storm. I have many glowing reports to tell you, but as you are saving your anecdotes till I see you—I will save this. Ran into lovely Martha Kemp at a soiree. We exchanged very few words a la me and Jack Maher. She revealed that she has always considered you dumb but lovable and we laughed heartily over you. . . . Have become very fond of Stanford. Everyone is very friendly—the gals are quite attractive and it's a very good life. Feeling much better the last two weeks."

For a while, Jack shared an apartment in the Hollywood Hills with actor Robert Stack, who later achieved fame as FBI crime fighter Eliot Ness on the television show *The Untouchables,* a big hit for ABC while Jack was president. In his 1980 autobiography, *Straight Shooting,* Stack discusses Jack's attractiveness to women. "I've known many of the great Hollywood stars," he wrote, "and only a very few of them seemed to hold the attention for women that Jack Kennedy did, even before he entered the political arena. He'd just look at them and they'd tumble."

After his sojourn in Hollywood, Jack returned to the East Coast in time for the Christmas vacation period, during which he liked to spend time with his family and Lem. It would be the last Christmas in which the United States would be at peace for four years. For Jack and Lem, the carefree period of their lives—their school and college years—

Harry Dixon, Kick Kennedy, John Coleman, Charlotte McDonnell, Jack, and Lem, Palm Beach, Christmas, 1940.

were now behind them. Like millions of other young Americans, they faced an uncertain future. In less than a year, the country would be at war.

The British and French, however, already were at war, and struggling to stay afloat. Americans looked on the situation from afar with concern and even alarm. Most backed FDR's policy, which skillfully moved public opinion toward aiding the British and the French while reaffirming U.S. neutrality.

FDR's task was not made easier, however, by the America First movement and the Lindberghs, or by Joe Kennedy, who was a friend of theirs. Joe thought that FDR's policies would draw the United States into a war that clearly the American people did not want. But he was mostly motivated by his concern for his sons' safety. He didn't see why any American boy should die to save the British Empire, which at that time oppressed one-quarter of the world, including part of Ireland.

As a Republican, Lem didn't necessarily agree with FDR about the European war and what the United States should do, either. He leaned toward isolationism, the predominant view of the Republican Party at the time. But Lem's views always reflected what Jack felt, so his position on appeasement likely moved as Jack's views evolved. The most important thing to Lem in any case wasn't politics but his friendship with Jack. When the Kennedys were still in England, all he wanted was for them to come back to a United States still at peace. He was delighted when Joe resigned his ambassadorship and the whole family was back on U.S. soil.

During 1941, Jack and Lem, increasingly viewing American involvement in the war as inevitable, began to think about trying to get into the military. Even though the country adopted its first peacetime draft in 1940, initially it was a lottery system requiring a limited number of recruits. Jack drew one of the earliest numbers but was rejected by the army because of his health. Both men were concerned that medical issues would stand in their way. Jack was worried that his bad back and the string of serious ailments from which he had suffered during his youth would disqualify him. Lem thought he would be barred because of his atrocious eyesight. As it turned out, both were right—at first.

In September 1941, however, Jack was granted a commission as an ensign in the Naval Reserve. Lem desperately tried to follow in Jack's footsteps but was also rejected by the army and the navy, and even the Coast Guard, because of his eyesight. So he bided his time in Baltimore, wondering what to do. Fortunately, Jack was in Washington, D.C., at this time, so Lem could easily make frequent trips to the nation's capital to see him, since it is only about an hour's drive between the two cities. "He had a very nice apartment in a brand-new building—the Dorchester on Sixteenth Street," Lem recalled. "I was down all the time trying to find out what I could do, so I spent a lot of time with him during this period."

Both men were frustrated over their circumstances—Lem because he had been unable to follow in Jack's footsteps and get into the service—Jack, because he had a desk job with the navy that he thought was a waste of time. "He was very frustrated and unhappy," remembered Lem. "So was I." They spent their free time during the last days of prewar peace in Washington going to parties and movies and visiting old friends.

5

COURAGE UNDER FIRE
(WAR, 1941–45)

"There is always inequity in life. Some men are killed in war and some men are wounded, and some men never leave the country, and some men are stationed in the Antarctic, and some are stationed in San Francisco. It's very hard in military or personal life to assure complete equality. Life is unfair."
—John F. Kennedy, March 1, 1962

Jack, being a Kennedy, was fanatical about touch football, a game Lem hated. But Lem forced himself to play to please Jack. Jack was always trying to start a game or join one. The morning of December 7, 1941, was just such a day. Jack dragged Lem down to the Washington Monument grounds for a game of touch football. Lem later recalled what happened. "We found a game near the Washington Monument. We'd just finished the game and were driving back to his apartment. All of a sudden, the news came over the car radio that the Japanese had attacked Pearl Harbor." Jack and Lem were together driving back uptown when they heard the most dramatic news of the century. They knew instantly that the country was at war, and that it would be total war.

As Jack and Lem drove past Massachusetts Avenue—Embassy

Row—they could see smoke billowing out from the Japanese embassy as diplomats there desperately tried to destroy incriminating documents. The United States was now in World War II whether it liked it or not. The two friends, together at this pivotal moment in twentieth-century history, turned to each other wondering what this would mean for them and for their country.

From that moment, events moved quickly. On December 8, President Roosevelt addressed a joint session of Congress. Jack and Lem, and almost every American alive that day, listened to FDR's powerful opening words on the radio, "Yesterday, December 7, 1941—a date which will live in infamy—the United States of America was suddenly and deliberately attacked by naval forces of the empire of Japan."

At the close of his speech, FDR asked Congress for a declaration of war against Japan. It was approved, with the exception of one lawmaker— Montana's Jeannette Rankin, the first woman elected to Congress, who declined to vote for the war because of her pacifist principles. She was maligned for that vote for the rest of her life and, needless to say, was kicked out of Congress at the next election by her constituency.

After the congressional approval of war against Japan, Germany met its obligations to its ally. On December 11, Germany declared war on the United States. At the beginning of the week, the United States was at war in the Pacific. By week's end, it was at war in Europe, too. Everyone knew the survival of the nation was at stake. There was a swelling of patriotic fervor across the land. In one horrific act, the Japanese had united the country in the worldwide fight against fascism. Everyone, whether in the military or not, wanted to lend a helping hand. Jack and Lem were no exception. They were in their midtwenties, and soon their lives, like those of millions of others, would change beyond their wildest expectations.

The war was the first big event to affect Jack and Lem's friendship. Up until that point, they saw each other frequently. At Choate, they saw each other every day and frequently spent much of their school vacation time together as well. For the one semester that Jack joined Lem at Princeton, they saw each other every day there, too. After Jack enrolled in Harvard, they often met in New York on weekends. But both men knew that they would likely go their separate ways during the war, that it would be impossible to enlist in the same unit together.

Neither saw military action immediately. For the moment, the two remained in the States while the war raged overseas. It was during this time that Jack had a serious involvement with a Danish woman. His sister Kick, who was working for the *Washington Times-Herald,* introduced him to Inga Arvad, a beauty who also worked for the newspaper. Jack could not resist her but kept his new love secret from his mother, Rose, because Inga wasn't a Catholic and had been married and divorced twice.

Jack raved to Lem about how gorgeous "Inga Binga" (as he called her) was and how he couldn't stop thinking about her. Lem must have found that tough, but by now he was used to Jack's many infatuations with women and he knew they were usually superficial and short-lived. This one, however, looked like it would be serious and more durable. But then a Washington newspaper discovered a photograph showing Inga sitting next to Hitler at the 1936 Olympic Games in Berlin. She was also reportedly acquainted with Goebbels, Hitler's minister of propaganda, and it was even rumored that Inga was a Nazi spy. The FBI began an investigation and learned of Jack's involvement with her.

At this point, Joe stepped in. He didn't care so much that his son was dating a non-Catholic. During his Hollywood days, he'd dated women of all religious affiliations, even though he was married, including—most scandalously—the movie megastar Gloria Swanson. He didn't care one bit about the religion of the women Jack saw. But he did care about his son's future, and Inga Binga was damaged goods. He tried to scare Jack off, but Jack defended Inga and would have none of Joe's meddling.

Joe then went behind Jack's back and arranged to have him transferred, initially to Naval Intelligence in Charleston, South Carolina. But Inga went down there to see Jack, as well. The FBI followed her and bugged her hotel room, capturing Jack discussing his intelligence work in between the lovemaking and pillow talk, which included Inga's concern about becoming pregnant. Jack's phone calls were also intercepted, although most of his conversations were routine.

The FBI tracked all of Inga's movements and conversations. The navy, too, was checking things out. At some point, Jack discovered that something was up, as a recorded conversation with Inga on February 10, 1942, reveals:

JACK: I hear the hotel clerk at the Sumter is an investigator.
INGA: For what?
JACK: The navy.
INGA: Oh really. Cater (sp)?
JACK: No, one of the other ones.
INGA: Wonderful. You'll soon be kicked out.
JACK: There is more truth than poetry to that.

Jack also discovered that his mail was being opened and copied. But the two lovers apparently were not deterred by the knowledge that they were being observed. The FBI reported that "at 6:25 P.M. on February 20, 1942, the above named subject [Inga] arrived at Charleston, South Carolina, by plane from Washington, D.C. She was met by John Kennedy at the airport, and the two of them drove directly to the Francis Marion Hotel where the subject registered as Barbara Smith. By 7:05 P.M., the subject was in room 926. At 7:52 P.M., on the same date, the subject received a phone call from Kennedy, at which time she told him what her room number was and that she was just finishing dressing. At 8:12 P.M., Kennedy came to room 926. The subject and Kennedy remained in room 926 until 9:01 P.M., at which time they went to Henry's restaurant on Market Street in Charleston, where they had dinner. They returned to the Francis Marion Hotel at 10:32 P.M. At 11:20 P.M., the subject sent the following telegram, presumably at the instigation of Kennedy,

Mr. K. Billings
C/o Dr. F. T. Billings
Vanderbilt University Hospital
Nashville Tennessee

Returning Monday, check in at Fort Sumter Hotel, will call you there. Regards Jack."

There are numerous references to Lem in Jack's telephone conversations with Inga, perhaps because Inga had met him by this point. For example, the FBI report indicates that on February 24, 1942, "Jack Kennedy told Inga that Billings is with him and that he is coming to Washington, D.C. He asked Inga to be nice to him."

As the surveillance indicates, the relationship between Jack and Inga was his most involved relationship with a woman to date. Inga seemed to understand Jack, which is one reason she may have been more than just another sexual adventure for him. In one letter, she wrote, "Maybe your gravest mistake handsome . . . is that you admire brains more than heart." The buggers at the FBI must have been amazed at Jack's chutzpah, dating a girl with Inga's background while working for Naval Intelligence, no less. But there is no doubt the relationship was genuine. The FBI transcripts of their meetings reveal a warm and close relationship. The suspicion that she was a foreign agent was never substantiated.

Meanwhile, Lem had moved from Baltimore to Connecticut to work for the Coca-Cola Bottling Company in Bridgeport. Hundreds of miles apart, Jack and Lem nevertheless kept up their letter writing to each other, both complaining of not being involved in the war. Lem wrote Jack, noting a telephone call to Inga, "I called up Inga, but learned from a strange male voice that she was on vacation in the East. Kick wrote me that Torb [Torbert Macdonald, Jack's friend from Harvard] had married Phyllis Brooks. Is he on the West Coast? I didn't imagine he has enough points to get out unless he married her before August 15."

In one letter to Lem, Jack makes a curious reference to Lem's having been called a fairy and Lem's lack of resentment over the matter. "After you hear someone call you a fairy," wrote Jack, "and discuss it for two solid hours, and argue whether you did, or did not go down, on Worthington Johnson, you don't write a letter saying you think that fellow is a great guy—even if it's true, which it was." There is no record of what Lem thought of Jack's remark. But for once he had more important things on his mind than what Jack thought. He was about to be accepted by the American Field Service (AFS), a paramilitary ambulance corps. The AFS, established in 1915 as the ambulance arm of the American Hospital in Paris, was an elite institution that recruited U.S. college graduates mostly for service in North Africa during World War II. It was organized into units by college—the Harvard unit, the Princeton unit, etc.—and attracted people who were rejected by the military for one reason or another but wanted to be in the thick of combat operations. Many of the ambulance drivers had been rejected by the services because of bad eyesight—not exactly a recommendation for vehicular safety on the combat trail. Ernest Hemingway, for example, an ambulance driver in World War

I, was virtually blind in one eye. Lem's eyesight had always been terrible. Even so, his driving skills were considerably better than Jack's.

Joe helped Lem get into the AFS by writing a letter of recommendation for him. In a letter dated February 9, 1942, Joe wrote, "I am writing one of my rare letters of recommendation on behalf of K. LeMoyne Billings who is anxious to become identified with the American Field Service. . . . Now as to this boy Billings, he has been my second son and Jack's closest friend for almost ten years. He is a high type of boy and would have been in active service long before this if it were not for his having bad eyes."

Jack, unable to resist some fun at Lem's expense, wrote him back from Charleston in a letter dated February 12: "Rumor had it you were going to Africa and I gather for once the rumor was correct. I received a letter from dad to Mr. Gallatti recommending you for the Field Service. You should feel rather complimented, as he had not been doing any of that lately. As I imagine he sent you a copy of the letter, may I refer to paragraph 4, line 6, beginning, 'To go on and add to this his peculiar qualities would be rather superfluous.' What could he possibly be referring to?—your habit of picking your chin—your paranoiac desire for a sunburn—or perhaps he means that rather 'peculiar' expression that comes over your face when you start inhaling your asthma medicine. All of these, of course, are peculiar and I'm just interested to know which particular ones he is talking about?"

Joe's letter on behalf of Lem did the trick. Lem proudly wrote Jack informing him of his acceptance and of the AFS intention to send him to North Africa, where the Allies were in a fierce struggle with Axis forces. "I at last have heard from the AFS after their long trying silence. They want me to be ready by the 20th of April, which, if they are their usual form, means we'll sail around August 1st. Maybe this is the real thing, but I've been waiting so long that the news isn't particularly exciting anymore, perhaps a bit boring. I imagine, however, that the first torpedo will knock this out of me completely. As a matter of fact, I'm all ready to go, feeling like an angel of mercy. I hope Rommel [Field Marshal Erwin Rommel, commander of the German Afrika Korps, known also as the "Desert Fox"] treats me as such."

Jack responded, "You know, I think it's an excellent idea you're going to Africa, first of course, because you would get more and more restless not being in uniform as things began to get going more and more—and secondly it will be a damned good experience for you to get away on your own without any buddies to go and see. When you lack that escapism you will find yourself much better equipped for the changing world, if you will excuse me sounding a bit like George St. John [their headmaster at Choate]."

Kick decided to throw Lem a party in New York to celebrate the occasion. "Try and make NY next weekend altho I hardly expect it," Lem wrote Jack plaintively. Pat Kennedy said that she "nearly fell over backwards when I heard [the news of Lem's acceptance]. . . . It doesn't seem the kind of thing Lem would do." Jack, too, was surprised but was happy that his friend was going to be able to make a contribution to the war effort, in whatever capacity. He was unable to make the party, however. "I talked to Kick on the phone tonight and she said you weren't coming up to the party after all," wrote Lem. "I'm not as disappointed as I might have been, as I really never expected you to come anyway. She said you are having trouble with your back again and this time you might need an operation. I hope like anything that this isn't true as it would mean you would be out of the navy for quite a while—& I know what a big pain in the ass that would be. I can't imagine what started it up again. I hope it wasn't an overdose of Charlie Atlas exercises. You remember he doesn't guarantee anything unless his exercises are accompanied by a rigid schedule of good clean living." (In fact, Jack escaped a back operation this time but had to suffer yet another round of hospitalizations and tests.)

Since Jack did not make the party in New York, Lem lost no time in heading down to Charleston. He was going down South in any case to attend the wedding of his brother, Josh, in Nashville. He sent Jack an invitation, but Jack declined, although he encouraged Lem to make it over to South Carolina to see him. Jack wrote back, "I got an invitation to your brother's wedding. Does that mean a present? As he is a Billings, I imagine that it does. I won't be able to get there. A look at the map will tell you why. Try to drop down on your way down or back. I am going up to training school in Norfolk in a week or so and I will probably go over to Washington for weekends. If you will be down in Baltimore, let me know."

Lem wrote back to Jack, "Just a note because I'm really rushed now but I'm going to try to get over to Charleston on Sunday following Josh's wedding. I resigned from Cokie [Coca-Cola] on Sunday, so now I'm free until I leave in the middle of March sometime. I'll let you know later more definitely when I arrive. . . . Frankly the only thing that worries me about this ambulance thing is that the British will have been completely defeated in Africa by the middle of March."

Of course, Lem did make it to Charleston to see Jack after Josh's wedding. He was thrilled to spend a few days with him there, not knowing for sure when the next time would be since he would soon be heading to Africa with the AFS. Lem found that Jack hated his navy desk job and was working off his frustration with Charles Atlas workouts to build up his body. It was in the southern city that Lem saw Jack give his first speech. Its content was rather dull—about two different kinds of incendiary bombs, which Jack knew little about. But it was given with panache and went over well with his audience.

"When he was all finished, I was very pleased and proud and I thought he had done a terrific job," Lem remarked. Lem congratulated his twenty-four-year-old friend. He was impressed, but of course Lem was impressed with anything Jack did. When Lem got back home, he found a letter from Jack waiting for him. "Dear Lemmer: I finished the Atlas courses and believe I'm well on my way to health, strength and personal power, whatever personal power is. I can see that with time I will be powerful, graceful, and magnetic."

For a change, it was Lem who took ill not long after he saw Jack in Charleston. He wrote to Jack explaining his condition. "I've pulled myself from a feverish sick bed into which I have been cast by the ravages of the dreaded streptococci germ to write you a letter. By the way do be careful about touching this paper. There really may be germs hopping all over it and they're as active in leaping as the crab—with which you are so familiar. Everyone who comes in here wears masks, etc. But why should I tell you more about how contagious this disease is when you're much more interested in hearing about all the latest news no matter how germ-ridden the paper is that it's written on. I traced this darn thing straight back to Charleston anyway—it's one of those tropic germs— though I admit I have to stretch the imagination a lot to call that chilly Charleston, tropic. I don't know why it's so hard to stop talking about what's wrong with me. Maybe it's because it interests the hell out of me.

My sister [Lucretia] is in the hospital too so we're all one big happy family. She had a miscarriage which is a pretty tough break."

Lem got so sick that he missed the boat that would have taken him to Africa with the AFS and had to wait weeks for another one. "I know you won't understand this because you're completely ignorant as far as the medical world is concerned," he wrote Jack. "But as long as there are any strep germs I can't go. This usually takes about 3 weeks. I'm fighting this as hard as I can because the suspense while I sit around here in Baltimore is too much. I have my name in now to go on the next boat and they haven't called me yet—but when they do I'll know there will be quite a battle. One of my Canadian cousins with bad eyes joined the AFS also, so things are looking up, or down."

Meanwhile, Jack, who had made a habit of not getting too involved with women, was depressed about his affair with Inga, who clearly had gotten to him in a way that most women had not. He wrote to Lem, "I haven't seen Inga but I understand she is headed for Reno." He then told Lem the bad news. "As you probably haven't heard, Inga Binga got married, and not to me. She evidently wanted to leave Washington and get to NY—so she married some guy she had known for years who loved her but whom she didn't love."

In fact, Inga married Tim McCoy, the cowboy movie star. She was only sixty years old when she died in 1973. Her love for Jack Kennedy appears to have been the real thing. Her son said that when she heard the news of Jack's death in Dallas, she went into her room and sobbed for hours. For Jack, it appears to have been the real thing, too. He felt closer to Inga than he had to any other woman to that date.

Despite his obsession with Inga, Jack remained deeply interested in the political situation. His letters to Lem at this time reflected his view that the United States was not prepared for war. "I wonder what's happening in this country," he wrote Lem. "I never thought on my gloomiest day that there was any possible chance of our being defeated. But ignoring the military defeats we are suffering, which seems to be what everyone else is doing . . . while all around us are examples of inefficiency that might lick us, Nero had better move over as there are a lot of fiddlers to join him." He added: "It seems a rather strange commentary that it will take death in large quantities to wake us up, but I really don't think anything else will."

He continued, "I don't think anyone realizes that nothing stands between us and the defeat of our Christian Crusade except a lot of Chinks who have never heard of God, and a lot of Russians who have heard of him but don't want him. I suppose we can't afford to be very choosy at a time like this. When you get to Africa, make friends with every brown or black or yellow man you happen to meet. In *The Decline of the West,* Mr. Spengler, after careful study of the waves of civilization, prophesied that the next few centuries belong to the yellow man. After the Japs get through uniting Asia, it looks as if the wave of the future will certainly have a yellow look."

After he recovered from his strep germ, Lem managed to make it back down to Charleston one last time before Jack left the city and before Lem finally set sail for Africa with the AFS. He received a letter from Jack after the visit, teasing him. "In regard to your good-humored remark about owing me dough for your stay in Charleston, you are right, you do. The plane trip was 28.00 and the meals were about 4.00. You gave me 20.00. So you owe me 12.00. As I knew you would be bothered by it the entire time you were traveling, I have deducted it from a present I'm giving you, as I can't wait 15 years, I need the money now. So consider it deducted. Let me know when you're going to sail. If it was a weekend, I'd try to get up."

"I hope like hell you'll be up before I sail," responded Lem in a long letter to Jack. "I don't imagine you will be if you're going to PB [Palm Beach] first—however keep in touch and let me know when you're in Washington or New York vicinity . . . Thanks again for the very generous going away present. I'm not going to cash it until I leave—so that I can spend it at Shepherd's hotel at the bar with Marshall Rommel." It was a plaintive appeal for yet more time with Jack before they both ended up overseas, where they knew anything could happen. Time was running out on the prewar innocence of their friendship. Soon, like millions of others, they would undergo the life-changing experience that war always is.

On April 9, Jack wrote to Lem from Charleston, "In regard to my own plans, I expect to be leaving here in about ten days for my operation. If you're still here why don't you come down—I thought I might go home for a couple of days or at least as far as Jacksonville to see Joe. From there we could drive to Washington as I am giving Kick my car. I'll let you know more definitely later, but keep it in mind." It is not clear whether Lem had the time to make that trip, however. Meanwhile, Joe, not sure Jack's affair with Inga was over, decided against taking any chances. He made more calls in an attempt to transfer Jack out of Charleston, which he eventually succeeded in doing.

In the summer of 1942, Lem was finally on his way to Cairo with the AFS while Jack remained at his desk job in the States. Lem may not have been in the military, but his assignment was nevertheless dangerous. Ambulances were required to go deep into the combat zone. "Ours was one of the bigger units that they sent, nearly one hundred people, and we had to wait for a freighter that could take us. We finally got one that was going to Cape Town," recalled L. Brookman Cuddy, Lem's ambulance partner. They had no protection against German attack, "so we went criss-cross over the Atlantic avoiding the direct route so that our progress and location could not be predicted. We knew that there were German submarines everywhere. It took us a tremendous amount of time to get there, much longer than you would imagine—two and a half months to get to Cape Town."

On the long journey, Lem "would talk about all of the things that he liked about the Kennedys. I knew everything about the Kennedys," Cuddy continued. "And Lem and I would sit on the bridge of the ship singing Cole Porter, George Gershwin, and all these other great tunes." At Cape Town, Lem, Cuddy, and the other men transferred to a troop carrier for the final leg of the journey to Egypt. The AFS mission was to support the British Eighth Army's campaign to defeat Rommel's Afrika Korps. The largest battles with the German and Italian forces took place at El Alamein, about 150 miles west of Cairo, particularly the second battle there—with the Eighth Army then under the command of British lieutenant general Bernard Montgomery—which lasted from October 23 to November 3.

Lem and Cuddy were amazed by all the activity when they finally completed the long journey from Cape Town at the tip of South Africa to the Cairo region in Egypt in North Africa. "Lem and I got along very well; we decided to be ambulance mates," said Cuddy. The two young Americans could not have known at the time that the victory of the Eighth Army at El Alamein would be one of the most decisive battles of World War II, giving a much-needed boost especially to the British but also to the Allied cause in general. Lem and Cuddy reached there in time for the decisive second battle, a major turning point in the war but one that came at a high cost—at least 23,500 dead and wounded. Lem was one of the injured. He suffered minor shrapnel wounds.

In a letter that was included in an AFS field bulletin, Cuddy refers to Lem in describing the dangers the men confronted. "October 24th [the day after the second battle of El Alamein began] was a busy day for us. And we were tired when it began. Our subsection 6 of 15 American Field Service Car company had moved the night before to a central stem of Quattara road. We were near a little railroad crossing known as El Alamein. The road was a desert track, ankle-deep in dust and gutted with ruts from heavy armored equipment. It ran south to an impassable depression that flanked the 8th Army's battle line. That night, there was no chance to sleep, for the Allies had laid down the heaviest barrage in Western Desert history."

Cuddy continued, "At first, in the evening, there were the hectic moments of digging in as the barrage began. The horizon was marked by giant white and red flashes. A moment before our convoy had pulled up in silence. Shrouded in moonlight, we were like Arabs on a lonely desert plain. Then thunder burst out all around us. A hundred yards on either side of the post was a battery of 25-pounders. When their shells were fired, our faces lit up in the brilliance of each explosion. I could feel the ground shake as the nearest one went off. In the flash, I saw Lem digging madly, Freddie [Frederic Meyers] doing the same. We were far too busy to worry or mind. We shoveled our slit trenches. We helped erect the main tent which would protect the wounded and provide a covering under which the doctors could work."

After the battle ended with an Allied victory, Lem and Cuddy drove their ambulance with Montgomery's triumphant Eighth Army to Tripoli and then on to Tunisia, where the Axis troops surrendered to the Allied armies on May 12, 1943. Despite the heat and exhaustion, and strafing from German planes, Cuddy remembers Lem as energetic and full of curiosity about the local people they met on their journey. Although he didn't speak one word of Arabic, he found a way to communicate, he added. "We chased the German Army 4,500 miles along the desert coast of North Africa." Along the way, they dodged land mines and enemy fire. On one occasion, Lem was bitten by a black scorpion and miraculously survived the encounter. He also had to contend with frequent asthma attacks. On another occasion, "The whole back end [of their ambulance] was shattered by a Messerschmitt," said Cuddy. Despite all the mishaps, Lem managed to read *War and Peace* along the way, he added.

Lem examines a damaged ambulance door following the Messerschmitt attack, Sirte, Libya, 1943.

Jack was anxious to reach Lem and to find out how he was doing. "Haven't heard a word from you," Jack wrote. "What the hell have you been doing? I was pleased to note that things picked up after your arrival," referring to Montgomery's battle with Rommel at El Alamein. He sent one letter to Lem's mother addressed to the American Field Service PO Box in New York. "Dear Mrs. Billings, I'm enclosing a letter to Lem, which I wish you would forward, as I haven't any idea where he is. Have you heard from him?" Eventually, the two friends made contact, however, and began exchanging letters just as they had when both were at home.

Meanwhile, Jack, bored and restless with his job in Naval Intelligence, was eager to see action overseas. He left Charleston and enrolled in the Naval Reserve's midshipmans' school at Northwestern University in Chicago. The school was committed to producing seagoing naval officers within three months. As usual, Jack's rebellious nature did not take kindly to the rigorous discipline at the school, and he quickly became disillusioned. He soon developed an interest in PT boats, not least because he thought he would have a good deal of independence on the flimsy vessels, well away from the navy brass.

"I have applied for torpedo boat school under Lt. Bulkeley," he wrote Lem. "The requirements are very strict physically—you have to be young, healthy and unmarried—and as I am young, healthy and unmarried, I'm trying to get in. If I last, we get command of a torpedo boat—and are sent abroad—where I don't know. Everyone is away at schools and by winter's end will be abroad in different directions. You are therefore not missing a damn thing and are relatively the master of your own destiny—which I am definitely not—this god dam place is worse than Choate—and Lt. J makes Jack Maher [Jack and Lem's old teacher at Choate] look like a good guy—well, maybe not a good guy, but a better guy. But as FDR always says, this thing is bigger than you or I—it's global—so I'll string along." After his sojourn at the PT boat training unit in Melville, Rhode Island, and a short stint as a trainer with Squadron 14 in Jacksonville, Florida, Jack was ready to ship out.

On March 6, 1943, Jack left San Francisco on his way to New Hebrides, northeast of Australia, as a replacement officer for Motor Torpedo Boat Squadron 2. Jack wrote to Lem care of his mother, Romaine, telling him it would probably be his last letter "for a good while." He was finally en route to combat. "I am rather glad to be on my way—although I understand that this South Pacific is not a place where you lie on a white beach with a cool breeze, while those native girls who aren't out hunting for your daily supply of bananas are busy popping grapes into your mouth. It would seem to consist of heat and rain and dysentery + cold beans, all of which won't of course bother anyone with a good stomach." He added: "If it's as bad as they say it is, I imagine I'll be voting Republican in '44."

Jack had seen what he thought was a photograph of Lem in a Harvard alumni bulletin article on the AFS. He also included a note to Romaine with his letter to Lem. "He looked very well," he said. "He is certainly doing his share—and more—and deserves a great deal of credit for doing much more than he had to. I hope he gets back soon. Though the South Pacific is mighty large, I hope I shall run into Tremaine [Lem's older brother, better known as Josh] some place. Best always. Jack Kennedy." Jack also mentioned a photograph of Lem in a Baltimore newspaper. "How did they get a copy of the picture," he asked. "Or did they just happen to find it in their morning mail from Cairo?"

The young navy lieutenant, as he now was, saw combat soon enough, even before he reached his destination. As his ship approached the north coast of Guadalcanal, there was a major encounter. "The day I arrived, they had a hell of an attack," he wrote Lem. "As we were carrying fuel and bombs—and on a boat that was a tub, I thought we might withdraw + return at some later date, but the Captain evidently thought he was in command of the USS *North Carolina* as he sailed right in. Well, they dropped all around us—and sank a destroyer next to us but we were OK. During a lull in the battle—a Jap parachuted into the water—we went to pick him up as he floated along—and got within 20 yards of him. He suddenly threw his life-jacket + pulled out a revolver and fired two shots at our bridge. I had been praising the lord + passing ammunition right alongside—but that showed me a bit—the thought of him sitting in the water—battling an entire ship. We returned the fire with everything we had—the water boiled around him—but everyone was too surprised to shoot straight. Finally an old soldier standing next to me—picked up his rifle—fired once—and blew the top of his head off. He threw his arms up—plunged forward + sank—and we hauled our ass out of there. That was the start of a very interesting month—and it brought home very strongly how long it is going to take to finish this war."

When Jack reported to PT boat HQ in the Solomon Islands, he found out how dangerous PT combat service was. The fatalities were much higher than for service in the navy in general. But he didn't allude to that in his letters to Lem. "Received your latest saga and am glad you are in one piece—and probably badly in need of one," he wrote. "You have certainly had your share of thrills and if I were you, I would return safely to the U.S. and join the quarter master corps & sit on your very fat ass for a while. . . . Am writing this bit of advice from the South Pacific—sitting in a native hut. Have been here for a bit more than a month and am with Motor-Torpedo Boat Squadron 2. It's not bad here at all, but everyone wants to get the hell back home. The only people who want to be out here are the people back in the States—and particularly those at the Stork Club."

Eleven days after his arrival in the Pacific, Jack was made commander of his own boat—PT-109. He wrote Lem saying he wished he was part of his crew: "Received your letter and noted with interest your description of the 'dull beige of the desert,'" Jack wrote. "It was interesting but I could see you were writing with one [eye] on your publishers and the other on posterity. . . . Well Lemmer that is about all the news. This job on these boats is really the great spot of the navy, you are your own boss, and it's really like sailing around as in the old days, though these motors take a bit of understanding, as motors were never my strong point. Wish you were along, however. Let me know your activities."

Lem knew that Jack would eventually maneuver himself into a role where he would see combat, for all kinds of reasons. Years later, he said, "Jack always had something to prove physically. He was always so behind the eight ball with his health that he would engage in this bravado—right?—to overcompensate and prove he was fit when he really wasn't. So, he turns into a killer football player and he turns into a voracious womanizer, a stud. Then what's next? It was the logical next step given the times. Nothing surprising. I always thought that it was kind of interesting that Jack read Hemingway an awful lot, with all those flawed heroes coming on strong; striving, enduring, spoiling for fights and for opportunities to prove themselves. That was Jack."

On August 3, 1943, Jack did prove himself. While on active duty in Blackett Strait in the North Solomon Islands, PT-109 was cut in half and sunk by a Japanese destroyer. Two of the crew were killed instantly. The rest, including Jack, were thrown into the water, where oil fires erupted in the wake of the retreating Japanese ship. The survivors clung to wreckage until morning, when they managed to swim to a nearby island, Jack towing one seaman five miles despite having badly injured his already weak back. They were rescued a short time later. Although Jack has been criticized in recent years for allowing the incident to occur in the first place—the only one of its kind during the war—no one has questioned his heroism once the boat was struck. It was the making of the legend of John F. Kennedy as a war hero.

The story of PT-109 was a sensation back in the States. John Hersey's stirring account of the incident garnered a huge readership when it was reprinted from the *New Yorker* in *Reader's Digest.* On June 12, 1944, Jack was awarded the Navy and Marine Corps Medal and a citation for "extremely heroic conduct." But in later years, Jack would always play down his heroism with his famous quip, "I had no choice. They sank my boat." He told aide Kenny O'Donnell when he decided to run for Congress in 1946 that he had no taste for "trying to parlay a lost PT boat and a bad back into a political advantage."

In September, after not hearing from Jack for weeks, a worried Lem received a *New York Times* story from his mother. The article described the harrowing events involving Jack and the rest of his crew. Lem started

a scrapbook of newspaper stories about Jack's heroism aboard and over-
board PT-109. When Lem finally got a letter from Jack, he only casually
mentioned the incident that had almost cost him his life and that had
made him a hero. "What are your plans? When do you figure on getting
back to the States? Bobby said you were staying there another six
months—so I figure you should be home by Dec. or January—which
should be good as I ought to get back around then myself. It would certainly be nice to put in a month down at P.B. [Palm Beach] or in Canada
skiing—as I'm getting god-damned tired of the boat. . . . We have been
having a difficult time for the last two months—lost our boat about a
month ago when a Jap cut us in two + lost some of our boys. We had a
bad time for a week on a Jap island—but finally got picked up—and
have got another boat." Lem no doubt smiled. He knew understatement
was part of Jack's personality. For his part, Jack wrote Lem's mother
saying how proud he was of Lem's service in North Africa with the
ambulance corps.

Later, Jack wrote Lem and further commented on PT-109. The cel-
ebratory nature of the coverage made him uncomfortable, since two men
had died in the incident. He also knew how much of a role luck played
in the event—and in life in general. He thought that whether any man
survived any war was as much due to chance as to skill or bravery. "It
really makes me wonder if most success is merely a great deal of fortu-
itous accidents. I imagine I would agree with you that it was lucky the
whole thing happened—if the two fellows had not been killed which
rather spoils the whole thing for me."

By November 1943, Lem was home and out of the AFS. While he was
waiting for Jack to return on leave, Lem asked Joe to help him get into the
U.S. Naval Reserve. Lem's eyesight was still awful, but since his last navy
eye test, new, more practical, and easier-to-wear contact lenses had been
developed. Lem's brother, Josh, said Lem got hold of some of the first
lenses ever made, and they helped him pass the eye test. The contact lenses
were huge and he could barely stand putting them in his eyes for more
than a few minutes, but that was enough to fool the navy examiners.

Jack was happy that Lem finally got his chance to be in the service.
"Was extremely glad to hear that you had gotten into the Service Corps.
It's a good organization and has some damn good guys in it." It's not

clear whether Lem wanted to join the
navy and see combat because Jack had, or
because he wanted it for himself. Lem's
sister, Lucretia, who knew Jack as well,
said, "I think he had to do something
because Jack was doing so much." Either
way, it was a courageous move in view of
the casualties the navy was suffering in
the Pacific at the time. "It was very hard
for him, but he wanted to do it and he
stuck with it," Lucretia added. When
Jack reached home, the two friends
greeted each other in Palm Beach like
there was no tomorrow. Despite the fact
that they had been apart longer than at

Lem's Navy portrait, circa 1944.

Jack and Lem on leave, Palm Beach, 1944.

any time since their friendship began, and also the fact that they had changed under the impact of their wartime experiences, both men resumed the friendship at home with as much enthusiasm and devotion to each other as before. They enjoyed the luxury of a two-month reunion until Easter 1944. But all too soon, it was time for Lem to leave

Lem, Teddy Kennedy, Boston Police Commissioner Joseph F. Timilty, and Jack, Palm Beach, 1944.

for the South Pacific on the USS *Cecil* for the duration of the war—and beyond. His duties aboard the supply ship consisted of organizing and operating the ship's store and supervising forty-five enlisted men. Occasionally, he performed the role of acting supply officer aboard the ship.

Jack, however, supposedly home only on leave, had to delay his departure because of a further deterioration in his

USS *Cecil*, the supply ship on which Lem served in the Navy, 1945.

condition, particularly his back, which had been aggravated by the PT-109 incident. He also might have become infected with malaria while in the Pacific. In June 1944, after being diagnosed as having "chronic disc disease of the lumbar area," Jack underwent the first of a series of back operations. It was a serious operation with terrible side effects that kept him in the hospital for two months. In August, his condition was still precarious. He also suffered acute abdominal distress. Heavy doses of narcotics were needed to ease the pain. Questions were raised as to whether he really should have undergone the neurosurgery in the first place. It was clear that he was in no condition to return to the Pacific. Jack's navy career was over.

Almost a year after the PT-109 incident, on August 12, 1944, Jack's brother Joe was killed when his Air Force plane blew up shortly after takeoff from an airfield in England while on a dangerous mission. The plane was loaded with explosives. President Roosevelt's son, Elliott, flying a fighter alongside Joe's plane, was taking pictures when the plane was suddenly engulfed in a ball of flames. The wreckage was strewn over the Suffolk countryside. Joe's body and that of his copilot were never found.

Joe had to have known the assignment was hazardous. But there is no way of knowing whether he volunteered for it because of the heroism of his younger brother in the South Pacific. The Kennedy family was devastated by Joe's death. He was the oldest son, the greatest achiever, the one whom everyone thought stood the best chance of being the first Catholic elected president. Jack was at Hyannis convalescing when a telegram announcing Joe's death arrived. According to Rose, he left the house immediately and walked on the beach—alone with his thoughts.

Joe's father retired to his room. He completely withdrew. He grew even more bitter about the war he had tried to stop and more critical of FDR—although he stopped short of supporting the Republican nominee in 1944, Thomas Dewey. When Joe finally emerged from his self-imposed exile, Jack knew that his father's political hopes rested with him. Now the burden fell on his shoulders, even though Jack always said that his father never demanded that he seek political office.

In memory of his brother, Jack put a book together, *As We Remember Joe,* which was published privately. He wrote to Joe's old teachers, friends, and service buddies and asked them to contribute to it but also wrote an article himself, which he thought was his best writing effort to date. Lem said, "When two brothers are growing up and they are two years apart you aren't aware of a great love between them, but Jack's editing of Joe's memorial book was a real work of love. There's no question about it. Jack had a fantastically strong admiration for what his older brother had accomplished in the very short time he lived." Even Choate headmaster George St. John praised the book for capturing the essence of Joe's life.

In November 1944, Jack was told that his continuing medical problems could not be cured with further hospitalizations, and that he would receive a medical discharge from the navy with the full rank of lieutenant, although he was not formally released from the navy until March 1945. He had been in and out of hospitals since he'd come home on leave, had suffered through two operations, and was in frequent pain as a result of the injuries that were inflicted during the PT-109 calamity and other incidents. He had also been diagnosed with a duodenal ulcer, later changed to colitis. His stomach, as well as his back, was a wreck. It was time to stay home for good.

Lem remained in the South Pacific and told Jack he didn't know when he would be back home. The Japanese were still far from defeated, even though the war in Europe was winding toward its conclusion. Jack wrote Lem about his "now seeing a bit of the war," off the coast of Iwo Jima. "Iwo is getting a terrific play lately—it must be tough as hell. What do you think of the marines? You are the only person in the world who has seen both the marines and the Eighth Army in action—you could write a damn good article comparing them I think." It was not an empty remark. In his own way, Lem had been something of a war hero, as well. Although he could easily have avoided the war on medical grounds, Lem was determined to serve. At Iwo Jima, where some of the worst fighting of the war occurred, Lem had a narrow escape when a wounded Japanese soldier pulled a hand grenade from behind him and threw it toward Lem, who was helping with a stretcher.

But for Jack, with the war now over, it was time to take it easy and regain his strength. Joe once again sent him to Arizona to recuperate. Jack wrote Lem, "I've been out here for a month but the back has been so bad that I'm going to Mayo's about the first of April unless it gets a little better." Jack also talked about Choate. "I got a letter from Tinker a couple of weeks ago that I am saving for you as it will make you very ill. I'm still planning to go up there and make a speech and give the faculty hell indirectly and JJ Maher directly. I'm going to wait till he comes back from fighting the war which he is doing out in Tennessee. I have gathered together all my reports from Choate and when you read what that son-of-a-bitch wrote—it makes me sore as hell. The only laugh I ever got out of that guy was the night he backed you up against the fireplace for making faces at him and shook the hell out of you while you trembled and tearfully apologized. Well, we all have our bad days." Lem probably didn't want to be reminded of what reads like a scene from *Tom Brown's Schooldays,* but it was their times together at Choate that was the link to their past and to their youth. So presumably he didn't really mind that much.

Not content to rest up in Arizona for long, Jack again took a trip to Hollywood, where he was once again on the prowl for girls. Lem teased Jack for a change. "Haven't you found any girl that will have you, Kennedy?" he wrote. "It seems to me you are destined to never fall in love with anyone unless she's married or divorced. You know, you're no spring chicken any longer—twenty-eight in a couple of weeks, as I recall—when I last saw you your hair line was receding conspicuously. . . . So what the hell have you? Take it from me, you'd better cut out being so particular. You're on the road down. Leaving you with that in mind, I remain looking very well with a bronzed and stern appearance."

Lem was proud that, like Jack, he had finally served in the navy and seen action in the Pacific, but now he was eager to return home as soon as he could. Jack was already in the States planning his future in postwar America. Lem wanted to catch up with Jack, help him in any way he could, and determine his own future, as well. What would they do with their lives in postwar America?

6

TURNING POINT
(1945)

"For time and the world do not stand still. Change is the law of life. And those who look only to the past or the present are certain to miss the future."
—John F. Kennedy, June 25, 1963

I n the spring of 1945—after hostilities in Europe had concluded—Jack felt sufficiently well to turn his attention to what he wanted to do in civilian life. He was eager to make his mark in the postwar United States.

Jack had always been interested in journalism and thought that might be the profession that would bring him the most satisfaction. Using his father's connections, he soon found himself with top-notch reporting assignments with Hearst newspapers—covering the first United Nations conference in San Francisco, where the United Nations Charter was drafted, and the British elections. He also got a chance to attend the Potsdam summit of the Big Three—the United States, Britain, and the Soviet Union.

The UN conference in San Francisco was convened in April 1945 as the war in Europe drew to its dramatic close with the fall of Berlin. Jack's assignment was to cover the meeting from the point of view of the ordinary GI, a task for which he was eminently qualified. Even though he had been a lieutenant, Jack mixed easily with fellow officers and enlisted men alike and was close to all the guys with whom he had been in combat. He said that his image of the reader of his articles was the average guy returning home with hopes for a better world.

When Lem heard about Jack's assignment in San Francisco, he plainly was not happy, perhaps because Jack had not kept him informed of what he'd been up to since he'd returned from the war. "You certainly are a rotten correspondent," he wrote from the Pacific. "Bobby tells me you are now writing up the San Francisco conference for some Chicago papers—why they are trusting you with so important a job I do not know, it must be rather an unimportant paper. Before they get too involved with conferences anyway, they should be damned sure they have the Japs on the way to being licked." Lem also questioned what he regarded as too rosy a view of the situation in the Pacific back home. "The Japs do not seem to have the slightest intention of quitting—and apparently plan to carry this war on to the bitter end," he said.

Although Jack supported FDR's idea for a new international organization to succeed the League of Nations—without the latter's fatal flaws—he was no pie-in-the-sky idealist concerning the question of whether the United Nations could head off future conflict and avert another world war. In fact, he was downright skeptical that a new international organization could succeed. He felt that big power rivalries and realpolitik would inevitably trump good intentions and noble efforts.

In a letter he wrote to a PT boat friend from San Francisco, he voiced his doubt. "When I think of how much this war has cost us, of the deaths of Cy, and Peter, and Orv, and Gill, and Demi, and Joe, and Billy, and all those thousands and millions who have died with them—when I think of all those gallant acts that I have seen, or anyone who has been to war—it would be a very easy thing for me to feel disappointed and somewhat betrayed." He continued: "You have seen battlefields where sacrifice was the order of the day and to compare that sacrifice to the timidity and selfishness of the nations gathered at San Francisco must inevitably be disillusioning." His viewpoint was also reflected in the stories he filed from the City by the Bay.

In an article datelined May 7, one of sixteen he filed on the UN conference, he wrote, "The world organization that will come out of San Francisco will be the product of the same passions and selfishness that produced the Treaty of Versailles. There is here, however, one ray of shining bright light. That is the realization, felt by all the delegates, that humanity cannot afford another war."

After covering the UN meeting, Jack—still working as a reporter for Hearst—headed once again to Europe. It was one of the most crucial summers in the history of the continent. The war in Europe had just ended with the unconditional defeat of Germany and Italy. The Allies—the United States, Britain, France, and Russia—were struggling to decide Europe's future and already arguing among themselves. The Soviet Union was emerging as the biggest problem from the point of view of the Western powers.

For Jack, it was a dream assignment. He would be present at the creation of a new Europe, to be built from the ashes of a devastating war that worldwide had cost fifty million lives. It was a great opportunity for a young man whose interest in international relations had grown immeasurably during his years at Harvard and during his time in England just before the outbreak of the war, when his father was U.S. ambassador to the country. His primary assignment was to cover the British election, among the most important in that country's history.

The election was set for July 5, 1945, even though the war with Japan was not yet over. Britain's wartime leader, Winston Churchill, strongly objected to the voting even taking place while the war with Japan was still under way, but he was overruled by the opposition. Britain had not had a national election in almost ten years, since Stanley Baldwin's National (mostly Conservative) government was elected in 1935. Unlike the United States, Britain had canceled elections during World War II.

Churchill presided over a coalition government during the war. But now, with victory against Germany behind them, the British faced a full-fledged election battle between Churchill's Conservative Party and Clement Attlee's Labour Party, which at that time was committed to orthodox socialist principles. A much-smaller third party, the Liberals, which had once been dominant, also competed for votes.

After six years of war under a national government that understandably relegated all domestic programs to the back burner, the British people were eager for a new beginning and the election of a government committed to large domestic expenditures to rebuild the country, significant parts of which were in ruins as a result of massive German bombing. The Labour Party offered a radical rebuilding program together with a cradle-to-grave welfare state that would provide free health care, enhanced social security, and free college education for those who qualified.

Jack conveyed the feelings of the British people in his reports back to the States. "Britishers will go to the polls on July 5th in the first general election in almost ten years and there is a definite possibility that Prime Minister Winston Churchill and his Conservative Party may be defeated," he wrote. Jack clearly sensed that change was in the air and that Churchill was in trouble, despite the small lead he had in some polls.

In a later report, Jack tried to explain to American readers why England, and much of Europe, was moving left. "Churchill is fighting a tide that is surging throughout Europe, washing away monarchies and conservative governments everywhere, and that tide flows powerfully in England. England is moving toward some form of socialism."

On June 21, Jack confided these thoughts to his diary: "Tonight it looks like Labor and a good thing it will be for the cause of free enterprise. The problems are so large that it is right that Labour, which has been nipping at the heels of free enterprise in England for the last 25 years, should be faced with the responsibility of making good on its promises." However, in the same diary entry, he left no doubt that he was skeptical of socialism. "Socialism is inefficient. I will never believe differently. But you can feed people in a socialistic state, and that may be what will insure its eventual success."

Jack's instincts proved correct. On July 5, the British threw out Churchill and elected the Labour Party in a landslide. Official Washington, along with most Americans, was stunned. But Jack had accurately predicted the outcome. The colorless Attlee, whom Churchill once derided as "a sheep in sheep's clothing," was now prime minister. When he was offered an award—the Order of the Garter—for his wartime service, Churchill boomed, "Why should I accept the Order of the Garter when the British people have just given me the order of the boot."

But Jack understood that the British parliamentary system is radically different from the U.S. structure of government, with its separation of powers and direct election of the president. In Britain, all political power stems from the election of lawmakers from hundreds of constituencies. The British do not have the opportunity to directly elect the prime minister. The new Labour government wasted no time in fulfilling its promises. During its five-year term, it set about transforming British life—rebuilding the cities and establishing the welfare state. Major industries were nationalized. In 1947, the Labour government also placed the first nail in the coffin of the British Empire by granting independence to India, although Africans would have to wait a decade longer and more for their freedom.

FDR tried unsuccessfully to persuade Churchill that after the defeat of the Third Reich and the Italian and Japanese empires, imperialism had no future—craftily coaxing Churchill into signing the wartime Atlantic Charter in 1941, which committed the signatories to the principles of self-determination and independence in the postwar world. But Churchill was unpersuaded, despite his signature on the charter agreeing to "respect the right of all peoples to choose the form of government under which they live." The young Kennedy, who was witness to the battle over colonialism in Britain during the election campaign, was much more attuned to FDR's view. He sympathized with those who were against colonialism.

The debate in Britain about colonialism was of tremendous interest to Jack, who felt that the days of empire in the postwar world were numbered. In 1957, he raised eyebrows in Western Europe when, as a junior U.S. senator, he blasted French colonialism in Algeria. He referred to "the powerful force of man's eternal desire to be free and independent. The worldwide struggle against imperialism, the sweep of nationalism, is the most potent factor in foreign affairs today." The speech angered many Europeans, and some Americans, but earned him the respect, and even devotion, of Africans from one end of that continent to the other.

Since the United States had once been a colony, there had always been sizable opposition to colonialism in this country. However, in 1945 many white Americans, as well as Europeans, still harbored entrenched racist views. They evidenced the same paternalistic attitudes to colonized peoples in Africa, Asia, and the Caribbean as many white Europeans did and were therefore not as moved to oppose the Western European empires as they might have been had the victims been white. But Jack was not one of them. Early on, he developed an instinctive opposition to the Western European colonial empires. He was cautious when he spoke in public, but in private he was vehement. In Lem's FBI file, obtained through a freedom of information request, there is a reported phone conversation in which Jack criticizes Churchill and describes "the British as the worst colonizers in the world . . . and very cruel to their subjects."

But Jack's views were clearly in the minority in the United States at the time. In the immediate aftermath of World War II, the United States caved to Western European demands to reestablish their empires, partly because of then prevailing racial attitudes and partly because the country ultimately saw the need to contain communism as paramount, particularly after Churchill's speech in Fulton, Missouri, in 1946, in which he warned that an "iron curtain" had fallen across Europe. So the Western Europeans got their Marshall Plan aid and an alliance with the United States in the form of NATO in 1949—and kept most of their colonies for the foreseeable future. Few at the time saw the hypocrisy of opposing Stalin's empire in Eastern Europe while turning a blind eye to the Western European colonial domination of much of the third world. Jack witnessed these battles over colonialism firsthand at the end of the war in Europe, from both the European and American perspectives, and formed views and ideas that would be crucial to his thinking in the years ahead.

As a pragmatist, Jack thought the European desire to hold on to an empire was not only wrong morally but also impractical and doomed to failure. That was also his view as president, at a time when the Europeans still retained sizable colonial possessions. "The revolution of national independence is one of the most fundamental facts of our era. This revolution will not be stopped," he said. He thought that those European countries trying to retain their colonies even into the 1960s, such as France and Portugal, were fighting a battle they could not and should not win.

While Jack was getting an education on British politics and the future of Britain's empire, Lem remained in the Pacific still fighting an empire that had not yet been defeated—Japan. Lem agreed with Jack on the whole issue of colonialism and empire. He had seen what the Japanese empire had done to the peoples of Asia and believed in the American effort to defeat it. But Lem was less interested in what was going to happen in the future, especially in Europe, than he was in victory over Japan. It was clear from his letters to Jack that Lem thought too many Americans had turned their attention to the postwar peace in Europe and underestimated what still needed to be done to defeat the Japanese in the Pacific.

"From what I have gathered from the newspaper and magazine articles there is rather an unhealthy optimistic attitude in the States that the Japs are just about finished," Lem wrote to Jack. "If any of these people would talk to some of the men who have recently returned from Okinawa they [might] have a bit of a different story to write. The Japs do not have the slightest intention of quitting and apparently plan to carry this war on to the bitter end." He added: "Out here, the general feeling seems to be that unless Japan quits now—she can carry this war on for a long time. Of course we do not know how much raw material she has on hand and how much else she can draw from other sources—this will also hasten or lengthen the war. However, our experiences at Iwo Jima and Okinawa have not been encouraging."

But Jack continued to be preoccupied by events in Europe, especially since he spent much of the spring and summer of 1945 in England or on the continent. After a brief trip to Ireland to see his sister Kick, the next stop for Jack during his whirlwind summer was occupied Germany. His main purpose was to attend the Potsdam summit. Using his father's connections, Jack flew in the same plane as President Truman's secretary of the navy, James Forrestal (who, in 1949, committed suicide under mysterious circumstances). Flying over Germany, Jack saw firsthand the devastation the country had suffered. He confided his thoughts to his diary. "All the centers of the big cities are of the same ash gray color from the air—the color of churned up and powdered stone and brick. Railroad centers are especially badly hit, but the harvest seems to be reasonably good and the fields appear as though they were being worked fully."

Jack had been in Berlin just before the war started in September 1939, when he was almost arrested by storm troopers. Then, the city was clean and prosperous. Now, it was laid waste. "The devastation is complete. Unter [den] Linden and the streets are relatively clear, but there is not a single building, which is not gutted. On some of the streets, the stench—sweet and sickish from dead bodies—is overwhelming," he wrote. The young Kennedy also saw Hitler's Reich Chancellery, describing it in his diary as a shell. "The walls were chipped and scarred by bullets, showing the terrific fight which took place at the time of its fall. Hitler's air raid shelter was about 120 feet down into the ground—well furnished but completely devastated. The room, where Hitler was supposed to have met his death, showed scorched walls and traces of fire. There is no complete evidence, however, that the body that was found was Hitler's body. The Russians doubt that he is dead."

Jack wasn't only interested in the fate of Germany's criminal leadership, however. He was also curious about the lives of ordinary Germans in a country where even getting adequate food was now difficult. He had a journalist's eye for the seemingly inconsequential detail. "One or two of the women wore lipstick, but most seem to be trying to make themselves as unobtrusive as possible to escape the notice of the Russians," he wrote.

The Forrestal party, including Jack, was met at the airport by General Dwight D. Eisenhower. Potsdam was just a short drive from Berlin. In Jack's privately printed book, *As We Remember Joe,* there is a photograph of General Eisenhower greeting Forrestal at the airport. Jack is in the background of the shot—not bad company for a young reporter. Jack, apparently, didn't have too high an opinion of Ike, either then or later, according to Lem. "Jack told me that Eisenhower was, surprisingly, a kind of naïve type of person and that he was very jolly. He said Eisenhower made a big effort with everyone, and that he was primarily interested in telling little stories about sports. He seemed to be a man's man. What surprised Jack was that intellectually he was most unimpressive." He added: "Frankly, I don't think the president's impression of Eisenhower ever changed." As for Lem's opinion of Eisenhower, it wasn't much better than Jack's. "I feel that Eisenhower was too shallow to really appreciate Jack Kennedy. He probably resented so young a man replacing him."

The Potsdam summit featured new players on the world stage. Harry Truman succeeded FDR in April and Clement Attlee replaced Churchill. Stalin was the lone holdover. The purpose of the meeting was to clarify and implement decisions taken earlier at Yalta by Roosevelt, Stalin, and Churchill. It didn't help that the two great leaders of the United States and Britain were no longer around for this second summit.

Truman and Attlee were on unsure footing with the wily, scheming Stalin, who proceeded to get most of what he wanted. The two new Western leaders were widely blamed for handing over Eastern Europe to Soviet control when the details of what was agreed to at Yalta and

Potsdam eventually became known. But, significantly, Yalta and Potsdam also ensured Soviet involvement in the war against Japan. Many Americans, and certainly Lem and his comrades in the Pacific, whose lives were still under threat, cared much more about that than the future of Eastern Europe. It is also undeniable that nothing could have been done to prevent Soviet hegemony in Eastern Europe—short of starting World War III a few months after World War II had ended. Soviet control of Eastern Europe was a fait accompli no matter what stand the Western leaders would have taken at Potsdam.

Jack wrote to Lem about his experiences in Berlin and Potsdam. But he didn't provide much detail. Nor did he mention that he had met General Eisenhower, the Supreme Allied Commander during World War II and the man whom Jack would eventually succeed as president in 1961. Lem, for his part, was more interested in whom Jack had been hanging out with while he was there. He seemed most upset by how chummy Jack had become with Navy Secretary Forrestal. "I hope my pessimism in regard to the length of the war did not in any way jeopardize your fine friendship with the secretary of the navy," he wrote. "Possibly, you passed it on to him in one of your eloquent speeches at these dinners." For Jack, this was typical Lem. He likely chuckled when he read it. Teasing and needling had always been a part of Jack and Lem's friendship. It went both ways. In this instance, they didn't allow lofty thoughts about the fate of Europe to get in the way.

Jack was deeply affected by his time in California and Europe during the summer of 1945. In San Francisco, he witnessed the birth of the United Nations. In Britain, he covered one of the greatest political contests in British history, resulting in the election of the first majority socialist government. And at Potsdam, he watched the big powers struggle with the shape of the postwar world, making decisions, in a few days, that would impact the lives of millions for decades. The whole experience stimulated his interest in international relations and deepened his desire to run for elective office.

By the end of the summer, Jack was back in the States and thinking about a political career. "I was reluctant to begin law school again," he said in a recording made with a Dictaphone. "I was vitally interested in national and international life. . . . In my early life, the conversation was

nearly always about politics," Jack explained, but he hadn't seriously considered a political career until his brother Joe died in the war. "One
politician was enough in the family.

"I was at a loose end at the end of the war," Jack continued. "I was
not interested in a business career. The first speech [as a potential candi-
date] I ever gave was given at an American Legion post. Somebody, a
politician, came up to me afterwards and said that I should go into politics, that I might be governor of Massachusetts in ten years. Later in the
fall, a congressional seat became vacant. This was the Eleventh Congressional District, which my grandfather had once represented fifty years
before. Suddenly, the time, the occasion, and I all met." The speech he
gave at the American Legion was titled, "England, Ireland, and Germany: Victor, Neutral, and Vanquished." In a letter, Jack told Lem that
he was "making speeches around. I'm getting ready to throw my slightly
frayed belt into the political arena any time now. I'm expecting you back
to vote early and often."

Commenting on Jack's growing political ambition, Lem wrote, "I
believe that last time I heard from you was back in August when you
enclosed the most depressing card from the St. Johns indicating to me
that you had even been lining their votes up. I have had reports from
Eunice, Pat and Bobby that you have not only been stomping Massachusetts but have even competed with Jimmy Burus at the Al Smith dinner.
You must have become as gabby as Pattie's pig." Lem also teased Jack
about his prominence in the Choate *Alumni News.* "I never seriously
objected when he [Harold Tueller] put your picture in the front piece—
nor did I object when the first half of the issue was taken up with
Kennedy pictures—and write-ups—but Gordon Barlow and myself
draw the line when 'Jack Kennedy's Challenge' is announced in large letters on the cover—followed by a long and boring article on the content
of the challenge—as though this wasn't enough for your old roomie and
Jack 'Muscles' Ross to swallow—75% of the 1935 alumni notes space
must be taken up with a day by day description of your life."

Still far from home, Lem had no clear plans for his future, although
he was thinking about going back to college, particularly Harvard. For a
time, before he learned of Jack's political plans, Lem thought Jack might
return there also to go to law school. He wrote Jack, "I believe I've told
you I've darn near decided to go to Harvard Business School as soon as

possible—not because of its proximity to the Cape—although this may enter into it. I haven't been able to find out definitely whether I am entitled to one year of the GI's education. I certainly should be. If I am, that will help a lot—because I understand Harvard is not at all cheap. Since I've been in the navy, I've managed to save almost $3,000. I don't have any particular urge to go back to Cokie—but that seems to be all I have to offer. From what I can gather, a Harvard B.S. gives you about as good a business training as you can get."

All that seemed a long way in the future when Lem wrote those words, since most of America's fighting men in the Pacific believed that the battle to defeat Japan would be long and bloody. But in August 1945, everything suddenly changed. The United States dropped two atomic bombs on Hiroshima and Nagasaki. On September 2, the Japanese surrendered. It was over. Lem, like everyone else, was taken by surprise and ecstatic that a war he thought might drag on for years was abruptly terminated. As he sailed into Tokyo Harbor aboard the USS *Cecil,* Lem was amazed at the number of American ships converging there. It was a sea of Stars and Stripes as far you could see, he said. He couldn't believe the Japanese had surrendered so quickly. "Actually I was not the only one over there who was damned surprised the Nips folded so soon. Certainly those Kamikaze kids at Okinawa gave us no indication that they were ready to throw in the rag," he wrote Jack. But it was indeed over.

However, if Lem thought that would mean a quick passage back to the States, he was mistaken. It took months—into 1946—before he finally made it home. "The Army and Navy are really fouled up on this 'getting the boys home from the Pacific,'" he wrote Jack. Lem couldn't wait to return home and see what all this talk about politics and Jack was going to lead to. At the end of 1945, members of the Kennedy family were telling Lem that Jack was now talking politics nonstop and eager to get his political campaign under way. Remembering his father's constant admonition to his kids, "We don't want any losers around here; in this family we want winners," Jack was determined to win his first political race.

Lem got the message. From now on, he would have to commit to John Kennedy, politician, as well as John Kennedy, friend. It would be yet another big change in their friendship. Lem fretted that in the future his contact with Jack might not be as frequent as it had been before. In fact, after the end of the war, as Jack's attention turned more to politics, his letters to Lem diminished rapidly. Most of their contact after 1945 when they were apart was over the phone. Lem wasn't above complaining about the decline in their correspondence. "I think I've gotten one letter from you in 1945," he wrote Jack. Months later, he was still upset. "I wish you'd take a few minutes away from stumping and throwing your hat in the ring and agreeing to run and drop me a line." But once he got home, discharged from the navy with the rank of lieutenant junior grade, his concerns were allayed. They wouldn't write as many letters to each other from now on, but they would see each other just as often as before. Despite all the time they had spent apart during the war, their friendship was secure.

Lem and Jack, Palm Beach, 1945.

The fact is that after the war there wasn't the need for as many letters or telegrams. Both men were back in the United States, where it was just easier to call, especially since long distance had become more feasible and affordable. Moreover, both men, especially Jack, were becoming busier with their careers, and using the telephone was more practical. Unfortunately, however, phone calls are not kept the way that letters are, so they are not available to us to grant further insight into Jack and Lem's friendship after the war—aside from one phone call between them that was taped when Jack was in the White House. "We wrote each other a lot during our younger days," said Lem. "Of course, Jack never wrote any personal letters in his later years. He always used the telephone. I have about 175 letters from Jack. I don't know why but for some reason I kept them all."

In the mid-1940s, neither Jack nor Lem could have foreseen that Jack would choose a path that would lead directly to the White House just fifteen years later. At first, Lem seemed surprised by his friend's increasing zest for politics, and certainly by his interest in running for Congress. "I never thought he'd go into politics. Neither did he. I figured he must be about as surprised as I was," Lem recalled in a letter to Rose Kennedy. But Lem knew that Jack always had been interested in history and current events. And he also knew that since Joe's death in 1944, Jack's entry into elective politics was likely. So it probably was not as big of a surprise as he indicated.

Jack's summer in Europe as an eyewitness to history also likely encouraged his interest in politics and winning elective office. By the end of the year, all doubts were gone. He would run for Congress in 1946. He was just twenty-nine years old. Lem was eager to get back to the States to help him win. "It was exciting for me to have him running for Congress, which at that time seemed a very high office indeed," he later said.

7

SEEKING THE TORCH
(1946–59)

"We must reject oversimplified theories of international life—the theory that American power is unlimited, or that the American mission is to remake the world in the American image."

—John F. Kennedy, March 26, 1962

J ack's grandfather, "Honey Fitz" Fitzgerald, had always been an inspiration to him. He once told Jack, "You are my namesake. You are the one to carry on our family name. And mark my words, you will walk on a far larger canvas than I." Honey Fitz and Jack "were absolutely crazy about each other," said Lem.

In January 1946, Jack followed in the footsteps of Honey Fitz and announced he was running for a seat in Congress from the Eleventh District of Massachusetts. It was an ideal choice for the young Kennedy, even though he had not lived there. It included Boston's North End, where his mother and Honey Fitz were born, the East Boston waterfront area, where his father was born, the West End, including Beacon Hill, and the whole of Cambridge and the Charlestown community, which were solidly Irish.

Jack adopted the Bellevue Hotel in Boston, where Honey Fitz lived, as his official address. He later rented an apartment on Bowdoin Street that he kept for the rest of his life as his permanent address. He then set about lining up the help of old Bostonians who were familiar with the district—people like Dave Powers, a war veteran like himself, who knew the Charlestown area like the back of his hand. Next, he enlisted the help of his family—from little Teddy (then only fourteen) to Grandpa Honey Fitz. All the Kennedys were expected to actively campaign. In addition, he persuaded his old friends to help out—chief among them Lem, of course. The campaign slogan was "The New Generation Offers a Leader, John F. Kennedy."

Joe's money was indispensable to the effort. But the cash was a hindrance as well as a benefit. Many in the mostly working-class district regarded Jack as a millionaire's son on the make with not much of a résumé. What was his agenda? How could he relate to the problems of the average man? Plus, Jack was an unseasoned campaigner in his first run for office. His speech was halting and his shy demeanor sometimes made him seem remote and aloof. He also had been to Harvard, which, he said, was "not a particularly popular institution in the Eleventh District."

Fortunately, Jack was his own best advertisement. Despite being rich, he had the common touch. He came across as an average guy, not as a member of the wealthy elite—even though he was. One of Joe's favorite lines was, "You must remember. It's not what you are that counts, but what people think you are." Jack also had a well-known name, good looks, and great hair (which is why he never liked wearing a hat). Add to that the fact that he was a bona fide war hero, spoke about issues that people cared about, and already had that winning smile that could disarm a roomful of skeptics in an instant. In addition, no one worked harder to win the support of the voters. He stood outside factory gates in the predawn hours to shake the hands of workers clocking in for the early-morning shift.

For Lem, Jack's decision to enter politics and run for Congress was the second big change that impacted their friendship. First there had been the war, and their separation during the conflict, and now there was politics. From here on out, Lem knew that he would have to adjust to a different Jack Kennedy, who was now surrounded by a new group of friends. First there were the buddies Jack had acquired in the navy, with whom he felt especially close. Then, there were the political operatives whom he needed to help him with his new career. Lem knew this meant less time with Jack. But he also felt confident that their friendship would continue to prosper, as it always had, and that Jack would want him around not just as a form of relaxation away from politics but also to participate in the political process with him, especially campaigning. Lem said later that Jack's entry into political life didn't impact their friendship in any meaningful way. "There never was any change in our relationship," he said.

Indeed, in some ways the friendship grew as Lem became involved in Jack's career for the first time. Jack asked for Lem's help as he climbed the political ladder, despite Lem's obvious lack of political acumen. Lem told Jack he would come up to Boston to help for a few weeks, but he ended up staying with him at the Bellevue Hotel for the whole campaign. Lem was supposed to begin studying at Harvard Business School that spring, but he ended up delaying graduate school till the fall. He just couldn't bear to leave Jack there with all those old pols once the campaign got under way. Lem remembered the hotel suite as a beehive of activity. "Jack and I would go to bed and there'd be these Irish politicians smoking cigars and talking strategy in the next room. We'd wake up the next morning and they'd still be there smoking and talking."

The old political pros viewed Lem as a bit strange, to say the least. Sure, he was Jack's old chum from Choate. But he was a Protestant and a Republican in a city that had become Catholic and Democratic. He seemed out of place and lacking in political skills. "He was never that interested in politics; it was never his milieu," said his niece, Sally Carpenter. Nevertheless, Jack put Lem in charge of his office in Cambridge. "When Lem said, 'I'm a Republican, a native of Pittsburgh, and an Episcopalian,' I said to Jack, 'Keep him out of Cambridge,'" Dave Powers recalled. But Jack wanted Lem there, and that was that. Nevertheless, Jack *was* nervous about his prep school pal putting his foot in it, remembered Teddy. Jack's instruction to Lem as he went about the working-class district was, "Wherever you go, Lem, don't tell anyone you went to Choate."

Jack's other friend from Choate and Princeton, Rip Horton, recalled Jack saying, "Every district that poor Lem ever had from 1946 to 1960, when he ran the campaign in Wisconsin, he managed to lose." But Jack didn't care. He felt comfortable just knowing he could call upon his best friend whenever he needed him. Lem's political skills and his ability to get along with Boston Irish politicians just weren't that important to him. As it turned out, Lem's performance in Cambridge was none too shabby. Lem worked fifteen-hour days and "was very popular with the women volunteers, keeping them in good humor with stories about himself and Jack at Choate, and anecdotes of their 1937 trip to Europe," Dave Powers said.

Francis McAdoo, Lem's friend from Princeton, said that Jack had the people to whom he related politically, and that was quite separate from his personal friendships, chief among which was his friendship with Lem. "Lem was a relaxation for the president, a wonderful witty companion. They had the same sense of humor." After so many years, Jack also felt he could be himself with Lem, who knew everything about him, the minuses as well as the pluses. Jack liked having Lem around during the campaigns not because of his political expertise, but because Lem helped smooth the rough edges and made him feel more at ease.

But Jack knew also that the help of the political pros, especially the local political operators, was crucial. Some would become well-known members of Kennedy's political team in the years ahead and would go with him into the White House—Dave Powers and Kenny O'Donnell chief among them. They both made sure the campaign was run efficiently. Dave also introduced Jack to all the right people in the Eleventh District, which he knew inside and out. He also gave Jack tips on how to frame issues in a way that would most appeal to the voters in this part of the commonwealth.

Jack's sisters, Eunice, Pat, and Jean—and Jean's roommate Ethel Skakel (who would later marry Bobby)—worked in the Boston office while twenty-one-year-old Bobby was assigned to Cambridge. Although Bobby and Lem knew each other well by this time, Bobby didn't like taking orders from Lem and eventually took off on his own, knocking on almost every door in East Cambridge. Meanwhile, Lem organized house parties all over the district where people who might support Jack were invited. Joe, of course, managed the campaign expenses and tried to pull all the right strings. Jack's mother, Rose, hosted gatherings all over the district—the famed Kennedy tea parties—giving the first of what would be many accounts of the way she raised her children.

But no one worked harder than Jack, who exhausted himself to the point where he could hardly talk. "In this first campaign, he demonstrated his ability to work harder than any other candidate was willing to work. He was tireless," said Lem. "He had a natural ability to speak in public," and the people responded, he added. Lem was concerned that Jack's grueling schedule would trigger more illness. But this time he did not become sick, and all the hard work paid off. On June 17, 1946, he easily won the Democratic primary. His family was immensely proud, no one more so than Joe. Lem, of course, was thrilled. "It was really one of the great experiences of my relationship with Jack," he said later of the campaign. "His victory was terribly exciting and it was Jack Kennedy's first taste of victory, one of the most exciting nights I can remember. I had never been so proud of anyone in my whole life." Lem must have worried that from now on especially it might be difficult to get time with Jack. But when Lem finally left Boston to enroll at Harvard Business School in the fall, he felt good that he had been able to help Jack win and get what he wanted. Jack's victory in the general election in November was pro forma. The real contest in the Eleventh District had been the Democratic primary.

In January 1947, Jack proudly took his seat in the Congress. At twenty-nine, he was no longer just Jack Kennedy. He was Representative John F. Kennedy, Democrat of Massachusetts. He was assigned a two-room office suite in the old House Office Building on Capitol Hill. He was back living in the nation's capital again, a city he once quipped was "full of southern efficiency and northern charm." He found a house on Thirty-first Street in Georgetown, an upscale neighborhood about seven miles from the Capitol. He was still a bachelor and soon earned a reputation around the city (in the then small-town atmosphere of Washington, D.C.) as a ladies' man, the preferred term for a man who liked a lot of women before he was married, as opposed to a womanizer, the term used for a man with this lifestyle after marriage.

Jack hosted frequent parties at his house, but he also had serious gatherings as well, at which the key issues of the day were discussed, as his father had done at the Kennedy dinner table when he was a kid. Jack was somewhat frustrated with the cumbersome nature of the legislative process, but he was glad to be in a place where important decisions were being made. Although his record as a congressman wasn't outstanding, he was reelected in 1948 and 1950 by sizable margins by the people of the Eleventh District.

Despite his much-busier life, Jack still made time for Lem. "The business school was of course in his district and he came up a lot," recalled Lem. "I remember seeing him whenever he came up to Cambridge. I remember he spent a lot of time encouraging me [in Lem's studies]. He was a very sympathetic guy." When he could get a break from school, Lem often went down to D.C. to see Jack. "I stayed at his house a lot. When he was invited out to dinner, he'd take me along and he was invited to a lot of interesting houses," Lem remarked.

In 1950, Honey Fitz died. Jack was saddened by the death of his grandfather, who had taught him so much about politics, and Boston politics in particular, and, just as important, how to act the part. "There was something in the pageantry and the richness [of Honey Fitz's funeral] that really got to Jack," said Lem. "It made him realize the extraordinary impact a politician can have on the emotions of ordinary people, an impact often forgotten in the corridors of Capitol Hill. It was as if he were seeing for the first time that he really might be able to touch people as a politician and that if he did, then they could give him something back."

After he returned from the war, equipped with an art and architecture degree from Princeton, Lem also had to decide what he was going to do with his life. Unlike Jack, he did have to worry about money. He didn't want to spend his adult years being broke, as he was during his Choate and Princeton days, or relying on Jack for a helping hand. He was not nearly as political as Jack, and in view of his navy experience as chief purser aboard the USS *Cecil,* the obvious practical choice was business. That was his reason for going to Harvard Business School. It had the advantage of being relatively close to Hyannis Port as well as being within easy reach of D.C. by train or plane.

Lem finished graduate school in 1948 and took a series of jobs in sales and advertising, even returning to Coca-Cola for a while. A family member said he left for good when the soft drink giant demoted him. On one occasion, a talent agent even offered him a job as the "Marlboro Man." His first major job after the war, however, was an executive position with General Shoe in Nashville, Tennessee, where his brother, Josh, who was a doctor, lived. Lem found an apartment that would allow him to keep his two Dalmatians, whom he adored. He had quite a few Dalmatians during his life. While at General Shoe, he designed a pair of shoes for his mother with the tallest heels ever manufactured. Lem liked the job but wasn't happy about being in Nashville, so far from Baltimore and Washington, D.C., which is where he really wanted to be.

In 1952, Lem moved back to Baltimore. Not only was the city much closer to Washington than Nashville, his mother, Romaine, lived there. Lem's relationship with his mother had always been close. When he moved back to Baltimore, there was no question but that he would stay with her. Even after he moved to New York, he would frequently return to Baltimore to spend time with her. You only had to walk through his apartment at any point during his life and see the many photographs of Romaine to see how much he adored her.

Romaine also liked Jack and was always happy to see him when he came up from Washington. But Jack was not universally popular with the Billingses. For one thing, the family tradition going back to the days before the Civil War was to support the Republican party. Even Lem remained a Republican until 1960. But the main concern focused on what was seen as Lem's excessive devotion to Jack, and the Kennedy family in general, at the expense of his own family.

Speaking on condition of anonymity, one Billings family member said that Lem's closeness to Jack "went too far." Eventually, he became "more of a Kennedy than a Billings. He was a Falstaff [the humorous, lovable friend of Prince Hal in Shakespeare's *Henry IV*] for the Kennedy family, their comedian. They thought it was just great. And Lem enjoyed the notoriety of it all," the person said. In addition, "Lem knew all about the disastrous sex life of Jack Kennedy and he wasn't as religiously opposed to it as I was. In fact, he never told us about it. We found out later," the person added.

This feeling is not held by all members of the Billings family. While some said that Lem spent too much time with Jack and neglected his own family, others said he was scrupulous about attending family events, such as birthdays and anniversaries, and was devoted to all members of his family, especially his nieces and nephews. On one occasion, Lem dragged his friend, singer Andy Williams, to a college party organized by one of his nephews who was desperately trying to find a replacement for his guest singer, who had canceled out. They both drove for hours to get there. While Andy delighted the surprised students by singing "Moon River," Lem regaled them with his many stories and jokes. Before the evening was over, Lem had pushed Andy from the stage and was singing himself—"We're No Angel," of course.

It isn't surprising that Lem's nieces and nephews were perhaps more appreciative of him than the adults in the family. For them, he was the madcap uncle who never played by adult rules, who always remained a kid at heart. They all loved his gigantic laugh, which he never toned down even when it offended more sedate adults. Some of JFK's advisors, for example, seemed embarrassed by Lem. But Jack, as well as the young Billingses, found Lem's flouting of convention to be one of his most appealing characteristics.

Lem was particularly close to his niece, Sally, the daughter of his sister, Lucretia. She continues to adore her uncle more than a quarter century after his death. Lem would come to see her often when she was a child, she recalled, and not just on holidays or for special occasions such as her birthday. Lem left many of his possessions to Sally. Ten years after he died, she and Robert F. Kennedy Jr. put together a privately published book in tribute to Lem. In it, hundreds of people—his nieces and nephews as well as many of the friends he had acquired in life—paid tribute to him, proof, it seems, that Lem's gift for connecting with people and the appeal of his magnetic personality extended far beyond Jack Kennedy. While it was clear that Lem was devoted to Jack, this didn't mean he neglected the many other people in his life, said Sally, and there were many.

However, it is clear that Lem's devotion to Jack caused tension among some members of the family. "I am very anti-Kennedy," said one person, "so I don't really want to talk about it. Lem and I could never talk about it. We would get mad at each other."

Some members of the Billings family wondered about Lem's sexual orientation, given the fact that he didn't marry, "which was the usual thing to do back then," said one relative. The person added, "I wondered whether he was gay. But I never asked him about it. That wasn't the sort of thing you did back then. He certainly never had any close involvements with women. I thought he might be asexual." For his part, Lem never brought up the subject with his family, either. One relative said that Lem's great gift for friendship, not only with Jack Kennedy, but with many other people, would not have been possible had he married.

After he moved to Baltimore, Lem took a job with the Emerson Drug Company, a veteran business whose most famous product was Bromo Seltzer, a remedy designed to cure all manner of maladies, especially stomach upsets and hangovers. Francis McAdoo, Lem's old friend from Princeton, was a vice president at Emerson and offered Lem a job working directly for him as head of advertising. More than half a century later, Mac, as everyone called him, remembered Lem as a "good and efficient" worker, but he would always be talking about Jack Kennedy. Mac, who served in the South Pacific on the PT boats, knew Jack slightly from the war. "I saw Jack off and on," he recalled. "He was in the Solomons. I was in New Guinea. Jack would come to social reunions after the war and we'd chat a bit. So Lem knew I knew Jack and that's probably why he talked to me a lot about him."

At the time Lem started working for Mac, the Emerson Drug Company was in trouble. Unlike its rival Alka-Seltzer, Bromo Seltzer didn't contain aspirin and was not marketed in tablet form. By the time Lem joined the company, Emerson's sales of Bromo Seltzer had fallen dramatically behind those of Alka-Seltzer, marketed by Miles Laboratories. So in 1954 Emerson changed course and began marketing Bromo Seltzer tablets. The first batch of the new tablets was shipped overseas for test-marketing.

Meanwhile, the machinery for making the tablets in Baltimore lay idle and Lem came up with an idea. Since Bromo Seltzer had a kind of salty taste that many people didn't like, why not add fruit flavoring to hide the taste of the sodium citrate? More to the point, why not make a new kind of fizzy drink altogether that was not formulated just to cure aches and pains? The new effervescent tablet could be placed in water, like Kool-Aid, producing a new, flavorful drink, but fizzy—as kids liked. After their scientists confirmed it was feasible, Lem's bosses agreed to try the experiment while they were waiting for the test results on Bromo Seltzer. Thus was born—Fizzies.

Lem asked the New York advertising firm Lennen & Newell, for which he later would work, to take charge of the marketing campaign. Fizzies came in four flavors originally: orange, grape, cherry, and lemon-lime. Lennen & Newell's promotion effort emphasized that Fizzies contained no sugar and was full of Vitamin C. It also stressed that no storage space was needed for Fizzies, unlike bottled drinks, since the tablets could just be dropped into a glass of water. Eight tablets cost nineteen cents.

The new product was test-marketed in Harrisburg, Pennsylvania. Lem oversaw the effort so he could personally assess how popular it was with customers. To his delight, it was a hit. His bosses gave the go-ahead for the new product. Within months, Fizzies captured 45 percent of the nonbottled soft drink market in locations where it was available. The kids, as Lem had hoped, were crazy about it. It wasn't the taste of the drink that appealed to them so much as the fact that they could see it sparkle once they dropped the tablets into the water. Kids loved watching the bubbling and sizzling.

Fizzies became a fad and was so successful that soon Emerson marketed the drink in eight different flavors nationwide. It became a ten-million-dollar industry for the company. Lem remained proud of Fizzies for the rest of his life, even though, by the 1970s, the fad was history. But it was not forgotten. In 1989, a writer for the *New York Times*, Dena Kleiman, penned an article titled, "When Fizzies Left, So Did the Sparkle," in which she called the Fizzies phenomenon "a hula hoop like craze." Why did Fizzies fade? According to Kleiman, the touted benefit of the drink—no sugar—spelled its doom. When reports surfaced in the 1960s that cyclamate, the artificial sweetener that was used in the product, might cause cancer, Fizzies was pulled from the market and never replaced. Fizzies returned in the mid-1990s with a new artificial sweetener, NutraSweet. But this time it didn't catch on and quickly went out of production. In the early twenty-first century, Fizzies has been introduced yet again. It has become the soft drink that refuses to die.

At one point, during the heyday of Fizzies, Lem thought of buying the rights to the drink and marketing it himself. But he found it hard to secure investment partners. He considered trying to interest Jack and other Kennedy family members, but he eventually decided not to, preferring to keep his friendships and his business dealings separate. Lem was always careful not to exploit his friendship with Jack. Although he was tempted to do so at various points in his life—the Fizzies era being one of them—he knew what was most important to him. He never wanted to use Jack in any way, never had, and wasn't going to do it at this time just to advance his career, even if it would have made him rich.

Author Lester David, who interviewed Lem toward the end of his life, said, "Never in our conversations through the years had Lem Billings told me anything but the truth as he saw it. He never was a PR man for Jack or anyone else in the family, although he defended them against what he considered unfair attacks. In short, Lem was too honest to be devious." Lem "was a terrific advertising man, very creative," recalled Dave Hackett, a friend of Bobby Kennedy's who got a job working for Lem at Emerson. "He gave me a room in his mother's house in Baltimore, where he was living at the time," he recalled. "We didn't have much money and we ate fried chicken every night. Lem used to get furious with me for putting the bones in the wastebasket at his mother's house." But Hackett was grateful for the help. Lem's friends "were his life," said one of those who knew him well. "His closest friends were his heroes. To them, he gave everything he had to give."

While Lem was at Emerson, the company enrolled its executives in a speed-reading course, another fad of the time. Lem invited Jack and Bobby up to Baltimore to join him and the other Emerson brass. It didn't take Jack and Lem long to revive their old schoolboy shenanigans even though they were both grown men and Jack was a member of Congress. "I can remember that a sort of officious little guy was running it," who didn't know who Jack was, Lem said. "He'd never set eyes on him before. During the course, I was sitting beside Jack and I remember we were talking during the time this little guy was lecturing—just like we probably had at Choate—and this guy turned on us." Asked how Jack responded to that, Lem said, "He thought it was very funny."

Contrary to the oft-stated view, Lem said that Jack didn't improve his reading speed "since he already read terribly fast." But he said Bobby did.

Lem's career at Emerson lasted until a merger occurred with Warner-Lambert in 1958. In that year, he moved from Baltimore to New York and took a position as a vice president at Lennen & Newell, the top New York advertising firm with which he had had dealings at Emerson. He hated being farther away from Jack, but his financial situation improved as a result and he could easily afford to take the train or plane down to Washington.

In addition to his regular job in advertising during the 1950s, Lem also took great delight in restoring old houses and in collecting antiques and art. According to his sister Lucretia, she and Lem bought a number of old houses, overseeing their restoration and then selling them. It was a passion that lasted for the rest of his life. In the process, he helped save old neighborhoods that otherwise might have gone on the chopping block, she added. One of them was Fell's Point in Baltimore, then a run-down part of the city. "I will say that it was Moyne's enormous enthusiasm which carried me through the lengthy battle to save Fell's Point, a fight that ensued for years," she said. At one point there was a plan to build an interstate highway through the area that would have destroyed Fell's Point, she said. "It was with his great help and encouragement that it was saved at all."

Later, Lem also helped friends and relatives with the selection and renovation of homes elsewhere, especially in the Philadelphia area. "I think in terms of his achievements in life, he was most proud of his renovation of homes, more so than his work in business," noted Lucretia. In the late 1960s and early 1970s, he joined with the Stroud family to renovate houses that were deteriorating in the rural Pennsylvania Quaker area where they lived. And he also enjoyed buying and restoring old brownstones in Manhattan, where he lived during the last years of his life.

Lem was never much of a sportsman, but he did enjoy skiing. There was nothing that gave him greater pleasure than to organize a skiing trip to upstate New York or a location out West, accompanied by one or more Kennedy family members, or some of his friends. He was never very good at it, by most accounts, and his thick eyeglasses were always freezing up, making it difficult for him to see. On one occasion, he fell off the ski lift, yelling, "Where are you, Eunie baby?" A ski instructor wrote him, in jest, offering him free ski lessons for the rest of his life, provided only "that you agree never to wear your overcoat during a class lesson."

∽

Robert F. Kennedy, Pat Lawford, and Lem, White
Peak Cabin, Waterville Valley, New Hampshire, 1967.

In the summer of 1947, Jack, now Representative Jack Kennedy, returned to Europe. First, he went to Ireland to see his sister Kick, who'd lost her husband, Billy Hartington, heir to the estate of the duke of Devonshire, in the war. He also visited the home of his ancestors in the village of Dunganstown, not far from New Ross on the banks of the Barrow River in County Wexford. It was from here that his grandfather emigrated to the United States in the 1840s.

After Ireland, Jack spent time in London, where he was finally diagnosed with Addison's disease. He was so sick that on the journey back home, he was given last rites. But once again he pulled through. Predictions about his premature demise were of course something Jack was used to by now.

Commenting on Jack's Addison's disease, which was kept secret for years, Lem said, "Of course he had it. But he wasn't terribly sick with it. This was never a problem with him in his whole life. I mean, Addison's disease was one of the lesser problems. . . . He got it during the late forties. That was before they had the drug cortisone, which of course made his life completely normal." Lem didn't likely realize when he spoke, however, that the various illnesses from which he had seen Jack suffer—at Choate and later—were connected to Addison's, which had not been diagnosed at that time.

Almost a year after his trip to Europe—on May 13, 1948—Jack received a telephone call from a reporter at his home in Washington. Kick had been killed in an airplane crash in France. Again, the agony of a premature death. Jack was devastated. He loved Kick deeply. She was exuberant and fun loving, always looking forward to the next chapter in her life. Now, just four years after Joe died in the war, she, too, was gone. It was all too much. Jack not only loved Kick's carefree ways, he also respected her determination to be independent from Joe and Rose, which even included marrying a Brit, and a Protestant Brit at that. During Jack's time in England before World War II, it was Kick who'd introduced him to all the right people. He was so distraught over his sister's death that he was unable to attend her funeral in England. He got as far as New York but then returned home. He was too upset. The sad task of representing the family fell to Joe, who was the sole Kennedy to make the journey to attend the service and burial.

For a while, Jack found it difficult to sleep. He told Lem that as soon as he shut his eyes he would start to think about Kick and all the times that they had talked long into the night. He also told Lem that eventually he found it easier to sleep with a woman by his side. Imagining the woman was a friend of Kick's, he would think of the three of them having breakfast together the next morning. This would help him fall asleep.

Later, when he was president, Jack, speaking on the occasion of Robert Frost's death, said, "His sense of the human tragedy fortified him against self-deception and easy consolation. 'I have been one,' he wrote, 'acquainted with the night.' And because he knew the midnight as well as the high noon, because he understood the ordeal as well as the triumph of the human spirit, he gave his age strength with which to overcome despair."

The loss of Kick and Joe, the friends killed during the war, and his own brushes with death made Jack more fatalistic. He became increasingly conscious of the fact that any one of us can be wiped out in an instant, that nothing is for sure, that life, as he would say as president, is unfair. He determined to live his own life to the fullest, to never delay or hold back. Lem noticed the changes in Jack as he tried to come to grips with everything that had happened. He began, Lem said, "living for the moment, treating each day as if it were his last, demanding of life intensity, adventure, and pleasure." He was not yet forty.

Anyone who has had his own confrontation with death, or who has been diagnosed with an illness that can kill instantly, can relate to these kinds of psychological effects. Jack's comments to friends, as well as the speeches he gave as a congressman, began to be imbued with a new sense of urgency and an unbending impatience with delay. It animated everything he did, whether at work or play. He became caught up in what Martin Luther King Jr. called "the fierce urgency of now." As the 1950s began, Jack Kennedy was a man in a hurry.

Kick's death had a profound effect on Lem, as well. Of all Jack's sisters and brothers, Lem probably was closest to Kick. There had been a voluminous correspondence between Lem and Kick, especially when she was living in England. Lem loved Kick for the same reasons that Jack did—her incredible warmth and joie de vivre, and her loyalty to both of them. Lem had experienced the impact of death and loss at an early age when his father died while he was still at Choate. Kick's death in 1948, when he was in his early thirties, was his second great loss. Because they both loved her so much, Kick's passing was one of the events that drew Jack and Lem closer together. They were marching through life as great friends knowing that, in their case, tragedy and loss had become a permanent part of their lives.

In 1952, after just three terms in the House of Representatives, Jack decided to take on a Massachusetts icon, incumbent senator Henry Cabot Lodge, who was thought to be unbeatable. Joe again bankrolled the effort. Campaigns had become more costly since the advent of television. Some of the pros said that Jack was crazy to take on Lodge, who was well financed and well liked in the commonwealth. "It was a very daring thing for him to do in a Republican year to run against the incumbent senator with a name like Lodge," said Lem. "It was damned ambitious."

Joe, who never liked losing at anything, was all in favor of entering the race. He thought that defeating a Protestant blueblood would be a gigantic feather in Jack's cap and would move him closer to a run for the White House. Bobby, now twenty-six, managed the campaign, earning a reputation for being just as ruthless as his father. The Kennedys once again became famous for their tea parties across the state, presided over by Rose and Jack's sisters. They were enormously successful. Lem did not participate in Jack's Senate campaign because he had just moved to Baltimore and taken the new job with Emerson. "This was a big break in my business career and I was a little above my head in that job at first," he remarked. But Jack talked to Lem about the contest frequently on the phone. Lem's influence in this regard has often been discounted. But

Washington insider Rowland Evans later said that Lem was "a major family player who seemed to be on the edge of every family decision and opinion, and every tribulation and triumph—not always on the right side perhaps, but really with a strong opinion."

Once again the Kennedy money and organization kicked into gear. But this time the candidate's performance was much improved. Jack now spoke with more confidence and assurance than he had when he'd first pressed the flesh in Boston. When the results came in, against the odds, Jack had beaten Lodge by more than seventy thousand votes. Although he had not participated in this campaign, Lem was there to savor Jack's victory. "The night of his election, I went up there and spent the evening with him and his family." On January 3, 1953, Jack was sworn in as a United States senator. He moved to the Senate Office Building, Room 362, located directly opposite Richard Nixon's room. The two had grown to be quite chummy in their early days in Congress. But Nixon was elected to a new position as well that November, as vice president of the United States, after Dwight Eisenhower, at the top of the Republican ticket, won a landslide victory over Democrat Adlai Stevenson.

Now Jack and Nixon increasingly became rivals as their political ambitions took precedence over their friendship. Nixon, as vice president, felt he would be in a good position to run for president in 1960 after Ike's two terms were up. But Jack also had his eye on the job. There was just one problem as far as a bid for the presidency was concerned. He wasn't married.

"By the time he was approaching his mid-thirties, his father and I had really begun to wonder if he was going to remain a bachelor for several years more and then marry late in life," recalled Rose Kennedy. Joe felt that Jack must marry if he wanted to use his seat in the Senate as a springboard to the White House. Coincidentally or not, Jack already had met someone he liked. During his campaign for the Senate, Jacqueline Bouvier came into his life.

Charlie Bartlett, a Washington correspondent for the *Chattanooga Times,* and his wife, Martha, invited Jack to a dinner party at their house. Charlie, who had earlier dated Jackie, still recalls that famous get-together half a century later. Jackie was one of a number of guests "and I could tell that Jack was interested in her," he said. Jack later remarked, "I leaned across the asparagus and asked her for a date."

Jackie was twelve years younger than Jack, and, like him, a child of privilege. Before graduating from George Washington University in Washington, D.C., Jackie studied at Vassar and also at the Sorbonne in Paris. She was fluent in a number of foreign languages, including French, Italian, and Spanish. In one major respect, however, she was different from Jack. She did not share his interest in politics. Her great love was the arts.

"Jackie was different from all the other girls Jack had been dating," said Lem. "She was more intelligent, more literary, more substantial" and had a "certain classiness that is hard to describe." This made her more of a challenge for Jack "and there was nothing Jack liked more than a challenge." Lem added: "I think he understood that the two of them were alike. They had both taken circumstances that weren't the best in the world when they were younger and learned to make themselves up as they went along."

At the time she met her future husband, Jackie was the "inquiring photographer" for the *Washington Times-Herald.* She earned $42–50 a week to ask questions like, "Are men braver than women in the dental chair?" and, "Some women should be struck regularly like gongs [a Noël Coward line]. Do you agree?" Later, she did a piece on Jack for her column. She asked him what was his best quality, to which he answered, "Curiosity." And his worst? "Irritability and impatience with the dull or mediocre," he responded.

The dinner at Charlie Bartlett's place has become legendary as the occasion on which Jack and Jackie met. But it was another dinner, shortly thereafter, that sealed the deal. Jackie was living at the time in McLean, Virginia, a Washington, D.C., suburb, with her half-brother Hugh Auchincloss III. Not long after the visit to Charlie Bartlett's place, Jackie told Hugh that she wanted to bring a congressman home for dinner. "But don't get into any arguments with him, Hugh, because he's a Democrat and you're a Republican and he's a liberal and you're a conservative," he recalled her saying.

"The dinner went well," Hugh said. Jackie "really liked him. It was a physical attraction. But it was more of an intellectual attraction. He had a great deal of knowledge about American history and she knew a great deal about European history and about the arts. Jackie could talk about any subject. So they talked about history, World War II, and the

Middle East. He got a lot of information from Jackie and he respected her knowledge. They both were quite taken with each other." Hugh added, "Within the first five minutes, even I was taken over by Jack's charm. He always asked questions. He was a great listener. He treated you as if you knew more about a subject than you did. We got along wonderfully and became good friends."

Although Jack was campaigning for the Senate at the time, he called Jackie frequently after that dinner and asked her out. "Jack was intrigued by Jackie, perhaps because she always seemed to hold back some of her personality, in contrast to the other women he dated," Hugh said. As far as Jackie was concerned, she was crazy about Jack and considered his intelligence to be way above average. "He has this curious, inquiring mind that is always at work," she said. "If I were drawing him, I would draw a tiny body and an enormous head." Jackie knew she had found the man she wanted to marry.

Jack felt that Jackie would be a hit with his parents. He never cared about anyone's religion, but he was well aware that her Catholicism would be a big plus, with Rose especially. Joe, once he got to meet her, thought Jackie would be the perfect political wife. He liked her and she liked him. They formed a bond in those early days that only grew, and that was particularly important to Joe after he suffered a devastating stroke in late 1961. "When Jackie and Jack had problems, she would unburden herself to Joe," Lem said. "He admired her strength, the fact that she was born with her own identity. She was the one person who could stand up to the old man and get away with it." Strangely, Jackie never seemed to object to Joe's womanizing. Lem said that "for hours he would tell Jackie about Gloria Swanson, Marion Davies, and countless others, past and present. He and Jackie shared personal feelings and private jokes."

Of course, Lem knew about all the other women in Jack's life, as well. He had seen many come and go over the years. At first, he saw no reason why Jackie would be any different. "Through all the years that I had known Jack, I had met many of his girls so, to me, this was just another," Lem remarked. He was well aware of Jack's line, "Give me a beach and a girl and that's about as good as life can get." But Lem did remember Jack telling him he had "met an attractive young girl and that she was engaged to somebody else." However, when Lem asked Jack whether she was different, someone special, Jack said no. But things quickly changed, Lem remembered. "He began taking her out all the time. Instead of taking out a lot of different girls, he concentrated on Jackie."

It wasn't long before Jack introduced Lem to Jackie. "I can remember we were going to Bobby's for dinner at one of Bobby's many different houses in Georgetown," recalled Lem. "I was staying with Jack at the time and we drove out to Merrywood and picked up Jackie to take her to Bobby's." Lem quickly got the sense that Jack was more serious about Jackie than any other girl he had dated. Lem also knew that sooner or later Jack had to get married if he were to go for the top political prize—the presidency. This was yet another adjustment—the most important adjustment so far—that Lem would have to make in his friendship with Jack. If Jack had to get married, then for Lem, Jackie seemed like the right kind of woman. Most importantly for Lem, Jackie seemed to accept him as part of the marriage package.

Relationship experts and psychologists have long argued that marriage, as one of the key shifts in life, can easily jeopardize a friendship, even one of long standing like Jack and Lem's. The reaction can be worse if the single friend has abandonment issues and/or low self-esteem, as was the case with Lem, especially if the newly married person begins focusing on the marriage and spending less time with the friend. However, all the evidence shows that this did not happen with Jack and Lem. First, Jack never abandoned Lem, or even noticeably decreased the time he spent with him. Second, Lem knew that marriage was inevitable for Jack because of his political ambitions. He felt he could get along with a woman like Jackie—and he did.

The more relevant question was, could Jack get along with Jackie? Jack's relationships with women, for the most part, had been fleeting. He wanted to meet women primarily for sexual enjoyment. "He had never been involved as a friend with girls—he had never wanted to spend a lot of time with any of them," said Lem. "He was crazy about girls but he never really settled down with one girl. . . . I think that possibly Jack maybe had, in this one area, an immature relationship with girls—that is, while he was terribly interested in going out and having fun with them at night, I don't think that he really was terribly excited about girls as friends."

However, Jack had reached the point "where he felt it was politically important to marry—fortunately, Jackie came along at the right time," said Lem. Even so, Lem felt that Jack really liked Jackie and that he wasn't dating her just because he needed a wife to run for president. As the affair between them became more serious, however, Lem decided that Jackie should at least know what she was getting herself into. Lem was staying with Jack during the early part of 1953. As a senator, Jack was invited to the 1953 Eisenhower inauguration and subsequent festivities. He decided to take both Jackie and Lem with him to the events. The first inaugural ball provided an opportunity—while Jack was mingling with all the dignitaries—for Lem to take Jackie aside and let her know what Jack was really all about.

"I felt I should prepare her a little bit for what I felt were some of the problems that Jack might have in marrying at thirty-five. She was terribly young, and it might be best if she were prepared for it," Lem said later. "So I told her that night that I thought she ought to realize that Jack was thirty-five years old, had been around an awful lot all his life, had known many, many girls—this sounds like an awfully disloyal friend saying these things—that she was going to have to be very understanding at the beginning, that he had never really settled down with one girl before, and that a man of thirty-five is very difficult to live with. She was very understanding about it and accepted everything I said. Of course, later I told Jack everything I said to her—and he was pleased because he felt it would make her better understand him."

"Later, after they were married, I talked with Jackie on this subject again, and she said, 'When you discussed that with me, I realized all that, and I thought it was a challenge,'" Lem said. Jackie apparently told the same thing to her stepbrother. She was not offended by Lem's warning, said Hugh Auchincloss. She liked Lem in the same way that Jack did. "He was a cozy funny fellow with her," as well. Importantly, she knew that Lem was Jack's best friend and that they went way back. She was glad to learn everything she could know about Jack from Lem, he added. "I don't think she regarded Lem as a very serious person. But she did like him. There is no question about that."

In fact, Jackie did take Lem's chat as a challenge. By all accounts, it made her fall for Jack even more. She liked men who weren't pushovers, who had something exciting about them. Even though she didn't care that much for politics, she was impressed by Jack's idealism and ambition. She considered what Lem said about Jack's view of women. But at this time, before she was married, it didn't really register. She told friends all she wanted to do was marry Jack. Perhaps she thought she could change him, but no one really knows if that was the case.

Even though Jack was taken with Jackie, it is clear that he didn't really want to get married, said Jackie's cousin John H. Davis. In Jackie, Jack "saw primarily someone of 'class,' as his father would say, who would advance his social status and his political fortunes," Davis said. Although he liked Jackie, Jack enjoyed his bachelor life, which consisted of fleeting involvements with women and solid friendships with men—most importantly, Lem. "Jack Kennedy was terribly fond of his male friends and his family," said Davis, and always wanted them around, which frustrated Jackie on many occasions. He added: "Jack never 'fell in love' with Jackie, or with anybody, for that matter, but in time he definitely did come to love Jacqueline, as much as it was within his power to love one woman."

Priscilla McMillan, Jack's researcher during the 1950s, also thinks that Jack only considered marriage because of his political career. More than fifty years after she worked for him, she says she still vividly recalls his remarks about marrying Jackie. "I only got married because I was thirty-seven years old. If I wasn't married people would think I was queer," she recalls Jack as saying. Charlie Bartlett said that Jack told him the same story, adding that it was his father who first suggested the political image problem as regards his sexual orientation if he didn't get married. "He lived his life in compartments," McMillan said. Once when she questioned him about the number of women in his life, he replied, "I just can't help it."

Jack's political aide Kenny O'Donnell, said, "Jack Kennedy kept his personal affairs, his various friendships, his political activities, and other interests in separate compartments; when he was with Dave Powers, Larry O'Brien, and me, he talked Massachusetts politics and very little else." He added: "Getting to know him intimately was not easy."

An old Harvard friend of Jack's, Langdon Marvin, who was his advisor on aviation issues, recalled a conversation with him during this time that further clarifies his thoughts on marriage. Marvin said that the discussion took place while Jack was in the bathtub and he was sitting on the toilet seat. Jack was saying he didn't want to marry a girl who was an "experienced voyager," a metaphor used by Lord Byron. "I mean, I don't want to marry a girl who's traveled sexually," Marvin recalls Jack saying. "There are too many complications with a girl who's an experienced voyager. They make comparisons between you and other men. I want someone young and fresh. I want to marry a virgin."

Marvin was the kind of guy Jack liked, witty and urbane. He was also good-looking, athletic, and attractive to women. But like Lem, Marvin was gay (although it is not clear that Jack knew this at the time). In any case, Jack didn't think twice about going into the bathroom and taking his clothes off while someone he knew was around, said Marvin. He surmised that Jack liked being the object of attention, even the attention of men. "He was used to it, in fact. He had a perpetual tan, a great big mop of hair, and natural good looks that just drew people to him—men and women," Marvin said. "He'd been used to it since he was a young man and it didn't bother him in the slightest. He enjoyed it."

"Jackie Bouvier's different," Jack told Marvin. "She's definitely different." Marvin listened intently as Jack went on washing himself, all the while talking about women and marriage to a guy who was probably more interested in watching Jack in the bathtub. Appropriately enough, Marvin remembered that Frank Sinatra was singing "All or Nothing at All" on the record player in the background. Frank's records often helped Jack relax. The two eventually would become pals—and bad boys on the Hollywood party circuit.

After going back and forth, and no doubt after many discussions with Lem, Jack decided that Jackie would be the one, but he didn't want to rush into marriage. Joe and Rose were both in favor of her, but Jack's sisters were not nearly as impressed. Jack's sisters were much more casual, down-to-earth, and athletic than Jackie. "The debutante" and "Babykins" were just two of the nicknames they lumbered her with, in part because of her soft voice. Despite the cool reception Jackie got from Jack's sisters, however, Lem was convinced Jack had finally found the right girl for him. "They were kindred souls, two halves of the same whole," he remarked. Lem felt that his friendship with Jack would not be too adversely affected by a marriage with Jackie, which, in fact, proved to be the case. But Jack remained scared of taking the plunge.

While Jack hesitated, Joe pushed, according to Lem. "Joe Kennedy not only condoned the marriage, he ordained it," he said. "Joe said, 'A politician has to have a wife, and a Catholic politician has to have a

Catholic wife. She should have class. Jackie probably has more class than any girl we've ever seen around here.'" Jack finally suggested to Jackie that they get engaged. But even then he had politics on his mind. He wanted to delay the announcement of the date for their engagement because a magazine was about to print a story about him. When he saw the title of the piece at the office, however, he went ballistic. It was named, "The Senate's Gay Young Bachelor." The word *gay* didn't mean then what it means now to most Americans. But the word was not unknown. Clearly, Jack had heard about the other meaning of *gay* and was none too pleased by the publication's choice of headline.

While Jack procrastinated in setting a date for their engagement, Jackie decided to give him a shove. She went off to London, accepting a plum assignment from the *Washington Times-Herald* to cover the coronation of Queen Elizabeth in London. Her series of front-page articles about the coronation—and what ordinary Britons thought about the dawn of a second Elizabethan age—was the talk of the town. Jack relished all her stories—mostly because they were written by her.

Jackie had been gone a week when she received a telegram in London from Jack: "Articles excellent, but you are missed." After that, they talked on the phone, and sometime during the transatlantic conversation Jack set the engagement date—June 24—and asked Jackie to marry him. It had taken him almost two years to pop the question, but he finally threw caution to the winds. Lem said later that he couldn't picture Jack proposing, and even more so, expressing his love for a person. "I don't think he was the kind of person (and again, Jackie is going to have to answer this) to say 'I love you.' He just never wanted to show his inner emotions. He would rather have it happen without talking about it." But however Jack did it, he did it. It was a go. Jack and Jackie would tie the knot. "I know it was a very big step for Jack Kennedy. He was scared," said Lem.

The wedding of the year took place on September 12, 1953, in Newport, Rhode Island. Jack asked his brother Bobby to be best man and Lem to be an usher. On the night before the wedding, a bridal dinner was held at Newport's Clambake Club. Jack gave Lem and each of the other ushers a Brooks Brothers umbrella engraved with initials and the wedding date. The next morning, all eyes were on Jack and Jackie as they arrived at St. Mary's Church for the ceremony, which was presided over by Archbishop Richard Cushing. Lem, along with the other ushers, was busily helping latecomers to their seats. As Lem bent down to pick up some change someone had dropped, Ethel's brother, George Jr., gave him a kick in the ass, sending him—gray morning suit and all—crashing to the floor. Ethel and her siblings roared with laughter. But one imagines that Lem was less than thrilled to be the victim of a prank on this particular day, even though they all usually engaged in such antics with equal enthusiasm.

The reception following the wedding was held at Hammersmith Farm, the Auchincloss estate overlooking Narragansett Bay. All the arrangements for the wedding and reception were stage-managed by Joe as if it were a Hollywood production. He arranged for photographers and press coverage, cajoling the *New York Times* and the *Boston Globe* into placing Jack and Jackie on the front page. His objective was to introduce Jackie to America as not only a beautiful wife but also as a potential First Lady. Jack was thrilled at how great Jackie looked, according to Lem. He soon began taking an interest in women's as well as men's clothes. "He did have something to say about every single thing Jackie wore," remembered Lem. "I think he had an awful lot of influence on Jackie's clothes." It wasn't so much Oleg Cassini, the fashion designer, who was later credited with creating the Jackie look, but Jackie herself, advised by Jack, added Lem.

The whole Kennedy family was at the reception, in addition to thirteen hundred other guests, including the Newport aristocracy, Washington pols, and Boston-Irish chums. It was a happy day for Jack and Jackie, for Lem, and for everyone else who attended. Jack's old navy buddy, Red Fay, brought along an 8-millimeter color movie camera and captured the event on film. After their wedding, Jack and Jackie left for New York and then went on to Acapulco for their honeymoon.

After the wedding was over, Joe took steps to try to curtail Jack's womanizing—not because he thought it was immoral, but because now that Jack was married, any indiscretion could trigger political damage were it to become public. Joe knew that Lem would help Jack restrain himself. But he also talked to Jack's other friends, as well. Joe told George Smathers, a Florida congressman who was also Jack's friend, "George, you better try to keep Jack more discreet. He can't do it in the public eye. Jack can't afford to have people talk about his messing around."

What Joe should have realized, however, is that it would be difficult for Jack to change his lifelong bad-boy habits. Before the wedding, Jack—and Lem—leveled with Jackie about some of the past behavior, but Jack didn't stop. She rarely confronted him with it, but she did notice what he was up to, according to people who knew them well. After the marriage, "she wasn't the same carefree, happy Jackie Bouvier anymore," Charlie Bartlett said. "She was much more solemn."

Jack couldn't understand why her moods would change, not realizing that he was the cause much of the time. "While on one level Jackie must have known what she was getting into by marrying a thirty-six-year-old playboy," Lem said, "she never suspected the depths of Jack's need for other women. Nor was she prepared for the humiliation she would suffer when she found herself stranded at parties while Jack would suddenly disappear with some pretty young girl. Before the marriage, I think she found Jack's appeal to other women tantalizing—I suspect it reminded her of the magic appeal her handsome, rakish father had had with women all his life—but once she was married, and once it was happening to her, it was much harder to accept."

Jackie's moods used to drive Jack crazy, according to Lem. "He wasn't moody in any way and he couldn't bear anybody around him who was moody," he remarked. "If someone was moody around him, he'd go to every extreme to get them out of that mood." He added: "When I might get in moods, he wouldn't say, 'I'll see you after you're through.' He'd get you out of the mood, and he would do it very successfully, by taking your mind off yourself. . . . Through my thirty years with Jack, I suppose I had moods. Anytime that I was in those moods and had to be around him, instead of just walking off, Jack Kennedy would get me out of these moods. . . . Of course, I don't know if he did this with anybody but myself."

Lem was understating his temperament a bit. The evidence shows that he threw tantrums from the earliest days at Choate, especially when he felt Jack wasn't spending enough time with him. But compared to Jackie's moods, Lem's were small fry. "He did marry a girl who had these ups and downs, and certainly here it was more important than any other time in his life," said Lem. "He was living with her and to have her moody really drove him out of his mind. He couldn't stand it. It was the worst thing that could happen to him. He spent a great deal of his time, when she was in these moods, cheering her up—and he worked very hard at it."

Of course, neither Lem nor Jack understood that at least some of Jackie's moods were a result of Jack's womanizing, and possibly even frustration over his friendship with Lem, especially when she felt he was around too much. But whatever the cause, Jack would try his level best to get rid of her lows. "He wouldn't just talk to her about why she was in a mood and all that," said Lem. "He'd be understanding about it. He'd try to think of all the things that were fun. He was bright. He knew how to get her mind on others than herself. At least, he always talked me out of it, and I saw him talk Jackie out of it, many, many times." Despite Jack's ability to raise Jackie's spirits, however, he never changed his behavior, the root cause of much of her distress.

Charlie Bartlett, who admired Jack, concluded that he just wasn't marriage material. "Introducing Jackie and Jack wasn't one of the smartest things I've done," he said. "I don't think Jack should have been married. He had this thing about him, which was not under control." Jack's promiscuity, and his sometimes uncaring indifference, almost guaranteed that the early years of their marriage would be difficult. Lem was a bridge between Jack and Jackie especially during this time, said Peter Kaplan, one of the people who knew Lem in his later years. Lem had a way of breaking any tension between them with his playfulness and humor. Jackie, as well as Jack, felt comfortable talking to Lem. Despite some emerging friction, Jackie and Lem had one overriding thing in common—they both loved Jack.

The occasional tension between Jackie and Lem was caused by his omnipresence as much as anything. If Jackie thought that, after the wedding, Jack and Lem would see less of each other, she was mistaken. Sometimes, she enjoyed having Lem around, and the three of them got on famously together. Other times, however, especially when she was in a more introverted mood, she just wanted to be with Jack. "She liked him, but she didn't like him," said Kaplan. "He appreciated things. He had an aesthetic sense that she wanted Jack to have. But she got fed up with his ubiquitousness and she made fun of him . . . although he did help her in various ways."

If it wasn't Lem who was there, it was Jack's brothers and sisters—and often it was both. Jackie sometimes resented the presence of the large Kennedy brood, as well. Lem unwittingly tells a story of just how overpowering it could all be for Jackie. It was the Christmas in Palm Beach after Jack and Jackie were married. Jackie had given Jack a beautiful painting set as a Christmas present. Jackie had always painted a little, and she was eager to get Jack interested, as well. "I'm sure she pictured them going down to the dunes and painting together in a romantic sort of way," said Lem. But once Lem and the rest of the Kennedy family found out Jack had a new painting set, they all got into the act. "This beautiful set was divided up amongst the entire family—we took the canvases, and we all, every one of us, started painting," Lem recalled. "It was the first time any of us had ever had a paint set." Lem and the rest of the family conveniently forgot it had been a present from Jackie to Jack. "It wasn't exactly what Jackie had in mind when she bought it," Lem sheepishly conceded years later.

Jack, Lem, Pat, and Peter Lawford enjoying the day painting, Palm Beach, 1953.

However, Jackie was happy that Jack loved his gift and took his painting seriously, despite all the commotion as Lem and the Kennedys painted up a storm—even causing Rose to eventually issue an edict that they could only paint in the bathrooms since they were making a total mess of the house. Lem was impressed at how good Jack was. "I always thought that I was much more culturally endowed than he was. I always thought that I had much better taste and more talent in this area," said

Lem. But Jack excelled at his new hobby. "He had a tremendous color sense. Isn't it funny? It really killed me," said Lem. Jack did a series of paintings, mostly landscapes. "There are in existence today about five Kennedys," said Lem. "Had his life not gotten so busy, he would have loved to have gone back to painting." Lem didn't comment on what Jackie thought of everyone taking control of Jack's painting set. He likely knew she was upset.

During his time in the Senate, Jack had become interested in the political careers of men who had taken an unpopular stand and paid a high political cost. He thought political courage was a rarer commodity than bravery in battle. He determined to turn his thoughts into another book, his first since *Why England Slept* in 1940. The result was *Profiles in Courage,* a tribute to political valor. For years it was alleged that Ted Sorensen ghostwrote the book, though Sorensen has always denied this. Lem attested, "I saw him [Jack] writing the book. I saw it all in his own handwriting. And I saw him crossing out and rewriting, etc. . . . By God, if at twenty-one years of age, he could write *Why England Slept,* why the hell couldn't he write *Profiles in Courage?*" But that is as far as Lem went in agreeing with Sorensen's account.

Lem claimed that Sorensen, whom Lem described a decade later as "almost all the way to the left," started the rumor that Jack didn't really write the book. "I heard Jack Kennedy bawl Sorensen out, frankly, because he knew that Sorensen had leaked that story," Lem said. There appears to be no evidence to support Lem's claim other than his own statement, however. Whether this occurred precisely as Lem described it is open to question. Clearly, Lem was somewhat resentful of Sorensen's growing closeness to Jack at the time. "Sorensen just adored Jack," said Lem, grudgingly adding, "Sorensen was one hell of a speechwriter for Jack."

Published on January 1, 1956, the book became a bestseller just as *Why England Slept* had been sixteen years earlier. It also won the 1957 Pulitzer Prize for biography. Jack contributed the $500 prize to the United Negro College Fund.

Some critics wryly remarked that Jack would not be eligible for a chapter in *Profiles in Courage* himself, since he failed to stand up for his convictions during the McCarthy era. McCarthy had wreaked havoc on the American body politic without a peep from Jack.

‿

For Joseph R. McCarthy, communists were the enemy within, threat-ening the security of the Republic and the very fabric of society. The actual number of communists was few, but McCarthy roped in even the mildly liberal, and that was a lot of people. It was a time when the loyalty of every American was suspect and when neighbor turned against neighbor. The significance of McCarthyism, since communism was largely dead in the Unites States at the time McCarthy came to prominence, was its threat to liberalism and progressive thought, not communism.

The blacklist that resulted from McCarthyism led to hundreds of thousands of people losing their jobs, not only in prominent profes-sions, such as the entertainment industry, but also in ordinary lines of work, such as teaching. Many millions of others watched what they said and to whom they said it. The prudent course was to keep your mouth shut. For a time, "Are you now, or have you ever been, a member of the Communist Party?" became the scariest question in the land.

Although Jack ultimately disagreed with McCarthy, he chose not to confront him because he was a fellow Irish American Catholic and an old family friend. McCarthy had been a guest at the Kennedys' homes. Lem met him one time at the Cape, describing him as a "rather jolly, masculine fellow." Jack's sisters Eunice and Pat each dated McCarthy at one point, and Bobby served for six months as an attorney for McCarthy's subcommittee. He was asked by McCarthy to look into the hiring of homosexuals at the State Department. Moreover, Joe Kennedy had helped fund McCarthy's campaigns. For these reasons, and perhaps because Jack feared McCarthy's popularity in the early days, he failed to appreciate the scale of the threat to civil liberties, missing the opportu-nity to speak out during one of the darkest periods in the history of the Republic. It was a severe blot on his record as a U.S. senator.

One issue before the nationally televised Army–McCarthy hearings, some of which Lem attended, was whether homosexual parties had been held on army bases. Army Secretary Robert Stevens was grilled by sen-ators who, at one point, fell over each other seeking assurances that no such parties had been held on army bases in their state. At another stage in the hearings, the lawyer for the army, Joseph Welch, used the word *pixie.* When McCarthy asked Welch what he meant, Welch responded that a pixie is a kind of fairy, prompting laughter throughout the hearing room. It likely was a veiled reference by Welch to the rumors circulating that McCarthy was in fact gay and possibly involved with his aide, Roy Cohn, who died decades later of AIDS. It is more likely, however, that Cohn was seeing the handsome G. David Schine, an army private, and not McCarthy. One of the issues at the hearings was the allegation that McCarthy and Cohn had both pressed the army to give favorable treatment to Schine. "We used to sing, 'Come Cohn or come Schine,'" Gore Vidal quipped.

The rumors about McCarthy being gay first surfaced publicly in 1952 in the *Las Vegas Sun*. A story dated October 25 talks about McCarthy being a bachelor who "seldom dates girls, and if he does, he laughingly describes it as window dressing." McCarthy considered suing the newspaper but decided the safer course was to get married instead. He promptly did, to his secretary. The irony is that thousands of gays, in addition to politically targeted individuals, were losing their jobs as a result of McCarthy's antics. There is no record of what Lem thought about the proceedings unfolding in front of him, but he must have considered them to be intimidating, to say the least. And he must have been relieved when McCarthy ultimately self-destructed.

McCarthy's downfall largely resulted from his own performance in the Army–McCarthy hearings and from an exposé by Edward Murrow on the CBS program *See It Now*. The veteran newsman relentlessly attacked McCarthy's tactics, ending his broadcast by quoting Cassius, from Shakespeare's *Julius Caesar*, "The fault, dear Brutus, is not in our stars, but in ourselves." It was a profile in courage by a journalist willing to take a stand against a man who commanded the support of millions, a far cry from the vacuous blow-dried anchors of today who take earnest, ardent stands in favor of motherhood and apple pie—and without any quotes from Shakespeare, either. With double blows from CBS and Congress, it was good night to McCarthy, even though CBS a month later gave him his own airtime to respond to Murrow. McCarthy said that Murrow was a propagandist for the communists who at one time was "a member of the IWW, the Industrial Workers of the World, a terrorist organization." But it was too late. The counterattack failed. A badly wounded McCarthy lingered on for a few more months. Then, on

December 2, 1954, the U.S. Senate voted to censure him. Three years later, he was dead of cirrhosis of the liver at the age of forty-nine.

Jack, however, absent for the vote, was the only Democrat not to censure McCarthy. He was in the hospital struggling to recover from the first of his two back operations. It would prove a more difficult procedure than anyone imagined. His Addison's disease complicated the operation and resulted in a major infection that once again threatened his life. At one point, the doctors said he had only a fifty-fifty chance of survival. He was so close to death that he was given the last rites of the Catholic Church—again. Lem was frantic. "We came close to losing him," he said. Jack went home to Palm Beach, but within four months underwent the second operation. He was determined to try to reduce the pain in his back so that he could lead a more comfortable life and make a more effective run for the presidency. The second operation was more successful, although it only dented the problem rather than solving it. Jack spent months recovering in Palm Beach with Jackie and Lem by his side. Francis McAdoo recalled how devoted Lem was during this period. "Lem helped take care of him. He just wouldn't leave his side."

Years later, Lem described how bad it was. "The area where they cut into his back never healed. It was oozing blood and pus all the time. It must have been painful beyond belief. . . . It was an open wound that seemed to be infected most of the time. And now and then a piece of the bone would come out of the wound. His pain was excruciating. You know he was in bed for almost a year with this thing." But Lem added: "I don't remember any time he wasn't pleasant. I mean it. I don't remember any time he wasn't fun to sit in a room with or when I didn't feel it really was fun for me to be with him. I felt I was lucky to be there." Jackie, who was only in her early twenties at the time, also stayed constantly by Jack's side and was dedicated to helping him in any way she could. "She was really terrific," said Lem.

Lem always defended Jack's failure to cast a vote against McCarthy, saying people didn't understand how sick Jack really was at the time. "I know the real story on that, because I was down in Florida at the time [with the indulgence of his understanding boss, Francis McAdoo] this vote came to the floor. At that time, Jack Kennedy was probably the sickest he'd been during the entire period. If he had sent up a vote [casting a "pair," vote with a colleague on the opposing side] it would have been a vote that he hadn't thought out." He added: "I know that, had he been well enough, he would have wanted to censure McCarthy because he was highly critical of McCarthy's methods." But most liberals did not buy this explanation at the time. Joseph Rauh, a prominent activist in Americans for Democratic Action, a leftist lobbying group, remarked, "A man who does not believe in the civil liberties of white citizens cannot be trusted to stand up for the civil rights of Negro citizens."

In 1956, Jack was ready to make his next big move. The party's nominee for president at the Democratic National Convention that year was again Adlai Stevenson, who had been the standard-bearer four years earlier as well, losing big to the wildly popular Dwight Eisenhower. Stevenson decided to let the convention decide who his vice presidential running mate would be the second time around. So Jack decided to throw his hat in the ring, even though his father warned him that Stevenson was already a loser and would likely lose again against Eisenhower and Nixon.

Lem didn't go to the convention, because he thought it would just be a routine event for Jack. On the day the delegates voted for the vice presidential nomination, "I remember I left my office about five that day, got in my car, and turned on the radio," Lem said. "The first thing I heard was Kennedy within something like fifty votes of being the vice presidential nominee. I've never been so shocked in my life. I left the car immediately and went to a place that had a television set. I couldn't believe it. I think this really emphasizes the fact that we hadn't been talking about this before he went out there. . . . He did not go to the convention with the vice presidency in mind," added Lem.

As it turned out, Jack narrowly lost the vice presidential nomination bid to Tennessee senator Estes Kefauver. But his concession speech, televised nationally, earned him millions of new admirers across the country. At thirty-nine, he looked terrific on television, with movie star looks that seduced not only the convention but also the millions watching at home. He conceded defeat gracefully and called for the convention to make Kefauver's nomination unanimous. "I believe that the Democratic Party will go from this convention far stronger for what we have done here today," he remarked.

Chet Huntley and David Brinkley covered the convention for NBC News that year, the first time the famous duo teamed together. After Kennedy was defeated for the vice presidential nomination, Huntley turned to Brinkley and said, "We haven't seen the last of Senator Kennedy, David." David replied, "I'm sure that's true." It was the understatement of the decade. Stevenson and Kefauver went on to lose again to Eisenhower and Nixon in the 1956 general election. But Kennedy's failed bid for the vice presidential nomination ironically helped him. By losing the contest, he escaped identification with the 1956 Democratic failure while gaining stature as a national leader in his party. From that moment on, party leaders, still powerful in this age of comparatively few primaries, took him seriously as a possibility for the Democratic nomination for president in 1960.

Lem saw Jack immediately after he returned from the convention "and of course he talked about nothing else but the convention. I remember at the time he was still disappointed at not making it." But, he added, "he later was very, very happy and felt that it was a narrow escape." In Lem's opinion, Jack's experience at the convention was the spark that lit his presidential ambitions for 1960. He remembered a particular day after Jack returned from the convention when they discussed the situation. "We talked about that. Now that he had become a national figure, he realized that he had certain responsibilities to the party. He knew he had to do a certain amount of campaigning for Governor Stevenson. However, he certainly didn't want to overdo it. I think he was going to do what he felt was the minimum. Let's face it, with presidential ambitions himself—Stevenson's defeat was to his advantage."

Jack's increasing concentration on presidential politics, however, came at a price. He was frequently neglectful of his marriage, but particularly in 1956. At the time of the 1956 Democratic convention, Jackie was pregnant and worried about the baby, since she had had a miscarriage in the first year of their marriage. But she dutifully attended the convention in Chicago with him even though he barely saw her there. After the convention, Jackie went to Newport to await the arrival of the baby. Jack, however, went off to Europe. While he was gone, Jackie suffered a life-threatening hemorrhage. She was just under eight months pregnant and her placenta had prematurely separated, causing the uterus to contract and to go into spasms. There was a danger of deadly blood clots. So the baby had to be delivered early. On August 23, 1956, Jackie had a Caesarean section.

When she regained consciousness, the first person Jackie saw was not Jack but Bobby, who had flown down from Hyannis to be with her. The first question she asked was whether it was a boy or a girl. But Bobby had to tell her that the baby girl, who would have been named Arabella, was born dead. Jackie was devastated. She wanted to know where Jack was and if he knew about the baby. Bobby was unable to reach him. He had gone on a cruise off the coast of France accompanied by Teddy, Senator George Smathers, and a host of young women. What Bobby apparently didn't know was that Jack was reachable. He always left instructions with his secretary, Evelyn Lincoln, on how he could be reached. Evelyn eventually made a call to Jack and told him what had happened with the baby. "I'll be right home," he told her. But in fact he delayed his return to the States. It is not entirely clear why. Kennedy critics have written that it was largely because he and his friends were having such a good time with the women they had invited aboard the yacht. But others say it was because he was hit hard by the loss of the baby and just couldn't face returning immediately.

Still, his wife needed him at the time and, for whatever reason, Jack failed to come home as quickly as he could. Once the newspapers got hold of the story that he was vacationing in the Mediterranean after his wife lost their baby, he was back pronto. He realized the press coverage could be particularly damaging to a rising politician with eyes on the presidency. Once he arrived back in Washington, however, he devoted his full attention to Jackie until she recovered from the loss. The Kennedys eventually moved out of their home at Hickory Hill in Virginia and into a more modest house in Georgetown.

Lem visited frequently, usually accompanied by his gigantic poodle. Not only was Lem an almost permanent houseguest, so was his dog. Jackie often found herself left to take care of it while Jack and Lem went off playing backgammon or otherwise enjoying themselves. Bobby and Ethel moved into the house on Hickory Hill, which was located about fifteen miles outside of Washington in the Virginia countryside.

For Jackie, 1956 had been a bad year. Jack had been on the road most of the time and she had lost their baby. Fortunately, 1957 was much better. On the day after Thanksgiving, she gave birth to a healthy seven-pound, two-ounce girl, Caroline Bouvier Kennedy, although again by Caesarean section. Jack was elated and was determined to be a good father. But again he was not there for the birth. "I'm never there when she needs me," he said. When Jack finally saw Caroline, he could not have been happier. By all accounts, he developed a warm, loving relationship with his first child, whom he called "Buttons." Caroline's birth also helped his marriage. He and Jackie became closer after their family expanded to three. For the first time in his life, Jack was experiencing feelings of intimacy and attachment.

Nevertheless, during the next four years, he would be away more than he was at home. He embarked on a grueling speaking schedule across the country in search of the 1960 Democratic nomination for the presidency of the United States. It was an exhausting effort for him, given his health and also the fact that he was a terrible sleeper, especially when he was on the road. The slightest noise would wake him up, Lem said. "I remember the first time I ever stayed with Jack, back during the early days at Choate, we were staying at the Cape. I don't know what I did, but I remember I woke him up and he screamed, 'God damn you Billings, shut up.' Well, I didn't know him so well then and I was furious. . . . He just hated being wakened during the night and he didn't like to have people in the room who made noises, like snoring, which would wake him up." With so many people around on the campaign trail, it was even harder.

However little sleep he got, however, Jack always managed to look fresh and energetic for his growing legion of admirers across the country. As 1957 drew to a close, he led polls as the number-one choice of Democrats to become the party's standard-bearer in 1960. As usual, Joe was running around trying to ensure that nothing happened that would jeopardize his son's election to the presidency. On one occasion in 1958, Jack and Lem were up to their usual antics at the Kennedys' Palm Beach estate, laughing and joking about some of Jack's past sexual escapades. But Joe heard them and directed his ire at Lem, who vividly remembered the dressing-down he received. "He said, 'LeMoyne, you've got to understand here and now that Jack is going to be president. You are one of the people who have got to understand this. You cannot ever say anything about him—anything in joking, except good things. In a public place, you can never know whether the table is rigged or not. You can't ever tell who's listening. From now on, you've got to not think of Jack Kennedy as a friend as much as you've got to think of him as a potential candidate for president of the United States.'"

If Joe was alluding to Jack's sexual activities, he didn't have to worry too much. In those more discreet times, people didn't readily talk about private behavior in public. If someone were inclined to talk to a reporter about sexual matters, it most likely would not be printed. But there were no absolute guarantees, and Joe constantly fretted that his son would do something that would get him into hot water with the press. Fortunately for him, most reporters loved Jack and his name stayed out of the papers, at least as far as scandal is concerned. Instead, the press ran adoring stories about the charismatic young senator and his picture-perfect wife and child.

In 1958, Jack won a landslide victory in his reelection bid for the Senate. The road to the White House was now wide open, a quest that would require the help of everyone around him. As always, Lem was more than ready to do his part. "I don't think there was any question in his own mind after he had won the greatest majority in the history of the state of Massachusetts that he was going to go for broke," Lem said.

But although he wanted Jack to get whatever he wanted, Lem must have had mixed feelings once again. Their friendship would be impacted as never before by the huge changes in Jack's life required to run a successful presidential campaign. His political travel, already burdensome, became virtually nonstop. And new people began to surround Jack, including a group of Harvard intellectuals who had been Stevenson supporters, such as the historian Arthur Schlesinger Jr. and the economist John Kenneth Galbraith. "Weekends at the Cape were no longer as much fun as they were now centered around such people as Arthur and the Galbraiths, etc. There was an enormous influx of new people," said Lem with obvious regret. Moreover, he was not sure that all of them were as loyal to Jack as he. Nor were some of the other family members sure about them. But they had no doubts about Lem. "Dearest LeMoyne," Rose wrote Lem. "I shall always love you for your abiding loyalty to my son."

Although from now on Lem would see much less of Jack, their friendship, as always, remained much the same when they were able to spend time together. But it was yet another adjustment for Lem to make, one that took him some time. "Of course, having a friend who is approaching the presidency or even aspiring to the presidency is an unusual experience for anybody, and one that you have to get accustomed to," he said. "I mean at first it was strange to have Jack recognized on the street—and the complete lack of privacy that came with the fame." It was the beginning of Lem's realization that from here on out, getting time with Jack would be much tougher, but as it turned out once the campaigning was over, not as tough as he thought.

8

ROOM AT THE TOP
(THE 1960 ELECTION)

"The presidency is the most powerful office in the free world. Through its leadership can come a more vital life for our people. In it are centered the hopes of the globe around us for freedom and a more secure life."
—John F. Kennedy, January 2, 1960

The election of 1960 was one of the most pivotal in American history. At home, African Americans were seething over their second-class citizenship, which they were no longer prepared to tolerate. In the world at large, the cold war conflict between the United States and the Soviet Union was raging, the threat of nuclear annihilation a constant danger as a consequence of either deliberate aggression or miscalculation.

It is important to remember that Jack ran for the highest office in the land just fifteen years after the end of World War II, a war in which he and Lem had participated and which took the lives of more than fifty million people around the world. Jack felt that the United States was not doing enough to control the arms race and to prevent another war, which, in the nuclear age, would be catastrophic. He also felt that the time had come for the United States to fulfill its unfinished promise of full citizenship rights for all Americans.

For Jack, the Eisenhower years were a wasted opportunity. He was impatient, eager to make his case to the American people. In this respect, his political message blended with his temperament, bred of the personal crises and disappointments that marked his life. There always was a sense with him that time was running out, that the moment would pass if not seized, that action should always be taken today in preference to tomorrow. His message to his fellow citizens was laced with urgency. He saw change as not only desirable but imperative.

On January 2, 1960, the man and the moment came together. John F. Kennedy threw his hat into the ring, announcing his candidacy for the presidency of the United States in the Senate Caucus Room. "I believe that the Democratic Party has a historic function to perform in the winning of the 1960 election comparable to its role in 1932," he remarked, harking back to the presidency of Franklin Roosevelt, which had influenced him so much when he and Lem were at Choate. He was just forty-two years old.

The first task was to win the Democratic nomination. It would not be easy, given Jack's youth and Catholicism. Key players such as Adlai Stevenson, Eleanor Roosevelt, and former President Harry Truman were less than enthusiastic about his candidacy. Stevenson coyly refused to rule out being drafted as the party's nominee for the third time. Eleanor Roosevelt openly voiced her opposition, and Truman, accused by some Kennedy loyalists of being against a Catholic nominee, said, "It's not the pope I'm worried about, it's the pop."

In addition, Jack's call to get America moving again, his emphasis on solving the country's problems, such as rural and inner-city poverty, inadequate health care for the aged, and substandard education, fell on deaf ears in many places. The country was largely prosperous and contented in 1960, not readily receptive to a message of radical change at home.

Abroad, Americans had been contented with Eisenhower's fatherly stewardship. Jack's call for bolder leadership to stem the communist tide was largely ignored. The United States is "the only sentry at the gate," he repeatedly said, warning of "the campfires of the enemy on distant hills." He also—more accurately than he could ever have known in 1960—predicted that Americans' "courage will be tested" as never before during the coming decade. He decided to enter key primaries to persuade party bosses that he was electable.

To win in the primaries, Jack needed money, political professionals, and volunteers. Jack had always relied heavily on his personal friends and his family in his runs for office. He felt that their commitment to him and willingness to work hard more than compensated for their lack of political skills. Early on in the campaign, Jack asked Lem to work full-time on helping him win the Democratic nomination for president. "I told him I didn't see how I could possibly get time off from my job. He said he would like to meet Toigo [Adolph Toigo, Lem's boss at Lennen & Newell]," said Lem. Jack not only persuaded Toigo to give Lem the time off, he seduced Toigo, who was a Republican, into backing him as well. From that meeting on, Lem's boss became a staunch Kennedy supporter. "Dolph told Jack I could take a leave of absence at any time Jack wanted me," Lem said.

In addition, Jack also persuaded Francis McAdoo, Lem's boss at his previous job in Baltimore, to work on the campaign. McAdoo was a friend of Jack's as well, having met him during the war and seen him at numerous veteran gatherings in the early postwar years. Mac, who was also a Republican, not only supported Jack, he helped raise funds for him in Maryland, where he was living at the time.

Early on, Jack's chief rival for the nomination was Minnesota senator Hubert Humphrey, a liberal with strong civil rights credentials and plenty of support from organized labor. The first big primary contest between the two of them was in Wisconsin, a neighboring state for Humphrey. Jack knew it would be an uphill battle. Nevertheless—and surprisingly in view of Lem's less-than-spectacular political record to date—Jack asked Lem to be a key coordinator of his campaign in the Wisconsin primary.

Lem and Teddy Kennedy, Kennedy Campaign headquarters, presidential primary, La Crosse, Wisconsin, 1960.

At first, Jack hesitated to enter the contest there because of Humphrey's popularity, but Joe was insistent that Jack could win and goaded him into making a go of it by suggesting he would be "yellow" if he didn't. Joe was always pushing his son, always urging him to go one step further, climb one more ladder. But he could be disarmingly witty in doing so. "Dear Jack," he wrote, "Don't buy a single vote more than is necessary. I'll be damned if I am going to pay for a landslide."

Lem was among the first to arrive in Wisconsin, assigned to coordinate activity in the Third Congressional District. Journalist John Seigenthaler, who later would become a key aide to Bobby Kennedy at the Justice Department, covered the Wisconsin primary for the *Tennessean.* Seigenthaler had known Lem in Washington and liked him. But that didn't mean he thought Lem was the best person to work on Jack's behalf in Wisconsin, the first critical primary of the campaign. "Lem was in Milwaukee and Madison when I was in both those places," he remembered. "This was more political responsibility than Lem ever had." He was somewhat disorganized and inept as a political operator, he added.

"Lem could be quite judgmental about candidates," Seigenthaler continued. "For example, most of the people who worked in that campaign had some degree of respect for Hubert, but I don't think Lem ever did. For Lem, Hubert was the enemy. Clearly, he was a stalking horse for the president from the outset." To some degree, Lem's loyalty to Jack and his passionate desire to see him win made up for his defective political skills, which, he was the first to say, were clearly limited. "I actually didn't even know where to start," Lem said.

Wisconsin was already a problem state because two groups of Democrats were warring against each other. Lem caused additional problems by upsetting an important congressman there. The issue concerned where the lawmaker would be seated in a car carrying Jack and Jackie when they visited the state, Seigenthaler recalled. One can imagine Lem telling the congressman where to put his you know what, given his penchant for in-your-face humor. This wasn't necessarily the smartest thing to do in a political campaign, however. But Lem always apologized when he realized that what he had done hadn't helped, Seigenthaler added.

Lem's mistakes did not endear him to Jack's longtime political aides and campaign strategists. But few dared to criticize him because they knew he was so close to Jack. Even Bobby was careful about criticizing

Lem, though he bawled out other people at the drop of a hat. Lem had his own style and had a great sense of humor, Seigenthaler said. "Some thought him a court jester. That may be fair. It's easy to call him that if you don't know him. For all the laughs, however, the president and the family took him seriously and that included politics. They sent him to Wisconsin, after all. I wouldn't have done that. But they knew he would do his best.

"I think his sense of humor was self-defeating with professional politicians who didn't take him seriously, though," added Seigenthaler. He also wasn't as good at meeting people who were unfamiliar to him as the pros were. "Lem was not comfortable with people he didn't know. He was aloof. Now, if their support for Jack was unqualified, and particularly if they were adoring, he felt very comfortable with people like that."

Lem found the hustle and bustle of the presidential campaign trail to be irritating and stressful. He felt that Jack's run for the presidency was much more taxing than his earlier runs for election to Congress. So much more had to be done—and in the whole country, not just in one state. In addition, Lem found it much more difficult to deal with the media. There was much more press, both television and print, to contend with now that Jack was a presidential candidate.

It was so different from the New York advertising world. "The problem is if you take a New York advertising executive and put him in Wisconsin, he is out of place. He is looking forward to cocktails at five o'clock. But politics is a twenty-four-hour business," Seigenthaler said. "He also wasn't used to a situation where your every word might be quoted in the press. He didn't realize his vulnerability" in a presidential campaign.

But Lem did well at the famed tea parties organized by the Kennedy family—mostly aimed to attract female voters. Almost every day, Pat or Eunice or Rose hosted tea parties around the state, and Lem was a great help in putting those together. They felt comfortable with him, and he felt at ease with them. "He was as loyal to Kennedy's causes as his brothers and sisters were," Seigenthaler said.

As the campaign got under way, Americans saw a primary covered as never before. Robert Drew pioneered a new kind of film record—cinema verité—made possible by the introduction of smaller, more portable equipment. For the first time, viewers could watch the campaign through the candidates' eyes, as the cameras tracked their every move, both formal and informal, even capturing strategy discussions in the car on the way to campaign events. That had not been possible with the earlier, bulkier cameras. In Wisconsin, both Jack and Humphrey gave Drew unfettered access to put together this new form of electronic journalism.

Humphrey relentlessly pandered to the rural vote there, stressing his Senate record of supporting farmers. But Jack was not above pandering to the ethnic vote in the state's big cities. Jackie even spoke a little Polish at one campaign event in Milwaukee, an early indication to Jack of her value as a campaign asset.

Jack's friend Frank Sinatra recorded a new version of his hit record "High Hopes"—"Jack is on the right track 'cos he's got high hopes"— that was played at all the scheduled events. This was in the days when campaign songs were commonplace. But Humphrey had his song, too— sung to the music of the hit record "Davy Crockett, King of the Wild Frontier"—"Vote for Hubert, Hubert Humphrey, the president for you and me." The irony of Hubert's song harking back to the old frontier, while Jack's slogan was the New Frontier, did not go unnoticed. Unwittingly, perhaps, the two songs symbolized the difference between Humphrey's old style of politics and Jack's new brand.

During the campaign, Jack repeatedly said that if he didn't win in Wisconsin, it would be difficult to secure the party's nomination at the convention in Los Angeles. In the final analysis, however, there was no need to worry. Against the odds, Jack won the first critical primary of the 1960 presidential campaign—although not by a huge margin. He won 56 percent of the vote, compared to 46 percent for Humphrey. For Humphrey it was a good enough showing to keep him in the race. The next primary, in West Virginia—a largely poor and Protestant state that was also friendly territory for the gregarious Minnesotan—would be where Humphrey would make his last stand.

Although Jack won Wisconsin, he lost the Third District—where Lem had been in charge. "In all fairness to myself," Lem said, "Humphrey was a very beloved figure in that district." Despite the loss, Jack asked Lem to go directly to Charleston, West Virginia, for the next and final battle with Humphrey. His job was "to be in constant contact with all the men in the field. I ended up being the troubleshooter," remembered Lem. He was also in charge of the television spots in the entire state because of his background in advertising. In Wisconsin, he had handled television only in the Third District.

Jack "had never been too anxious to go into West Virginia right from the beginning because of the 4 percent Catholic thing [only 4 percent of the population was Catholic]," Lem said. But "he knew that if he dropped West Virginia, particularly for a Catholic reason, this would be interpreted as meaning that a Catholic could never be president of the United States. Well, it was a hell of a problem and the president and everybody else were aware that they had to work twice as hard as before. You know that's a challenge, and to a Kennedy, anything like that— they're all at their best when they're up against the fence."

"Although the president pretty well avoided the religious question in Wisconsin, in West Virginia he jumped into it with both feet," Lem continued. "There he pounded home day after day after day about religion. This was really the issue there." Jack "convinced the voters" that if he lost West Virginia, he would have to drop out of the race, he added. In the end, against the odds, Jack won in West Virginia as well, finally knocking Humphrey out of the presidential race. Despite Lem's not being a natural in politics, Kennedy aide Dave Powers said later that Lem "worked his guts out" in Wisconsin and West Virginia. What he lacked in political skills he made up for in his passion to see Jack win, he added. Asked why Humphrey lost, Lem said, "He just didn't have it. That's all." He also said that Humphrey compared very badly to Jack on television. Lem had no doubt of the significance of the two primary wins. "All of us knew we had really elected a president."

The reality is that in those days, with far fewer primaries, it was difficult for a party nominee to secure the nomination for president before the convention. Much wheeling and dealing occurred behind closed doors both prior to and during the convention. Party conventions then were not, as they are now, stage-managed television spectaculars designed to promote the presidential ticket that has already been determined in the primaries. Real suspense and hard decision-making occurred at these gatherings, which were eagerly followed by American voters on television.

As with most conventions to that date, when Americans tuned in to the Democratic National Convention in Los Angeles in 1960, they had no idea who the party nominee would be. The favorite of many delegates was Adlai Stevenson, the standard-bearer for the party in 1952 and 1956.

But he had lost twice, and badly. Jack regarded him as a prissy liberal, the kind that lost elections all too often. There was also considerable support for Senator Lyndon Johnson, majority leader of the Senate, who pulled out all the stops to prevent Jack from winning a first ballot nomination, even telling delegates privately about Jack's Addison's disease.

But the tactic—and the challenge—failed. The Kennedy people out-maneuvered their opposition. Lem was in the thick of it all, "contacting the different delegates," and doing his best to help Jack win on the first ballot. As the roll call of the states proceeded, Lem was there, standing in the middle of the Wisconsin delegation, where he had worked in the primary, beaming with joy. The suspense was over when the state of Wyoming finally put Jack over the top on the first ballot. It was a satis-fying moment for Jack, who had harbored serious doubts about whether he could win the nomination. Lem was equally happy. Who wouldn't be, with his best friend as one of only two men who would be the next pres-ident of the United States?

Surprisingly, Jack chose his rival, Lyndon Johnson, as his running mate, causing consternation among his liberal supporters, since Johnson was a southerner and thought to be too conservative. In reality, Johnson was not a conservative. As a senator, he simply reflected the viewpoint of the people in his state of Texas who were. Nevertheless, liberals were upset. Bobby, especially, was flabbergasted. Here was Jack talking about the New Frontier and a bold progressive agenda and he chooses a Texan from the Old Frontier who was thought to be a reactionary. But Jack real-ized the election might be close, and he needed to balance the ticket and appeal to more conservative voters, and also get a shot at winning Texas.

(His judgment proved correct on election day when, with Lyndon's help, he won the Lone Star State. He would not have won the election without it.)

When Jack confidently strode to the podium at the Los Angeles Col-iseum on July 15 to deliver his acceptance speech, no one was more proud of how far he had come than Lem. He knew his best friend was a star, and so did the Democratic delegates assembled all around him. The coliseum was an outdoor football stadium facing west, as if to symbolize the New Frontier. As Jack began his speech against the backdrop of the Pacific Ocean, the sun began to set, providing added spectacle to his perform-ance. He began by outlining his vision of the New Frontier in the 1960s.

"The world is changing. The old era is ending. The old ways will not do," he said. "Abroad, the balance of power is shifting. There are new and more terrible weapons, new and uncertain nations, new pressures of population and deprivation. One-third of the world, it has been said, may be free. But one-third is the victim of cruel repression. And the other one-third is wracked by the pangs of poverty, hunger, and envy." The speech was a huge success both inside and outside the convention. His campaign was off to a flying start.

In Los Angeles, Jack sounded a theme that he would return to again and again during the campaign—that massive change was enveloping the world whether Americans liked it or not. He warned about the growing danger of big power confrontation and nuclear war and spoke of the new independent nations of Africa, Asia, and the Caribbean—"the lands of the rising people"—that, in his view, were going "through the greatest revolution in human history."

In those days, before it became a dirty word, Jack had no compunction about calling himself a liberal. But he was careful to define the word lest his opponents define it for him. "If, by a liberal, they mean someone who looks ahead and not behind, someone who welcomes new ideas without rigid reactions, someone who cares about the welfare of the people—their health, their housing, their schools, their jobs, their civil rights, and their civil liberties—someone who believes that we can break through the stalemate and suspicions that grip us in our policies abroad. If that is what they mean by a liberal, then I'm proud to say that I'm a liberal."

Richard Nixon, the unchallenged Republican nominee, had been vice president of the United States for eight years under President Dwight D. Eisenhower. John Kennedy, by contrast, had served just eight years in the U.S. Senate. At forty-three, he was widely considered to be brash and inexperienced. Even more problematic, he was a Catholic at a time when religious bigotry was a real force in American life. Only once before had the Democratic Party chosen a Catholic as its standard-bearer—Al Smith in 1928—and he was soundly defeated by Republican Herbert Hoover. It is hard to believe now, but many Americans thought—even as late as 1960—that a Catholic president would take orders from the pope in Rome.

As a Protestant, Lem was well aware of anti-Catholic prejudice in the country at the time. It was particularly strong in the South, where Lem's brother, Josh, now lived. Jack also knew only too well the dangers of the religious issue and believed that the level of bigotry in the country was understated. Few voters would tell pollsters that they would never vote for a Catholic for the presidency of the United States, but the reality was that many would not. Ultimately, Jack decided to address the issue publicly, before a group of Protestants. His speech is considered one of the most memorable of his campaign and one of the most powerful, if not the most powerful, speech ever given on the subject of religious bigotry.

Speaking on September 12 before a convention of Baptists, Jack said he was not the Catholic candidate for president but the Democratic Party's candidate for president, who happened also to be a Catholic. "If this election is decided on the basis that forty million Americans lost their chance of being president the day they were baptized, then it is the whole nation that will be the loser in the eyes of Catholics and non-Catholics around the world, in the eyes of history, and in the eyes of our own people." His forceful defense of the separation of church and state won over people of reason. But he realized that there still was an unknowable percentage of voters who would never vote for a Catholic for president—no matter what.

The general election campaign was one of the more contentious in American history. Both candidates attacked each other's records and qualifications to lead the country. The key event in the election battle—then as now—was the televised debates. The presidential debates in 1960 were the first ever to be televised and were watched by an estimated seventy million Americans. The first one was the most crucial. The two candidates appeared before a panel of journalists. At forty-three, Jack looked young and tanned. It's largely forgotten now that Nixon was only three years older. But he looked haggard and tired, having injured his leg just before the debate. Plus, he refused makeup, not realizing its importance in these early days of television. So his five o'clock shadow was clearly visible on the television picture, as well.

In addition, political campaigns were not as media savvy then as they are today, nor were network producers as skilled. The reaction shots of Nixon looked particularly bad and caught him looking nervous, shifty, and generally ill at ease. But Nixon did well in the exchanges with Kennedy, eagerly seeking to promote himself as the heir apparent to

Eisenhower, even though one question—from NBC newsman Sandy Vanocur—revealed the frosty relationship between Eisenhower and Nixon.

Vanocur asked Nixon about a statement that Eisenhower had made when he was asked to come up with an example of a Nixon idea that had been adopted. "If you give me a week, I might be able to think of one," Eisenhower quipped. Nixon barely recovered from the quip or the question, lamely citing Eisenhower's well-known penchant for humor. The power of the new medium was reflected in polls taken after the debate. Those who listened on radio thought Nixon had won, whereas those who watched it on television believed the reverse. It was a reaffirmation, if any were needed, of the importance of image in politics in the television age. The influential mayor Richard Daley of Chicago said that Jack "looked like Wilson, Roosevelt, and Truman put together."

Lem watched the debate in Janesville, Wisconsin, at the home of Kennedy volunteer Gertrude Corbin and her husband, Paul. Lem had returned there after the convention to help win the state for Jack in the general election. He spent the night at the Corbins' residence, riveted to the television set during the critical face-off between Jack and Nixon. As usual, he complained vociferously of what he viewed as Nixon's unfairness toward Jack. But by now, Lem realized the importance of appearance for a politician on television and he knew that Jack looked and sounded much better. Paul was away working for John Kennedy in New York when Lem stayed at the Corbins' home. "Paul called and I told him about Lem," Gertrude remembered, "and he said to be very nice to him—that he was a great fellow and very devoted to John Kennedy. So began our long and very happy friendship with Lem."

After the debate, Jack was surrounded by even more adoring crowds as he crisscrossed the country restating his message that it was time to get the United States moving again, that these need not be the years when the tide ran out for the country. "The time to repair the roof," he said, "is when the sun is shining." After the debates, he was more confident and more relaxed, more prone to let the Kennedy humor hold sway. "Do you realize the responsibility I carry?" he joked. "I'm the only person standing between Richard Nixon and the White House."

Joe, as usual, was taking no chances, pulling out all the stops. In those days, when television news was still in its infancy, the big kids on the block were *Time* and *Life* magazines, both of which were owned by media magnate Henry Luce, who had coined the term "the American century." Luce left no doubt he was backing Nixon. So Joe went to see him to try to persuade him to support Jack, or at least give him a fair shot. When Luce said that Jack was too liberal, Joe denied it, saying, "My son's no goddamned liberal." But of course he was, and Luce knew it. Luce's editorial stance against Jack didn't matter that much in the end, however. Luce's magazines may not have backed Jack editorially, but the pages of *Life* magazine were filled with great photographs of Jack and his photogenic family. The fact is that many more people saw the photographs than read the editorials.

The almost nonstop political campaigning during the summer and fall of 1960 were a constant drain on Jack's energy. But Lem was always there when needed—not so much to talk about politics or to discuss the status of the campaign, but to help his friend relax by distracting him with their traditional banter and humor. "Lem was very witty," recalled John Seigenthaler. "He had a sort of cryptic personality. He would take a serious subject and find something humorous in it—sort of tongue-in-cheek. He was funny, sometimes a little bawdy. And he laughed a lot." Jack was noticeably more relaxed after he saw Lem, he added.

Lem was a master at making fun of pretentious people in particular, and Nixon was a prime target, recalled Seigenthaler, especially since he had had the nerve to run against Jack. "I heard him make many cracks about Nixon. His five o'clock shadow was made for Lem. No one more than Jack enjoyed Lem's Nixon jokes. Most liberals despised Nixon, and Lem was among them," Seigenthaler said, even though he had been a Republican until Jack ran for president. But Seigenthaler described Lem as a John Lindsay or Nelson Rockefeller Republican, these two GOP stars belonging to the party's then still vibrant liberal or moderate wing. Even if Lem had been a rock-solid Goldwater conservative Republican, however, it wouldn't have made any difference. Anyone who was an enemy of Jack's was an enemy of Lem's. Anyone who ran against Jack would, at a minimum, be the butt of Lem's jokes, he said.

Despite Jack's message and campaign skills, the polls showed that it would be a close election, even though in those days it was easier for a Democrat to win the presidency, since the South was still part of the large Democratic coalition that also included minority and ethnic groups and organized labor, a powerful coalition in the early postwar years. In the final days of the campaign, Jack concentrated his efforts in the geographically small but electorally important Northeast, where sizable electoral votes could be won.

Jack relentlessly attacked Nixon on Soviet–American relations, coming at the Republican nominee from the right, arguing that he would be tougher with the Soviet Union. On domestic issues, he came at Nixon from the left, stating that he would stand for a fairer, more equitable society. Both candidates, however, avoided talking about civil rights, fearing that would alienate white voters in the South. Nixon scored points with black voters by promising he would appoint "a qualified Negro" to the cabinet. But Jack scored even more points with a call he placed to Coretta Scott King.

The reason for Jack's call to Mrs. King was the jailing of her husband, civil rights leader Martin Luther King Jr. in Georgia. He offered no specific help, however, and there was little he could give. The call was symbolic. But black voters noticed and appreciated the gesture. It gave him a tremendous boost with blacks—at least those who could vote at the time who were mostly in the North. The vast majority of African Americans living in the South faced literacy tests, poll taxes, and other impositions that effectively prevented them from exercising their constitutional right to cast a ballot.

On November 8, 1960, election night, Jack, Lem, the Kennedy family, and a large group of friends and political operatives gathered at the compound in Hyannis Port. Lem watched the election returns on television as closely as anyone. He felt totally confident that Jack would beat Nixon. He remembered that Jack had once described Nixon as a man without class. He couldn't believe that American voters would choose "Tricky Dick" over Jack. The early returns, however, indicated that no landslide was in sight for either candidate, that the election would be close. Nixon showed some early strength in suburban areas, which trended Republican, but Kennedy soon demonstrated his appeal to urban voters. As the night wore on, the lead went back and forth.

Lem tried to break the tension for Jack, as he always did, by cracking jokes. At one point, he engaged in mock crying, as if Jack were going to lose. Jack responded, making fun of Lem's less-than-stellar political skills. "He's lost another state," he said. "His record is still minus 100 percent. He's lost every county and every state of which he was supposed to be in charge."

Popular news anchors Chet Huntley and David Brinkley anchored the coverage for NBC. Chet and David constantly boasted about the network's RCA 501 computer, a huge machine that looked like something from a 1950s science fiction movie. It must have been low on computing power—and low on a lot of other things—because it consistently got things wrong. Even early the next day, when there was still no winner, the NBC RCA computer was predicting a Kennedy landslide, with odds of 331 to 1 in favor of Kennedy.

Then, at 7:19 A.M. eastern standard time, the network made its biggest goof—announcing "the NBC victory desk has just given California to Kennedy." By this time, Chet and David should have realized the RCA 501 computer was giving them bum information. But they stuck with it. In fact, Jack lost California, although narrowly.

The network did not officially announce that Jack was the winner of the election until after the noon hour, cautiously waiting till Nixon spokesperson Herb Klein read a wire from the Republican nominee announcing his concession. The electoral vote was 303 for Kennedy against 219 for Nixon. But the popular vote was much narrower. Jack won 49.9 percent of the vote compared to Nixon's 49.6 percent. This was the first election in which Hawaii and Alaska voted, and the last election in which the District of Columbia did not. (D.C. voters were given the right to vote for president in 1964. But the federal jurisdiction still has no voting representation in Congress.)

Jack didn't see much of the overnight coverage. Exhausted from the campaign, he went to bed not knowing whether he was the winner or loser. Before turning in for the night, Lem decided to go over to Jack's residence on the Hyannis compound, determined to see Jack one last time before he became president, an outcome Lem felt was certain to occur. Lem was approaching the door when several Secret Servicemen grabbed him and demanded ID. He had none, however, saying over and over again that he was Jack's best friend. While Lem stood there arguing with the Secret Service, Jean Kennedy Smith just happened to be passing by. The Secret Servicemen asked her to verify Lem's identity. But instead of confirming it, she replied, "Never seen him before in my life," and went into the house.

Lem was mortified; another demonstration of Kennedy mischief. He really wanted to get into the house to see Jack before he fell asleep. It might be the last time he saw him before he became president of the United States. His discomfort did not last long, however. A few minutes later, Jean came back outside and confirmed Lem's identity to the by then very aggravated Secret Servicemen. After extricating himself from the clutches of the Secret Service, Lem spent a few minutes with his friend before they both turned in for the night. The pendulum swung back and forth through the night, but finally, the next day, after it was confirmed, Jackie decided Caroline should tell Jack he had been elected president of the United States. Caroline went in to see her dad. She was the first person to call him Mr. President.

Jack Kennedy had been elected president of the United States by the narrowest margin in U.S. history—less than two-tenths of 1 percent of the total popular vote. He was ecstatic that he'd won, but disappointed at the margin. He had been sure he would win California, having spent a lot of time there. If he had, because of the state's size, it would have been an election landslide. But California then was not yet the largely Democratic state it is now. And a Republican win for Nixon there—it was his home state—was no big surprise in 1960.

In any case, victory was victory. As Jack prepared to assume one of the most powerful offices in the world, Lem wondered once again how this latest change in Jack's life would affect their twenty-seven-year friendship. It was yet another adjustment their long relationship would need to weather. Because their friendship had survived all the other twists and turns, Lem felt confident it would do so now. But what should he call Jack? Should he now call him Mr. President on all occasions? That would seem a bit ridiculous, especially after more than two decades of close friendship—and especially in view of all the nicknames they had for each other—or should he just call him Mr. President in public?

Lem knew that Jack did not stand on ceremony, especially with people whom he knew well, but he also knew that Jack had enormous regard for the office of the presidency. As a student of history, Jack was also aware that the American people attached symbolic, as well as substantive, importance to the highest position in government because he was not only becoming the nation's political leader but also head of state. Lem was determined to be respectful of Jack's new position in public, but he also resolved that their friendship would continue unchanged in private.

Red Fay, an old navy friend of Jack's who would become undersecretary of the navy during the Kennedy administration, told a story that is revealing about Jack's attitude toward the presidency. Once, as president, Jack was invited to a function at a neighbor's house. He went accompanied by Red Fay. The host repeatedly introduced the president as Jack—at one point asking him if that was OK. You can call me whatever you feel comfortable with, Jack politely responded, according to Fay. Later, when both Jack and Fay left the house, Jack turned to his old friend and said, "That son of a bitch, I hardly know him and he wasn't for me anyway."

Protocol, however, was the last thing on Lem's mind on the day after the election—November 9—as Jack prepared to address the American people for the first time as president-elect. The Secret Service had already moved into the Kennedy compound at Hyannis Port to provide round-the-clock protection. After some much-needed rest, the candidate emerged from his home and was seen on television sets across the land driving to the National Guard Armory about five miles away, accompanied by Jackie, Lem, other members of the Kennedy family, and friends and supporters.

Betraying a flicker of emotion, Jack told the American people he was grateful for their support. He predicted—more accurately than he could have known—that the 1960s would not be easy, that "the next four years are going to be difficult and challenging years for us all." Then he added: "Every degree of mind and spirit that I possess will be devoted to the long-range interests of the United States and to the cause of freedom around the world. And so my wife and I prepare for a new administration and a new baby."

The new baby was born just a few weeks later, on November 25 at Georgetown University Hospital. Jack and Jackie named him John Jr. He weighed just over six pounds. The baby wasn't due until December. Once again, Jackie had a difficult pregnancy and John was born early. Again, Jack wasn't there. After the speech, he went down to Palm Beach for a few days' rest before deciding whom he wanted to be in his administration. Lem went with him to help him relax. Jack quickly returned when he heard the baby would be born early, but John arrived before the president-elect's plane touched down in Washington. He comforted his wife, held the new baby, and lit a cigar to celebrate. Then, he set about preparing for his New Frontier. Asked later whether he wanted his son to grow up to be president, he said, "I just want him to be healthy."

On November 25, 1960—the same day John F. Kennedy Jr. was born—CBS, which still aired serious, hourlong documentaries back then, broadcast a *CBS Reports* program that is still discussed today. Reported by Edward Murrow, it was called "Harvest of Shame" and portrayed the devastating plight of migrant farm workers in the United States. The broadcast had enormous impact across the country. These were the days of just three major broadcast networks, when even documentaries garnered huge audiences. Many people who saw the program were shocked that such conditions existed in the United States and wanted something to be done. Americans, it seemed, were ready for John F. Kennedy's call for a new era of progressive change. They would not have long to wait.

The president-elect spent much of the remaining time before his inauguration preparing for his administration and relaxing in Palm Beach with Lem and members of the Kennedy family. Evelyn Lincoln also accompanied him. She recalls one Sunday morning in particular when Jack and Lem were having breakfast. As always, Jack was taking every opportunity to rib his old friend. Was he thrilled to be eating breakfast with the leader of the free world? "Not really," responded Lem. Jack then asked the same question to Mrs. Lincoln. "I am overjoyed," she replied. "See there," Jack said to Lem, "she is thrilled and you, Lem, don't feel a thing. It is a privilege for you to be eating breakfast with the president."

PART TWO

The White House Years

9

ONE FINE DAY
(THE INAUGURATION, 1961)

"So let us begin anew—remembering on both sides that civility is not a sign of weakness and sincerity is always subject to proof."
> —John F. Kennedy, inaugural address, January 20, 1961

You knew the inauguration of John F. Kennedy was going to be different. On inauguration eve, a heavy snow carpeted the nation's capital. Not since William Howard Taft took the oath of office in 1909 had so much snow fallen on Washington. Throughout the night, a crew of thousands cleared the eight-mile parade route from the White House to the Capitol. But the city as a whole was still largely immobilized as it prepared to welcome the new occupants of 1600 Pennsylvania Avenue.

Jack, armed with a speech that he believed was second to none, prepared for his inauguration like a king preparing to claim his crown. As he and Jackie exited their Georgetown home on N Street in the upscale northwestern section of the nation's capital, they both looked every bit the part. The television networks followed their short automobile journey to the White House, where, in a break from tradition, they had coffee with President Eisenhower and his wife, Mamie, before heading to Capitol Hill. Eisenhower had first met Jack sixteen years earlier, at the Potsdam summit. They could not have known at that time that they would each become president of the United States, one following the other.

The Kennedys then made the short journey to the Capitol, where the inauguration ceremony was to take place. Family members had the best seats in the house, although Rose complained that she was out of range of the cameras. The cabinet-to-be sat behind them. As a special guest, Lem was placed with the family. He sat in Row C with Teddy and his wife, Joan, ahead of Bobby, who was sitting farther behind, with the rest of the cabinet-to-be.

To signify his support for civil rights, Jack asked the great contralto Marian Anderson to sing the national anthem. In 1939, she had been prevented from singing in Constitution Hall by the Daughters of the American Revolution because she was black. Eleanor Roosevelt came to the rescue and arranged for her to sing in front of the Lincoln Memorial to a huge crowd of admirers. On this day, twenty-two years later, she sang at a presidential inauguration.

To highlight his support for the arts, Jack invited a host of literary giants to the inauguration, including W. H. Auden, John Steinbeck, Robert Lowell, and Robert Frost. He also asked one of his favorite authors, Ernest Hemingway, to attend, but Hemingway was too sick and depressed by then. He killed himself later that year. Frost, who was very old, was supposed to read a poem that he'd written for the occasion. He managed to deliver the first three lines without too much difficulty, even though a small fire erupted from short-circuited electrical wires beneath the lectern. "Summoning artists to participate in the august occasions of the state seems something artists ought to celebrate," Frost said. But then he called out that he couldn't see the words because of the blinding sun. Vice President-elect Lyndon Johnson came to his rescue, but Frost ended up choosing a different poem—"The Gift Outright"—which he could recite from memory.

As Jack boldly strode to the podium and took the oath of office as the thirty-fifth president of the United States, no one among the honored guests was prouder of him than Lem. To think that his best friend was now president of the United States. To imagine that a Choate Mucker was now the leader of the free world. It was hard to believe it was real. NBC anchors Chet Huntley and David Brinkley, both bundled up in topcoats and looking frigid, remarked on how cold the day was after the big snowfall the previous evening, telling their audience that the crowd was one-third the size of what it usually is for inaugurations because of the weather. In fact, at noon, although the snow had stopped and the sun was shining, the temperature was only twenty-two degrees. But Jack declined to wear a topcoat because he wanted to project an image of strength and vigor. As always, he was acutely aware of the power of imagery and symbolism, especially in the new age of television.

As Jack began his speech, it was so cold that his breath could clearly be seen on the television screen. His words were forceful and direct. "Let the word go forth from this time and place to friend and foe alike that the torch has been passed to a new generation of Americans, born in this century, tempered by war, disciplined by a hard and bitter peace, proud of our ancient heritage, and unwilling to witness or permit the slow undoing of those human rights to which this nation has always been committed and to which we are committed today at home and around the world."

The speech lasted less than twenty minutes, but it would come to be regarded as the best inaugural speech ever delivered, at least since Lincoln's Second Inaugural Address in 1864, almost a century earlier. But, unlike Lincoln's speech, Jack's remarks were instantly disseminated to millions of Americans watching their new leader on television. One line, more than any other, would become instantly memorable. "Ask not what your country can do for you . . . ask what you can do for your country."

Some old Choate alumni—not Lem, of course—charged that Jack had stolen that famous line from remarks made by George St. John, Jack and Lem's headmaster at Choate. St. John reportedly told his charges, "Ask not what Choate can do for you, ask what you can do for Choate." But Judy Donald, the current archivist at the school in Wallingford, Connecticut, said they have been unable to document the claim. In fact, the idea in the famous line has been expressed in many ways by politicians over the years. But no one said it exactly like Jack did on that day.

Jack worked long and hard on the speech, principally with aide Ted

Sorensen. He wanted it to be short and eloquent, in the mode of Lincoln's Gettysburg Address, which is only 269 words long. He asked Sorensen to research Lincoln's speech and he reported back that Lincoln believed in never using a two- or three-syllable word where a one-syllable word would do. Sorensen worked on the main draft, but others contributed words and ideas as well. However, Jack never delivered a speech written by a speechwriter without checking it. With important speeches, especially, he contributed key sections himself. His speechwriters, especially Sorensen, gradually learned the kind of language that appealed to him. On the morning of the inauguration, Jack was still penciling in changes on the typed draft.

After the speech, amid the goodwill of the entire nation, ex-President Eisenhower, at that time the oldest man ever elected president, turned to the youngest man ever elected president and said, "You're it now, boy." It was a fulfilling moment for Jack, who had begun his quest for the presidency a year after the death of his brother Joe in 1944. Now, he had stepped out of his brother's shadow and fulfilled his own, and his family's, expectations. It was also a dream come true for Jack's father, Joe, who had nurtured his own dream of being president but whose hopes were crushed by his support for the appeasement of Hitler in the 1930s. Joe was particularly proud that Jack had proved that an Irish American Catholic could be elected president. Religious bigotry was far from dead in the United States, but from now on it would no longer be a major factor in the country's political life.

For Lem, the feeling was different. He had never pushed Jack into anything but instead supported him in whatever he chose to do. He could not have known even during Jack's years in Congress that the road he traveled would eventually lead to the White House. But Lem was happy for him that it had. He knew Jack wanted to be president, and now he was.

In Ireland, where the journey of the Kennedys to the New World had begun more than a century earlier, bonfires were lit around the country in celebration that one of their own had been elected president of the United States. And all over the world, there was renewed hope that now that this intelligent, stylish, charismatic man had become leader of the free world, there would be a renewed American effort to help solve the myriad problems confronting the planet.

∽

Most of Lem's family attended the inauguration, including his mother, Romaine, his sister, Lucretia, and his niece, Sally. Jack had always liked Romaine, who was now seventy-eight years old. When they were boys at Choate, Jack had sometimes stayed at her home in Baltimore. He made special arrangements for her to come down to Washington to attend all the inauguration festivities as a guest of honor, including issuing instructions to arrange for transportation for her. "This comes from the President-Elect: Please have a car take care of Mrs. F. T. Billings (78 years old) and her four guests—by taking them to the Inaugural Ball and returning them."

Lem appreciated the effort, but he knew Jack would do no less. He also knew that the friendship between them wouldn't change now that Jack was president of the United States. No matter the burdens of the office, or the demands on his time, Lem knew that Jack would always make time for him. "This is one of the most astounding parts of the relationship between Lem and the president," said Lem's friend Peter Kaplan. "It puts a stamp on it that says, this is a lifelong friendship."

"Some people like to go on long walks alone," said Eunice Kennedy Shriver. "Jack liked to be with a friend like Lem. Just because he got into the White House didn't mean he was going to stop having a friend like Lemmie. If someone has always had friends, they keep them up, and Jack was that way. It was just a natural part of his personal life. He had a great capacity for friendship."

The inauguration was marked by much pomp and ceremony. Jack even wore a top hat, though he hated hats of any kind. He had always been informal, but he realized, said Lem later, that the American people expect a certain amount of formality in the office of president. "He recognized that even as the people would reject a king, their hearts tugged for the symbols of royalty. For that reason, he deliberately decided to invest his inauguration with pomp and ceremony. He wanted to use the moment to appeal to the imagination, to raise the ceremony to a heightened level of feeling. Perhaps it was his Catholicism that created in him the appreciation for tradition and majesty, or perhaps it was just his instinctive understanding of the American people. Whatever it was, it worked."

❧

After the speech, the traditional parade took place along Pennsylvania Avenue. In a highly symbolic moment, Jack stood in the car and took off his hat in a gesture of respect to his aging father, to whom he owed so much—despite their political differences.

Joe had mostly stayed behind the scenes during the election campaign, knowing he was unpopular with large sections of the American public. But now his son was president. He savored his moment in the sun. He was one very proud Irish American father.

While reviewing the Coast Guard contingent in the inaugural parade, Jack noticed that there were no African Americans among them. He called aide Richard Goodwin and asked him to find out why the Coast Guard unit had no black faces. Goodwin later said that he called the U.S. Treasury "with a rush of energy bordering on elation. Why, with a telephone call like this, we can change the world," he thought. Changing the world was one thing, desegregating the Coast Guard was another. Jack soon would learn how strong the resistance to civil rights for African Americans would be at this juncture in history. But his call to Goodwin on this first day of his presidency was an indication, albeit symbolically, of how strongly he felt about civil rights, an issue that would define his domestic record as president.

After the inauguration, Lem joined Jack in the White House. It was his first time there. Until that moment, it was hard to believe that his friend was now president of the United States. Entering the mansion with Eunice, Lem felt he was reenacting a scene from *Gone with the Wind*, his favorite movie. "I remember Eunice and I went in together and we were talking about how it felt almost like the part in *Gone with the Wind* when Scarlett's two old colored servants first moved in to her enormous mansion in Atlanta after suffering with her all during the war," said Lem. "As they walked into the house the old mammy said, 'Man, we's rich now,'" and we just felt the same way. We were really in. It was incredible."

Because he was crazy about antiques and period furniture, Lem took a special interest in the Lincoln Room, a high-ceilinged bedroom suite on the south side of the White House. Lincoln's furniture was arranged in the room just as it had been during his presidency. Lem and Eunice hopped on the bed and had their picture taken there. They marveled at being in the room of the man many historians consider the greatest American president. "We saw Lincoln's bed for the first time, which is really a thrilling experience," remembered Lem. After the long and exciting day, Jack and Lem and the rest of the family, with the exception of Joe and Rose, who left earlier, had dinner in their new home. "After dinner, we all went up and lay on the Lincoln bed," said Lem. "And I think some of us took pictures of ourselves on the Lincoln bed. It was really corny."

The previous evening, Frank Sinatra and Jack's brother-in-law, Peter Lawford, had organized a star-studded extravaganza that included a who's who of Hollywood's megastars of that era, including Dean Martin, Kim Novak, Angie Dickinson, Ella Fitzgerald, Gene Kelly, Sidney Poitier, Ethel Merman, Anthony Quinn, and even Laurence Olivier. It seemed almost everyone in Hollywood wanted to be seen with the first couple who had star power to match their own. Frank, Dean, and Sammy Davis Jr. were slated to perform along with Harry Belafonte, Mahalia Jackson, Milton Berle, Nat King Cole, Fredric March, Red Skelton, Bette Davis, Keely Smith, and even Eleanor Roosevelt, who read words from Lincoln.

However, in a snub that he would never get over, Sammy was disinvited at the last minute. The people around Jack apparently feared a southern backlash right at the beginning of his presidency because Sammy's soon-to-be wife, May Britt, was white. The three-hour show went on without Davis, even though he had been a strong backer of the Kennedy/Johnson ticket and had worked hard for it.

After the show ended, Jack went onto the stage, took the microphone, and said, "We're all indebted to a great friend, Frank Sinatra." Tickets for the extravaganza, which took place at the Washington National Guard Armory, cost $100.

Lem stayed at Bobby's house on Hickory Hill in nearby Virginia during the inauguration weekend, according to John Seigenthaler. "Lem was all over the place during the Inauguration—all over every party, every ball, having the time of his life," Seigenthaler recalled. He remembered one event in particular, a party at Paul Young's restaurant in downtown Washington, D.C. "All the celebrities from Hollywood were there. I walked over there in the snow from my hotel. The president stayed at the restaurant for a little while and I think Joe and Rose were there as well. Lem was having a great time and making everyone laugh as usual."

Lem also invited his friend and former boss, Francis McAdoo, and his wife to all the inaugural festivities. "Lem was at all the parties, more than we could keep up with," McAdoo noted. Asked what Lem thought of Jack's inaugural address, he said, "Well, of course, he thought it was wonderful. For Lem, the president could never do anything wrong. Of course, he thought it was great."

The main entertainment on the evening after the inauguration was the inaugural balls, five of them. Jack and Lem had the time of their lives, but Jackie quickly became tired. She was still weak from the Caesarean birth of John two months earlier. During the second ball—at the Statler Hilton—Jack slipped out and spent a half hour at a private party hosted by Frank Sinatra. He was curious, as always, about the goings-on of the Hollywood glamour set. Jack returned to the ball carrying a *Washington Post* under his arm, as if he had been checking out the news. Jackie gave him a chilly look, according to his aides, Dave Powers and Kenny O'Donnell. She returned to the White House long before the evening was over, perhaps annoyed at Jack's disappearing act.

Jack and his friends, however, partied all night long, even after the last ball ended at two the next morning. Then Jack decided to take a car to 2720 Dumbarton Street in Georgetown, the home of his friend and newspaper columnist Joe Alsop. As he was about to get in the car, Jack spotted his old navy friend, Red Fay, who had Angie Dickinson on one arm and Kim Novak on the other. Jack reportedly asked them to come with him to Joe's house.

When Red said sure, Jack caught himself and suddenly became conscious of what that would look like in the morning papers if reporters got hold of it. "JFK attends late-night party with glamorous Hollywood movie stars," or something like that. So he went over to Joe Alsop's without them. No doubt he was envious of Red standing there with two of Hollywood's sexiest movie stars. After celebrating a while at Alsop's home, Jack walked up to the White House in the frigid predawn hours and entered the building alone, saying good-bye to his friends on the steps outside. A presidency like no other in our history was about to commence.

Change was in the air in 1961, and not only politically. American culture, too, was tossing and turning in all directions, in part a response to the new beginning in Washington.

In California, 1961 was the year the Beach Boys first surfed their way onto the charts, the beginning of the West Coast sound that would take the world by storm. On the East Coast, that same year, Bob Dylan arrived in New York and became a sensation in Greenwich Village coffeehouses, triggering a folk song revival across the nation. Dylan's "Blowin' in the Wind" would become a theme for the civil rights movement. Another Dylan number, "The Times They Are A-Changin'" became an anthem for the decade. A new record company called Motown also burst onto the scene in 1961. Among the first artists it signed were Marvin Gaye and Diana Ross and the Supremes. Over in England, that same year, an unknown group named The Beatles first performed at the Cavern Club in Liverpool—though they would not conquer America until 1964.

In Hollywood, exploring the uglier side of the American dream became the fashion in a new breed of gritty drama like *A Raisin in the Sun, To Kill a Mockingbird, The Children's Hour,* and *Advise and Consent,* all of which were released during Jack's presidency. The former two movies cast a searing spotlight on racial injustice; the latter two were among the first to deal seriously and sympathetically with homosexuality. Television embraced the New Frontier, as well. This was the era of idealistic defense attorneys, compassionate doctors, and even crusading social workers (the latter depicted in the CBS series *East Side/West Side*).

The primary focus of attention, however, was the new president and his wife. Moviegoers were used to seeing Hollywood glamour. But nothing in Tinseltown could equal the appeal of John and Jacqueline Kennedy. Forget about Antony and Cleopatra or Gable and Lombard. In 1961, there was only one couple that people everywhere wanted to read about, and that was Jack and Jackie.

Even political opponents were entranced by the new occupants of 1600 Pennsylvania Avenue. They represented a sharp break with the drab leadership of the past. Almost as soon as they entered the White House, even before Jackie renovated it, the nation's home took on a new air of vibrance and excitement. The whole ambience of the nation's capital changed almost instantly. It glittered as never before. The first couple were viewed as American royalty, covered more like a fairy-tale king and queen than president and First Lady. It was Hollywood on the Potomac, and everyone loved it.

Lem couldn't believe the extent of the interest among press and public alike. For him, Jack and Jackie were not some mythical couple. They were his friends, the people with whom he palled around, with whom he laughed and joked. He loved them, but he certainly didn't think of them as royalty. He knew their flaws, their weaknesses, their likes and dislikes, their moods, even—certainly in the case of Jack—their most intimate secrets and their most embarrassing idiosyncrasies. In short, he knew them as real people, not international media sensations. It must have been hard for him to recognize the Jack and Jackie he read about in adoring magazine articles and watched on reverential television broadcasts.

Despite all the attention and the excitement, however, no one knew more than John Kennedy that the country and the world faced serious problems in the early 1960s. It was the way he responded to those challenges that would ultimately define his presidency. The first task at hand was to name the people who would serve in his administration. It was clear that Lem would be first friend at the White House. But what formal role, if any, should he have in the government? As he set about forming his team, Jack pondered what to offer his oldest and closest friend.

10

FIRST FRIEND
(1961–63)

"The presidency is not a good place to make new friends. I'm going to keep my old friends."
—John F. Kennedy, December 12, 1962

J ack had been advised to be cautious about appointing friends and relatives to posts in his administration, since there had already been press criticism of his top appointments.

Editorial writers blasted Jack for nominating his brother Bobby to be attorney general, which he did at the insistence of his father. Among the strongest critics was the *New York Times,* which attacked Jack for nepotism. Lem was quick to respond in his own inimitable way. He suggested a letter be sent to the newspaper discussing nepotism in the Sulzberger family, which owned the *New York Times.* "Nepotism? For God's sake, look at the *New York Times,"* he said. Democrats were upset that the president nominated two Republicans to serve in key positions—C. Douglas Dillon as secretary of the treasury and Robert McNamara as secretary of defense. Almost everybody complained about the influence of Jack's Boston political cronies, dubbed the Irish Mafia.

Despite the carping, Jack was determined to offer his best friend a job in the administration. He offered Lem the choice of three: director of the newly created Peace Corps, director of the proposed U.S. Travel Service, or ambassador to Denmark. Lem turned down all three. He was especially uninterested in the latter. "Can you imagine—my best friend becomes president of the United States and I spend his presidency in Denmark," he exclaimed. Lem recalled that his rejection of the Peace Corps job caused a problem when Jack then offered it to Sargent Shriver, his brother-in-law. "He offered me the Peace Corps, which of course is not well known. And this is one of the reasons Sarg had never thought about the Peace Corps," Lem said. "When he asked Sarg, Sarg knew I had been asked, too, and actually, he had a hard time selling Sarg on doing it."

In Lem's FBI file, obtained through a freedom of information request, there is a reference in May 1961 to Lem's "being considered for an appointment to the Peace Corps" and to another position that was not identified. Because sections of the report are blacked out even twenty-five years after Lem's death, it is not fully clear what J. Edgar Hoover's FBI was up to in reference to Lem. There is a curious section referring to an unidentified person being "instructed to cultivate a relationship with LeMoyne Billings, described as a close personal friend of President Kennedy." Another unidentified person is said to "welcome an opportunity to cultivate personages in influential positions of the United States government, particularly those with access to the president. The intelligence possibilities that can issue from a successful cultivation in this area are endless." It is quite possible that Hoover was trying to amass damaging information on Lem to use against Jack if he needed to. If so, this is extraordinary, considering the fact that Lem didn't accept any of Jack's job offers and never became a federal employee.

Lem did consider Jack's offer to become head of a U.S. Travel Service more seriously than the other two jobs Jack offered, however. He and Jack had held numerous discussions over the fact that there was no agency to encourage tourism to the United States, unlike in many other countries. Lem was very much involved in the effort to get Congress to approve such a body. "Needless to say, it was my first experience on the

Hill in lobbying for a bill," he remarked. "I discovered in the process that I basically did not want to work in government." But the main reason Lem turned down the offer was because he didn't want to become Jack's employee. Lem thought it would be better for his friendship with Jack if he accepted no formal role in the administration. "I realized that I didn't want to work for the president—because I felt it would change our relationship," Lem said. "Certainly my relationship with him was much more important than anything else to me." Lem wanted "to be a friend and not a political or business associate of the president's," said Lem's niece, Sally Carpenter. For Lem, being first friend was all he wanted.

Jack accepted Lem's decision and had probably known in advance that Lem would not accept a political job. In order not to hurt Lem's feelings, which Jack always knew could be so easily done, he felt he still had to make the offer. As Jack's administration got under way, Lem remained in New York and continued as an advertising executive with Lennen & Newell. The company "was very good in permitting me to keep my time flexible," said Lem. So he did take a small part-time position with the administration in September 1961. He served on the board of trustees of the National Cultural Center, which was to be built in Washington, D.C. (which was not completed until 1971, and then was named the John F. Kennedy Center for the Performing Arts). Lem was paid seventy-five dollars a day for the time he was working the assignment.

Jackie was cochair of the organization, but Lem was very insistent that the First Lady's role was pro forma, that he was Jack's point person for the effort. "Many people think that his interest in the arts was based on the fact that he was married to Jackie Kennedy and her influence was largely responsible for his interest in the cultural center," Lem said. "Possibly she made him more interested in cultural affairs generally, but I don't believe Jackie Kennedy knew anything about the center. I don't think he ever talked to her about the center." Lem added: "I discussed it with him to the point of boredom."

There was a minor scandal of sorts when the Associated Press reported that a government contract—worth about $250,000—was awarded to Lem's advertising firm. But the charge didn't cause too much of a stir. Everyone knew this kind of thing was a fact of life in Washington. The money wasn't that big, and most reporters didn't get too upset in those days if a president tossed a few bucks to his best friend's company.

"Of the nine or ten men who were close to the president, I would say that Lem was number one," Eunice Kennedy Shriver said, even though Lem had no governmental role. Jack, for his part, was probably glad that Lem did not accept a political job, as well. He, too, thought it might interfere with the friendship. And Jack knew, as president, that keeping old buddies was more important than ever. His old friends, most importantly Lem, made him feel secure and comfortable. From all accounts, the friendship between Jack and Lem didn't change at all during the White House years. Lem's sister, Lucretia, who knew Jack long before he was president, said, "They both saw each other a lot during the White House years as well and acted just the same." She said that Lem really didn't have any adjustment to make when Jack entered the White House, because the friendship didn't really change.

The transition to First Lady for Jackie, however, was much more difficult than Lem's transition to First Friend. Jack and Lem, by nature, were both extroverted and liked being around people. Jackie, by contrast, was introverted and enjoyed time alone or with a few close friends. Both Jack and Lem knew from experience that Jackie could easily feel overwhelmed. That was much more likely to occur now that she was living with Jack and the children in the nation's number-one fishbowl.

Jackie had never been a natural politician and had never really liked campaigning or public appearances. She needed frequent time alone to recuperate and rejuvenate, whereas Jack liked to be around people constantly and could easily concentrate on a book surrounded by aides and friends or even noisy pets and children. Lem said Jack could read a book even while holding a conversation. Jack drew energy from people. With Jackie, it was the reverse.

In the early days, she was constantly questioning her role as First Lady. What precisely should it be? Aside from being there for Jack—she once said her main job was "to take care of the president"—just exactly what should she be doing? As the Kennedys set about organizing their new home, Jack could see that Jackie was getting upset about all the routine household tasks that needed her attention. So he asked Lem to come down to Washington to help her out.

Lem promptly asked his bosses in New York for a leave of absence, a request the company probably felt unable to turn down, even if so inclined. Soon, Lem was winging his way to the nation's capital to help get the White House shipshape. Lem was always at Jack's beck and call. He never really thought of saying no. How could he now, when his best friend was the president?

In the first few weeks at the White House—when Jackie was very unsure of herself—Lem helped her focus on what she wanted to do, boosting her confidence. The most important priority for her was making the White House a warm, comfortable, and secure place for John and Caroline. So Jackie and Lem set about the task of preparing the children's rooms. Jackie wanted them to be ready before the children moved into the White House.

Consequently, Caroline and John remained in Palm Beach during the first few weeks of the administration. Since John was still a baby, it was decided that he should share his room with the children's nurse, Maud Shaw. Lem and Jackie also prepared the third-floor schoolroom. Jackie wanted the children to be educated at the White House along with other children who would be brought there. She thought their childhood should be as normal as possible. She would later say, "If you bungle raising your children, I don't think that whatever else you do matters very much."

On the afternoon of February 4, 1961, Jack, Jackie, and Lem left the White House for National Airport (now Reagan National Airport), where the plane carrying Caroline and John, who were attended to by two nurses as well as Secret Servicemen, was to land. Jackie and Lem were probably more excited than the children about the White House makeover of their rooms. They were really too young to notice. Caroline was a boisterous three-year-old, and John was just a few months old.

Almost from the beginning of his presidency, it was clear that Jack would need all the friends he could get. He was confronted with unprecedented problems at home and abroad. During the campaign, he had raised the expectations of the American people, and now they were watching to see that he delivered on his promises. He began a program of reform at home even as he prepared to face foreign crises unparalleled in gravity in the postwar world.

Despite major defeats and setbacks during John F. Kennedy's one thousand days in office (actually a few more than one thousand), he remained popular with the American people. This was due, in part, to his own personal appeal and to that of his family, as well as to his policies. For the first time since Theodore Roosevelt, the sound of young children playing could be heard in the White House. The American people, and much of the world, were fascinated by John and Caroline as well as Jack and Jackie.

Jackie tried to protect Caroline and John from the prying cameras of the press, but whenever she was away, Jack would always invite photographers to the White House—he knew what a great political asset the children were when they showed up in magazines and newspapers. He was also beginning to realize that his wife was a major political asset, too, and that the press was interested in photographing and writing about her as well as him. She set a new standard for elegance that women across the globe soon began to emulate.

It was clear that Americans, and non-Americans alike, had fallen in love with the First Family, who seemed to have it all. The public saw still photographs and video of them such as they had never seen before.

Lem, Jackie, Jack, and extended family, Hyannis Port, 1963.

The pictures of them sailing and swimming together off the coast of Cape Cod, of the children running up to the helicopter as the president rushed to greet them, and of the First Family at play surrounded by animals at Glen Ora, their weekend retreat in the Virginia countryside, are vivid in the memories of those who were alive at the time.

Jack and Lem getting ready for a golf game, Hyannis Port, 1963.

The public even saw the president driving his own car, usually a long, sleek convertible of the kind that was so much in style in the early 1960s. Most people didn't know that Jack had always been a terrible driver and that his family was taking a real risk by letting him take the wheel. But everyone loved the video. Everyone wanted to have the same kind of picture-perfect family—or so it seemed to Americans of that time, who were not privy to details about the private lives of their leaders.

Despite her love of Jack and the children and her determination to make sure Caroline and John led as normal a life as possible at the White House, there were times when Jackie needed to get away by herself, especially in the early months, when she was still suffering the effects from John's birth in late 1960. Her first trip was to Palm Beach, where she spent a few weeks with friends resting and recuperating.

With Jackie away, Lem took a leave of absence from his job in New York and stayed at the White House with Jack. The burdens of office had not yet descended on the young president. So the two friends found plenty of time to talk and laugh and play practical jokes on their friends. While there, Lem took over Jackie's hosting role. He arranged small dinner parties, frequently inviting old prep school and college chums of his and Jack's.

Lem even invited rival Torbert Macdonald, who was Jack's close friend at Harvard. Lem did not particularly like Torby, perhaps because he had grown too close to Jack. But first and foremost, Lem wanted to please Jack, and he knew that he liked Torby a lot. In his role as First Friend—and occasional host—at Camelot, Lem thrived.

Ted Sorensen, Jack's chief speechwriter and so close to the president professionally that he was considered his political alter ego, recalls seeing Lem frequently at the White House but said his role was purely social, as a longtime friend of Jack's. He described Jack and Lem as "fast friends" going back to prep school. "I never knew of any particular interest in politics or in his [JFK's] presidency," he said. However, he added, "I didn't know Mr. Billings very well at all. I know he was an admirer—almost a fawning admirer—of his friend for all those years. So he automatically liked everything the president did and stood for. Whether it tied into his own interests and biases, he never gave a clue."

As the administration got under way, Lem came to Washington almost every weekend, flying down from New York, where he was still working for Lennen & Newell. He stayed at the White House so often that he was given his own room on the third floor. He would leave some of his belongings there, so it effectively became Lem's room. No one else stayed in it. "Lem was in and out of the White House almost as much as the White House usher, and some people saw him so much they thought he was the Secret Service," said Jack's aide Dave Powers.

Lem "just moved into his room without anybody ever knowing he was coming. Maybe the president knew it, but nothing was ever said about it," said J. B. West, the chief usher at the time. The White House guards rarely quizzed Lem the way they would other visitors because he came so often and they got to know him so well. They all knew he was Jack's best friend dating back to school days.

"In all the books about Jack Kennedy," Lem said in an interview a few years before he died, "I'm referred to as a roommate from Choate and then dropped. I don't particularly want to be in books, but I resent always being treated as a childhood friend who could then be dropped. You never see me in the last pages, and yet I was at his house every single weekend he was president. . . . Jack was the closest person to me in the world for thirty years."

In another interview, Lem said, "Well, I did stay there a lot. As a matter of fact, of course the White House is very big and there were so many servants that there really wasn't any problem for them to have houseguests. The third floor has about six guest rooms and as a matter of fact, I did stay there enough so that I had a room of my own. Nobody else used that room so I could even leave my stuff there. Jack and Jackie were so nice about this that I didn't even have to tell them whether I was coming or going. If they were doing something else, dining or having people in and I wasn't necessarily included, it didn't make any difference. So I really was there a lot." He added: "It wasn't very long before all the Secret Service knew me . . . and all of the guards knew me. Actually, I never had a White House pass in my life."

Lem, north lawn of the White House, 1962.

The White House appointments book for Jack's presidency references Lem forty-nine times. But these were just the official appointments that were formally logged in when Jack met Lem, mostly in the
company of others at the White House, or went somewhere else with
him, most often with Jackie. Lem also visited the White House infor-
mally, and records of these visits were not generally kept, although
sometimes the newspapers would report Lem's presence. For example,
on October 16, 1961, the *New York Times* reported that "the president
had no official appointments or guests this weekend. Mrs. Kennedy
and their two children, John and Caroline, are with him, as is his
father, Joseph P. Kennedy. Their houseguest is LeMoyne K. Billings of
New York."

The first appointment that referenced Lem was logged in on February 4, 1961. "The president and Mrs. Kennedy departed the White
House and motored to MATS Terminal [at National Airport] to meet
their children who were arriving from Florida. Accompanying the president were the Hon. Pierre Salinger [Jack's press secretary], Mr.
LeMoyne Billings, Captain George Berkeley, USN, and the White
House physician." This was the trip that Jack, Jackie, and Lem took at
the beginning of his presidency to pick up the children, who had been
staying in Florida while their rooms at the White House were being
prepared. The last appointment referencing Lem was logged in on
October 27, 1963. It reads, "3:20 P.M. The president, LeMoyne
Billings, Contessa Medici, and John Jr. went for a ride to Glen Ora.
3:47 P.M. Returned to the residence. No further activity this date."

John Seigenthaler, who took a leave of absence from his newspaper to work for Bobby at the Justice Department, recalls seeing Lem
a lot during the White House years. "He was always around. He was
Jack's classmate from schooldays. He was very smart, as funny as hell
really. He also had a quick wit, which Jack liked. I never had a conversation with him that during it he would not say something very
funny, usually about somebody else. I liked him and I guess I knew
there was a loyalty there that was unfailing. But he sure could mix
it—exchange laughs and insults with anybody. Before it was over,
you'd be laughing a lot."

"I recall a birthday party I attended at Hickory Hill [Bobby and

Ethel's home in nearby Virginia]," Seigenthaler continued, "and at some point during that party Teddy shoved somebody in the swimming pool and then other people were dumped into the pool as well and finally Teddy got pushed in there. I recall Lem saying, 'I'm sure all America loves people who put on tuxedos before going into the swimming pool.' The story got into the newspapers and Joe Kennedy was credited as saying it, but I heard Lem say it."

Letitia Baldrige, Jackie's social secretary, remembers Lem at many of the social events, too, especially at the White House. "Jackie, as well as the president, liked to have him around," she said. "He was a big, attractive guy who told wonderful stories and cheered everyone up. The president could relax with him because he knew him so well." Some of Jack's political aides at the White House, however, resented Lem's closeness to the president and his presence in the White House, since they didn't see any particular reason for him to be there so often. Arthur Schlesinger Jr. wrote that Lem "used to glare at me when we occasionally encountered each other in the company of JFK, and for a time I took this rather personally. Soon I discovered that he glared with equal suspicion at anyone whose friendship with JFK postdated his own," which was of course everybody.

Bill Walton, another of the president's aides and thought to be gay, also felt that Lem resented his friendship with JFK. "I never was a friend of Lem Billings," he said. "He was in a totally different category. He's childhood, brought along for the ride sort of thing. I just could never bear him. He couldn't bear me." Even Rip Horton, the only person in Jack's circle who, like Lem, had known him since the Choate days, knew that there was a special relationship between Jack and Lem that transcended politics and that no one could really fathom.

Hugh Auchincloss III, Jackie's half brother, who was working with Adlai Stevenson, the U.S. ambassador to the United Nations, in New York, visited the White House frequently and often saw Lem there, particularly on social occasions. He said there was no mystery about Lem. It was just that Jack and Lem went way back together and were great friends. "Lem provided amusement," he remarked. "He was good with the children and he was fun loving." He added: "He helped Jack and Jackie relax." This was particularly important after Jack became president, he added.

Though many other people around Jack continued to be mystified by Jack's friendship with Lem, they knew better than to question his presence. "Lem Billings entered Jack's life at Choate and never left. He remained a bachelor and seemed to have subordinated his life to his friend," said historian Herbert S. Parmet. "Members of the president's staff thought of him as 'a handy old piece of furniture.'"

Some advisors no doubt wondered about Lem being gay but never brought the subject up with Jack. Paradoxically, the climate of homophobia and intolerance in the early 1960s might have protected Lem. The aides knew that the press would never print a story about the president's best friend being gay—no more so than they would print anything about extramarital affairs—unless something was so brazen it would compel coverage.

But there were no assurances, and one wrong move by Lem could have been disastrous. Jack's successor, Lyndon Johnson, found this out the hard way. In October 1964, one of his closest aides, Walter Jenkins, who was married and had six children, did do something brazen. He was arrested after having sex with a retired soldier in a public bathroom at the YMCA. The *Washington Star* got hold of the story and printed it, despite heavy pressure from Johnson. The scandal forced LBJ to let Jenkins go, but he remained close to the Johnson family for the rest of his life. Despite being a close aide, however, Jenkins was not the president's best friend. If he had been, the incident might have done more damage to Johnson politically, coming as it did just a month before he ran for election as president in his own right in November 1964.

In contrast to Jenkins, Lem was discreet at all times. There was never any hint of scandal surrounding him. Lem made sure of that. Whatever his thoughts and actions may have been during Jack's life, he kept them strictly private. He certainly was not inclined to take the kind of risks that Jenkins did. He may have been more careful partly because he was unmarried and knew that the slightest aberrant behavior would cause rumors to fly in the Washington of that time. In any case, Lem was devoted to John F. Kennedy. There was never any prospect of someone taking his place. "Lem was great around the president," recalled newspaperman Charlie Bartlett, who met Lem not long after he met Jack in the mid-1940s. "I never thought Lem was gay. It never occurred to me, although it is clear that he didn't share Jack's interest in women."

But other close friends of Jack thought otherwise. "I suppose it's known that Lem was gay," said Ben Bradlee, Washington bureau chief of *Newsweek* during the Kennedy administration and a personal friend of Jack's since the late 1950s. "It impressed me that Jack had gay friends." Bradlee, who recalls first meeting Lem at Hyannis Port, also encountered Lem at some of the White House social functions and at Glen Ora. "You're always interested in your friend's friends. I knew they had been friends for a long time. I think they had a teasing relationship," he added.

But Bradlee said that Jack never mentioned that Lem was gay to him. In fact, he never mentioned Lem at all in their conversations. "Jack tended to live his life in compartments and largely kept his friends separate from each other. He didn't mix his friends . . . but I'm fairly sure he didn't value Lem as a great political asset." He continued, "They were childhood friends and stayed loyal to each other forever." Ben agrees with others who were close to the president that Lem fiercely protected his access to Jack. "He had a natural jealousy. He didn't want to share his friendship with Jack, especially with newspaper types like me. He wasn't interested in the newspaper business.

"I don't remember anyone raising the gay issue as a potential political embarrassment to the president," Ben remarked. "But if it had come up, Jack could easily have handled that." But the issue didn't come up, because Lem was discreet enough never to cause Jack any problems. Lem had proved over and over again to Jack that he could be trusted. Recalled Charlie Bartlett, "He provided the solid link with past values and attitudes which a president needs always." Despite Lem's being discreet, these were dangerous times. The cold war was at its height. If the Russians had discovered that the president's best friend was gay, it would have been valuable information, to say the least.

In fact, the Russians did discover that another friend of Jack's was gay and attempted to blackmail him. The friend was Joe Alsop, a prominent Washington newspaperman of the time. Before he became president, Jack had been in the habit of dropping by Joe's home. Jack continued to visit Alsop, often accompanied by Jackie, after he became president. Known for the sophisticated gatherings he hosted in his Georgetown home, the stature of the effete Alsop grew once Jack was in the White House.

Alsop's lifestyle became known, however, at least among Washington's movers and shakers, because of an incident in Moscow in 1957. While he was visiting the Russian capital, Joe was seduced by a male KGB agent and then asked to become a Soviet agent. Alsop declined, dutifully reporting the entrapment to the CIA. No action was taken against him.

Eventually, photographs of the encounter found their way to the FBI and onto the desk of J. Edgar Hoover, who lost no time in passing the salacious material around town. Since the self-righteous Hoover undoubtedly knew that Jack and Alsop were friends, it is most likely that he put Jack on the mailing list for the photographs in a gleeful effort to let Jack know how much he knew. Hoover enjoyed letting Washington's elite know that he knew about everyone's sexual shenanigans. He would have been mortified, of course, if they knew about his own activities, which reportedly included cross-dressing.

The lifelong bachelor, who liked to think he was married to the FBI, nurtured a lifelong friendship with Clyde Tolson, his deputy at the agency with whom he lunched every day and took regular vacations. Rumors were rife, of course. Within the FBI, Hoover and Tolson were known as J. Edna and Mother Tolson. Writer Truman Capote nicknamed them Bonnie and Clyde. But most people were smart enough to leave Edgar and Clyde alone, including—given his own sexual secrets—Jack. There was no question but that Hoover would remain head of the FBI during a Kennedy administration. In fact, every president reappointed Hoover, who died in office in 1972.

Alsop was fortunate that the escapade in Russia never became public knowledge until after his death, since he was a conservative who railed against communists. His position as an elite Washington columnist of enormous influence in the 1950s and early 1960s remained secure. It is another example of the press—in that very different era—not reporting private behavior if it didn't impinge on public performance. In Alsop's case, it did not.

Jack, as always, remained a loyal friend. He really didn't care what Alsop was up to under the sheets one way or another, although he probably had a prurient interest. But in those days, you couldn't be too careful if you were gay. So Alsop took steps to improve his social standing. He did what many gay men of his generation did—he got married. On Valentine's Day night 1961, the Kennedys were sent, and dutifully accepted, an invitation to a dinner party at the Alsop home. Joe introduced his guests to Susan Mary Patten, whom he said he was going to marry two days later. He did. After Alsop got married, Jack quipped, "Now if only we can get Bill [a reference to his friend Bill Walton] and Gore [Vidal] married off."

When Jack died, Alsop wrote that "the Washington landscape seemed to me to be littered with male widows," an apparent reference to the legions of men, as well as women, who were emotionally affected by the president's death. If that was the case, then Lem "was probably the saddest of the Kennedy 'widows'" according to writer Sally Bedell Smith.

Among the guests at Alsop's dinner that Valentine Day's evening was David Bruce, who would become the U.S. ambassador to Britain in the Kennedy administration. Susan knew Britain quite well, as did Jack. Jack and Susan got into a discussion about then British prime minister Harold Macmillan, known as Supermac in England due to his political dexterity. Jack had not yet met him.

Jack would eventually become quite close to Macmillan, not only because of the prime minister's savvy political knowledge, but also because of his iconoclastic wit, which Jack enjoyed. Macmillan's sense of humor was most in evidence during a famous incident at the United Nations. While Macmillan was speaking, Soviet premier Nikita Khrushchev took off his shoe and began banging it on the desk to protest what the British leader was saying. Looking totally unflustered, Macmillan paused for effect and then responded, "Could I have that translated, please?"

Macmillan had been prime minister since 1957 and was a veteran in dealing with the Russians. He was a moderate Conservative—well to the left of the Labour Party's Tony Blair today—who favored independence for Britain's remaining colonies and moderate-to-progressive policies at home. But the story Susan told Jack that evening about Macmillan had nothing to do with politics. It concerned Dorothy, Macmillan's wife, an aunt of Jack's late brother-in-law, Billy Hartington, who was the husband of his sister Kathleen.

Dorothy was the dutiful British political wife of the time, seen but not heard. But behind the scenes, years before Macmillan became prime minister, Dorothy carried on a passionate love affair with Conservative lawmaker Robert Boothby, who later achieved notoriety suing the *London Daily Mirror* over the newspaper's implication that he was carrying on a gay affair with a British gangster. Her relatives decided that, to end the embarrassing affair between Dorothy and Boothby, a wife had to be found for him.

Everyone was relieved when that goal was achieved. But Dorothy ended up going on vacation with Boothby and his new wife, a ménage à trois that triggered another round of scandal and embarrassment. Even more astounding, Macmillan stuck by his wayward wife and continued to love her, although the situation apparently sent him into a deep depression. These were the days when man and wife tended to stay together even in the face of obvious adultery.

The story amused Jack. He found it astonishing that a man of Macmillan's stature had stayed with his wife in the face of such blatant infidelity. He was bowled over by a story whose humor rested on how pathetic it was for a man to continue to love his unfaithful wife. The irony was not lost on Jackie, who had been aware of her husband's tomcat ways since before they were married. She must have wondered whether Jack thought she was foolish for staying with him in view of his affairs. But the thought probably never crossed Jack's mind.

When Jackie eventually met Macmillan, they formed a bond that grew quite strong. They would remain close even after Macmillan left office. Susan said her source for the story about Macmillan and wife was Lord David Cecil, author of the *The Young Melbourne,* a book that Jack had read years before and that had made a deep impression on him. Cecil was related to Dorothy.

Jack always liked hearing about the sex lives of other people. It was just part of his makeup. It's not known what he thought about Joe Alsop's marrying Susan—if anything. He probably felt that Joe would continue having affairs with men, if that is what he was really into, although Joe was certainly no stud in the Kennedy mold and likely found cruising other men difficult.

Several Kennedy insiders were thought to be gay, although only Joe Alsop ever acknowledged it, and then probably only because he had to after the KGB incident. According to Gore Vidal, who knew Jack and who socialized with him both before he became president and afterward,

"Jack had acquired a number of fag friends, as Bobby liked to call them." Jackie, too, had gay and bisexual friends, including Leonard Bernstein, Rudolph Nureyev, and Truman Capote. It never seemed much of an issue to her, having been raised in an elite circle where gays were part of the woodwork. But neither Jack nor Jackie ever mentioned the subject in public. Any talk about gays at the time was safely behind closed doors and not for mass consumption. It may have been the swinging, liberal sixties, but most gays still were invisible. Outwardly, the Kennedy administration maintained a macho, heterosexual image. But there is no doubt that Jack and Jackie were decades ahead of their time in their comfort level with gay people.

Gore Vidal, who has always declined to classify himself by sexual orientation but who has written that he had many sexual encounters with men, agrees with that viewpoint. "I think he [Jack] felt quite comfortable in the company of homosexuals as long as they were smart enough to hold his interest." It might be more accurate to say that Jack felt comfortable in the company of men, straight or gay, who could hold his interest. Questions of sexuality as distinct from emotional involvement are of course enormously complicated. Some heterosexual men disdain close friendships with other men, while others welcome them and seem to need them. Jack was clearly in the latter category. Despite his sexual interest in women, Jack's closest attachments were with men, most saliently, of course, with Lem.

Author Seymour Hersh quotes a woman who had an affair with Jack as saying that she "came to understand that Kennedy's most significant attachments were not to women but to men." Jewel Reed, the wife of Jack's navy friend James Reed, said that she eventually became disturbed by Jack's "tremendous power over men—more than women. Jack was more comfortable with men than with women," she said. This may be one reason men were so comfortable with him. Even hard-nosed reporters in Washington wanted to be close to Jack. Seduced by his charm and charisma, many placed their friendship with him above their responsibility to the public as journalists.

Seasoned authors, as well, were seduced by Jack's allure. Gore tells of a lunch he attended with Jack and playwright Tennessee Williams, whom Gore called "The Bird." It was in 1958, two years before Jack became president. Before the lunch, Jack told Gore he knew exactly how to flatter writers: "Always say you admire their least successful work," he said. As the lunch got under way, Jack looked at The Bird approvingly and proceeded to praise his play *Summer and Smoke*. The Bird's mood instantly improved. He was immediately convinced that the future president must be a fan. Jack knew that both of his luncheon companions were gay before they all sat down together, but of course that subject would not be raised in the staid 1950s. When Jack got up to leave and walked away, The Bird said, according to Gore, "Look at that ass." "Bird," Gore said, "you can't cruise our next president." The Bird responded that the American people would never send a couple as glamorous as Jack and Jackie to the White House. Gore said he later told Jack about the incident and Jack replied, "That's exciting."

Gore, who also knew Lem, said he often wondered about the friendship between Jack and Lem but never really pursued the issue with Jack. He was not in the habit of discussing his own sexuality at the time, let alone anyone else's. But Gore has no doubt that Lem was gay. In his memoir, *Palimpsest,* he says that Lem picked up a friend of his in Times Square and "while Billings was in the hotel bathroom, my friend noticed his unusual name on a tag sewed to a sock," a habit acquired in boarding school. "One night at the White House, I was tempted to remind Lem of that encounter, but refrained," he added. It can now be confirmed that the man whom Lem met that night was George Armstrong, a former longtime reporter for the *Guardian* newspaper in England.

Even though Jack was very loyal to his friends, he was always sensitive to criticism, according to Lem. "Nobody read his press criticism with greater displeasure than Jack Kennedy," he remarked. "In fact, he read his bad press much more thoroughly than his good press, and usually got himself all excited about it, calling up to find out this, that, or the other. I think it was a form of excitement for him. He certainly got more adrenaline going with bad press than with good. . . . He did seem to really be upset about any criticism, from whatever source." This was particularly the case if the criticism came from a friend, Lem added, but it had to be very strong and continue for a long time before he would eventually ditch the friend.

Two examples of Jack eventually discarding a friendship were Clare Boothe Luce, whose egotistical war reporting was once hilariously satirized by Dorothy Parker as "All Quiet on the Claire Front," and Arthur

Krock. Jack had once been very close to the wife of Henry Luce, the founder of *Time* magazine. But she had gradually become more critical of him; she became downright scathing when he was president. Lem, who also knew her, said she seemed to think that Jack was insufficiently grateful for the help and encouragement she had given him when he was a young congressman. Nevertheless, Jack invited her to the White House. "I think that was the end of it, because I think right after that she wrote something again. That was the end of her as far as he was concerned," Lem remembered.

More disturbing to Jack was the end of his friendship with Arthur Krock, Lem recalled. The *New York Times* columnist and Kennedy family friend had also become increasingly strident in his criticism of Jack's presidency. Krock had seen the potential in Jack as a very young man and was instrumental in helping Jack publish *Why England Slept* in 1940. When Jack was unable to find an established publisher himself, Krock helped him secure a contract with a new publisher—Wilfred Funk—who was prepared to commit to the book. Because of their long association, the criticism by Krock was "very, very hard on Jack," recalled Lem. "He seemed to pick on him with purpose."

Jack could also be tough on a newspaperman whom he considered a friend. Ben Bradlee and Charlie Bartlett were both on the receiving end of complaints by Jack about coverage. But he thought their reporting was fair, remembered Lem. "I know he always read what they wrote and he called them if he didn't like it." But they didn't do anything "mean or spiteful," he added. Jack did distance himself from Ben for a while, however, because he felt that Ben "had taken advantage of his friendship in his reporting" on a few occasions, said Lem. But it didn't affect the friendship. "Ben continued to be a friend of his till the day he died."

Not long after the Alsop dinner, Jack and Jackie were to be the guests of Mahomedali Currim Chagla, the Indian ambassador to the United States, who wanted to show the Kennedys an Indian film said to be the work of one of his country's greatest artists. The Kennedys' acceptance of the invitation was a signal to the diplomatic community of the great importance attached to U.S.-Indian relations.

Even though India was a neutral country, it was the world's largest democracy and exercised enormous influence at the time under the charismatic Jawaharlal Nehru, who had led his country since independence from Britain in 1947. No matter. Jackie feigned illness and backed out of the engagement shortly before she and Jack were supposed to show up.

Jack had to go to the deadly event without Jackie. Senator John Sherman Cooper, who had been U.S. ambassador to India in the Eisenhower administration, accompanied the president in place of his wife. The Indian ambassador was deeply disappointed when Jack arrived without the First Lady. Jack, in turn, was deeply disappointed that the film lasted almost two hours and felt like three or four.

So Jack determined to get a little revenge on Jackie for leaving him in the lurch. After the event, he invited the Coopers over to the White House for one of the tours he always loved giving visitors. Halfway through, he told the Coopers that Jackie hadn't really been sick and he proposed that they knock on her door. Jackie was inside sitting up in her four-poster bed happily reading—obviously not sick at all. Jack teased her about the subterfuge.

Jack enjoyed practical jokes and loved nothing more than to tease and be teased. He saw no reason to stop the fun just because he was president. The chief targets of his teasing were Jackie and Lem. Jack was always introducing Lem to visiting leaders and dignitaries as General Billings, or Senator Billings, or some such title. Invariably, visitors would be impressed, believing that Lem really was a senator or a general. Sometimes it became embarrassing, however, when Lem was asked his opinion about a particular bill in Congress or an important military matter about which he had no idea. Jack derived enormous pleasure out of seeing Lem squirm his way out of these situations. "I remember he introduced me to Chancellor Adenauer [of West Germany] as Mr. Billings, one of our top cultural people, and to the first astronaut, Captain [Alan] Shepherd, as Congressman Billings," Lem said.

On one occasion, Indian premier Jawaharlal Nehru and his daughter, Indira, were visiting. While Jack met with Nehru, Jackie and Lem met with Indira in another room. After the meetings, Jackie mentioned to Jack that Lem had gotten along very well with Indira. Later, a series of messages was sent to Lem from Blair House, where Indira was staying, requesting the pleasure of his company. Each one would be more inviting than the last—first a luncheon invitation and then a dinner invitation, and so on. Lem was pleased with himself. He would return the calls, but each time he was told that Madame Gandhi was not available. Eventually, Lem found out that Indira's longing for his company was a game that Jack had played, with the cooperation of the White House switchboard. It was Jack who was behind the calls. Madame Gandhi had scarcely given a thought to Mr. Lem Billings.

On another occasion, later in Jack's presidency, Lem returned from France boasting that he had become friendly with screen legend Greta Garbo. He had been introduced to her by a mutual friend in Europe. Lem told Jack that not only was Garbo as beautiful as her screen persona, she also had a terrific sense of humor. Lem also told Jack that he and Garbo were an item and that they had gotten to know each other so well they had taken a tour by car together along the Italian Riviera.

Jack decided that Lem had boasted and name-dropped enough and decided to teach him a lesson. So he hatched a plan. He invited Garbo to the White House and asked Lem to come, as well. The evening was planned so that Garbo would arrive before Lem, giving Jack a chance to chat with the actress and lay the groundwork for his scheme.

When Lem arrived—a little full of himself—Jackie came over to greet him with Garbo at her side. Jack hovered around mischievously as Lem prepared to greet the special guest. "Greta," said Lem. Garbo looked taken aback. She paused, looked at Lem with a blank stare, and said, "I have never seen this man before." Lem froze on the spot.

Then Jack, Jackie, Garbo, and a very uncomfortable Lem sat down for dinner. Jack let Lem squirm for a full half hour, during which time Lem tried to remind Garbo of all the occasions on which they had been together. Jack sheepishly pretended to help out, suggesting at one point that Lem might have met a double of Ms. Garbo. Finally, Lem was let in on the joke and told that Jack had persuaded Garbo to play along with his scheme. Jack, Jackie, and Garbo laughed uproariously, while Lem grinned nervously. Lem eventually recovered enough to enjoy the dinner.

It was a night to remember—Jackie, Jack, and Lem—and Garbo. But it would always be an unbearably sad memory for Lem. As he said good night and walked out of the White House into the chilly autumn air, he had no way of knowing that it would be the last time he would see Jack. The dinner took place on November 13, 1963. Just over a week later, Jack went to Dallas.

In view of Lem's interest in the arts, architecture, and decoration, it was natural that he would be interested in Jackie's desire to refurbish the White House. After much thought, she became convinced that its renovation should be a defining achievement of her time as First Lady. She was appalled at how run-down the White House had become, and how few American works of art adorned its walls. She felt that since it was an eighteenth- and nineteenth-century house, the furnishings and decorations should reflect the period. She resolved to do something about it, with Jack's full support. Lem was there to help her as she set about the task. Although he gave her advice, particularly about the renovation of the second and third floors, most of the ideas were her own.

A year after Jackie entered the White House, the results of her efforts were shown to a nationwide television audience. "Tour of the White House with Mrs. John F. Kennedy" was watched by over eighty million Americans, who saw Jackie guiding CBS veteran Charles Collingwood around all the various rooms. She also discussed her plans for completing the renovation. Jack appeared for a few minutes in the program, which unfortunately was broadcast in black and white.

Even though they were both devoted to Jack, Lem and Jackie knew that they could never have Jack all to themselves. Jack had never been the kind of person who could be satisfied with just a few people in his life. He wanted and needed friends of all kinds. Each one seemed to offer him something different. Chuck Spalding and Bill Walton were two of his closest personal friends. Newspapermen Charlie Bartlett and Ben Bradlee also became trusted pals. He was also enormously devoted to the friends he'd made in the navy during the war years.

Chief among these was Red Fay, who became his undersecretary of the navy. Jack liked to reminisce about old times with Red. He also liked to go out on the town with him. He saw no reason why that should change just because he was now the president. With Red, Jack developed the habit of sneaking out to the movies—trailed by anxious Secret Service agents— even though there was a movie theater in the White House.

In the first few weeks at the White House, for example, when Jackie and Lem were working on the children's rooms, Jack and Red went to see *Spartacus,* with Kirk Douglas. It was playing at the Warner Theater just a few blocks down the street. Jack was very interested in the script, which was written by Dalton Trumbo, one of the blacklisted writers from the early 1950s. Douglas made a big dent in the blacklist by insisting that Trumbo be listed in the credits under his own name and not under a pseudonym, as had hitherto been the practice for blacklisted writers who could still find work.

Jack and Red's trips to the movies were a nightmare for the Secret Service, which had a great deal of difficulty keeping up with the pair. For example, they had to make sure no one was sitting behind the president and Red as they were watching the film. But Jack loved this kind of time alone with old friends. He needed and wanted male companionship, especially men who were intelligent and had a good sense of humor. "I just seem to be attracted by men like that," he said once. "Maybe it's chemical." Despite his need for a wide variety of male friends, however, everyone knew that Lem, his oldest friend, was number one.

The president would frequently skip out of the White House onto the streets of Washington with Lem, usually wearing some form of disguise. On one occasion, just a few weeks after his inauguration, he put on slacks, a sports jacket, and old shoes and went with Lem for a forty-five-minute walk on the busy streets in the vicinity of 1600 Pennsylvania Avenue. He even donned a hat (he generally hated hats) and carried a walking stick, just to make sure he would not be recognized. The two old friends no doubt enjoyed the subterfuge.

"The great thing about Jack Kennedy is that nothing changed him, not even the presidency. He was always the same guy with the same sense of humor," said Charlie Bartlett, who met Jack before he got into politics. He loved to relax with Lem, "who was always there to help him unwind. Lem was a stable presence for Jack," he added. "Lem's raison d'être was Jack Kennedy. I don't think it's true that he did not have views of his own, as some have said. He had a very independent mind. He had interests of his own that Jack didn't necessarily share. He certainly didn't have the same interest in politics and women that Jack had." What was the connection? "I think they had the same understanding of what life was all about."

∽

Jackie and Lem continued to get along well during the White House years. She respected his love of the arts, his interest in antiques, and his skill with home renovation. He was always willing to help her, as well as Jack, in anything that she asked. Lem was someone she knew well and with whom she could converse easily without the stiffness and artificiality that often crept into conversations with aides. Their senses of humor also generally meshed. But it was not a friendship made in heaven, as was the case with Jack and Lem. "His relationship with Jackie never seemed to me to be that easy," said Charlie Bartlett. "I didn't have the feeling that they had enormous rapport. He was always the third person at dinner." Lem's live-in dog sitter during the early 1970s, Sigrid Gassner-Roberts, said that Lem "did not particularly like her, but he admired her and respected her. He thought she was a terrific mother."

To the extent that there was tension in the friendship between Jackie and Lem, Lem's omnipresence was the essential problem. But although Jackie sometimes resented Lem's constant desire to be with Jack—and Jack's need for Lem—she knew that they had developed a close bond over many years and that it was there to stay. It was a fact of life that she accepted, one of many required to be the wife of John Fitzgerald Kennedy. She never really tried to figure their friendship out. What Jack wanted was usually good enough for her.

It is difficult to dissect precisely what role Lem played in Jack and Jackie's marriage at this stage. She didn't see Lem as an intrusion most of the time. Sometimes, Lem acted as a kind of intermediary between Jack and Jackie, as he had in the early years of their marriage when there were rough patches. In some ways—and sometimes—Jackie wanted Lem to be there as much as Jack. In addition, in some ways she had more in common with Lem than with Jack.

Most of all, Jackie and Lem were drawn to each other by their love of the president. They both wanted the best for him and were committed to helping him make his presidency a success. And in one way, they were in the same boat. They both struggled to keep his attention as he went off in a million different directions with legions of admirers clamoring for his attention. Jackie was also used to having Lem around long before the White House years. Lem had been a fixture at their home when the Kennedys lived in Georgetown during the 1950s.

The White House usher, J. B. West, tells of Jackie going to great lengths to ward off unwanted houseguests at the White House. He says she once instructed the White House staff to put open paint cans, drop cloths, and ladders in both the Lincoln and Queen bedrooms to make it seem that the rooms were being renovated. It was a ruse to keep visitors away.

But she made an exception for Lem, whom she was glad to see—on most occasions. "He was always at the White House," said West. And he was always full of surprises. On one occasion, Lem flew down from New York and arrived at the White House with two hamsters, a gift from a little boy in Manhattan, for Caroline's birthday. They were named Debbie and Billie. The two furry creatures were a handful, however. They were always breaking out of their cages—taking their own White House tour whenever they felt like it—usually with Caroline and the White House staff in hot pursuit.

There were times, however, when Jackie felt that Lem came to stay too often, times when she wanted to be alone with Jack on the second floor of the White House. On these occasions, she resented Lem's presence. "Lem Billings," Jackie told West, "has been a houseguest every weekend since I've been married." The comment reflected the frustration she sometimes felt with the mysterious, almost inexplicable bond between Jack and Lem and their need to spend a lot of time with each other. But, according to those who knew Jack and Jackie, there is no doubt that she appreciated Lem most of the time.

Jackie learned that, whatever the nature of the bond between Jack and Lem, it would not lessen now just because Jack was president. She sensed that Jack needed Lem more than ever. As president, he carried enormous responsibilities and burdens. Who better to help him shoulder them than his oldest friend, who knew everything about him? If Lem was good for Jack, Jackie felt that it was good enough for her despite the protective net she built around her immediate family. Through all the ups and downs of Jack's years in the White House—Cuba, Berlin, Vietnam, relations with the Soviet Union—it was Lem, as well as Jackie, upon whom he most relied when he needed to regroup.

The relationship between Jackie and Lem was complicated, said Sally Carpenter, Lem's niece. "They were quite different in temperament. But he helped her a lot and she appreciated him. He also was wonderful with the children. He was involved with them a lot and would take them out," especially in the years when Jackie was on her own. "I have a wonderful letter that she wrote to him. And I know that letter meant a lot to him." In 1978, at a birthday party for John and Caroline, who were eighteen and twenty-one, respectively, that year, Lem was one of her honored guests.

During Jack's time in the presidency, the White House switchboard got used to Lem's telephone calls. Whenever he possibly could, Jack would take them. He had a recording system and taped many of the telephone calls he received, and made, by pressing a hidden button. The person at the other end didn't know he or she was being recorded. Jack installed the system to compile a record of important developments in his presidency. Few personal calls were taped, but on one day in 1962, Jack hit the button and recorded a phone call from Lem.

The telephone conversation between the two friends took place at 2:30 on the afternoon of September 29, 1962. Jack and Lem were trying to arrange to get together in Newport, Rhode Island. Interestingly, Lem mentioned the "Mississippi thing," a reference to the battle of wills then under way between President Kennedy and Mississippi governor Ross Barnett over the admission of African American student James Meredith into the University of Mississippi. Clearly, Lem wanted Jack, who sounds somewhat distracted in the conversation, to know that he understood what he was dealing with. Jack was unsure whether he would be able to make it to Newport that night to see Lem and his friend from Harvard, Torby Macdonald. Lem seemed to be having his own difficulties in getting there, too.

The following is a transcript of their short telephone chat:

PRESIDENT:	Lem, hello, Lem.
LEM:	Hello.
PRESIDENT:	Where are you?
LEM:	Oh hi, I'm a . . . I missed my damn plane so I'm gonna have to shoot up to Boston and back to Providence.
PRESIDENT:	Oh, I see. Well, I'm still . . . doesn't look like I may be able to go there.
LEM:	Oh, go at all?

PRESIDENT:	That's right.
LEM:	Oh, I better not go until . . . until you know.
PRESIDENT:	OK. You're in a. . . . Just leave your message where we can—.
LEM:	I'm at LaGuardia now. When do you think you'd know or don't know?
PRESIDENT:	Well, it looks like it will be sometime. . . . Why don't you go back in to New York?
LEM:	All right.
PRESIDENT:	And then I will be in touch with you.
LEM:	OK. Good.
PRESIDENT:	Because I . . . because you can always come up later.
LEM:	OK. I guess it's not going too well, huh?
PRESIDENT:	Where?
LEM:	For you, because of the Mississippi thing.
PRESIDENT:	Yeah.
LEM:	OK. Well, I'll see you later.
PRESIDENT:	OK. Bye.

For Lem, some of the best times during the White House years were spent with Jack and Jackie at Glen Ora, the Kennedys' home in Middleburg, Virginia. They went there on weekends whenever they could. "Jackie would usually go down Friday, spend Friday night there, and we would come down Saturday and spend Saturday and Sunday night and come back the very first thing and be in the White House about nine o'clock Monday morning," Lem said. "But then sometimes Jackie would stay over Monday, but usually she'd come back with us. She really loved it at Glen Ora because of the horses. Remember, riding was very important to Jackie—and she felt she had to be in the horse country during weekends. Jack didn't like the place too much because there was nothing to do there," added Lem. "He didn't like it at all except for the restfulness of it."

"I'll give you an exact schedule because even there he lived by schedule," Lem continued. "I probably went down about as many weekends as he did. I really was there a lot. The funny thing is that he didn't ask me as much as Jackie did. This may sound strange but I think the reason they asked me—and of course I loved going—but the reason I think that they had me was because there was so little for him to do and Jackie wanted to do some riding but she certainly didn't want to leave him alone. She would have felt guilty, I suppose, about going riding, so I'm sure that's why Jackie made tremendous efforts to get me there every time they went down." Lem added: "I didn't like Middleburg particularly, but I always have enjoyed him and I welcomed the opportunity to spend so much time with him."

In fact, it was Lem whom Jackie asked to find a suitable place for the Kennedys during the summer before the presidential election. "Here I am, a bachelor, looking for a big house, which was rather difficult to explain to the real estate man," Lem remembered. On one occasion, Jackie went with him. "And she wore a wig and dark glasses and fooled nobody. . . . Needless to say, she didn't like anything I liked and we had to start all over again. I think Bunny Mellon [a friend of Jackie's] finally found Glen Ora and instead of buying, they rented," said Lem.

Jack wasn't crazy about paying what he regarded as excessive rent for Glen Ora, Lem recalled. But Jackie loved the place, and Jack said that Jackie would often sulk if she didn't get her way and Jack would most often give in to her. "Jackie usually got what she wanted with him," Lem said. "It wasn't worth any problems with Jackie. Jackie had discovered his Achilles' heel, which was the fact that he couldn't stand sulkers. I discovered that thirty years ago and it doesn't take long to discover that if you know somebody well. He just couldn't stand anybody around him sulking." Not long before he died, Jackie persuaded Jack to have a new house, which they would own, built in the country on Snake Mountain. But they were together there for only a few weekends before Dallas. Jack was in "complete shock" about how much money Jackie had spent on it, Lem said. "He was very close with a buck."

Lem said Jack would have preferred a place on the Chesapeake Bay, because he loved the water so much, or rather just stuck with Camp David in Maryland. "There were so many things you could do at Camp David. Sometimes we would take the helicopter and go to visit the different Civil War battlefields in the area," Lem said. "He was a real nut on the Civil War and he knew as much about the Civil War as anybody." Of course, there was always Cape Cod in Massachusetts when the president wanted to be near the water, Lem remarked. On some weekends, Jack

Jack, Lem, and Caroline enjoying the water, Hyannis Port, 1963.

and Lem would go up there. "I would take the shuttle down to Washington, go to the White House and we would be picked up by helicopter there—flown to Andrews [Air Force Base] and taken Air Force One to Otis on the Cape. From there we would helicopter right to his father's front lawn. Of course, he had always loved the Cape and was completely happy there." He recalled that Jackie "complained bitterly," however, about eating every meal with the family, and so sometimes they ate separately. On other weekends, Jack and Jackie might visit her family at Hammersmith Farm in Newport, Rhode Island. Lem even went there with them sometimes.

For Lem, the best of times during the presidential years was sailing with Jack and Jackie off the coast of Cape Cod, lighthearted occasions at the White House, and the weekends at Glen Ora. The latter, especially, was one of the few places Jack could get away from politics. Here, the two lifelong friends would engage in their passion for backgammon. "We'd always play backgammon," Lem recalled. "We'd have these terrible arguments about what we were paying for each point, and we'd really fight and argue over that every single game because I never wanted to play for high stakes, and he did."

"We would sit around after dinner and watch television or talk and

he would go to bed quite early," Lem continued. "I'd say he'd go to bed
at about eleven o'clock and usually Jackie would go to bed then, too. And
they didn't really go to bed, because I could hear the television going
and the records going." Sometimes, Jackie would go to bed later and stay
up talking with Lem. "Jackie had a lot of other friends there, but he
[Jack] never wanted to see them," Lem added. "We [Jack and Lem]
would drive around and we would go look at old houses and look where
people lived and then we would come back for lunch." Jack liked to drive
himself, although the Secret Service would not be far behind.

Lem knew that if a political problem was really bothering Jack it
would affect his mood. But he also knew from long experience how to
improve Jack's disposition. This happened many times during Jack's presidency. The first occasion occurred early in the administration following
the Bay of Pigs fiasco. The attack on Fidel Castro's regime in April 1961,
by Cuban exiles bankrolled and trained by the CIA, was a disaster. This
failure so early in Jack's presidency triggered not only a mood change but
a virtual depression. Jack felt that his entire presidency might already be
down the tube. Lem kept a diary for the two weekends after the Bay of
Pigs, when he was with Jack at Glen Ora, the only time he ever kept one
with the exception of their vacation together in Europe in 1937. But he
did not keep it for long. "I stopped after two weekends because I felt I
was being dishonest to him," Lem said, presumably because he did not
tell the president what he was doing.

During the weekend at Glen Ora after the Bay of Pigs, Lem talked
with Jack extensively about it, helping him to put it in perspective and
bolstering his self-confidence and sense of purpose. "He constantly
blamed himself for the Cuban fiasco," Lem wrote in the diary on April
29, 1961. "I asked him if he had bawled out those responsible and he
said he hadn't, but they were well aware of their responsibility in the mistake. Of course, he has lost confidence in them and this makes the Laos
situation that much more difficult. He knows he cannot afford to make
another mistake. He asked me if I wanted to send troops into Laos—of
course, I would rather not if there were any other way. . . . He said Rusk
[Secretary of State Dean Rusk] wanted to get into Laos."

Few people remember the Laotian situation today compared with
that in South Vietnam. This is because Jack favored a negotiated settlement between the communist and noncommunist factions there that

eventually led to a neutralist coalition government under Prince Sou-
vanna Phouma in 1962. Unlike in South Vietnam later, the situation in
Laos was diffused without the involvement of American forces. If the Bay
of Pigs fiasco had not occurred, Jack might have been tempted to send
thousands of U.S. military advisors into Laos, as he later did in South
Vietnam, although Lem always said Jack would never have sent combat
troops there and involve the country in a war that Lem later said "did no
good for anybody." We do not know what effect Lem's advice to stay out
of Laos if possible—one of the few occasions on which Lem offered an
opinion on foreign policy to Jack—had on him. Jack likely was more
influenced by the views of General MacArthur, who "advised him
strongly against sending troops to Laos," Lem wrote in his diary. No
doubt, McArthur was thinking of the U.S. experience in Korea and
feared intervention by Red China once again.

What we do know is that after the Bay of Pigs, Jack became
extremely cautious about another involvement. "He was desperately
unhappy about the result [at the Bay of Pigs] and he, as we know, publicly took complete blame, as he should have. But, as we all know, it was
so damn unfair really, because he had only been in the White House,
what, a month," Lem said later in an interview. "It was hard to console
him. . . . He became more somber." Lem recalls Jack saying, "Lyndon can
have it in 1964." In his diary, Lem wrote, "All during the weekend, he
said he certainly wasn't interested in a second term—that this was the
most unpleasant job existent."

One clear consequence of the crisis was that Jack would never again
blindly rely on the CIA and the Joint Chiefs of Staff, a fact of critical
importance during the Cuban Missile Crisis a year later, when most of
his advisors were urging an invasion of the island. Although Lem was
always willing to listen to Jack talk about political situations and discuss
them with him, he rarely offered political advice—Laos and Cuba being
the major exceptions. He saw his role as doing for Jack what he always
had done—supporting him, soothing him, relaxing him. The only difference was that he was now providing solace and comfort to a friend
who was the president of the United States.

The extent to which Jack confided in Lem about the political crises
during his presidency has not been widely known. It was not just confined to the Bay of Pigs. Lem also learned about the Cuban Missile Crisis

long before even key members of the government knew what was going on, let alone the public. "I'm sure he knew I wouldn't repeat anything," said Lem. "I knew about Cuba. . . . I was with him during the Bay of Pigs episode as well as the Cuban Missile Crisis." A close friend of Lem's tells of a conversation he had with Lem years later about the issue. Thales Vassilikiotis, who met Lem on Aristotle Onassis's yacht while visiting the Greek island of Mykonos in the early 1960s with Jackie, recounts Lem saying that Jack was very concerned about the near-unanimous advice he was getting to invade Cuba during the missile crisis. "Lem said he encouraged the president to follow his instincts and not listen to his advisors. 'You're the president. If you don't want to do it, don't do it,' Lem said." Vassilikiotis added, "JFK had wisdom enough to trust his boyhood friend."

Again, this was not because Jack valued Lem's political input on the crisis or wished to discuss with him the choices he faced in trying to successfully remove the missiles from the island without triggering a nuclear war. Rather, it was because during this supreme test of national will and endurance, Jack needed someone he could totally trust with whom he could vent—someone who was a calming influence, someone who believed in him, who could reassure him that his instincts were sound. During a crisis when one wrong move could have led to massive destruction and loss of life, the importance of the role that Lem Billings played behind the scenes cannot be overestimated. We now know that, had an invasion of the island occurred, a nuclear war almost certainly would have been triggered.

There is also a reference in Lem's diary on April 29, 1961, to the situation in Algeria, where the National Liberation Front (FLN), whom the French labeled terrorists, was fighting a war to free its country from foreign rule. Jack had always been sympathetic to the various struggles for national independence against the European colonial powers, even though most of them were members of NATO and U.S. allies. As a senator, he had made a major speech condemning French rule in Algeria. He didn't change his viewpoint after becoming president. His assistant secretary of state for Africa, G. Mennen "Soapy" Williams, infuriated the Europeans with just one sentence: "Africa for the Africans." And Jack backed him up at a news conference, famously saying, "Who should Africa be for?" Lem held the same viewpoint as Jack. "Ridiculously enough, they [the French] are blaming the United States for encouraging the insurgents," Lem wrote in his diary. "He [Jack] said that he wished he wasn't going over to see de Gaulle and he would call it off if it were possible." But the trip in fact occurred the following month.

On May 7, 1961, Lem wrote, "He asked me if I would like to go to Paris—he might have been kidding in that when I inquired if I would be able to attend the big dinner and entertainment at Versailles—he said he didn't think that would be possible. I would like to go anyway and will check with him again on this." In fact, Jack did take Lem, as well as Eunice, on that European trip in June, though Lem didn't make it over there in time to attend the dinner with Jack and Jackie at Versailles. "Of course, it was terribly disappointing to miss this," Lem said. "But it was the last official function I missed for the entire trip, except, of course, the small private dinner given at Buckingham Palace by the queen." But he expressed regret about that, as well. "I was quite fed up because I was not invited—only the president's family went."

Not all Lem's diary entries were about politics or affairs of state. Earlier on April 30, 1961, he wrote, "No one called the president for church this morning until about ten minutes before Mass time. He burst into my room and asked why I hadn't wakened him—which of course was silly." It was an indication that Jack could still get steamed up even if the issue was trivial. At the weekend getaways in Glen Ora, Jack and Lem made a point of watching *Meet the Press* and *Face the Nation,* although Lem wondered whether it was worth it. Jack would often get riled up about something someone said that he thought was unfair. He had a pretty thin skin as far as the press was concerned. Lem remembers him throwing a copy of *Time* magazine into the fire rather than reading it because something about the issue annoyed him. Even though the media largely adored him and gave him overwhelmingly favorable coverage, he was still upset if he felt a story was unfairly critical. Lem would reassure him that it really was not that important.

Lem also bolstered his resolve and determination whenever he saw evidence of it flagging. In his diary entry for May 7, 1961, Lem wrote, "He told me again that he probably wouldn't run in '64. He feels things can't get better—that the Communists will constantly be making inroads by creating crises all over the world. He believes they will be tougher and tougher. I said I couldn't believe he would like to turn over the country to Lyndon. He agreed that this would be bad as he hasn't been too impressed with Lyndon in the different crises that have come up to date."

Most often at Glen Ora, however, Lem would try to get Jack's mind off politics—not an easy task for the number-one political animal in the country. In this informal setting, they would often talk about the old days and all the good times at Choate and Princeton, during the weekends they met in New York, and in Palm Beach and Hyannis Port. It was here at Glen Ora, away from the White House, that their friendship most resembled the way it used to be. Glen Ora was not only a good place for Jack to unwind, it was also an opportunity for him to rejuvenate and to rest his back, which continued to cause pain that was sometimes debilitating. Lem said that Jack told him that he would trade all his political success and his money for Lem's health if he did not have to suffer back pain any longer.

Asked a year after Jack died why they were so close despite their differing interests and temperaments, and why their friendship had changed so little over the years, Lem said, "I suppose it must have changed a little, but I probably spent more time with him than any of his friends, even during his years in the presidency. . . . He relaxed with me because I didn't really talk to him about any political matters, or any of the matters he had on his mind all during his workweek, and I mean this from the time he was congressman on through the presidency. I don't know that we had a lot of things in common. I guess just the fact that we'd known each other intimately for thirty-two years is a pretty strong bond in itself, so I felt that I understood him, understood his sense of humor and he understood mine. I guess, just by habit, that we continued to enjoy each other. It's very easy to see why I enjoyed him. I suppose that he felt the same way. I think that was it. Probably having me around was relaxing, because he knew me so well. I don't know what else it was."

Later, Lem expanded on his comments. "Perhaps this was our common bond. He had never really been secretive with me. We grew up as boys together and we shared secrets, or whatever you might call them. He always told me things and he never held anything back from me. . . . I knew more about his personal life than his family did. I certainly did in his youth. You asked why we were close. Maybe it was because he could really tell me everything. He knew through the years that I never told anybody." Despite his closeness to the entire Kennedy family as well as Jack, Lem said that the friendship with Jack was of a totally different nature. He was never as close to other members of the family. "I really don't know any of them as I knew Jack and the longer he is dead, the more I realize this. No one in the family shares their confidences with me as Jack did, and with reason. Why should they? I think they are extremely careful of what they say on every personal subject."

Newspaperman Charlie Bartlett thinks the explanation for the bond between Jack and Lem is really quite simple. Lem "was devoted to Jack and wanted to help Jack get what he wanted. He was cheerful and upbeat, an enormous asset to the president," he said. "I think it was a very healthy relationship. I always thought Lem was a classy guy and Jack would have liked that. Jack trusted Lem totally."

Despite Lem's comments, there were occasions when Jack did seek Lem's advice on official matters, mostly in areas where he thought his friend had expertise. This included anything to do with the arts or social etiquette. Before his June 1961 trip to Europe to meet de Gaulle in Paris and Khrushchev in Vienna, Jack went up to Hyannis Port with Lem. He told Lem that he didn't have any gift for the Russian leader and asked him for his ideas. Lem suggested he give the Russian leader his model of the USS *Constitution*. This had been a gift to Jack from Joe. Jack had wanted to buy it himself but thought the price too high. He asked Lem whether he thought Joe would buy it for his birthday, knowing full well that Lem would pass on the message to his father. Lem did, and Joe bought it for Jack. Now he had his gift for Khrushchev—not that it made the Russian leader any more pleasant during their meeting in Austria.

But before Vienna there was Paris. The president was taken aback by how popular Jackie, who spoke fluent French, was with the French people in general and with de Gaulle in particular. "I am the man who accompanied Jacqueline Kennedy to Paris and I've enjoyed it," Jack famously said at the state dinner given in honor of the American president and his wife. The American couple was a gigantic hit in France despite the growing tensions in the U.S.-French relationship. Rose also went to Paris. But, according to Lem, Jack wasn't too happy about it. "He was very fed up with his mother going." But he felt that there was nothing he could do about it, he added.

In Vienna, too, the Kennedys were greeted like movie stars. Lem was on this leg of the journey, where Jack met a bombastic Nikita

Khrushchev. "Of course, I have arrived with the president on Air Force One at the airports of many American cities—but this was the first time I had been with him on the arrival in a foreign city," Lem said. "His ovations as president had always been tremendous but in Vienna there were many more people than I had ever seen before—all of them roaring with enthusiasm." The Austrian government gave an enormous dinner for the two heads of state. Lem recalled chatting with Mrs. Khrushchev about her apparently hardworking daughter-in-law. "Madame Khrushchev shot back that of course she has a cook and a maid and a nurse," not exactly Lem's image of life in Russia among the ruling class.

The major story out of Vienna was Jack's meeting with Khrushchev. The American leader seemed unable to get his Russian counterpart to engage in a rational discussion. Even Jackie's presence at the social events did not seem to soothe Khrushchev, who, in his meetings with Jack, was surly and ill-tempered and given to long ideological harangues. On Air Force One en route to England, Lem saw how disturbed Jack was by the confrontation. "I only saw him really upset once in my life and that was after he left Austria after he confronted Khrushchev." Jack told Lem that he had "never come face-to-face with such evil." Lem was always able to calm Jack's nerves and distract his attention from affairs of state. His skills in this regard were tested as never before on this occasion.

The following year, Lem went on an official trip without Jack. In 1962, Lem, Jean, and Eunice visited Poland, a visit that almost resulted in a diplomatic incident. They all attended a state dinner at the former Radziwill Palace, which the communists had nationalized. Lem noticed that the silverware was engraved with the Radziwill coat of arms and quietly pocketed some of it to give to Stash Radziwill, the husband of Lee, Jackie's sister. When he heard the story, Jack was furious with Lem for being so cavalier while on an official trip to a communist country. But Lem was unapologetic. He had done something for a friend. The larger political picture, and the damage that could have been caused to Polish–American relations, escaped him.

The most spectacular of the overseas trips was the president's visit to Germany, Ireland, England, and Italy in late June and early July of 1963. Jackie stayed at home on this occasion. Lem, Eunice, and Jean accompanied the president instead. Lee Radziwill joined them when they reached Europe for part of the trip. Of course, as befits a head of state, Jack and

Lem and the rest of the presidential party traveled in style aboard Air Force One and were afforded the finest accommodations by the Europeans, a far cry from the way the two men had toured Europe as young students in 1937.

The political highlight of the European visit was West Berlin, where Jack gave his famous "Ich bin ein Berliner" speech on June 26. "Two thousand years ago, the proudest boast of any man was 'Civis Romanus sum,'" he said. "Today, in the world of freedom, the proudest boast of any man is 'Ich bin ein Berliner.'" The Berliner line was followed by a pause and the sheepish Kennedy smile that Lem, looking down on him from a balcony above where he was speaking, knew only too well. "I appreciate my interpreter translating my German," he ad-libbed. As everyone now knows, he should have said, "Ich bin Berliner," since "ein Berliner" is a jelly doughnut. West Berliners, however, knew what he meant. They roared their approval.

The film of John F. Kennedy on that day, his chestnut hair blowing in the wind, his voice full of energy and defiance, remains among the most vivid images of his presidency, the speech among the most memorable. However, Jack told Lem later that the enthusiasm of the crowd had disturbed him. He felt they had been too easily swayed by his rhetoric. But it wasn't just his words. West Berliners had fallen in love with the Kennedy magic. They probably would have embraced him even if he had read the New York telephone directory. "I'm sure this was one of the high points of the president's life," Lem said later. "It was a hell of an experience to witness the acclaim of a multitude that large. . . . We talked a good deal about that experience."

Although Lem was not there when Jack was attending the political meetings in Germany, he said, "I would always see him whenever he was alone, when he was relaxing . . . whenever he was finished with his official duties. But I was included on all the official dinners and appearances." After the visit to Berlin, the presidential party "flew to some small city where we all stayed together at a hotel" to unwind, said Lem. "It was at that hotel in Germany when we really talked about his experiences. This was an evening off schedule for him, one for relaxation. We all had dinner together in his suite, and his enthusiasm was infectious. There was always a crowd outside the hotel roaring 'Kennedy.'"

After Germany, it was on to the sentimental part of the journey—

Ireland. "I'm pleased to be back from whence I came," Jack said. "It took 115 years for me to make the trip, and six thousand miles, and three generations, but I'm proud to be here." The Irish people are notoriously undemonstrative, but they suspended this aspect of their national character while Jack was there. Jack and Lem and the other Kennedys were overwhelmed by the welcome. They knew that, in part, it was for the country they represented. Jack was the first American president ever to visit Ireland. He was the first Irish American Catholic president, and the Irish laid claim to one of their own. Quoting Joyce and Yeats, Jack addressed the Irish parliament, referring to the country's long struggle for independence. He also went to Arbour Hill Cemetery in Dublin, the gravesite of the Irish patriots who were executed by the British in the Easter Rebellion of 1916. On a cool, rainy day there, he laid a wreath in their memory.

Some of the most informal film ever taken of Jack was shot on his visit to the towns and villages of this ancient country. Telefis Eireann produced a color documentary that shows him—and Lem, Eunice, and Jean—looking relaxed, clearly enjoying themselves. In Dunganstown in County Wexford, not far from New Ross, where Jack's grandfather lived before he emigrated to America, Jack and company visited Mrs. Ryan, the president's cousin. "We want to drink a cup of tea to all the Kennedys who went and all the Kennedys who stayed," he said. In an emotional farewell at Shannon Airport, Jack said, "I'm going to come back and see old Shannon's face again." But it was the last time the Irish would see him.

After their four days in Ireland, Jack and Lem and the rest of the presidential party went to England for a quick twenty-four-hour visit. They landed at the Royal Air Force Base in Waddington in the English Midlands. From there, they flew by helicopter to the estate of the duke and duchess of Devonshire in Chatsworth, apparently causing quite a stir. The duchess later recalled the reaction of one local resident. "The wind from that machine [the president's helicopter] blew my chickens away and I haven't seen them since." Jack wanted to stop off there—before going to see British prime minister Harold Macmillan—to visit the grave of his sister Kick. Jack placed a small bouquet of flowers on Kick's grave, located on a hill near an old Anglican church. The stone marker was inscribed with the words: "In loving memory of Kathleen, 1920–1948, widow of Major, the Marquess of Hartington, killed in action, and daughter of the Hon. Joseph P. Kennedy, sometime ambassador of the United States to Great Britain. Joy she gave—joy she has found."

The most memorable part of the 1963 trip for Lem was the last, the visit to Rome, where "the government gave an enormous official dinner for him at the presidential palace," he recalled. "Of course, I was the only civilian on the trip with absolutely no protocol status. . . . I was always placed as far down the table as possible. I always sat next to a couple of men—as they usually had run out of women by that time." The visit provided an opportunity for Lem to regale Jack with his knowledge of Italian art. Jack decided to test Lem's knowledge. "He sent word down to me that he would like to see me at the head of the table. He told me he was scheduled for an audience with Pope Paul the next morning and that while he was there he would like me to visit the different antiquity shops and bring back to the embassy residence some choice items for him to choose from."

With only ninety minutes available to search the city, Lem was assigned an aide to the president of Italy and a prominent archeologist. The three of them raced from shop to shop, with the Italian officials apparently warning shop owners not to sell any fakes to the representative of the president of the United States. Lem collected twenty-seven pieces in all and brought them back to Jack. He chose two—a little Greek horse from the sixth century B.C. that cost $900 and a life-size head, a Roman copy of Praxiteles' Hermes, that cost $500. The remainder were returned. "God, I don't know why we didn't get more," Jack reportedly said to Lem on the plane back to Washington. Lem then phoned the Italian president's office after they landed, and within a couple of days the Italian ambassador delivered a treasure trove of statues and jewelry to the White House. Jack selected a few more pieces, giving them to Jackie, then passed the rest back to Lem and other friends to make their own choices. This time, nothing was returned.

After he returned from his triumphant trip to Europe in the summer of 1963, Jack was feeling much better about his presidency than he had during the earlier period, when he made serious mistakes. The Peace Corps and Food for Peace programs were now a reality. Major efforts were under way to combat poverty and unemployment. The country was on its way to the moon, "before the decade is out." Major changes were proposed in health care that eventually would become Medicare and Medicaid. Most importantly, he placed his administration squarely behind the struggle against racism and sent a comprehensive civil rights bill to Congress. Overseas, he had stood up to the Russians over West Berlin and the placement of nuclear missiles in Cuba and now felt able to pursue a path of conciliation that would later be called détente. In September, he signed the partial Nuclear Test Ban Treaty with the Soviets—the first major arms control agreement—which set a standard for future negotiations between the superpowers.

In the fall of 1963, Jack was at the top of his game, popular at home, respected overseas. Lem and Jackie and everyone who was close to him said he never felt or looked better.

11

A TOUCH OF CLASS
(1961–63)

"If art is to nourish the roots of our culture, society must set the artist free to follow his vision wherever it takes him. We must never forget that art is not a form of propaganda, it is a form of truth."

—John F. Kennedy, October 26, 1963

Nothing before or since has quite equaled the Kennedy White House. Jack and Jackie occupied the nation's home only for a brief one thousand days, but their time there has lived on in our memories as an extraordinary, even enchanting, period. "Let the skeptics snort about Camelot," said Hugh Sidey, who covered Jack's presidency for *Time* magazine, "but there was something during the Kennedy years that was magic." It is doubtful that either Jack or Jackie—or Lem— thought of it in that way in the early 1960s, however. But they did want to liven things up a bit.

Prior to the Kennedys, official guests invited to the White House had found the atmosphere dull, even stuffy. During the Eisenhower years, for example, the State Dining Room was painted an austere dark green that overwhelmed everything in the room. The furniture was also decidedly dowdy. "It looks as if it's been furnished by discount stores," Jackie said. She called the upstairs family quarters "early Statler" and referred to the oval sitting room as "the Lubianka." The bedroom curtains were "seasick green." The ground floor hall, in Jackie's view, looked like a "dentist office bomb shelter."

More significant than the White House décor for many of the guests when Ike was in charge was the fact that alcohol was forbidden, further dampening the mood. Visitors had to stand in the East Room drinking punch prior to meeting the president and Mamie. No music was allowed until the First Couple appeared, either—sometimes almost an hour later.

This all changed with the arrival of the Kennedys. Champagne and cocktails now were served—a relief to Lem, for whom a drink, or drinks, was really a requirement on social occasions. Jackie overhauled the menu. Prior to her arrival, guests frequently left with a feeling that they had just dined out at a steakhouse chain. But with the hiring of chef René Verdon, the menu was lighter and more varied. "White House entertaining had not merely undergone a change with the Kennedys. You might call it a revolution," said Letitia Baldrige, Jackie's social secretary. "She changed the White House from a plastic to a crystal bowl."

In addition, the guest list underwent a makeover. Artists and scientists were mixed with politicians and statesmen for the first time—including André Malraux, the French minister of culture, who was also an author and had been a World War II resistance leader. At a dinner Jack and Jackie gave in his honor, the great violinist Isaac Stern played for them.

The White House makeover wasn't just Jackie's idea, according to Lem. "The kind of things that were done in the White House during that administration Jackie discussed with him before she did anything," he said. "It was all designed not to please, let's say, Charles de Gaulle, it was designed to please Jack." But Lem said there was no question but that Jackie knew more about art, cuisine, and the finer aspects of life than Jack did, which is why he usually went along with her recommendations. Jack was already interested in art, but Jackie broadened his taste, he added. For example, Jack "would never have gone to a ballet without Jackie's influence," Lem said.

As far as the White House menu was concerned, Jack was concerned only that it curb his growing weight, Lem quipped. During the election campaign, it had surged. "If you look at pictures of him in July 1960 and then look at pictures of him taken in January of 1961, you'll find he was much heavier," Lem remarked. The total weight gain was about fifteen pounds. "Frankly, he was concerned about it," he added.

That was one reason Jack was rigid about his daily exercise in the White House swimming pool, said Lem, although the pool area, which was not air-conditioned, was unbearable to many visitors, including Lem. "Judas Priest, that place was hot. Jack had ideas of getting air-conditioning in there but, while he was alive, they never did." Nevertheless, Lem grudgingly swam with Jack when he was in Washington because he was always happy to have company in the pool. "Actually, Dave Powers was always available but, if there was somebody else like myself there, I'd swim with him instead. Then I'd go up and have lunch with him. After lunch, he always slept for about an hour and a half." What Lem didn't say to interviewers was that whenever Jackie was away, Jack often would have female company in the pool as well.

A steady stream of world-renowned figures made the pilgrimage to what was increasingly being viewed as an American Versailles—without the pomposity. Even legendary cellist Pablo Casals came to the White House to entertain the Kennedys. A strong backer of a return to democracy in Spain, Casals said that he wouldn't play in any country that recognized the fascist government of Francisco Franco, still in power in the 1960s. But Casals made an exception for the America of Jack and Jackie.

Jack always looked forward to the social occasions. It was a chance for him to relax, enjoy good conversation, and be playful. He seldom lost an opportunity to display his wit. At a dinner honoring composer Igor Stravinsky, Leonard Bernstein, the conductor of the New York Philharmonic Orchestra, greeted the musical legend and kissed him on both cheeks, European style. Stravinsky responded in kind. Jack was standing some distance away, noticed the intimate greeting, and called over to the two men, "Hey, how about me?"

Bernstein, who was bisexual, called the episode "endearing and so insanely unpresidential." But the maestro—all the Kennedys' guests really—loved their spontaneity, informality, and joie de vivre. Of course, the alcohol helped. Guests could even smoke, at least in the State Room. Jackie had been a closet smoker for years, although she preferred not to be photographed while she was puffing away. Jack enjoyed the occasional high-priced cigar and had no objection to the photographers snapping him enjoying one.

But Jack and Jackie most enjoyed socializing at the White House when they were with their closest friends—small dinner parties for six or eight with people like Lem, the Fays, the Bartletts, and the Bradlees. The partying often went on till the early hours of the morning, but then the next day Jack and Jackie would be up looking radiant, Lem somewhat less so. Jack wasn't as big a drinker as Lem, usually sipping back a cocktail or two all evening. Lem "sometimes had one too many," recalled Hugh Auchincloss III, Jackie's half brother, who visited the White House frequently and stayed in the Lincoln Bedroom. "Jack put me there because I was a Republican."

When he was among friends, Jack loved letting loose about politics, usually blasting some foreign leader or homegrown opponent who had upset him recently. At these private gatherings, his language was far different from his eloquent public pronouncements. He usually referred to people who annoyed him as "shits" or "bastards." Jawaharlal Nehru was one man Jack didn't like who fit both these categories, in his opinion. "That sanctimonious bastard," he called him. Jackie had a softer spot for the Indian leader, however. Nehru later famously hosted Jackie and her sister Lee Radziwill on a much-reported trip to India in 1962 during which they both were photographed riding on an elephant.

The legendary former *Washington Post* editor, Ben Bradlee, Washington bureau chief for *Newsweek* at the time and Jack's neighbor when the Kennedys lived in Georgetown, before they moved to the White House, said that, in private, Jack's language was old navy talk, commonplace among men who served in World War II. When Lem was there, the atmosphere was even more electric. Jack, Jackie, and Lem had, of course, known each other for years, unbeknownst to some of the guests. Humor was the glue that held them together.

Often, they were the butt of each other's jokes and gibes, but when other people were there, they had fun at the guests' expense. Even though all three of them were from an upper-crust background, they remained mischievously rebellious even at the pinnacle of power. Many of Jack's speeches have a defiant tone even though the presidency is about as establishment as you can get, and Lem was always poking fun at authority and pretentiousness. There was a sense in which they both never ceased to be Choate Muckers.

Jackie could be quite a Mucker, too, in her own way. She had a gift for mimicry and would frequently lampoon the guests, especially bombastic heads of state and pompous homegrown pols, particularly when they weren't looking, or better still, once they had left. The shah of Iran was one of her favorite targets, as was German chancellor Konrad Adenauer, who avoided cracking a smile even when amused. "Jackie was a mimic, and Jack loved mimicry," said Lem. "There was a sort of sardonic quality to Jackie's humor which he liked. He used to try to elicit humorous stories out of her for the sake of seeing what would come out. I think he respected Jackie. There was a respect there, despite the stories to the contrary."

The Eisenhowers were a favorite Jackie target. When the First Lady visited them at the White House just before they vacated it, she said of Mamie, "Not even a cup of tea did she offer. But the upstairs sitting room, the oval one, was worth the whole tour. They had two TV sets— his and hers—with little tables in front of them, where they had their TV dinners, he watching the Westerns, and she her soap operas." She dubbed Vice President Johnson and his wife, Lady Byrd, "Colonel Corn-pone and his little pork chop." These were among her more affectionate characterizations, however. In fact, she liked the Johnsons and got on particularly well with Lyndon, who later said that she was the only person in the Kennedy White House who treated him well.

One of the most memorable social events during the White House years for Lem was Jack's last birthday party, on May 29, 1963. It was carefully choreographed by Jackie, who was five months pregnant with their son Patrick at the time. She wanted to do something special, so she arranged a cruise down the Potomac on the presidential yacht, the *Sequoia,* and sent out invitations that said "Come in yachting clothes." Of course, she invited Lem. In addition, Bobby, Ethel, and Teddy, the Shrivers, the Bartletts, the Bradlees, the Fays, and movie star David Niven and his wife also attended. Bill Walton and Lem were the two most prominent bachelors at the party. Unfortunately for Jackie, the evening was less than successful. She had searched for days for a unique gift for Jack, finally settling on a rare antique engraving that Lem, with his love of antiques, must have thought was the perfect present. Just as Jack was opening the gift, however, one of the guests who had had too much to drink—Clem Norton—lurched forward and put his foot right through the engraving. But, as was her style, she didn't make a fuss in front of people. "I can get it fixed," she said.

Author Gore Vidal was skeptical of the Kennedys politically, but he enjoyed their love of life and their sense of humor. Jackie, to whom he was related (he was Jackie's stepfather's stepson), "was very malicious, but in the most enchanting, life-enhancing way," he said. "She had a very black humor. She hardly had anything good to say about anyone. Jack was very much the same way, but of course he had to be much more guarded. Alone with friends, the two of them were just devastating about everyone else, and when you left the room, you knew they'd be doing it to you, too. That was one of the reasons I liked them so much. We got on famously."

Gore and Lem, however, did not get on famously at all. At the first private party given at the White House in November 1961, honoring Italian auto magnate Gianni Agnelli, Lem and Gore started to quarrel. "He came up to me and attacked me for never going to any of the meetings of the Council on the Arts," remembers Gore. "I said I didn't go because I don't believe in government interference in the arts, whether it's benign or malign. 'Then why did you join it?' Lem asked. I said I didn't join it. Jack put my name on it without asking me. So I responded by never going to a meeting. 'Why did you do that,' Lem persisted. I didn't go to a meeting to show that I didn't believe in the thing, I said. Jack should never have put me on it. But I wasn't going to object to him. He thought he was doing me a favor." And so it went with Lem that night, Gore recalled.

The encounter with Lem, however, was nothing compared with what was to come. The story always varies depending on who is telling it, but according to Gore's account, he went into the Blue Room, where he found Jackie seated in a straight-backed chair. Gore knelt down to talk to her, and when he got up he put his hand on her shoulder for support. At that point, Bobby Kennedy appeared, no doubt tired from a long day at the Justice Department fighting for truth, justice, and the American way. Bobby apparently was offended when he saw Gore's arm on Jackie's shoulder. So he pulled Gore's arm away. This is the part of the story on which everyone agrees.

After that, versions differ, although Gore says there were no witnesses to what precisely occurred except him and Bobby, because they left the room when they began arguing. After Bobby pulled his arm from Jackie's shoulder, Gore says that he told Bobby, "Don't ever do that again." He says Bobby responded, "What do you mean, buddy boy? You're nobody." After that it escalated, with both men using the F-word against each other. Gore left later in the evening in the company of some other nota-bles who were at the dinner. Since the incidents with Lem and Bobby were "back to back, I was steaming," said Gore.

The incident was more of a "dustup" than a major fracas, according to Ben Bradlee, who says Lem was involved in the second incident as well, backing Bobby up against Gore. "Fisticuffs were suggested," he said, "but averted." According to writer Truman Capote, Gore's great nemesis, who wasn't there that night, Gore didn't leave the party. He was bodily thrown out by Bobby. Worse, Truman made the allegation in *Playgirl*. Gore denied this and proceeded to sue Truman for libel—and won. The settlement required Truman to give Gore a signed letter indi-cating he'd lied. "Dear Gore," Truman wrote, "I apologize for any dis-tress, inconvenience or expense which may have been caused you as a result of the interview with me published in the September 1975 inter-view of *Playgirl*." He added: "What I am reported as saying does not accurately set forth what occurred." Gore no doubt relished the apology.

This was Gore's last visit to the Kennedy White House, despite the fact that he got along great with Jack and genuinely enjoyed Jackie's com-pany, as well. This was no doubt fine with Lem, whose dustup with Gore had started the fracas in the first place. In fact, Gore was permanently expelled from the Kennedy White House not because of the much-remembered incident with Bobby but because he had crossed swords with Lem, a point underlined by, among others, George Plimpton. Jackie told Plimpton that "the real reason for Gore's 'expulsion' from the White House circle was that he had cornered Lem Billings, a former roommate of the president and practically a family member, and had verbally humiliated him in the hallway."Asked why he thought Lem attacked him that night, Gore said, "Well, he knew that Jack and I had a relationship which was far more interesting than anything he had. He's the guy who carries the coat. That's all he does. He's the guy who runs errands. Kennedy was very much in awe of the fact that I had two hit plays on Broadway and that my books were being read here, there, and everywhere and that I ran twenty thousand votes ahead of him in upstate New York in the 1960 election—the Twenty-ninth Congressional Dis-trict. Jack respected success. To Jack, Lem was a kind of idiot friend."

That viewpoint is disputed by, among others, Eunice Kennedy Shriver, who always said that the friendship between Jack and Lem was equal and not one-sided. And despite his characterization of Lem as "the guy who carries the coat," Gore conceded that the two men were close. It stemmed from their Choate days and Jack's precarious health at that time and for the rest of his life, he noted. "Jack was an invalid all the time. Till the day he died, he was an invalid. He needed all kinds of help. He'd take Lem Billings with him. In other words, he needed Lem Billings to get around—better than a trained nurse, which would have been the obvious thing to do. But then he would not have been able to have a political career because the word would have been spread around that he was not in good health. So Lem was there to get him through the day and to serve him loyally in all things."

In addition, Gore said Lem took care of Jack in other ways. "Jack never carried any money. He didn't know the price of anything. He was kind of helpless. Lem was always there to assist Jack with anything he needed," he added. Asked what Jackie thought of Lem, Gore said, "I think she thought he was kind of a nothing. But Jack needed him and she was practical. I thought he was absolutely nobody. But I certainly thought it was a good idea that Jack had somebody he could trust like that around him." As to whether Lem was in love with Jack, Gore responded, "I suspect so, yes."

Needless to say, Lem's opinion of his friendship with Jack did not comport with Gore's. "I've often wondered why, you know, all through the years why we continued to be such close friends because I never kept up on politics and all the things which interested him," he said. "However, we had so many things in common over the thirty years we had known each other. I knew everything about everybody he'd ever met in the past. Actually, I was just talking to Jackie this weekend and we were discussing why he'd rather have me around than [Secretary of Defense Robert] McNamara for a weekend. She said it was because he and McNamara would talk of nothing else but business in the White House. What he really wanted to do, on weekends, was to get away from anything that had to do with the White House."

On August 22, 1961, the first of a series of concerts—performed by young people for young people—was held on the south lawn of the White House. "I'm leaving my door open so I can hear the whole concert," Jack quipped, even though he couldn't be present at them. But he wanted them to know that his administration was young at heart and committed to them as well. He wanted to send a signal that every American—young and old—should be exposed to the finest of the arts.

The most celebrated social occasion during the Kennedy administration was the dinner Jack and Jackie gave in 1962 to honor forty-nine Nobel Prize winners. Actor Fredric March read an unpublished work of the late Ernest Hemingway, whom Jack much admired. In addition to the Nobel winners, over one hundred writers, educators, and scientists were invited. Jack loved to pick the minds of his guests, "although he never picked mine," Lem said. "But he was a great listener," he added. Two of the guests that night were controversial scientists Dr. Linus C. Pauling and J. Robert Oppenheimer. By inviting them, Jack wanted to telegraph that the era of the blacklist was over.

Rarely, if ever, had there been such a gathering of major intellects at the White House. But the most memorable line of the evening was uttered not by any of the guests, but by Jack himself. "I think that this is the most extraordinary collection of talent, of human knowledge, that has ever gathered at the White House, with the possible exception of when Thomas Jefferson dined alone," he said. It was the perfect remark for a flawless evening.

The children were not usually present during these evening events, but during the daytime, they frequently had the run of the place, and Jack played with them whenever he could. Unlike for most dads, it was easy to do so, since he worked at home. When he had the time, Jack would clap twice if they were around and they would come running. Jack also loved telling stories to his children. A famous one that Kennedy insiders still talk about today involved whales and socks. One day on his boat, the *Honey Fitz*, named after his grandfather, Jack told Caroline a story about a white whale that loved to eat old, sweaty socks. Franklin Roosevelt Jr. was aboard the boat at the time, wearing old, sweaty socks and no shoes. The president reached over, took off one of Roosevelt's socks, and threw it in the water.

Caroline was amazed to see the sock disappear, thinking a whale had eaten it. Then, Jack took off Roosevelt's other sock, and the same thing happened. Jack would repeat this trick many times when Caroline was aboard the boat—so much so that Lem said that whenever Jack would "start telling the story of the white whale, I'd move to another part of the yacht." Jack told Caroline many stories about white whales, "all of them very different. Caroline loved these stories," Lem added.

The Kennedy years were not only filled with children—his and those of others—but also dogs. Jack loved dogs from the time he was a small boy. But he was allergic to them, as he discovered when he and Lem took their two-month trip to Europe in 1937. They'd had to give up their little dachshund, Dunker, their beloved companion as they drove across Europe, because Jack's allergy to dogs was so bad. But he still wanted dogs, lots of them, around when he was in the White House.

At one point, the family had nine, including an Irish wolfhound, a Welsh terrier, and a cocker spaniel. They also had a canary, a cat, two hamsters, several ducks, and two ponies, named Leprechaun and Macaroni.

To Americans looking on, the First Family seemed ideal, the kind everyone would want to have. But the reality is, of course, that no family is ideal. The Kennedys had problems just like everyone else.

Jack could sometimes be insensitive and self-absorbed, Jackie temperamental and unavailable. Some of Jackie's moods no doubt were caused by the president's womanizing, which continued in the White House, although the thought never seemed to occur to Jack and Lem. Jack seized the opportunity to continue his philandering particularly when Jackie was absent. She knew about it, of course. Like any woman, she didn't like it, but she also considered it the price of marrying Jack Kennedy, whom she once described as a whirlwind. Jack always knew he could count on Lem's support and discretion for his activities. It was the pattern since the earliest days when their friendship first formed. Lem accepted everything about Jack and always kept his secrets.

The public did not know about Jack's extramarital affairs while he was alive or in the immediate years after his death, but Lem made what may have been one curious allusion to them in his mid-1960s oral history. "Certainly, Jack and Jackie had their share of rumors," he said. He was responding to an artfully worded question about why they spent so much time apart. But Lem explained it at the time as being a consequence of their different interests.

In addition to sexual promiscuity, there was another issue that was potentially damaging to Jack, although this, too, was unknown to the public during the years in the White House—drug use. For some time, Jack had used the services of a doctor named Max Jacobson, nicknamed Dr. Feelgood, who would periodically inject him with a concoction that Jacobsen claimed was made up of vitamins, enzymes, and hormones, but which in reality was speed. Jack felt the shots helped deaden his back pain. Dr. Feelgood sometimes gave injections to Jackie as well. It is not known whether Lem ever availed himself of Dr. Feelgood's services, but it is likely that he did.

The White House doctor, Dr. Janet Travell, also gave Jack Novocain injections for his back pain but did not prescribe any exercise. Lem was concerned about the treatments she gave to Jack, even though he took the opportunity to avail himself of her Novocain injections as well—for what he described as his bursitis. Eventually, Jack got a new doctor, who prescribed spinal back exercises, which strengthened his back enormously during the last two years of his presidency, according to Lem. "You never saw him on crutches in the latter years of his life," he said. As for Travell, "She didn't leave the White House . . . but he lost complete faith in her and never personally used her services again." Eventually, Jacobsen was also barred from treating Jack.

It seems that Jack could handle it all during his years in the White House—the duties of the office, Jackie and Lem's need for time with him, the demands of other friends and family, casual affairs, his health, even potentially damaging drug use. But two great personal tragedies that occurred while he was president tested him as few events before in his life had.

On December 19, 1961, Joe Kennedy suffered a massive stroke while playing golf in Palm Beach with his favorite niece, Ann Gargan. The stroke left the seventy-three-year-old patriarch paralyzed on one side and unable to speak. He never spoke again during the remaining eight years of his life, except for one word. He could say "no," which he apparently meant to mean "yes." Joe had been told about the possibility of a stroke and prescribed medication, but he'd refused to take it.

Now Joe would never again be able to chat with his son about the presidency or anything else, giving this or that piece of advice about the problems Jack faced as president. Joe had dreamed of his son becoming president of the United States for decades and had schemed and planned for it, but he had enjoyed good health for only eleven months of Jack's time in the White House—a lifetime of struggle for less than a year.

From then on, he would be a silent observer of Jack's presidency, although he retained his faculties and understood what was happening around him. Jack was devastated, according to Lem, who said it was a shock to them all when it happened. No one saw it coming. Jack always dreaded aging. "Old age is a shipwreck," he said. Now, his father had suffered a catastrophic stroke. He had his differences with his dad, like most sons. But he knew that Joe loved him, respected his independence, and had always watched out for him. Jack felt that Joe had done his best. Jack also knew that without his dad he likely never would have become president. He felt the loss deeply, even though his father was still alive.

Jackie, too, was devastated by Joe's stroke. Outside of Jack, and probably Bobby, Joe was the Kennedy to whom Jackie felt the closest. When the Kennedys were playing touch football on the lawn at Hyannis Port—which seemed like all the time—she would frequently be sitting on the porch with old Joe, reminiscing. They loved and respected each other. Some members of the Kennedy family treated Joe differently after the stroke, but not Jackie. She spent as much time as she could with him and touched him in a way that others were afraid to. He responded to her affection and always seemed better after one of her visits. Joe was always glad to see Lem as well, but no one seemed to be able to console him as much as Jackie after his stroke.

In August 1963, Jack and Jackie suffered the second major personal tragedy of their time in the White House. Their son, Patrick Bouvier Kennedy, died just two days after his birth. This time, Jack was there and profoundly moved by his son's death, reportedly crying openly, something Bobby Kennedy said he had seen Jack do only one time before in the White House—when he was thinking about the millions of children who would be killed if nuclear war broke out. Adults had a chance to lead their lives, he remarked. But the children hadn't. When British prime minister Harold Macmillan heard about Patrick's death, he wrote to Jack saying, "The burdens of public affairs are more or less tolerable. But private grief is poignant and cruel."

Perhaps because of the loss—again—perhaps because they had grown much closer during their years at the White House, Jack and Jackie leaned on each other more than ever as they struggled with their grief over their child's death. Lem went down to help them and console them in any way he could. Jack and Jackie's friends said that the death of Patrick Bouvier led to a greater level of intimacy. "Their marriage never seemed more solid than in the later months of 1963," said Arthur Schlesinger Jr. Perhaps, at long last, Jack was learning how to love his wife. It was just two months before Dallas.

In September, Jack and Lem and the rest of the Kennedy family gathered at Hyannis Port to celebrate Joe's seventy-fifth birthday. Despite the effects of his stroke, the photographs taken on the occasion showed him enjoying the attention. It was the last time Jack would be together with Lem and the entire Kennedy family.

Lem (left) joins in on the singing for the family birthday celebration of Joe Kennedy Sr., Hyannis Port, 1963.

Lem (seated at the table at left) joins the Kennedys for dinner on Joe's birthday.

On Wednesday, November 20, two days before the fateful trip to Dallas, Jack and Jackie held their last social event at the White House before attending a birthday party for Bobby Kennedy at his home in Hickory Hill. The guests were the Supreme Court justices and their wives, as well as more than five hundred other judges and party supporters. The Marine Band and the Air Force Strolling Strings played popular tunes from the era, including songs from *My Fair Lady*. They also played music from another one of Jack's favorites: "Don't let it be forgot, that once there was a spot, for one brief shining moment, that was known as Camelot."

The next morning, November 21, Jack and Jackie left the White House at 9:15 on their journey to Texas. Before he left, Jack kissed Caroline, who would be six the following week, and said good-bye. "Bye Daddy," she said, before running off to school. Her brother, John, whose third birthday would occur on the day of the president's funeral, went with Jack and Jackie to Andrews Air Force Base, just outside Washington, because he loved to ride on the helicopter and Jack wanted to give him the chance to do so again. At 11:00 A.M., Jack gave his son a farewell hug and kissed him good-bye. "I want to come," John told his father. "You can't," Jack responded, handing him over to the care of Secret Service agent Bob Foster. "You take care of John, Mr. Foster," he said. Then Jack and Jackie boarded Air Force One, destined for an unbelievable tragedy.

12

Blood and Tears
(November 22–25, 1963)

"For in the final analysis, our most basic common link is that we all inhabit this small planet. We all breathe the same air. We all cherish our children's future. And, we are all mortal."

—John F. Kennedy, June 10, 1963

The common wisdom is that John Kennedy went to Dallas on November 22, 1963, to heal wounds within the Texas Democratic Party. But the underlying cause of the trip was his stand on civil rights.

Earlier that year, in June, he had finally placed the full force of his administration behind the cause of equal rights for African Americans. His nationwide television address that month was the most forceful statement made by any U.S. president, before or since, on ending discrimination. It was the first ever to define white Americans' treatment of black Americans as a moral issue. A week after he addressed the nation, he forwarded to Congress a landmark civil rights bill.

Many white southerners were already furious with the president because of his support of James Meredith's admission to the University of Mississippi and his confrontation with Alabama governor George Wallace over the admission of James Hood and Vivian Malone to the University of Alabama. They also resented his very visible public statements in support of equal rights. The civil rights bill he sent to Congress was the last straw. If passed, the whole structure of legally mandated segregation in the South, erected following the Reconstruction period after the Civil War, would crumble. Some white southerners welcomed that prospect. Most did not.

Jack was in political trouble in the South and he knew it. Even his national popularity dropped in the wake of his actions on behalf of civil rights in the summer of 1963. It nose-dived from 76 percent in January to 57 percent in October, just before he went to Dallas. The issue was politically important because the "Solid South" had always been in the pocket of the Democratic Party since the Civil War ended in 1865, and that included Texas. Now, the Democrats faced the very real prospect of losing the South in the 1964 election. "In 1963, by irreversibly insisting upon full equality for the Negro, both [Kennedy] brothers knowingly cut themselves off from this traditional Democratic source of electoral votes," said Kennedy aide Ted Sorensen.

Most white southerners voted Democratic not only because the region was generally poorer than other parts of the country and the programs of the Democratic Party appealed to them but also because Abraham Lincoln, the first Republican president, had presided over the defeat of the South during the Civil War. The majority of black southerners—the few who could vote there—voted Republican for the opposite reason. But beginning with FDR's second term, most blacks switched to the Democratic Party because of FDR's programs to help the poor.

Even though FDR held pronounced liberal convictions, he did not move against the system of segregation in the South during any of his four terms because he didn't want to alienate white southern congressmen whom he needed to pass the New Deal. Although blacks, like whites, benefited from New Deal programs, little or no effort was made on behalf of civil rights during his presidency. FDR's successor, Harry Truman, made the first big dent in segregation when he integrated the U.S. armed forces by executive order in 1948. Truman also tried to build support for civil rights legislation in Congress. His groundbreaking program was titled "To Secure These Rights."

Had it passed, African Americans would have obtained their citizen-ship rights in the 1940s instead of having to wait two more decades. But the legislation went nowhere in a Congress still dominated by southern segregationists. And Truman was punished for his efforts when he ran for election in 1948 by not only having to face Republican Thomas Dewey but also Dixiecrat nominee Strom Thurmond, who ran on a segrega-tionist platform. Henry Wallace also ran against him from the Left.

Jack was well aware of the political risks of championing the cause of African Americans. In September 1963, just two months before he went to Dallas, he was asked a question about civil rights at a news conference. A reporter cited a Gallup poll indicating—incredibly—that 50 percent of Americans thought he was pushing too hard, too fast, on civil rights. In his answer, Jack tried to look on the bright side. "The fact is," he said, "that same poll showed 40 percent or so thought it was more or less right. I thought that was rather impressive because it is change. Change always disturbs, and therefore I was not surprised that there wasn't greater oppo-sition. I think we are going at about the right tempo."

When the civil rights bill was signed into law by President Johnson on July 2, 1964, LBJ famously predicted that the Democrats would pay the price by losing the South. That, in fact, has happened in most elections since the law was passed. Bobby Kennedy agreed, saying that if Jack would have lived to run in 1964, "he wouldn't have won any of them [the Southern states], and I suppose he might have lost—probably lost—Texas." Knowing that he had won the 1960 election by a wafer-thin margin, Jack was determined to win as many southern states as he could.

Lem always remained proud of what Jack achieved in his fight for racial equality. Lem's family had been involved in supporting civil rights for African Americans decades before the Kennedys had even thought about the subject. Lem's mother, Romaine, was a direct descendent of Dr. Francis LeMoyne, who founded the Washington County Anti-Slavery Society in Pennsylvania. He also ran as a vice presidential candi-date on the Abolitionist platform. The successful doctor, reformer, and builder of the first crematory in the Western hemisphere also allowed his home to be a stop along the Underground Railroad, the network of hiding places for runaway slaves from the South. Later, he established what became the LeMoyne College for African Americans in Memphis,

Tennessee. It is now LeMoyne-Owen College and still has a predominantly African American student body.

During Jack's time in the White House, Lem "stopped by the all-black college on impulse," remembered Robert F. Kennedy Jr., to demonstrate his own support for civil rights and his backing for Jack's stand on the issue. Lem gave a speech there on civil rights and answered questions from students, who were amazed to see the founder's great-grandson show up virtually unannounced. Lem discussed the civil rights situation in the South, but he knew that racism wasn't just a southern problem. He remembered a time when the Ku Klux Klan was visible in his hometown of Pittsburgh. "It was not only that he was a principled man who despised intolerance and fought it, but Lem had a good heart," said Robert F. Kennedy Jr. He was opposed to prejudice of any kind. It was a family tradition.

Since members of Lem's family lived in the South, including his brother Josh, Lem was well aware that many white southerners were violently opposed to Jack's civil rights agenda. John Seigenthaler said, "I don't think Lem had as much of a committed interest to civil rights as the president had, but I know that when I was injured in Montgomery [by an angry white mob opposed to racial integration] he was very solic-itous of me and worried about me. He was outraged by it really. I recall that he telephoned me. He may have talked along the lines of referring to cowards with white sheets. There is no doubt he looked upon southern racism with contempt. But I don't think he really saw that there was a problem in the North as clearly.

"But you know," Seigenthaler continued, "Lem was proud of anything Jack did, including on civil rights. If he had not initially been supportive of civil rights—which in fact he was—he soon would have been converted to the cause. Whatever Jack thought, Lem thought. Lem's mind was an echo of whatever he could read in Jack Kennedy's mind. He really identified with the president. He was family. He was family to every Kennedy brother and sister, too, as well as Jack."

There is no record of Lem having been concerned about the president's safety because of the opposition his civil rights stance had triggered. Lem probably thought that Jack was sufficiently protected by the Secret Service now that he was president. In any case, Jack had overcome so much adversity in his life it was inconceivable to Lem that he could be vulnerable to a gunman when he had more protection than anyone in the country.

Jack knew the likely Republican nominee in 1964 would be Barry Goldwater, a far-right candidate who opposed the civil rights bill. This stand was likely to hand Goldwater many of the southern states in the election, including Texas. Moreover, deep divisions in the Texas Democratic Party—between conservatives championed by Governor John Connally and liberals supported by Senator Ralph Yarborough—had emerged. Jack decided he must go to Texas to try to heal the divisions within the party before the 1964 election. He planned to take Vice President Johnson and Mrs. Johnson with him on the trip as well as Jackie, whose popularity among Americans transcended ideology.

Jackie had not accompanied Jack on his triumphant trip to Europe earlier in the summer (Lem and two of Jack's sisters had accompanied him instead). So she was determined to be there for him this time, even though it had only been a few months since she'd lost their baby, Patrick.

U.S. ambassador to the UN Adlai Stevenson, however, warned Jack not to make the trip. Stevenson, in Dallas earlier in November, had been physically assaulted by conservatives there who objected to Kennedy administration positions on civil rights and other issues. Journalist Marquis Childs reported back to Jack that he had been stunned by the hostility toward the president. He said he often heard the phrase, "Soft on the blacks, soft on the commies." Childs told Jack, "I heard hatred reminiscent of the hatred of Franklin Roosevelt a generation before." But Childs said Jack was just baffled by the opposition to a policy that was self-evidently morally right to him. He ignored the advice and pressed ahead with the trip.

As he boarded Air Force One, Jack's health was better than it had been for a long time. "I feel great," he said to aide Kenny O'Donnell. "My back feels better than it's felt in years." The Kennedys landed at Love Field near Dallas at 11:37 A.M. central standard time on the warm, sunlit morning of November 22. Just under two hours later—at 1:33 P.M.—acting press secretary Malcolm Kilduff (press secretary Pierre Salinger was on a plane en route to Japan with Secretary of State Dean Rusk) spoke to a group of reporters. "President John F. Kennedy died at approximately 1 P.M. central standard time today here in Dallas," he said.

"He died of a gunshot wound in the brain. I have no other details regarding the assassination of the president."

It was all that need be said. He was gone. It was over—in an instant—just like that—the way life can be—the way John Kennedy knew life could be. Jack had once told journalist Joe Alsop that he didn't think he would live past the age of forty-five, one reason he always lived life like there was no tomorrow. As it turned out, Jack's prediction about his fate had been eerily accurate. It was nearing six months after his forty-sixth birthday when he boarded the plane for Dallas.

After the seconds of madness in the Texan city, everything moved quickly. The president's body was removed from Parkland Hospital to Air Force One. Jackie, and Vice President Johnson and Mrs. Johnson, were on board. Johnson took an oath to become president on the plane, but constitutionally he was already the nation's chief executive when Jack died. The plane landed back in Washington in the early autumn evening.

When he learned that the love of his life was dead while on his lunch hour in New York, it was as if Lem had been struck by lightning. He couldn't move or think. How could this be? How could this have happened? Consumed by grief, he walked along Madison Avenue just a few blocks to St. Patrick's Cathedral. He entered the church and prayed. The whole nation, indeed the entire world, was stunned at losing a popular and even beloved president, but for Lem the fact that Jack was president was secondary. He lost his best friend, the person he cared about more than anybody or anything in the world. He would willingly have tossed the presidency out the window in a second if it meant that Jack would live.

Lem had always been there when the Kennedy family needed him. Despite his anguish, he determined that he would do so now. Shortly after the shooting, he took a call from Eunice Kennedy Shriver in Washington. Lem was the first person Eunice called after she contacted her sister Pat. He offered to fly to Santa Monica where Pat lived with her husband, actor Peter Lawford, and accompany them back to the nation's capital. Pat told Lem, however, that she didn't think it would be necessary, and in fact it wasn't. Bobby Kennedy had already reached Pat and arranged for a flight.

Crushed by grief, Bobby Kennedy was waiting at Andrews Air Force Base just outside Washington for the plane to return from Dallas. Lem later said, "It was much harder for him than anybody." He added: "I think the shock of losing what he's built everything around . . . aside from losing the loved figure, was absolutely devastating . . . he didn't know where he was. Everything was just pulled out from under him."

But Francis McAdoo, Lem's old friend from Princeton and his days at the Emerson Drug Company in Baltimore, said that no one was more distraught than Lem. "I talked to him that week. He controlled himself on the phone, but I could tell he was in bad shape. It was terrible," he said. "He didn't want to live anymore. He was devastated for a very long time. At first, he was just stunned, shocked. Then he became morose— not at all the fun-loving person he had been. He just couldn't pull himself out of it. He just couldn't believe it had happened—couldn't believe that the president—who had survived so many near-fatal illnesses, and the war and everything, was now dead. That relationship was an important part of his life." Lem's sister, Lucretia, said, "Well, he could never get over it. I think Jack was terribly important to him. Jack was his best friend. I think he often was sad after it happened. I don't think it changed his personality, but you could tell it was something he thought about a lot and that was very upsetting to him."

John Seigenthaler recalled that Lem "was devastated—emotionally distraught. It was the only time in his adult life that he could find nothing to laugh and smile about. I never talked to him about it. What could you say? You knew he was decimated. You knew every time you saw him he was about to burst into tears. The death of Josh [Lem's brother] could not have affected him more. Jack was a brother to him." His niece, Sally Carpenter, said Lem told her, "I always was afraid of losing him to the presidency, but I never thought I would lose him this way."

When the plane arrived, Bobby boarded it and rushed to embrace Jackie. The late president's aides—Dave Powers, Kenny O'Donnell, and Larry O'Brien—placed the casket carrying the president's body on the plane's hydraulic lift. An honor guard of six men carried it to a waiting ambulance. There was a heartbreaking moment when Jackie repeatedly tried to open the ambulance door herself without success, her dress still carrying the bloodstains from earlier in the day. "I want them to see what they have done," she said. The ambulance was driven to the Bethesda naval hospital, where an autopsy was performed.

Americans watched on television as President Lyndon Johnson walked to the microphones with his wife and spoke to the nation. "I will do my best. That is all I can do. I ask for your help—and God's." NBC anchor David Brinkley remarked on the mind-numbing speed of the tragedy. "It has all been shocking," Brinkley told viewers. "But perhaps one element in the shock was the speed. By the Washington clock, at a little after one o'clock this afternoon, President Kennedy was about as alive as any human being ever gets—young, strong, vigorous—looking forward to, no doubt, five more years, he hoped, of leadership in this country and of the Western world. His wife—young, beautiful, looking very happy—was beside him and seeming to have a very wonderful time, and leaning against the backseat of the car to say to him 'You can't say Dallas hasn't been friendly to you.'"

Brinkley continued: "That was a little after one o'clock. Five hours later—at six o'clock—Mr. Kennedy had been murdered, Lyndon Johnson was president of the United States, Mrs. Kennedy was a widow—a brave and composed one that nobody could fail to admire. All of them were back in Washington in the same airplane that took them to Texas, and an incredible tragedy. The sheer speed of it all was just too fast for the senses. . . . There is seldom any time to think anymore and today there was none. In about four hours, we had gone from President Kennedy in Dallas alive to back in Washington dead and a new president in his place. There is no more news here tonight and really no more to say except that what happened today has just been too much, too ugly, and too fast."

Frank McGee, his voice breaking, concluded NBC's coverage in the early hours of Saturday morning, November 23, with words that seemed to express the sentiments of the entire nation. "There is no way of calculating the millions of words that have been uttered in the course of this day in all countries of the world as human beings fumble for words to express their offended senses about what has happened in the United States. I seriously doubt that any words uttered by anyone, anywhere, have succeeded in expressing what you feel yourself. I would suppose that the answer for that is only to be found deep within the hearts of each of us."

On Saturday, Lee Harvey Oswald was charged with assassinating the president. On Sunday, as he was being transferred to a higher-security jail, he was shot by a nightclub owner with underworld connections named Jack Ruby. He died a short time later. Many Americans saw the shooting on television, as it occurred. The unbelievable turn of events would lead many to question the circumstances surrounding the assassination for decades to come. But Lem had little time for that. He could not get beyond the fact that he'd lost Jack. The circumstances surrounding the assassination were not of much interest to him. Nothing would bring him back.

During the weekend, the casket carrying the president's body was moved from the White House to the Capitol Rotunda. It was visited by hundreds of thousands of ordinary citizens who wished to pay their respects. Over a third were African Americans, an indication that John Kennedy's civil rights stand was appreciated where it counted the most. The night before the funeral, *Washington Star* reporter Mary McGrory gave a dinner at her house. She said to Daniel Patrick Moynihan, "We'll never laugh again." He responded, "We will, but we'll never be young again."

Early on Monday afternoon, Jackie stood at the north portico of the White House with Caroline and John Jr. by her side. They watched the honor guard lift the casket onto the artillery caisson. Three pairs of horses drew the carriage past the White House to St. Matthew's Cathedral a short distance away for the service. It was followed by a riderless horse. In accordance with Jackie's wishes, the funeral was patterned on Lincoln's in 1865. John Jr., who was three years old on the day of his father's funeral, saluted the coffin from the steps of the cathedral. A still photograph of his salute ran in newspapers all over the world. Caroline reached out to comfort her mother, who remained stoic throughout the day. Jackie would later say, "It is children who allow widows to go on."

John F. Kennedy, the thirty-fifth president of the United States, was buried in Arlington National Cemetery alongside his daughter Arabella and his son Patrick. A set of whale's-tooth scrimshaw that Jack had kept on his desk in the Oval Office—a gift from Lem—was buried with him. Jackie lit the eternal flame that rises from his grave. It flickered in the autumn air and in all the autumns since. Arthur Schlesinger later said that he had never really understood the function of a funeral. "Now I realized it is to keep people from going to pieces."

Speaking of his generation, John Kennedy once said that there were only two days that people remembered so well they could recall where they were at the time: the day Pearl Harbor was attacked and the day Franklin Roosevelt died. Now, there would be a third. A new generation of Americans would always remember the day John Kennedy died and exactly where they were when they heard the news. To see this remarkably youthful-looking man struck down in an instant reminded everyone of his and her own mortality, of the line between life and death, the length of which is so unknown.

There was an extraordinary outpouring of grief not only in the United States but also across the globe. To some degree, this was because, in an age of mass media, people thought they knew John Kennedy much more than they had great leaders from earlier times. But it really went beyond that. People felt that a unique human being and statesman had passed from the scene, that the world would be less safe and more chaotic now that he no longer was there to preside over the most powerful political office in the world. Indeed, it proved to be so.

The feeling of irreplaceable loss was expressed in many of the eulogies to President Kennedy, but perhaps none was more eloquent than that given by his old rival, Adlai Stevenson, U.S. ambassador to the United Nations in the Kennedy administration. "President Kennedy," he said, "was so contemporary a man, so involved in our world, so immersed in our times, so responsive to its challenges, that he seemed the very symbol of the vitality and exuberance that is the essence of life itself. Now he is gone. Today, we mourn him. Tomorrow and tomorrow, we shall miss him. And so we shall never know how different the world might have been had fate permitted his blazing talent to live and labor on man's unfinished agenda for peace and progress for all."

The violinist Isaac Stern also spoke to the feeling of lost promise that still haunts the American political landscape today. "With him, you always could believe in the ninth home run, in winning the fifth set at Wimbledon, in making a three-and-a-half-minute mile . . . with hope, with clarity, with intelligence, with compassion and with an immensely broad view of history—and an understanding of people."

Historian Arthur Schlesinger Jr. remembered John Kennedy's optimism despite all the tragedies and all the disappointments. "He voiced the new generation's longings for fulfillment and experience, for the subordination of selfish impulses to higher ideals, for a link between past and future, for adventure, and valor, and honor. What was forbidden were poses, histrionics, the heart on the sleeve or the tongue on the cliché. What was required was a tough, nonchalant acceptance of the harsh present and an open mind towards the unknown future."

∽

It is impossible to know what ran through Jackie's mind in these first days after her husband's death. She had traveled a difficult road in her marriage to John Kennedy, but everyone close to them agrees that in the last years they had finally found a way to love each other that worked for them. A month after the funeral, she talked to Teddy White of *Life* magazine and told him how she had tried to tell her husband that she loved him as the bullets entered his brain. "I kept saying . . . 'Jack, Jack, can you hear me, I love you, Jack.' But I knew he was dead."

On the first anniversary of the assassination, she paid tribute to her late husband in an article published by *Look* magazine. "I don't think there is any consolation. What was lost cannot be replaced," she wrote. "Now I think I should have known that he was magic all along. I did know it . . . but I should have guessed it could not last. I should have known that it was asking too much to dream that I might have grown old with him and seen our children grow up together. So now he is a legend when he would have preferred to be a man." She added: "His high noon kept all the freshness of the morning . . . and he died then, never knowing disillusionment."

During all of her remaining three decades of life, Jackie rarely spoke again in public, or privately to reporters, about the events in Dallas or anything else, perhaps because of what Teddy Kennedy so eloquently called "unbearable sorrow endured in the glare of a million lights." In the weeks and months after Jack's death, she grappled with the enormity and finality of what had occurred. We know little about her inner thoughts or the foundations of her outer strength during this sad time. She told her friend John Russell, "I think that my biggest achievement is that after going through a rather difficult time, I consider myself comparatively sane. I'm proud of that."

The proof of her love for John Kennedy, if any were needed, is in the way she set about preserving his legacy and his memory. In the interview with *Life* magazine, she revealed that Jack had loved reading about King Arthur and the Knights of the Round Table as a boy, and that his favorite music was the final refrain from *Camelot,* as interpreted by lyricist Alan Jay Lerner, whom Jack knew from Choate and Harvard. "Don't let it be forgot—that once there was a spot—for one brief shining moment—that was known as Camelot." Thus was born the modern legend of Camelot. The word had never been used before to describe the Kennedy presidency. Now, after his death, in just one rare interview, Jackie had created a new way to remember Jack's one thousand days in office. From that moment on, their time in the White House would forever be America's Camelot.

For Lem, his grief—unlike Jackie's during those four terrible days between the shooting and the funeral—was private. No cameras focused on him, nor did any reporters seek him out; and he likely could not have talked to them if they had. Indeed, he was barely recognized among the mourners except by the people in the administration who knew him, and of course members of the Kennedy family. From the time he'd met John Kennedy thirty years earlier, there had never been any doubt of his love—total love—for the man who would become the nation's thirty-fifth president. It was an unqualified, uncritical, unconditional commitment that never wavered throughout all the ups and downs of their lives throughout all the years. They had always been there for each other. Now Lem would face the rest of his life alone and never, according to those who knew him best, recover from the events of November 22, 1963. "In many ways, Lem thought of his life as being over after Jack died," said Bobby Kennedy Jr. Lem lived for eighteen years after Dallas. But in a very real sense, the assassin's bullets ended his life on that day as well. He was never the same again. For all his remaining days, he would think of Jack every day, finding comfort only in talking about him to the younger Kennedys—and to anyone else who would listen.

John Kennedy didn't have a chance to say good-bye—to Lem, to Jackie, to his children—to all of us. On one occasion, however—in Ireland—he came close. As he was leaving the country, he said, "This is where we all say good-bye." Then he read a poem that had been given to him the previous evening by the wife of the Irish president:

> *Tis the Shannon's brightly glancing stream*
> *Brightly gleaming, silent in the morning beam*
> *Oh the sight entrancing*
> *Thus returned from travel's long*
> *Years of exile, years of pain*
> *To see old Shannon's face again*
> *O'er the water's glancing.*

~

PART THREE

Lem After Dallas

13

The Sea Change
(1933 v. 1973)

"There should be no place in America for bias against persons because of their sexual preference. Yet evidence abounds that gays and lesbians are frequent victims of discrimination and even violence because of their sexual orientation."
—Senator Edward Kennedy, *America: Back on Track*

To understand Lem at the various stages in his life, it is important to know the climate of the time for gay men in the United States and how it changed. When Jack and Lem met at Choate in the spring of 1933, the concept of a gay identity was unknown. The word *gay,* or even *homosexual,* was barely used. There were no gay political organizations to speak of and no openly gay politicians. Writers, artists, and celebrities who even hinted at same-sex relations in their work were firmly in the closet. There were a few gay bars, social events, and private parties, but most were hidden from view and disguised to appear as something they were not—especially after the vice laws, often directed at gays, became rampant following the repeal of Prohibition in 1933. When gay people realized they were attracted to members of their own sex, they thought there was no other person in the world like them, for this was an era in which there was no public discussion, no recognition, and no acceptance. Consequently, most gays waged an unrelenting struggle against themselves, against who they were—a losing battle for most that resulted in endless psychological pain and confusion.

Unable and unwilling to accept their sexual orientation, most gays allowed themselves to be defined by a society that regarded their inclination as at best unmentionable and at worst evil. Shame, self-hate, and rock-bottom self-esteem were the inevitable result. The psychiatric view—that "sexual inversion" was an illness—was considered enlightened in comparison to the opinion of society at large. The treatment that was offered included aversion therapy, electroshock, and even, on occasion, castration and lobotomy. In every state of the union, and in most other countries in the world, homosexuality was illegal. Gays who were indiscreet risked imprisonment, and worse. To survive, what was required was a secret life, not only from society at large, but also from family and friends. The concept of "coming out," a phrase not even in general use until the 1970s, was unimaginable in all but the most bohemian circles.

By 1973, however, just forty years after Jack and Lem met, a sea change had occurred. In this country, as well as others, millions of people self-identified as gays and lesbians. Gay political and social organizations had proliferated across the nation. Political candidates appealed to gays for their votes. Some candidates were openly gay themselves. Gays freely marched for equal rights and an end to discrimination, demanding, not asking, for their American birthright. Gay bars and other meeting places mushroomed, no longer disguised and no longer targeted by the police. Some establishments welcomed straight, bisexual, and gay people and became the in places to see and be seen. In 1973, the most famous of them, Studio 54, which Lem went to occasionally, was just four years away from first opening its doors in New York.

Books, movies, and television shows dealing with all aspects of gay life were routine, no longer provoking the kind of shock and disgust that would have been the near-universal reaction in 1933. Journalists were reporting on the gay and lesbian community, as it was now being referred to, instead of ignoring it as they had done ever since the first newspaper came off the presses. Although this was just the beginning and gays still faced rampant discrimination and disapproval, it was a different universe for gays coming of age in 1973 compared with 1933. Even the American Psychiatric Association (APA) got into the act. In 1973, it finally decided that being gay wasn't sick. For gays who came of age in the earlier period, however, and who were now middle-aged or older, it was at best a confusing time. They had been told they were either evil, or ill, or both, all their lives. But now the educated opinion was that they were neither. What was expected of them now? What should they do? How could they adapt?

For Lem, who turned fifty-seven in 1973, this new world was daunting and frightening. What was required of him seemed so different than when he was a young man. Should he stay in the closet, or boldly step out—perhaps inch out to some people, but not to all? What would that mean to his friends, to his family, and most of all to the Kennedy family? If his being gay became public knowledge, would it tarnish the image of Jack Kennedy, the one thing that Lem cared more about than anything else? Or would it enhance it with most people, who would feel that Jack was an even more heroic and caring person for having maintained a friendship all his adult life with a gay man despite all the risks it posed to his political career? These and many more questions must have entered Lem's mind at the beginning of the tumultuous decade of the 1970s, when gays felt freer than they had at any other time in history.

In the early-morning hours of June 28, 1969, eight officers from the public morals section of the First Division of the New York City Police Department raided the Stonewall Inn, a gay bar located on Christopher Street in the heart of New York's Greenwich Village. There was nothing particularly different about the police assault that night. The same thing had happened at gay bars across the nation for decades. Four gay bars in the Village had been raided in the previous few weeks. What made this raid different, however, is that this time the patrons of the bar resisted. Over the following three nights, the resistance grew and became politicized.

The demonstrators didn't know it at the time, but they had given birth to the modern gay rights movement. A new slogan was born, "gay power," and a new phrase, "the gay liberation movement." Gays were on the move, influenced by the idealism of the 1960s unleashed by John F. Kennedy and inspired by the civil rights movement he embraced, particularly during the last year of his administration. The antiwar movement, radical feminism, and the New Left also shaped the infant gay militancy.

On the anniversary of the Stonewall rebellion in 1970, more than twenty thousand gay men and women marched from Greenwich Village to Central Park. It was the first sizable demonstration by gays in memory. But it would be only the first of many, both in the United States and overseas. According to a close friend, Lem was not an activist and did not participate in any of the growing gay political activity. But like many gay people of his generation, he quietly welcomed it, perhaps realizing for the first time the price he had paid for his secret life.

The increasing gay political activism took place against a backdrop of an emerging gay culture, what some were calling a gay consciousness or gay sensibility. Gay men and women, aware of their sexual orientation as never before, began to devour gay history, gay literature, and other aspects of a lifestyle long hidden from view in the majority culture. There was a new sense of solidarity, a deep-seated commitment to purpose. Rather than being ashamed of their lifestyle, for the first time gays embraced it.

It was all so different from the times during which Lem had come of age. In 1933, the word *gay* wasn't even in general usage. Although *gay*—to mean homosexual—dates back to the 1920s and perhaps even earlier, according to most sources, it wasn't employed widely among the general population until the 1960s were well under way. Most people in the 1950s still thought *gay* meant "happy." Television programmers in England, for example, could cavalierly broadcast *The Gay Cavalier* without its audience thinking the show's hero was about more than defeating the Roundheads (as the supporters of parliament and opponents of the king were called during the English Civil War).

Even the word *homosexual* wasn't commonplace when Jack and Lem were young men. It was probably first referenced in the United States in the 1880s. Its first recorded use in an American text was in the *Chicago Medical Recorder* in 1892, in an article titled "Responsibility in Sexual Perversion." The *New York Times* didn't get around to using the word *homosexual* until the 1920s, but it still was not in regular usage before World War II.

Many straight Americans were totally unaware that homosexuality existed, except perhaps on the fringes of society. Ironically, the widespread ignorance provided a good deal of cover. In the early 1930s, for example, Cary Grant and Randolph Scott lived openly together and attended social events and parties as a couple. Paramount even provided the press with "at home" photo shoots that look startlingly suggestive today, but that raised few eyebrows during that more naïve time.

When newspapers reported arrests for homosexual activity, they would most often use euphemisms like "morals charge." Even as late as 1964, when Lyndon Johnson's aide Walter Jenkins was arrested for propositioning a male undercover police officer in a bathroom, the newspapers did not openly refer to his sexual orientation. In a phone call to her husband about the matter, Lady Byrd Johnson suggested that Jenkins, who was married with six children, had been stressed out and overworked. LBJ lost no time calling J. Edgar Hoover to have a little fun at the closeted FBI director's expense. How can one recognize someone of that persuasion? he asked. (Johnson couldn't bring himself to use the word *gay*, either.) Hoover assured him it was difficult. Listening to the telephone call today, you can sense Hoover squirming under the pressure and Johnson's obvious pleasure and amusement.

It is important to note that Jack and Lem's friendship formed less than four decades after the trials of playwright Oscar Wilde, who was foolish enough to sue the father of the young man, Lord Alfred Douglas, with whom he was having an affair. Even though Wilde was married and was most likely bisexual rather than gay, he ended up in prison, ruined and disgraced in the Victorian society he so effectively satirized in his plays. "We know no spectacle so ridiculous as the British public in one of its periodic fits of morality," he declared. But his uptight public had the last laugh. Wilde died in 1900 at the age of only forty-six.

Although during the latter half of the nineteenth century, particularly, homoerotic literature flourished both in Europe and the United States, and an increasing number of thinkers and scientists addressed the issue of homosexuality sympathetically, Wilde's conviction ushered in another era of repression. A new wave of fear gripped the gay community, not only in Britain, but also in other countries, such as the United States, where the trials were reported. It would not subside significantly until the late 1960s, when Lem was well into middle age.

In World War I and during the interwar years, homosexuality remained "the love that dare not speak its name," in the famous words of Bosie, as Wilde called his young male lover, although there were pockets of tolerance during the Roaring Twenties. Even such bon vivants as Noël Coward, in many ways Wilde's successor, were circumspect when it came to sexuality. Coward even embraced right-wing causes as he grew older, perhaps to deflect attention from his decidedly nonconservative lifestyle.

During World War II, when both Jack and Lem were serving their country along with millions of other young Americans, the military was busy discharging thousands of men they determined to be gay, despite the fact that the United States was in a struggle for survival. In the navy and the army, gays were referred to as "sexual psychopaths" and regarded as mentally ill even by the more enlightened medical personnel. For the first time, recruits were asked if they were homosexual, a question Lem would have had to answer in the negative when he enlisted

Fortunately, the military still thought of gays in terms of effeminate stereotypes (or masculine stereotypes for women), so most gays in the service were able to escape the net, if they chose to do so, some honing their gaydar to spot others of the same persuasion. It was risky, though. Gays who too obviously displayed a queer eye for the straight guy were booted out of the military. British servicemen fared no better, even though the leader of Britain's war effort, Field Marshal Bernard Montgomery, was also a closeted gay man, as author Nigel Hamilton has documented in his biography of the British officer. That didn't stop Montgomery from speaking out against the legalization of same-sex relations in Britain, declaring, "This sort of thing may be tolerated by the French, but we're British—thank God!"

However dire the situation was in Britain and the United States during World War II, in many other countries gays faced a much graver threat. In Germany, Hitler declared that homosexuality was incompatible with Aryan manhood during his first year as führer even though his own sexuality has long been suspect, and numerous top Nazis, including Ernst Roehm, leader of the SA, openly cavorted with young Nazi studs.

During World War II, an estimated one hundred thousand gay men were arrested under the country's infamous Paragraph 175 law. The law had existed since 1871, but the Nazis toughened it and enforced it. (Lesbians were not covered by the law and were not included by the Nazis, either.) An estimated ten thousand to fifteen thousand gays, and suspected gays, were herded into concentration camps along with Jews, communists, and other undesirables. Presumably, some had the misfortune to be all of the above. In many camps, gays were forced to wear a "pink triangle" to symbolize their degeneracy. At least two-thirds of the gays died in the camps even though they were targeted for reeducation rather than extermination, the fate that awaited most Jews.

The deaths of the gay men were ignored for decades after World War II, and some of the men who suffered in the concentration camps even went to prison after the war for homosexual offenses, since Paragraph 175 remained on the books until 1968 in communist East Germany and until 1969 in democratic West Germany. Nobody wanted to hear about what gays experienced in the concentration camps, and even if they had, many of the gay inmates were so ashamed of who they were that they would have maintained their silence anyway. In fact, the German government didn't get around to considering compensation for the few gays still alive who had survived the concentration camps until the early twenty-first century, when journalists and others began seeking them out. Imagine suddenly being asked what you went through in a concentration camp a half century or more after the fact!

In the United States and Britain after the war, there were a number of high-profile trials that resulted in prison sentences. The most notorious was the arrest and prosecution of Peter Wildeblood, diplomatic correspondent for the *Daily Mail* in England, who was sentenced to eighteen months in prison along with Lord Montagu of Beaulieu and Michael Pitt-Rivers. Wildeblood's book about the ordeal, *Against the Law,* became a cause célèbre for reformers in England whose greatest achievement during this period was the 1957 Wolfenden Report. It urged legalization of same-sex activity between consenting adults in England. The goal was not achieved, however, until 1967.

Reformers in Britain had been helped enormously by the release—in 1961—of the groundbreaking movie *Victim,* in which matinee idol Dirk Bogarde, who previously had starred mostly in light comedies, risked his career to play a gay married barrister who was blackmailed because of his secret life. The movie eloquently demonstrated not only the fear of blackmail among closeted gays during the repressive era but its reality. There is no evidence of any blackmail attempt against Lem at any time during his life, but he must have feared the possibility, as millions of other gays did during this era, especially those in high-profile occupations.

The anxiety was especially palpable in Hollywood. Rock Hudson, for example, lived in fear throughout the 1950s that his career would be ended if his homosexuality were revealed. A muckraking movie magazine—*Confidential*—threatened to expose him. Even respectable publications, such as *Life* magazine, got into the act—and without much subtlety. In its October 9, 1955, issue, the magazine wrote, "Fans are urging twenty-nine-year-old Rock Hudson to get married—or explain why not." That was all the prodding that Universal and Rock needed. He married his secretary Phyllis Gates a month later, although it didn't fool anyone in the know in the industry. Phyllis later wrote a book about the marriage saying, surprisingly, that Rock was a darn good lover.

Although there were a few scares here and there, Rock managed to keep his lifestyle hidden, at least from the public, something that would be impossible today—even if it were desirable. In 1959, he tantalized Hollywood insiders when he starred with Doris Day in the movie *Pillow Talk,* in which the gay guy played a straight guy pretending to be a gay guy in order to get the girl. The comedy was an enormous hit with moviegoers and even funnier for insiders who knew the real scoop. Interviewed not long after Rock died, Doris Day captured the climate of the time in Hollywood, saying, "Many people at parties would ask me, 'Is it true about Rock Hudson?' and I always said to them, 'I have no idea.' . . . I think that a lot of people knew, but more did not, I would think." Most gay stars of that era, like Rock, adopted the required secret life and didn't come out to the public until decades later, if they did it at all.

If the fifties were a time of fear and repression in Hollywood, three thousand miles away in Washington, the situation was even worse. This was the time of the McCarthyist witch hunts when being pink was almost as bad, if not worse, than being red—and thought by some to be one and the same thing. The worst epithet you could be called was "pinko commie faggot," which is ironic, because behind the Iron Curtain the communists labeled homosexuality evidence of bourgeois decadence.

Not to be outdone in the witch-hunt department, FBI director J. Edgar Hoover boasted that his agency had identified 406 "sexual deviates" in federal service. Of course, that did not include himself and his friend Clyde Tolson—Bonnie and Clyde, as they were later nicknamed by Truman Capote. Hoover was the classic self-hating gay man who felt the best way to deflect attention from himself was to finger others. After President Eisenhower signed Executive Order 10450 in 1953, which stipulated that federal employees holding security clearances be "of good conduct and character," thousands of gay men and women lost their security clearances and were booted out of federal agencies as security risks, particularly from the State Department. Some even committed suicide.

In the first sixteen months after the executive order was signed, an average of forty gays were removed from federal employment every month. The thrust of the order was not reversed until 1975, when the Civil Service Commission eliminated the ban on gays in most federal jobs. And it was not until 1998 that another executive order was signed—by President Clinton—adding sexual orientation to the list of prohibited bases for discrimination.

Lem was never a federal employee, turning down Jack's offer of a job in his administration—perhaps wisely. Nor did he work in a high-profile profession such as show business or journalism. But there is no doubt that his positions, as head of advertising with the Emerson Drug Company in Baltimore and later as a vice president at Lennen & Newell in New York, would have been jeopardized had he not stayed in the closet. In Lem's case, he likely didn't give the matter much thought because he had known all his life that, given the public attitudes of the time, to be Jack Kennedy's best friend, it was necessary for his sexual orientation to remain a secret.

Even during this repressive era, however—before Stonewall—there was evidence of grassroots efforts by a few gay people to fight back. In 1950, at the height of the red and gay scares, the Mattachine Society was formed in Los Angeles. It began a publication—*One* magazine—aimed at gay men. In San Francisco in 1955, a group of lesbians founded the Daughters of Bilitis. It had only eight members at the beginning but it soon grew, starting a national newspaper for lesbians named *The Ladder*.

In 1961, the year Jack's presidency began, astronomer Frank Kameny, who had been fired from a federal job for being gay, began a Washington, D.C., chapter of the Mattachine Society. In August 1963, Kameny mounted a spirited campaign on behalf of the Mattachine Society to oppose legislation under consideration in Congress that would have banned the solicitation of funds for gay causes. Small but visible demonstrations of gay activists took place throughout the 1960s—before Stonewall—especially in Washington, D.C., and Philadelphia.

These early efforts were spurred by the publication of the Kinsey reports of 1948 and 1953—the first major challenge to the "gay is sick" ideology. Kinsey's work revealed that homosexuality and bisexuality were far more widespread than was previously thought. Kinsey's view was that human sexuality was based on a continuum ranging from exclusively gay at one end of the spectrum to exclusively straight at the other, with most people falling somewhere in between. The importance of Kinsey was not just his findings but also the fact that the media—for the first time— gave such prominence to the story. Never before had the love that dare not speak its name been spoken about so widely. Kinsey became a household name.

The same year that Kinsey published his first report—1948—author Gore Vidal caused an uproar with the publication of his novel *The City and the Pillar,* which graphically and uncompromisingly portrayed a same-sex relationship. The book was considered so controversial that the *New York Times* declined to review it. Vidal complained that books of his were not reviewed for years in that newspaper because of *The City and the Pillar.* Nevertheless, the book sold like hotcakes, as did other landmark books published later, such as James Baldwin's *Giovanni's Room,* John Rechy's *City of Night,* Truman Capote's *Other Voices, Other Rooms,* and Hubert Selby Jr.'s *Last Exit to Brooklyn.*

Despite his writing, Gore did not identify as a gay activist or writer. He thought of himself as bisexual. Echoing Kinsey, Gore wrote, "There is no such thing as a homosexual or heterosexual person. There are only homo- or heterosexual acts. Most people are a mixture of impulses, if not practices." Kate Millett, in her book *Flying,* put it somewhat differently. "Homosexuality was invented by a straight world," she wrote, "dealing with its own bisexuality."

All the efforts during the 1940s, 1950s, and even 1960s, however, were limited in scope and in effect. Before Stonewall, most gays—and bisexuals—stayed, of necessity, firmly in the closet, some even adopting antigay stances and far-right conservative views to deflect suspicion. Many gays even laughed—nervously—at the many locker room gay jokes prevalent at the time. Some gays even told more antigay jokes than straights to deflect suspicion. The greatest fear of most gay men and women was that they would be "found out," and not only lose their jobs but also the affection of their friends and colleagues—and, in many cases, their own families. There is no indication that Lem engaged in any antigay rhetoric to mask his true nature. The evidence indicates he just avoided the subject, as most people did at this time.

A poll taken as late as the 1960s found that 82 percent of American men and 58 percent of American women believed that only communists and atheists were more dangerous than homosexuals. Moreover, anti-sodomy laws were still on the books in all states but one (Illinois) throughout the time of Jack and Lem's friendship. During these years when homosexuality was not only illegal but also deeply feared and resented, most gays knew better than to be open about their sexual orientation, even if they were inclined to do so. Simply put, for people of Lem's time and place, being in the closet was a necessity. There was no other course. Most gay people made that decision without even thinking about it.

Of course, if a person remained single beyond a certain age, it would be noticed, perhaps even commented upon. People would talk about so-and-so being a "confirmed bachelor" or "spinster." Another common code phrase of the time was, "He's not the marrying kind." The most a suspected gay person could expect in the repressive era was a little tea and sympathy. God forbid if he was actually gay.

In more enlightened circles, gay people might be accepted, but it was also expected that they keep silent about it. It was basically "Don't ask, don't tell," long before Bill Clinton was pressed to agree to that policy in the military by Colin Powell, then chairman of the Joint Chiefs of Staff. It is hard to imagine that such an era existed in the United States and most other Western countries—not to mention elsewhere in the world, where the situation was often worse. But it did, and millions of gay and bisexual Americans alive today lived through it and remember it vividly. This was the world gay people of that era had to come to terms with.

Is it any wonder, then, that during this repressive era people like Lem chose the closet? With his high-pitched voice, Lem was never the most masculine person in the world, but his behavior was not so overtly feminine that people automatically suspected he was gay (although many "feminine" men are not gay and many "masculine" men are). A friend very close to Lem during the 1970s said that he "never talked to me about that [his homosexuality]. But he was a homosexual." Lem would sometimes have intimate relations with men at home. The friend remembered an occasion when Lem was seeing a Latino man. "One time, the guy came naked out of his room. He and Lem had been in bed together. The man came to Lem's house on a number of occasions," the friend added. Another friend close to Lem said that he kept a supply of male-oriented magazines, which the friend came across. But Lem would never acknowledge or talk about his lifestyle with the close friend.

Lem's keeping his gay life separate from his straight life was of course nothing unusual, given the social climate at the time. Many, perhaps most gay men did the same thing. But there would be times when things would just pop out, the friend remembered. On one occasion the friend was talking on the phone at Lem's house to a person who had been seeking a security clearance for a sensitive job. Lem's friend told the job applicant that the FBI suspected him of being gay because he was unmarried and interested in art. Lem "overheard me talking on the phone and was very upset that I said that. 'You shouldn't have said that to him. Don't say it. Don't say it,'" the friend reported Lem as saying. Clearly, it had hit a nerve. On another occasion, the friend remembers Lem coming home with a female friend who reportedly said to him, "Why don't you marry Ms. [name omitted] just for cover."

But unlike some gays, then and now, Lem was not prepared to marry to disguise his sexual orientation. Some married gays were up-front with their spouses, while others lived a secret gay life on the side. Lem was not willing to get married under any circumstances. He was much too attached to Jack to opt for that. Lem remained a bachelor all his life and took his chances. As for Jack, he discovered Lem was gay early on during their friendship—although it is likely that, in the early 1930s, he did not conceptualize it as such.

Jack was too intelligent and politically savvy a man, however, not to have realized that his friendship with Lem was risky. But risk avoidance was not part of Jack Kennedy's DNA. He threw himself into life and took the kinds of chances that most people would only take if they were told they had a week to live. The thing he feared most, his friends said, was boredom, not risk. In addition, he had come face-to-face with death so many times that he knew life was unpredictable and a long life far from assured. He wasn't going to let anyone control his life, and he certainly wasn't going to let anyone choose his friends.

There is no doubt that Jack and Lem's friendship was light-years ahead of its time. How many straight men of that era would even have considered maintaining a close involvement with a man they knew to be gay even if the friend was totally discreet, especially if he was seeking high political office? How many straight men would invite a gay man, closeted or otherwise, to his home, have him stay there, and introduce him to his family and other friends?

By the time Jack reached the White House, he likely sensed that some of his aides were uncomfortable with Lem, although none of them dared question him about it. But Jack didn't base his friendships and attachments on what other people felt. He simply didn't care. If he liked someone, that was that. There is no record of Jack ever having discussed Lem's sexual orientation with other family members or with any of his friends. His old pal, newspaperman Ben Bradlee, for instance, recalls people realizing, or at least suspecting, that Lem was gay during the White House years. But asked if John Kennedy ever brought up the subject with him, Ben said no. "And I didn't bring it up with him, either."

If Jack raised it with anyone, it likely would have been his father, who was very much aware of gays, having worked with many in Hollywood. Joe sensed early on that Lem was gay but regarded him as a positive influence on Jack, helping to keep him out of trouble. Joe was also untypical. He didn't particularly care whether people were gay or not. So he had no particular objection to Lem. It is more probable, however, that Jack never discussed Lem's sexual orientation with anyone. He just accepted it as a private matter.

And it certainly was that for Lem during all the years that Jack was alive. After Jack's death in Dallas, Lem was rudderless, although his friendship with Robert Kennedy gave him some support—until Bobby, too, was killed, in 1968. But just over a year after Bobby's death, the Stonewall rebellion happened, and everything changed as far as being gay in the United States was concerned. Lem, like most older gays, now faced a new situation and a different set of challenges, with which he was ill equipped to deal.

Now gays were no longer expected to stay in the closet. They were told to rush to the nearest exit and keep going. Gay activists, in particular, excoriated closeted gays who seemed ashamed of who they were and who paid a terrible price, in their view, for "living a lie." Some prominent gays, in the worlds of politics and entertainment, were "outed," a practice that remains controversial even today. During the 1970s, Lem harbored a new fear—of being revealed as Jack Kennedy's gay friend. In the repressive era, ironically, that would have been much more unlikely.

For people of Lem's age, however, the situation was difficult. If he did come out to his family, his friends, the younger Kennedys—how could he explain all his prior behavior and statements that would now appear to be dishonest and deceptive? What would they think of his friendship with Jack, which for him was always the most important thing in the world?

For Lem, entering the last decade of his life, it must all have been bewildering. "Lem was terribly confused during the gay liberation years," said Larry Quirk, an author, film historian, and former editor of *Screen Stars* magazine. "Imagine when Lem and I were young, the gay thing was an abomination. Now it has become stylish, trendy really. I don't think he disapproved of the gay movement or anything like that. He thought it was good that things were changing. But his opinions varied depending on his mood. He was drinking more, and I told him that wasn't good for him."

Larry Quirk is the nephew of James Quirk, who edited *Photoplay* in the 1920s and 1930s, at that time the most influential movie magazine in America. James Quirk had earlier worked for Jack's grandfather, the legendary "Honey Fitz," when he was mayor of Boston. Through Honey Fitz, James met Joe Kennedy and introduced him to Hollywood (and to Gloria Swanson, with whom Joe had a legendary affair). Larry Quirk says he first met Jack just after World War II, when he was taking a stroll on Boston Common with Honey Fitz, to whom his uncle had introduced him. He then worked on Jack's first congressional campaign in 1946, which is where he says he met Lem.

"You could tell there was a strong friendship between the two of them even then," says Quirk. "Lem was so adoring that he went along with anything JFK needed or wanted. I'm not sure that was always for the best, because a true friend will tell you when he thinks you are wrong or when you should move in another direction. But Lem was not that type of guy, certainly not with JFK. He was a go-along type, really, and later in his life various people took advantage of him, I think."

"Lem and I became friends over time," Quirk continued. "We certainly didn't talk about anything gay in the early days. I was bisexual at the time. But later on we did. I also became involved with him sexually. But it was not a relationship. I didn't love him or anything like that." Lem would become more candid when he got into one of his moods or depressions, remembered Quirk. "I was practically his psychoanalyst," he said. "He told me a lot of things when he was thinking about writing a book around 1975, but of course he got cold feet and didn't. He talked to me because he was considering asking me to ghostwrite it for him since I had written books." Quirk, who does not drink alcohol, said, "Towards the end, I think Lem went into a decline with all the drinking and I kept my distance from him although we would still see each other from time to time and talk on the phone."

Inevitably, because of Lem's sexual orientation and the fact that he was spending a lot of time with people half his age, especially young Bobby Kennedy and Chris Lawford, rumors swirled around Manhattan for years concerning whether Lem attempted to seduce one or more of them. Despite the whispers and innuendo, however, none has said that he did. None has even said that they knew for sure that Lem was a gay man. Lem "was very upset over stories that he was gay, and when a particularly vicious rumor had it toward the close of his life that he was in love with the decades-younger Robert Kennedy Jr. and had aided and abetted his drug habit so as to personally control and use him sexually, he told me he had the first of what he was sure were irregular heart spasms," Quirk said.

A friend who was close to Lem at the time also considers the rumors vicious and unfounded. Asked if Lem kept his gay life separate from young Bobby and the Kennedys in general—in fact, from all the straight people he knew then, the friend said, "Absolutely, he kept it separate." The friend said Lem's friendship with young Bobby Kennedy was above reproach. "He was devoted to Bobby. If he got a phone call from Bobby to say he was on his way, he just dropped everything and got ready for Bobby." Lem "had hidden being gay all his life," added Quirk. "It's what he knew how to do and he wasn't going to change now. He felt that he would be letting the Kennedys down if it became known to them in particular." From all accounts, Lem's paternal concern for Bobby's future was genuine and always has been recognized as such by Bobby himself in the statements he has made.

Lem's association with the Kennedys made him more determined, not less, to keep his gay life secret. The easiest course for Lem—the one he chose—was to continue to cover his tracks, even though it became increasingly difficult to do so during the 1970s. He hid them so well that even Chris Lawford, who, like Bobby, visited and stayed at his house a lot, says he didn't know the nature of Lem's sexual orientation, though it occurred to him that he could be gay. Asked after the publication of his 2005 book, *Symptoms of Withdrawal*, whether Lem was gay, Chris said, "I don't know. He could have been. He certainly was flamboyant. But the answer is I don't know. I never saw any direct evidence of it."

It is interesting to speculate how Jack and Lem might have handled their friendship had it formed in 1973 instead of 1933. It is not at all clear that they would have fared better. Today, almost half the country still does not accept being gay as a legitimate alternative lifestyle, even though the overwhelming evidence is that gays don't consciously choose their orientation. Even now, many people reading this book may view the revelation that Jack Kennedy maintained a close friendship with a gay man for thirty years not as evidence of his open-mindedness and tolerance, but rather as proof that he was morally corrupt. Certainly in this post-Stonewall period, if a president maintained a close friendship with a gay man, the press, or sections of the press, would reveal it. It would not be covered up. And yet, there would still be a political price for the president to pay.

It's possible, therefore, that if Jack were running for the presidency today, he might be more wary of maintaining his friendship with Lem than he need have been in 1960. At least then he had a high degree of assurance that the friendship would not become fodder for newspapers and television. The Walter Jenkins affair hit the newspapers during the Johnson administration, but that was only because Jenkins had been arrested. Jack knew that Lem would never embarrass him in that way. He was always discreet—at least while Jack was alive. As long as that was the case, both men knew their friendship would remain private.

The question as to how Jack and Lem would handle their friendship if it formed today is, of course, impossible to answer, for Jack and Lem were men of their time. They came of age more than thirty years before Stonewall and more than a decade before the publication of the Kinsey Report. Neither they, nor the public, thought in terms of straight and gay at that time. Jack and Lem simply accepted their attachment for what it was and never questioned it. "Although there was a sexual element to his attraction to Jack, Lem loved Jack all his life beginning in the 1930s. His devotion to Jack was very touching," said Larry Quirk. "And Jack needed someone at that time who would love him unquestioningly. Lem did. Lem was the only person who loved Jack unconditionally who didn't want anything from him except to be with him, and Jack recognized that," he added. "At that time, they didn't put labels on it."

Nor, it is safe to say, did Jack and Lem ever put labels on it. They became friends when they were teenagers. They maintained their friendship over the years, through all the difficulties, all the crises, and all the tragedies. On the day John Kennedy died on November 22, 1963, his friendship with LeMoyne Billings was just as strong and committed as it was during the months it formed in the spring and summer of 1933.

14

HIS FINAL YEARS
(1963–81)

"I think you have one time around and I don't know what's going to be in existence in six months or a year, or a year and a half, or two years. So I think—you have to feel—that there are all of these problems and that you are here on earth to make some contribution of some kind."

—Senator Robert F. Kennedy

For Lem, Jack's death in Dallas was the end of his world. It wasn't so much that he never got over it. He didn't *want* to get over it. By all accounts, it took months for him to resume even the appearance of a normal existence. He just couldn't let go of the man who had been the most important person in his life since he was seventeen years old. Consumed by his memories, he talked about Jack constantly to his friends, and especially to the younger generation of Kennedys for whom he was the repository of so much information about the president in his younger days.

Lem became all too familiar with the intermittent ache that hits at unexpected and inopportune moments following a terrible loss even after the immediate period of grieving is over. For him, the jabs of pain were unbearable. Eventually, there is always someone in our lives whom we never get over, whom we think about every day. Self-evidently, for Lem, that was Jack. And yet the instinct for self-preservation is powerful, as well. Most people who have suffered irreplaceable loss choose to go on with their lives, despite never feeling whole again. And so did Lem. He chose to live, but the way in which he did so for the remainder of his life was the subject of much comment among those who knew him well. For Lem, it was as if John Kennedy was not completely gone. Almost everything he said and did for the rest of his days was somehow connected to Jack.

Moreover, even if he had been inclined to move on, it would have been difficult. Jack had been an immensely popular public figure. Images of him were everywhere. Books, television documentaries, records of his speeches were commonplace, a constant reminder to everyone who knew him of what had been taken away. Some people close to Jack avoided the coverage as much as they could, finding it too upsetting. But Lem did not. He welcomed anything that would cele-brate and preserve Jack's legacy. Lem had always stood by Jack and defended him when he was alive. He saw no reason to change course now that he was dead.

Lem readily made himself available to authors, scholars, and artists who lined up to document and explain—or try to—the Kennedy mys-tique. The artist Jamie Wyeth, who was asked to complete a posthumous portrait of President Kennedy, recalls immersing himself in everything he could get his hands on about JFK before beginning to paint. But it was Lem, he says, who "gave me an uncommon insight," stemming from the fact that he had been so close to the president. "Lem helped me see a JFK that no amount of books, films, tapes, and recordings could reveal," he noted. Lem spent not hours but days with him, talking about the JFK the public never knew, Wyeth added. "If you someday see my completed portrait of John F. Kennedy, look a little closer, for under the surface of the paint is a portrait of Lem Billings."

Most Americans felt a profound sense of loss on hearing the news of President Kennedy's death, but it faded over time. For Lem, it never did, because the loss was so deeply personal. He missed John Kennedy the man, John Kennedy the friend, much more than John Kennedy the

president. In the weeks and months after November 22, 1963, Lem
spent a great deal of time with Bobby and Jackie, mostly because he
knew they also loved Jack and felt a similar ache. It somehow helped to
be with them.

After they left the White House, Jackie and Caroline and John lived for
a short time in Georgetown, the elegant Washington neighborhood
where Jackie and Jack lived before he became president. But the nation's
capital harbored too many memories for her now. Georgetown in particular reminded her of all the evenings when she would greet Jack after
a long day in the Senate and Lem would come over for dinner, accompanied by his gigantic poodle. She also found that she had little privacy
there. Newsmen, photographers, and even curious citizens made her feel
under siege. She longed for the kind of anonymity that she knew Washington could never provide.

    After the family's short stay in Georgetown, Lem was ecstatic when
Jackie told him she and the children were moving to New York. Manhattan was his home, so it would be easier for him to see them. And he
often did, especially during the years between 1963 and 1968, when
Jackie was still single and still living in the United States. Sometimes he
would take John Jr. and Caroline to the movies or to other events
around town. But whatever they were doing, he would always tell them
stories about Jack, whether or not they asked. Often, Caroline and John
were just as interested in hearing Lem's stories about their father during
the old days as Lem was in telling them. "I grew up within a few blocks
of Lem's house and used to go over there to play with his dog, Ptolly
[Ptolly of Gramercy Park as Lem called his basenji, a barkless dog from
Africa], and to look at the pictures on his walls, or just to listen to his
stories," John F. Kennedy Jr. remembered. "He took an interest in me
and we would occasionally go on day trips during weekend afternoons
when we were both in the city." On one occasion, Lem took John to see
entertainer Jack Paar, a friend of Lem's. John wanted to see Paar's two
pet lions, which he kept in a nearby zoo.

    Jackie was delighted that Lem could tell John and Caroline so much
about their father that predated even the time when she'd met him in the
early 1950s. Lem had now been a part of Jackie's life for more than ten

John F. Kennedy Jr. and Lem, Warner Brothers' Jungle Habitat Wildlife Preserve, West Milford, New Jersey, 1972.

years, since shortly before she married Jack. There were so many memories of the late president that belonged only to Lem and to her. Although Jackie had always had a love-hate relationship with Lem, they had something deeply in common now—the passionate desire they shared, stemming from their love for Jack, to keep his legacy alive not only in the hearts of Americans but also in the world at large.

It was Lem to whom Jackie turned when the British government invited her and the children to attend the dedication of a memorial to Jack on British soil. She asked Lem to accompany them, which of course he did. The ceremony took place on May 14, 1965, at Runnymede, which is believed to be the most likely location of King John's 1215 sealing of the Magna Carta. Queen Elizabeth ceded the ground on which the memorial stands in perpetuity to the American people. The queen, who first met Jack in prewar London when she was a young princess, spoke warmly of the president, "whom in death my people still mourn and whom in life my people loved and admired." Jack's old friend, now former Prime Minister Harold Macmillan, also spoke. "I will never forget how touching Macmillan's speech was at the Runnymede ceremonies after the president's death," Lem later remembered.

Lem and John Jr., aboard Air Force One en route to Runnymede, England, with an inscrip-
tion from Jackie, 1965.

In Washington, D.C., a living memorial to Jack, the John F. Kennedy Center for the Performing Arts, opened its doors in 1971. The idea to have one major structure named after Jack in the nation's capital was Lem's. It should enjoy the privilege of singularity, he said. Other suggested tributes—for example, renaming Pennsylvania Avenue after Jack—were dropped. Lem served on the board of the new Kennedy Center, though he was forever complaining about the Nixon appointees with whom he had to work.

Lem was especially vociferous when Nixon replaced outgoing Kennedy members with his own people. He couldn't stomach the fact that, eight years after Jack had beaten him, Richard Nixon was now president of the United States. On one occasion, when the Kennedy Center roof leaked, Lem was convinced that Republican board members were conspiring to withhold the necessary funds to fix it. Eunice later said that neither the John F. Kennedy Library nor the John F. Kennedy Center for the Performing Arts "would ever have existed without Lem's love and dedication to Jack, his greatest friend."

After Jack's death, the most obvious person to whom the torch had passed was his brother, Robert Kennedy, now attorney general in the Johnson administration. Lem had met Bobby when he was nine years old, on the first of what would be many trips with Jack to the Kennedy family homes in Hyannis Port and Palm Beach. Although he never became as close to Bobby as he did to Jack, Lem always felt a special connection to Bobby. The feeling was mutual.

Robert F. Kennedy and Lem, Hyannis Port, 1964.

In the months after the assassination, both men were brought even closer together by their shared love of Jack and the pain of his loss. Gripped by immobilizing feelings of sadness, for months they could do little more than reflect, coping, and sometimes not coping, as best they could. For Bobby, the writings of the ancient Greeks and of modern existential authors such as Albert Camus became his consolation. He became more sensitive to suffering and injustice, qualities that would soon become evident to his fellow countrymen as he inched back into political life.

Lem noticed the changes in Bobby. The politician, who had been viewed as his brother's hatchet man, became more compassionate. Aware of his own pain, he somehow was more able to understand the pain of others, especially those in the neglected corners of American society who were poor and dispossessed. For Bobby, the cause of civil rights particularly, which his brother had embraced, became his passion. Black Americans sensed it and believed it, and believed in him. Slowly but perceptibly, he found his voice and prepared his return to the political arena. It was an outlet for his grief that Lem did not have. While Bobby wanted to move forward politically to fulfill Jack's dream, Lem remain trapped in the past, unable to move beyond Jack's death. Nevertheless, he was determined to help Bobby as best he could.

When Bobby rejoined the political fray, no one was happier than Lem. For many other Americans as well, Bobby became the last best hope for resurrecting Camelot, for a return to the kind of liberal idealism that Jack had epitomized. Bobby's decision to pick up Jack's torch was important to Lem as well. But, above all, Bobby was profoundly important to Lem personally. Although Jack and Bobby were very different in temperament—Jack, detached and cerebral, Bobby, intense and emotional—Lem saw so much of Jack in Bobby. He wanted to be with him, to be a part of whatever he wanted to do to continue Jack's legacy.

Bobby and Lem, Waterville Valley, New Hampshire, circa 1967.

Bobby and Lem on a diving trip off Lyford Cay, Bahamas, 1966.

Lem had first worked politically with Bobby almost twenty years earlier, on Jack's first campaign for Congress in 1946. Lem had headed the
office in Cambridge and remembered Bobby as a tough campaigner even
then. "He didn't want to work under me in Cambridge. Very shortly he
wanted to go out on his own, and there were eleven districts in Cambridge. He took over three." He added: "As I recall, it was the poorest
part of Cambridge. I'll never forget it—Bobby wouldn't let me anywhere
near the place."

But even though they often argued and sometimes got on each
other's nerves, they always made up in the end. After the 1946 campaign,
Lem and Bobby took a trip together to Latin America—visiting Brazil,
Uruguay, Argentina, Chile, Peru, Panama, and Mexico. They had a great
time, although Lem didn't care for the fact that Bobby drank Coca-Cola
instead of alcohol. Throughout the 1950s and the years Jack was in the
White House, Lem saw Bobby frequently, sometimes staying in his
house on Hickory Hill in Virginia, which Bobby had purchased from
Jack in 1957 for the then princely sum of $125,000, the same price Jack
had paid for it three years earlier.

After months of doubt and agonizing hesitation, on August 25, 1964, Bobby announced he was running for a U.S. Senate seat representing the state of New York. Two days later, he spoke at the 1964 Democratic convention in Atlantic City.

Lem was there and saw Bobby give one of the most moving speeches of his entire career. It included words from the definitive play about love and loss that Jackie had slipped to Bobby not long before he began his remarks. "When I think of President Kennedy, I think of what Shakespeare said in *Romeo and Juliet,*" he said. "'When he shall die, take him and cut him out into little stars and he shall make the face of heaven so fine that all the world will be in love with night and pay no worship to the garish sun.'" The main purpose of the convention was to nominate Lyndon Johnson to be the Democratic nominee for president in his own right. But Bobby was clearly the star of the proceedings.

After the convention, Bobby threw himself into the fall campaign, visiting all parts of the state of New York. This was Lem's home turf, and he was more than ready to place his advertising skills at Bobby's disposal. Lem was involved in the television spots, especially the last-minute advertising blitz throughout the state. His company, Lennen & Newell, was responsible for doing the polls and defining the issues. Some of the commercials revolved around staged man-in-the-street exchanges between Bobby and potential voters. "He was terrible," remembered Lem, "because he knew he was talking to someone who didn't give a damn about what he said. We changed from preplanned things to films of Bobby in action at places like Columbia University, where he was responding to students' questions, many of them pretty antagonistic."

Lem was never reverential toward the Kennedys and could argue with them ferociously at times as if—well—he were one of them. Anthony Shriver remembered that on one occasion Lem and his mother were going at it so fiercely that his dad, Sargent Shriver, attempted to intervene. He recalls Lem saying, "Stay out of this, Sarge, you're crazy to think Eunie baby [that's what he called her] could be right." Lem and Bobby had been having set-tos since Jack's first campaign, and they certainly had their share during Bobby's 1964 run for the Senate. But Bobby knew, as did all the Kennedys, that he was devoted to them and that being high-strung was just part of his temperament.

Despite their mutual disdain, President Johnson flew up to New

York to campaign for Bobby, mostly because he wanted a Democrat to win the seat—even if it had to be Bobby. "You had to feel sorry for them both," said Lem. "They were stuck with each other for forty-eight hours and it drove them nuts." Although it was a tough contest, Bobby beat Republican senator Kenneth Keating and became Senator Robert F. Kennedy representing the state of New York. He took his seat in the Senate in January 1965, just twelve years after Jack was first elected to the eminent body. Few of his colleagues had any illusions, however, that the Senate was the culmination of Bobby's political ambitions. They had no doubt that he would soon seek the presidency to complete the journey that Jack had begun on January 20, 1961.

As the Vietnam War worsened and racial strife increased during the powerful years of the 1960s, Bobby became increasingly alarmed at the direction in which the country was moving. After Minnesota senator Eugene McCarthy scored a strong showing in the New Hampshire primary in the spring of 1968, almost beating Johnson, Bobby decided he could wait no longer to run for the nation's highest office. Although many liberals felt he was jumping on the bandwagon that McCarthy had had the guts to begin rolling, on March 16, Bobby announced his candidacy—in the same Senate Caucus Room in which Jack had announced his run for president eight years earlier. "I do not run for the presidency to oppose any man," he said, in a thinly veiled reference to Johnson, "but to propose new policies." Again, just as in 1960, Lem, together with most of the people who worked for Jack in the earlier campaign, was there to cheer him on and to do all they could to help him win.

But it was not to be. On June 5, moments after giving his victory speech in the California primary, Bobby was shot at the Ambassador Hotel in Los Angeles. Again the bullets, again the agony. Lem was three thousand miles away on the East Coast when the shooting occurred. Gertrude Corbin, the wife of Paul Corbin, one of Bobby's advance men, called to tell him the heartbreaking news. Lem had worked with the Corbins to get Jack elected in Wisconsin and knew them well. At first, he couldn't grasp what Gertrude told him, couldn't believe it had happened all over again, that the same thing that had been done to Jack had now been done to Bobby, the two people who were irreplaceable for him. It seemed impossible that so much tragedy could befall one family. It was all so senseless. He just couldn't understand it.

But somehow, just as he had done five years earlier, Lem pulled himself together to do what he could to help the Kennedys get through the terrible days that lay ahead—even though he was just as stunned and crushed as they were. When she heard the news that Bobby had been shot, Jackie was traumatized all over again. She couldn't even think clearly, let alone sleep. She called the *New York Times* in the middle of the night seeking the latest news on Bobby's condition and then flew to Los Angeles. Her sister, Lee Radziwill, caught the first available plane from London to the United States to be by her side.

At Ethel and Bobby's home on Hickory Hill in Virginia, fourteen-year-old Robert F. Kennedy Jr. had been watching the primary election returns from California on television, but—since the East Coast is three hours ahead of the West—had gone to bed when his father was declared the probable victor. He didn't learn of the tragedy until the next morning when he picked up the newspaper and switched on the television. Experiencing grief beyond belief, he threw the newspaper into the fire. Bobby then spoke briefly with his mother, who, pregnant with her eleventh child, was by her dying husband's side in Los Angeles.

Ethel was with some of her younger children, including David, in many ways the most vulnerable. David was in an upstairs room of the Ambassador Hotel and saw his father shot on live television. He never got over it. By midafternoon in Virginia, the two oldest of Ethel and Bobby's children—Joe and Kathleen—returned to Hickory Hill from their respective New England boarding schools. Lem flew down to Washington to be with them, barely able to maintain his composure on the plane. But he knew he had to hold himself together for young Bobby, and Joe and Kathleen, while Ethel remained at her husband's side with the rest of her family.

Later in the day, Lem accompanied Bobby Jr., Joe, and Kathleen on the sad journey to Los Angeles aboard a plane provided by Lyndon Johnson. With them were two Secret Service agents. It arrived in L.A. at 11:30 in the evening, just a few hours before Bobby died. They rushed to the hospital, where Ethel was surrounded by family and close friends, including singer Andy Williams. But there was little that could be done. Since the bullets fired by Sirhan Sirhan had entered vital areas of Bobby's brain, the attempt to save him was hopeless from the start, even though the surgeons made a valiant effort.

The task of informing the world that another Kennedy was gone fell to Bobby's press secretary, Frank Mankiewicz. With restraint and dignity, his face etched with sadness and pain, Mankiewicz walked into the makeshift press room at the hospital. "Senator Robert Francis Kennedy died at 1:44 A.M. today, June 6," he said simply. "He was forty-two years old." That was all he said. It was all that needed to be said. It was a moment that anyone alive at the time watching on television can never forget, an image that will always stay with them.

Few could have known then that in that instant, the hopes of American liberals for a continuation of the progressive era that had begun thirty-six years earlier with the election of Franklin Delano Roosevelt, and that had been energetically continued by Jack Kennedy, were now dashed. Bobby was the last real liberal who had a good chance of becoming president. It was the end of an era, the end of a dream.

After the announcement of Bobby's death, events moved quickly. Lyndon Johnson sent Air Force One to bring the body back to New York. The immediate family, Lem, and other close friends were with Bobby for the final journey home. The casket was taken to St. Patrick's Cathedral on Fifth Avenue, where thousands gathered outside. During the weekend, the entire extended family descended on New York for the funeral. Bobby Jr., David, and cousin Chris Lawford spent most of the time that weekend at Lem's apartment.

"This became our refuge from the volatile intensity of our parents' pain and the place where we could be ourselves," Chris remembered. "With Lem we were connected to it all but had found a place where we could begin to exercise our independence while remaining tethered to the bright Kennedy light." Lem took them all to Saks on Fifth Avenue to buy new clothes. He was concerned that they all be properly dressed for the funeral so that they presented the right image to the public at a time when the eyes of the world were once again focused on them.

Just before 10:00 A.M. on Saturday, June 8, Cardinal Richard Cushing presided over a requiem mass. In addition to the family and Lem, many other friends and dignitaries came to pay their respects to another fallen Kennedy. They included President Lyndon Johnson, Senator Hubert Humphrey, Senator Eugene McCarthy, and even Richard Nixon. Coretta Scott King, who two months earlier had lost her husband to an assassin's bullet, was also there. The heartbreaking service lasted two hours and included the Adagietto from Mahler's Fifth Symphony, conducted by Leonard Bernstein, and *The Battle Hymn of the Republic* unforgettably sung by Andy Williams, who in the weeks to follow would become a good friend to Ethel at the time of her greatest need.

On the afternoon of June 8, a twenty-one-car passenger train carrying Bobby's body left Penn Station in New York City for what proved to be an eight-hour journey to Union Station in Washington, D.C. "It seemed almost interminable," remembered Lem, who was coming close to an emotional breaking point. At one point—incredibly—there was another tragedy. Near Elizabeth, New Jersey, a northbound train struck and killed two people who, in their zeal to get close to the train carrying Bobby, had wandered too close to the tracks. There was a delay but then the decision was made to continue on to Washington.

In the heat of a summer day, hundreds of thousands of people, perhaps as many as a million, lined the route to say good-bye to one of the most charismatic and committed leaders in the Republic's history. It was a spontaneous demonstration of respect—and love—rarely equaled before or since. There was an outpouring of emotion from ordinary people—young and old, black and white, male and female—some saluting, some placing their arm across their chest, some overcome by emotion, their eyes filled with tears. Chris Lawford recalled that he and his cousins ran between the cars of the train trying to make it onto the roof to wave to the people who lined the route. Bobby's casket lay in the last car. "I saw my aunt Ethel," he said, "kneeling by my uncle's casket. Her head was bowed down and her hands were clutched in prayer. She was crying with grief and pain of a loss unimaginable." The television networks covered the event for Americans watching at home. CBS anchor Walter Cronkite said, "It was the end of a brilliant public and political career."

The train took all day to reach Washington, arriving at Union Station shortly after nightfall. The family, Lem, and others accompanied the casket to Arlington National Cemetery, each of them carrying a candle. Lem was one of the pallbearers. There was a short fifteen-minute ceremony, and then Bobby was buried under a magnolia tree sixty feet southeast of Jack's grave. The two brothers who had epitomized the dreams of an entire generation were now together at rest forever.

As if sensing that America's progressive ideals were in mortal danger,

the statement the Kennedys released in the week after Bobby's funeral—
so typical of them—dwelled not on the loss but on the urgent tasks that
still lay before the nation. It asked Americans to pay tribute to Bobby by
supporting what he had stood for. "We shall honor him not with useless
mourning and vain regrets for the past, but with firm and indomitable
resolution for the future; attempting to relieve the starvation of people in
this society; working to aid the disadvantaged and those helpless inartic-
ulate masses for whom he felt so deeply."

However, difficult days lay ahead as the country fragmented politically and, at times, seemed to be coming apart at the seams. In the fall,
the country lurched right, electing Richard Nixon by a narrow margin.
The 1960s, which began amid so much hope and promise, ended with
the election of the candidate whom Jack had defeated in 1960 and who
had seemed destined then never to rise again. "You won't have Dick
Nixon to kick around anymore," he famously said after his defeat in the
1962 gubernatorial election in California. Lem was depressed even further. "Nixon always tries to undo what Jack did," he said.

But for Lem, Ethel and the children, Jackie, and all the others who
loved Bobby, there was little time for politics in the weeks and months
after he was laid to rest. They were trying to stay afloat, no one more so
than Lem. "He was ripped apart when it happened all over again," said
John Seigenthaler. "I don't think Lem was ever as close to Bob as he was to
Jack. It was not the same relationship. Bobby was more serious than Jack
and although he enjoyed Lem and laughed a lot with him, I think he took
Lem's needles with less tolerance than his brother. But Lem loved Bobby,
too. He had known him since he was a little kid. And Bobby loved him."

"Lem just couldn't get over what had happened no matter how hard
he tried," recalled his old friend and boss, Francis McAdoo. "He was devastated" by the events in Dallas, but after what happened to Bobby in
Los Angeles, "it was more than he could do to keep himself functional."
His behavior gradually became more eccentric. He also began drinking
more to bury what was for him an insurmountable mountain of pain. "I
just don't think he could ever get his hand back on the rudder," said
Seigenthaler. "Things were never quite as funny again. He lived every day
like he lost his friend, and then lost another friend. It's a cliché, but for
him the music died twice." Lem had barely handled Jack's death. He
simply didn't have the strength and fortitude to deal with Bobby's as well.

Jackie, too, grew increasingly distraught. Americans, people the world over, had admired the calm and dignity she had displayed during her husband's funeral. She had also been serene and regal during Bobby's funeral and tried to console Ethel and the children as best she could on the long train journey to Washington. But, as with Lem, once the funeral was over, she went off the deep end. She had become increasingly reliant on Bobby after Jack's death and had grown much closer to him in the years after Dallas than she had been earlier. Now he, too, was snatched away from her. She lashed out at the United States, a country that she believed harbored a culture of violence that was out of control. A day after Martin Luther King Jr. was shot, Bobby had spoken about the "mindless menace of violence in America which again stains our land and every one of our lives."

Now Jackie spoke out in understandable rage. "I hate this country," she said. "I despise America and I don't want my children to live here anymore. If they're killing Kennedys, my kids are number-one targets." She was determined to leave the country for a part of the world in which she felt her children would be safe. On October 20, 1968, the former First Lady of the United States married Greek shipping magnate Aristotle Onassis on the island of Skorpios in the Ionian Sea. She didn't love him the way she loved Jack, but with all of his wealth, which included a number of private islands, she sensed she and her children could be secure. Security, not love, was now her number-one concern. The American public was confused and baffled by her decision. How could the beautiful widow of the handsome president marry a short, unattractive foreigner? But the public was no longer the number-one concern for a woman who, not yet forty, had already suffered too much.

With Jackie now out of the country, Lem was unable to visit her and Caroline and John Jr. as easily as he could during the years before Bobby's death when they still were in New York. He began spending more time with Ethel's children, especially Robert F. Kennedy Jr., whom Lem had known since he was very young. "Lem and I were always friends," Bobby would say later. In the weeks and months after her husband's death, Ethel, who found solace in her religion, needed the help. On December 12, 1968, six months after Bobby died, Ethel's eleventh child, Rory, was born. She found it increasingly difficult to maintain discipline in a household of so many children. She searched out friends of Bobby's to help, especially with the boys.

One of those to whom she turned was Lem, since she had known him for decades and liked and appreciated him. Moreover, she knew how close Lem had been not only to Jack but also to Bobby. The problem was, however, that Lem was in no condition to help himself, let alone anyone else. "Ethel wanted various friends to help out," recalled John Seigenthaler, "but the truth of the matter is that Lem was in no shape to be a mentor to anybody. Nevertheless, Lem was determined to take young Bobby under his wing."

Larry Quirk said that Lem "had always been a person of low self-esteem. He never thought he accomplished very much on his own. It was always about the Kennedys. After Bobby's death, he became even more self-critical. He was basically depressed." Lem was not the right person to be helping anybody at this time in his life, added Quirk. But it is also possible that by helping young Bobby, Lem was helping himself as well. He always saw something of Jack in the other Kennedys, and in young Bobby, Lem saw Jack and Robert Kennedy. The time he spent with Bobby no doubt helped ease some of his pain.

In the late summer of 1968, Lem took Bobby on a trip to Africa, where the young Kennedy could revel in his lifelong love for animals. By all accounts, the two bonded on their African adventure. When they returned to the United States, young Bobby began spending a lot of time in Lem's Upper East Side Manhattan cooperative. Lem took Bobby under his wing, helped him with his problems in school, and reassured him by telling him that he and Jack had had troubles when they were young, too, and had been viewed as rebels by their families and teachers. "He helped Bobby a great deal during that

Lem and Robert F. Kennedy Jr., Valley of the Kings, Egypt, 1968.

terrible time and in the years after that. He was very good with Bobby," said Andy Williams, who met Lem at Hickory Hill some years earlier. "He went there a lot and I went there a lot. We became quite good friends" in the last decade and a half of Lem's life. "A couple of times, he [Lem] and Bobby came out to California and we would do things," Williams added.

Andy Williams and Lem, Waterville Valley, New Hampshire, 1970.

Younger son David and cousin Chris Lawford also spent considerable time at Lem's house, whose walls were adorned with Chagalls and other eminent works of art as well as scores of photographs of Jack and the other Kennedys. In some ways, Lem was a great person for the kids to be around. He wasn't as strict as Ethel, Eunice, Jean, and Pat, and he regaled them with stories about Jack and Bobby that only he could tell. Young Bobby and the other kids loved being around him. Remembering those times, none has spoken critically of Lem. Despite his sometimes eccentric and outrageous behavior, the older generation of Kennedys also felt he was doing them a favor by helping out at a difficult time. Ethel, Eunice, Jean, Pat, and Teddy evidently adored him to the end.

Lem and Ethel Kennedy, circa 1980.

Lem with Jean Kennedy Smith, Club 21, New York, 1981.

Lem and Ethel at annual Christmas skating party, Bedford-Stuyvesant, New York, 1975.

On his sixtieth birthday in 1976, Ethel gave him a big birthday splash. "He saw the ridiculousness of the human condition," she said, "and parodied it until tears came down his cheeks and an asthmatic coughing fit ended his glee."

"Lem Billings was an amazing person even in his decline," said John Seigenthaler. "I have never met anyone quite like him. I did not spend great amounts of time with him. But I never laughed more in the presence of anyone than I did when in his presence even when he poked fun at me—which he did often, making fun of my being a southerner. 'How can you touch that grits and red-eyed gravy,' he would say. And he would needle me about being a journalist. 'Gosh, you're all so common. Can't you get anything right?' I recall him saying. I'm sure the Kennedy kids enjoyed his sense of fun as much as I and many other people did." And that sense of fun sometimes came with a higher purpose. One friend recalls his dragooning her fourteen-year-old daughter into confronting women wearing leopard coats. Lem had no problem telling perfect strangers that they should be ashamed to be wearing furs when there were so few leopards left in the wild, she recalled.

"Lem was the most fun person I had ever met in my life," said young Bobby. "Lem's house was more than a fun house; it was a museum, a library, a classroom. Books lined the walls throughout. They were all histories, biographies, and art books." Recalling Lem ten years after his death, Bobby added, "Whenever I felt lonely, or sad, or left out, I would call Lem and laugh." But their friendship wasn't all fun and games. Sometimes the two would argue furiously, as Lem often did with everybody he knew well, including the other Kennedys. But later all would be forgiven, and things would go back to normal.

Lem had moods just like everyone else, said Peter Kaplan, Bobby's college roommate who also became a friend of Lem's. "Not all of it was giddy of course—there were depressed evenings and nights of disappointment when he felt that someone or another had not lived up to the values he assured [us were] part of all of us. There were nights in which he would just sulk, and it would take troops and assaults and marching bands to break him out of it." But break out of it he did.

"The stories he told and the examples he set gave us all a link to our dead fathers and to the generation before us," Bobby said. "The only person in my life who ever attempted to pass down any oral history of my family to me was Lem Billings," recalled Chris Lawford. "Lem was Jack Kennedy's best friend dating back to the days when they went to school together at Choate. He was a tall man with bad eyes, chronic asthma, and a roar of a laugh that announced his presence in any room, no matter how vast or crowded. He was as much a part of our family as anybody could be, traversing generations with his humor, fearlessness, and willingness to engage in all things Kennedy." Lem Billings, added Chris, "family friend and oral archivist, became my new godfather." Chris was in fact a godson, one of Lem's sixteen godchildren.

Lem seems to have been genuinely devoted to the younger Kennedys, according to the public statements they have made. All of them have spoken of him fondly and expressed particular appreciation for his willingness to discuss the family's past. No one in the family would talk about Uncle Jack's assassination except Lem, Chris noted. He said his parents, Peter Lawford and Pat Kennedy, avoided the issue at all costs. "Lem was the only one to try" and talk to us about it, he added.

Caroline Kennedy, Robert F. Kennedy Jr., Lem, and Chris Lawford, Forest Hills, New York, circa 1980.

Lem told Chris Lawford that Bobby felt the findings of the Warren Commission—which identified Lee Harvey Oswald as the sole assassin of President Kennedy—"were correct." Lem had his doubts, but he was certain that there was no one more invested in finding the truth than Bobby, added Chris. And if Bobby bought the commission's findings, so would Lem. "The day he told me this, I felt like I had been let in on a big secret. My uncle's assassination was first and foremost a murder of a family member, and knowing that my uncle Bobby had dealt with it made me feel better." However, Lem could not talk about the assassination with everybody. One employee of Lem's who asked him about it says, "He got extremely angry and said to me, 'Don't talk to me about JFK's death again.'"

Lem preferred to talk about what Jack and Bobby did while they were alive. He felt differently than the older members of the family, who found it too sad to discuss. Lem felt that the older generation had an obligation to pass on the legacy to the younger Kennedys. He was proud of what Jack and Bobby had stood for politically, and he wanted the kids to know as much about them as possible so that they didn't learn everything from books or newspaper articles, many of which, he felt, were overly critical and inaccurate.

The Kennedy boys felt that Lem was filling a void that their parents either couldn't or wouldn't fill. "His love for our parents' generation was transferred to ours," said Chris. "We were grateful that somebody connected to our parents was paying attention to us. There were thousands of people who claimed to love my family but only a few who gave love. Lem was one of them." He added: "Lem adopted our generation. He cared about us and treated us like the sons he never had." Because of his interest in the broad span of American history and not just the Kennedy era, Lem was able to place events in context for the younger Kennedys in a way that didn't seem paternalistic or boring.

Despite his affection and regard for Lem, however, Chris had no doubt that young Bobby, not him, was number one. Chris and David both resented Bobby being Lem's favorite. "I spent many years competing for Lem's attention and affection. When Lem was angry with Bobby, I became his favorite and the extra bedroom in Lem's Eighty-eighth Street apartment became 'Chris and Bobby's room,' but when they made up it was back to being just 'Bobby's room,'" Chris said. Despite the fact that young Bobby clearly was Lem's favorite, however, Chris seems not to harbor any resentment and remembers him with affection.

Two and a half years after Bobby's assassination in Los Angeles—in December 1970—Lem suffered another devastating blow, the death of his beloved mother, Romaine, in Baltimore at the age of eighty-eight.

Romaine had been a rock for Lem all his life, especially after the death of his father in the early 1930s, while he still was at Choate. It was Romaine to whom he would turn again and again in times of trouble, when he found it difficult to cope. "I think it was hard on him, harder than we expected or even knew," said Lem's sister, Lucretia. "He was really close to our mother and he missed her terribly." Said Lem's niece, Sally Carpenter, "They had a similar sense of humor. They both had a great time together." Ethel remembered that "his eyes filled with tears when he spoke of his mother. And she so doted on him. When Lem arrived home, all her social obligations were automatically canceled so she could be at his beck and call." Within a decade, Lem had lost Jack, Bobby, and his mother. Although Romaine, unlike Jack and Bobby, had lived a long life, it was another irreplaceable loss, one that further shattered his precarious hold on life, according to those who were close to him.

As he did after Jack and Bobby's death, Lem began to immerse himself more and more in his past. He would often talk about his mother, recalled Sigrid Gassner-Roberts, his live-in dog walker, art watcher, occasional cook, and most of all "the listener he needed," from 1969 to 1974. "He had an extremely close relationship with his mother. He called her practically every day," she said. She recalls one event in particular—about six months after Romaine died. "He woke up in the middle of the night. He said that I should go to the gravesite of his mother with him. We left at two in the morning [driving from Manhattan to Pittsburgh, where Romaine is buried] and on the way we had breakfast in a diner. On the way, he asked me to memorize the names of all the presidents and vice presidents we've ever had. This was his way of staying awake. After we saw the grave, we drove back to New York."

More than three decades after she left his employment, Sigrid still vividly remembers Lem. She says she had many conversations with him once they got to know each other. He loved talking about art and antiques, peppering his remarks "with all kinds of amusing comments." He also spoke of people he had known and gone out with over the years, including Ella Raines, the glamorous movie star who also had an early 1950s TV show titled *Janet Dean: Registered Nurse*. Sigrid said, "He told me he loved Ella Raines and Kathleen [Jack's sister] and that he would have married them." In addition, he discussed other people who meant a lot to him, including his beloved niece, Sally. And of course, he loved to have the younger Kennedys visit him. She recalls making popcorn for Jackie's children, Caroline and John, when they came over. However, Sigrid said she did not believe he was that close to his brother, Josh, a doctor in Nashville, Tennessee, who resented Lem's closeness to the Kennedys. "Every time his brother came up to New York, it ended up in a fight," she said.

"Lem and I developed a very good understanding," Sigrid continued. "We really liked each other. He was very understanding when I had a problem and I helped him when he had a problem." They got to know each other so well that she recalls his even giving her unsolicited advice about the men in her life—who was suitable and who was not. She remembers one night in particular, soon after she moved in to the ground floor of Lem's brownstone at 318 East Fifty-first Street. "He called me upstairs to the library. He told me he was happy with me and moreover that Ptolly [his dog] was happy with me. I recall asking him why he had so many photographs of President Kennedy on the wall. He said, 'Because I was President Kennedy's best friend.' He started to make Bloody Marys. And we stayed up till four in the morning drinking Bloody Marys and his telling me all about his relationship with President Kennedy. It was a very intense relationship." Lem never really got over losing JFK, she said. "He cried a lot about that."

During her years living with Lem, "the person he talked most about was John Kennedy," Sigrid recalled. "He was proud of the box of telegrams he and John Kennedy had exchanged. He relived his trip with John to Europe as I sat there listening, enraptured." There was no doubt of "his deep feeling for, and total commitment to, President Kennedy," she added. Sigrid, who now lives in Bludenz, a small Austrian town near the Swiss border, says she got to know Lem "very well" during the five years she stayed with him while she was a student at Hunter College, and that they confided in each other. "I was scared of him at first. He had the most unusual voice," she remembered. "I learned that whenever he said anything in a low voice, it was emotional and important. When I arrived to take the job, young Bobby answered the door [Bobby was staying with Lem during the college vacation] because Lem had twisted his ankle. I didn't see him for three weeks."

As to whether Lem was a gay man, Sigrid said, "I have a viewpoint on that, yes. I would say he was." She added: "He was a very kind and loving man. He had this gruff behavior, but underneath was a softy. If he loved you, he would do anything for you. He was so helpful to me and so generous," although she said he could be "stingy" when he wanted to be. She was particularly outspoken about his concern for the welfare of young Bobby, who had recently lost his father when she arrived at Lem's house. "He did an incredible amount for young Bobby. He would say Bobby has it in him to be president of the United States. He wanted to groom him for the presidency," she said. She remembered on one occasion, "Bobby ran away from college and joined a commune. Lem searched all night for him. He got a car from Mary Lasker [the philanthropist and a close friend of Lem's]. Eventually, he came back home at ten the next morning and said, 'He's now back in school.' He was totally, totally devoted to that kid."

Lem transferred a lot of his feelings about President Kennedy to young Bobby, Sigrid said. He saw so much of Jack in him. She said Lem did a lot for Bobby when it counted. She remembered that Lem would sometimes make deals with Bobby. "'I'll stop drinking if you'll stop smoking pot.' He made a lot of challenges like that," and kept to them for a time, she added. "For a while, he went back to drinking Coke." At the time, she said, Lem was working in an office on the thirty-second floor of the Pan Am Building, where he tended to financial matters involving the Kennedy family and was paid for doing so. In the fall of 1969, Lem moved to a new home on East Eighty-eighth Street, and Sigrid moved with him. During the time she lived with him, she said, there were four burglaries at Lem's two homes, during which he lost some beloved gifts from John and Robert Kennedy that could never be replaced.

With Sigrid taking care of Ptolly and doing some occasional cooking for him, and his beloved maid, Lucille, taking care of the house, Lem was free to indulge in his passion for art and antiques and restoring old houses. However, Lem considered that his most important task was to be a father figure to Chris Lawford and the other Kennedys, especially young Bobby. But eventually there was another side to Lem's substitute parenting. Unable to extinguish his own pain stemming from the assassinations of Jack and Bobby and the death of his mother, he began to drink more and also—a sign of the times—he began doing drugs, and doing them with the Kennedy kids. "Eventually all of them, including Lem, became addicted to drugs and booze," said Larry Quirk. "But Lem had the responsibility because he was much older and he procured some of the drugs for them," he added. Chris Lawford even remembers doing PCP at Lem's house "and watching the nuclear destruction of Manhattan from his first-floor window. This drug can definitely fuck with your perception of reality," he said.

Since Lem was a good thirty years or so older than the Kennedy kids, he has been blamed by some for their involvement with controlled substances. But the truth is, as Chris Lawford confirmed in his recent book, the kids were doing drugs before they did them with Lem and almost certainly would have continued doing so whether Lem was there or not. In fact, it was the kids who turned Lem on to drugs rather than the other way around. Lem always was a go-along, get-along guy, and he probably didn't think twice about taking the plunge, especially in this very different era when drugs were, if anything, fashionable. Also, as Sigrid Gassner-Roberts recalled, at times Lem would try to curb the substance abuse. But this was the era of "turn on, tune in, and drop out." Drugs were socially acceptable then to a degree they are not today, certainly in the United States. In those days, mainstream movies, and even some television shows, portrayed drug usage as routine and even attractive—sometimes funny and almost always pleasurable. Millions of American kids—and more than a few adults—were doing the same thing. Drugs were cool.

Inevitably, however, the excesses of the decade led to a counterreaction. People gradually realized the insidious effects of extreme drug use. The deaths of a number of prominent celebrities during the 1980s sounded the alarm. For every death, many others saw their lives spin out of control. Young Bobby and Chris Lawford, who had even snorted coke with his movie star father without batting an eyelash, survived their drug use, but not without deleterious effects. In this respect, Chris and Bobby were no different than millions of other young Americans during this period who regarded drug use as a rite of passage. Sadly, David Kennedy did not survive. On August 25, 1984, at the age of twenty-nine, he died of an overdose of Demerol and cocaine in a Florida motel room. It was a wake-up call for the entire family.

But it would be sensationalizing the lives of Lem and the young Kennedys to imply that their drug usage was an all-consuming lifestyle. Lem was probably doing more damage to himself at the time through drinking rather than drugs. One person who knew him well said that Lem tried at various times to give up alcohol—and did. But eventually he would return to drinking. Overwhelmingly, alcohol was his drug of choice. As he got older, it likely compromised his health more than he realized as his physician brother Josh, who knew Lem had a heart condition, no doubt warned him. However, it did not stop Lem from trying to keep up with the younger Kennedys and his other young friends.

During the 1970s, Lem and his twentysomething buddies took a series of memorable trips overseas. They hacked their way through the Colombian bush with machetes, rode horses across the Latin American llanos, confronted poachers in Kenya,

Lem and Robert F. Kennedy Jr. on a ranch in Mozambique, 1978.

Lem stages being held up by an official, after assisting with the capture of poachers on the Serengeti, 1968.

sampled ranch life in Mozambique, and navigated a previously unexplored
Peruvian River. The latter—a rafting trip down the Apurímac, a tributary
of the Amazon—was the most dangerous of their overseas adventures. In
addition to Lem and young Bobby, David and Chris went along. Three
non-Kennedys, Doug Spooner, Morris Stroud, and Blake Fleetwood, completed the group. Bobby was clearly the leader, with Lem now playing the
role of his number-one supporter, just as he had with Jack decades earlier.
Bobby "got a lot of magnetism from Lem's fixation," said Chris. "Lem had
decided that Bobby was the next bearer of Kennedy greatness—and none
of us were about to argue. These facts gave him gravitas. Lem's attachment
and anointing of Bobby defined him as the second coming."

Lem and the boys were on the river for ten days. Despite the risks, it
was a great adventure for all of them—not counting the bouts of diar-
rhea and other ailments they experienced during various parts of the
journey. It was on these trips that the old Lem was most often on display,
boisterous and full of fun despite the fact that he was a generation older
than his compatriots and found it hard to keep up with them. But he
matched all of them in his zeal to explore anything new or different. "He
burned with curiosity about everything and everyone," one of the boys

David Kennedy, young Bobby, Camilio (guide), Lem, and Chris Lawford, Apurímac River,
Peru, 1975.

Bobby and Lem with two Masai men, Kenya, 1975.

said. All the guys became familiar with his inimitable expressions, such as "golly neds" or "Judas Priest," when he was excited. He also used lines like, "Sister Anne Vigil," "bleeding like a stuck pig," "gabby as Patty's pig," and the more familiar "to the manor born." Bobby said later that Lem "taught me to love and appreciate people and things and how to be grateful for every day of my life."

These excursions with Lem were an important escape for a family that invariably felt it lived in a pressure cooker, constantly in the spotlight, always expected one way or another to continue Jack and Robert Kennedy's legacy. As the sole surviving son of Joe and Rose Kennedy, no one in the family felt this more strongly than Senator Edward Kennedy. In 1980, he seized the moment and challenged President Jimmy Carter for the Democratic nomination for president. Carter was furious that he faced a challenge from within his own party that was sure to weaken whoever the Democratic nominee was when he confronted his Republican opponent in the fall. But Teddy had long felt that Carter was too conservative. Twelve years after Bobby's death, he thought the time was right to restore Camelot. It was not. With his marriage to Joan barely intact, his campaign was a disaster from the start, beginning with an ill-timed interview with Roger Mudd on CBS. Asked by Mudd why he wanted to be president, Teddy could barely articulate an answer.

This time, Lem wasn't interested in helping out, as he had with Jack's and Bobby's campaigns so many years before. By 1980, Lem, at sixty-four, was worn out both physically and mentally, his health adversely affected by years of too much drinking and, in more recent years, too many drugs. He also felt that it was too dangerous for Teddy to run for

Jack, Teddy Kennedy, and Lem admiring an usher's gift, Teddy and Joan Bennett's wedding, 1958.

president and he feared that the stories about Kennedy missteps over the years both sexually and politically would surface all over again. The press was no longer as protective of the Kennedy mystique as it once had been— or anyone's mystique, for that matter. Teddy's behavior at Chappaquid-dick (Lem had rushed to the Cape to be with Teddy after that event), his reported womanizing and drinking, and his troubled marriage would all be dredged up again and again, Lem thought. His greatest worry was that the press would use Teddy's campaign to tarnish the images of Jack and Bobby, whose memory still was, and always would be, sacred to him.

"My god, why does he have to do it," Lem reportedly said. "He's just dragging the family through the mud. I don't know about everybody else, but I'm just going to sit this one out." As it turned out, he couldn't turn his back on Teddy, either. He was a Kennedy, after all. But the campaign to overturn an incumbent president proved too difficult even for

Teddy. Carter won twenty-four primary contests. Teddy won only ten. President Carter, however, was soundly defeated by Ronald Reagan in the fall, ushering in the conservative era in the United States that is still with us today.

At the Democratic convention that summer—the last summer of Lem's life—the Kennedy political magic was on display one last time. The liberals at the convention could still recognize one of their own and they jumped to their feet in joy as Teddy—in defeat—gave perhaps his best political speech ever. "The work goes on, the cause endures, the hope still lives, and the dream shall never die," he said. The delegates may have given their votes to Carter, but they gave their hearts to Teddy. After the cheers died down, Teddy left the stage satisfied he had made the attempt to restore Camelot on behalf of Jack and Bobby that always had been expected of him. Now he was content to bury his presidential aspirations forever. Henceforth, the political future of the Kennedys belonged to a new generation who were making their first, cautious attempts at running for political office in a country that had turned much more conservative than it had been a few decades earlier.

Jackie, who always kept her apartment in New York even when living overseas with Onassis, returned permanently to the city after his death in March 1975. No one was more thrilled than Lem, who was overjoyed to see her and also to be able to spend more time with John Jr., who was now fifteen, and Caroline, who was eighteen. Jackie's fear of living in the United States had subsided during her years abroad and she now felt more comfortable returning to the city she loved and that she felt would be a good place for her children to rediscover their American heritage. She also became a working woman for the first time since she had been the inquiring photographer for the *Washington Times-Herald* back in the fifties when she met Jack. She took a job as an editor first with Viking Press and later with Doubleday. Caroline, who was older now, frequently visited Lem's house by herself or with one of her boyfriends. Jackie, however, reflecting the mixed feelings she'd always had about Lem, saw him occasionally but not frequently. "Jackie was more cautious than people give her credit for," said Larry Quirk. "She saw that Lem was on a collision course and kept her distance, but she still saw him from time to time."

During the late 1970s, when Ethel's middle kids—Courtney, Kerry, and Michael—also discovered Lem, he was able to regale a new brood of young Kennedys with stories of Jack and Bobby from long ago. Nothing brought him greater pleasure. He would also take great pride in showing them his collection of Kennedy memorabilia, which spanned almost five decades. And he was not above giving them advice on fashion and etiquette, even though his tastes were now decidedly old-fashioned and stodgy. But Lem "always knew what was proper," said Michael Kennedy, whose middle name was LeMoyne, "everything from what you should get a person as a present on a particular occasion to how to handle yourself in various social situations—the things parents generally teach, but ours hadn't." Sometimes, Lem would take the younger Kennedys out drinking to Trader Vic's at the Plaza and then they would go back to the apartment and he would dig out all the old photograph albums and scrapbooks. They were there so much that Teddy said that whenever Ethel would call Lem's number, "one of her children would always answer the phone."

Lem at home, 5 East Eighty-eighth Street, New York, circa 1977.

Not all the young people Lem befriended were Kennedys. Donzaleigh Abernathy, an actress and daughter of the late civil rights leader Reverend Ralph Abernathy, recalls meeting Lem through Bobby. "We were kindred spirits," she said of Lem, even though she was in college and quite young at the time. "We had a mutual interest in the arts. He was elegant and classy, but with no pretension associated with it," she said. "He loved Bobby. That's for dog-gone sure. He was like a father to him." Donzaleigh, Bobby, and Lem would sometimes go out together to Trader Vic's, but she also talked to Lem one-on-one once she got to know him. "I knew him well enough to pick up the phone and ask him how he was doing," she said. "I remember talking to him not long before he died. He told me he wasn't feeling very well and had to work up his energy to walk his dog."

Another friend of Lem's at this stage in his life was Morris Stroud, the son of Joan and Gus Stroud, Lem's college pal from Princeton. Morris used to stop by Lem's house in the 1970s and sometimes stayed overnight. "I remember him as a very funny guy, very interesting. LeMoyne used to come to my parents' house in Pennsylvania for as long as I can remember. He used to love helping them with their antique store. He made a big effort if he liked you." Lem would go to auctions on the Cape and in Manhattan searching out quality items at a good price and then take them to Pennsylvania where the Strouds would place them in their antique store. Lem also loved working with the Strouds to renovate old homes in deteriorating rural areas of the state near where they lived. Antiques and early American art were Lem's passion all his adult life.

But at this stage of his life, Lem was not always in good spirits, Morris, who had been on one of the overseas trips with Lem, remembered. "Sometimes he could get angry and upset; he would pout. You couldn't say anything about the Kennedys. He would get very emotional. I recall when he visited our house sometimes, if someone was visiting and he didn't like what they said—he wouldn't leave the room, he would turn his chair around in protest." But mostly Lem was fun to be around, Morris said. "Being a bachelor, I think he could relate well to teenage kids. He wasn't judgmental. As for whether he went into decline, I don't know. I think there were fundamental parts of him that remained the same, particularly that sense of humor. . . . His sense of humor was so large it took over a room and captured everyone in it." He added: "He didn't talk to me too much about the Kennedys since all that had been years before. I guess he knew I was more removed from those events. But you could tell the president meant the world to him. The last time I saw him was probably not long before he died. I had some drinks with him and stayed overnight. The next day I had a hangover."

Indeed, it was different for Lem with the younger generation, for whom the tragedies of the 1960s were not as vivid, and who had not lived through the same permissive era. They were not as reliant on Lem as the older kids, who were now concentrating on building their careers and starting families. Lem was the godfather of Timmy Shriver, the son of Jack's sister Eunice and Sargent Shriver, who had been Jack's Peace Corps director. But Timmy regarded Lem as rather sad at this stage in his life—engulfed by his past and unable to forge a future for himself separate from his ties to Jack and Bobby. "He had grown out of touch with his old friends and even with his own family, letting go of the contacts which had once given at least a semblance of independence in his own life," he said.

Lem's old friend and boss Francis McAdoo recalls meeting Lem at the Princeton Club for drinks during these years. "Sometimes he was the same old Lem," he remembered, "but he would often show up at the club totally disheveled. He eventually didn't care about how he looked or dressed. It was sad to see, really." Other friends, too, began to notice a steep decline in Lem's appearance and demeanor. He would telephone Eunice, who had adored him ever since she'd met him in the early 1930s, almost every day, and say, "We're the only ones left of that early era," and then he would reminisce about better times when the world was at their feet and the future seemed limitless. And he would miss young Bobby, whom he was seeing less of now, although Bobby would still try to see him whenever he could.

Sigrid Gassner-Roberts recalls that during the time she was staying with Lem as his dog sitter and eventually his friend in the early 1970s, before his precipitous decline, he would have mood swings. "He had times when he was in a bad mood and wanted to be by himself and wouldn't take phone calls." But she recalled other times when she would come back from college "and he would call me up and say, 'Let's have some Bloody Marys.'" He loved to relax by lying in bed for hours watching television with his beloved Ptolly by his side, she said. She says the last time she saw him was in 1978, four years after she had left his employment to move to Adelaide, Australia, after she got married. Up till then, he had called her Miss G. and she had called him Mr. Billings. But she recalls his writing her after the visit and suggesting it was time they went on a first-name basis. "Shortly before he died, I wrote a letter to him in which I said, 'Who is going to look after you someday?' He wrote back to me saying, 'I don't intend to be sick long.'" He knew he was not in good health and didn't have much time left, she said.

Lem's live-in dog sitter during the last three years of his life, Retha

Gharzita, agrees that Lem sensed months before he died that he would not live a long life. He began trying "to patch things up" with people he cared about, she said. Retha did not become as close to Lem as Sigrid, preferring to keep the relationship more professional. But being in the same house, she got to know him to the extent that they sometimes discussed personal issues. She said that during these last years Lem did not talk to her much about his friendship with President Kennedy. "At that point, he was concerned about Bobby and whether or not Bobby was doing all right, whether he was making the right decisions, who he was dating, where he was going with his life."

She described the friendship between Bobby and Lem as close and caring although they "would go at each other" sometimes. Bobby would often come over with his French dog, Hogan, Retha recalled. "You knew the dog was French because Bobby spoke to it in French. It was always escaping from the house, sometimes taking off to Central Park," hotly pursued by Lem and Bobby. Lem always looked forward to Bobby's visits, Retha said, although toward the end they were not as frequent as when Bobby was younger.

Lem began spending more time alone in his room in his Manhattan townhouse. On long winter nights, how often must his mind have reeled back to his days at Choate and Princeton with Jack, to their summerlong vacation in Europe in 1937, to all the fun they'd had together after the war, and of course, during the White House years? His thoughts, fleeting and selective as thoughts are, became his support. The scores of photographs and hundreds of letters and telegrams that he and Jack exchanged when they were young, and that he scrupulously maintained, became his consolation, providing a link to a past that could now be recaptured only through memory. But nothing, not even the solace of memory, could take away the void left by Jack's absence. Each day, above all, was a day without him. In so many ways, his attachment to Robert Kennedy, and then to young Bobby, was a way of reliving his life with Jack, because he saw so much of Jack in them.

It is interesting to note that Lem never felt overshadowed by Jack even though it must have been difficult for him. When they were both at Choate, both Muckers, their lives were essentially similar. But Jack grew and evolved in very different ways than Lem did, eventually winning the nation's highest office and, after his death, becoming a national and worldwide figure of mythic proportions. Yet Lem never resented being the junior partner in the friendship, at least in the eyes of others. Lem remained proud of all Jack's accomplishments. Jack's success didn't make him feel less worthy. He reveled in Jack's triumphs, almost as if he felt a part of it. Indeed, he was. Remarkably, according to those who knew them, the friendship never seemed to change. Jack and Lem at the White House in the 1960s weren't that much different in the way they interacted with each other than Jack and Lem at Choate three decades earlier.

Larry Quirk said Lem told him that despite his various involvements, including with Quirk himself, Jack was the only person whom Lem had truly loved totally all his life. In the final analysis, Gore Vidal may be right. Gay and straight are merely labels to describe a complex range of actions and emotions that in reality defy categorization. "Only connect," one of the characters in E. M. Forster's novel *Howard's End* famously says—connections between people that at their core are difficult to fathom and impervious to will—but magical when they occur and are sustained. In the end, Forster suggests, there is only love—whom you love and how much.

One person who knew Lem well said that he was "more emotionally himself when he was with Jack Kennedy than at any other time." His deep and abiding love for Jack, he suggested, transcended everything, including sexuality, never wavering for one second from the time they met at Choate to the day he died. How many people are fortunate to have a connection like that, to be loved that much and so consistently? And it was clear that Jack loved Lem, too, in his own way and to the extent that he could, said Sigrid Gassner-Roberts. "Lem would never have forced himself on anyone," she remarked. "He wasn't that kind of person, so I'm sure JFK wanted him as a friend as much as Lem wanted him." She added: "It was a very unusual friendship. It was love, and not all love needs to be consummated."

Shortly after my interviews with her, Sigrid wrote to me. Here is what she said about Lem in full. "So many people comment on the fun person in him, and on so many photos he laughs. However, I am convinced that deep inside he was a sad and lonely person, in a sense a tragic antihero who didn't get what he wanted most—a life with and around JFK. I saw him cry and lock himself into his bedroom—unhappy, angry, disappointed—then again, overjoyed, totally devoted to young Bobby of whom he expected to carry on the torch of the Kennedys. His brother made fun of his close association with the Kennedys. I remember a phone conversation with Rose Kennedy. She was worried about him as he didn't answer the phone. I did, and she gave me advice on how he should treat a rheumatic problem. He was a bundle of emotions. His constant laughter, his being the live wire of any party, I am sure was a cover-up for his deep unhappiness. In my five years with him, I got to know him quite well—as far as he let anybody get to know him beyond the Lem-is-fun facade. He was a softy who liked to show a certain roughness at times. There was a lot of love in him that he bestowed on many people, but the one person that he loved most was torn away from him by an assassin's bullet. He transferred this love on to Bobby."

Although he distanced himself from some friends and acquaintances toward the end, Lem always looked forward to getting together with the Kennedys because they reminded him so much of Jack. And he still felt an obligation to pass the torch on to the younger generation. Courtney Kennedy's former husband, Jeff, recalls Lem being in good spirits shortly after he returned from a trip to Connecticut. "He had just come back from Timmy Shriver's graduation at Yale and was strolling around in that god-awful bathrobe he used to wear, making rum drinks and telling stories. He was in such a good mood. He sang *The Mikado* and acted out the whole thing. It was hilarious."

Earlier in the day, however, Lem's condition had been different. He told Retha Gharzita he was drained after taking a walk and that he was very tired, but she thought nothing of it at the time because later on he felt better. In the evening, Lem took his young friends to see the movie *Outland*. Lem seemed upbeat, talking about helping Michael Kennedy and his new wife, Vicki, design their new house in Virginia. He talked loudly through the movie, Michael remembered. "It was hilarious. . . . 'What the hell is going on,'" he would say. "We went back to his apartment and talked. It was a good night." It was Lem's last full night on earth.

Twenty-four hours later—on May 28, 1981, a day before the sixty-fourth anniversary of John F. Kennedy's birth—Lem died in his sleep following a heart attack. He was sixty-five years old. His friend Peter Kaplan, who stayed at Lem's place that night, found him the next morning. Bobby went to Lem's house when he heard the news, as did other members of the

Kennedy family and close friends, including Andy Williams. A heart attack may have been the technical cause of death, but those who knew Lem well, and loved him, felt that his fate had been sealed on November 22, 1963, when Jack Kennedy, the love of his life, was killed. Bobby's death five years later made it all the more certain that his last years would be clouded by pain, sadness, and regret. In reality, given his attachment to Jack, the miracle is that he lived on for so long after him with not one day passing that he didn't think of him and what he had lost.

In its obituary, the *New York Times* said, "K. LeMoyne Billings, a retired advertising executive and a friend of President John F. Kennedy, died Wednesday at his Manhattan apartment." Few New Yorkers reading the newspaper that day, however, could have known what those words really meant, could have realized what Jack Kennedy was to Lem Billings and what Lem Billings, in turn, meant to the most charismatic leader of our time. After his death, Teddy Kennedy referred to it as "a bond of perfect trust and understanding that served them all their lives." Jackie said, "So many grown-ups lose their sense of play. Lem never did. And how he loved his friends."

Lem was buried in Pittsburgh close to his mother and father. Most of the Kennedys went to Pennsylvania for the funeral, including Bobby, Jackie, and Caroline, as well as many others who knew and loved Lem. His friend Andy Williams sang "Ave Maria." Lem had asked the young Kennedy men to carry his coffin to its final resting place. But when they arrived at the cemetery, it was already in position to be lowered into the ground. The young men discussed what to do, not wanting to break their promise to Lem. "What are they doing?" Jackie asked Caroline. Then the young Kennedys moved toward the coffin, retrieved it from its position, and carried it around the gravesite before returning it to the burial spot. They all felt obligated to keep their pledge to Lem. And they did. "It says a lot about their relationship and what they thought of him," said Retha Gharzita, who was one of those present. "It was their way of saying, 'We respect what you did for us,'" she added.

In his eulogy, Bobby Kennedy Jr. said of Lem: "He felt pain for every one of us—pain that no one else could have the courage to feel. . . . I don't know how we'll carry on without him. In many ways Lem was a father to me and he was the best friend I will ever have." Eunice Kennedy Shriver said, "I'm sure he's already organizing everything in heaven so it will be completely ready for us—with just the right Early American furniture, the right curtains, the right rugs, the right paintings, and everything ready for a big, big party. Yesterday was Jack's birthday. Jack's best friend was Lem and he would want me to remind everyone of that today. I am sure the good Lord knows that heaven is Jesus and Lem and Jack and Bobby loving one another."

Godlike.

Jack and Lem, from Lem's scrapbook, circa 1935.

Acknowledgments

Over a period of two years, from 1964 to 1966, Lem Billings gave extensive interviews about John Kennedy and his friendship with him for the John F. Kennedy Library (JFKL). This 815-page oral history is under restriction at the JFKL. I want to express my profound gratitude to Robert F. Kennedy Jr., not only for giving me access to this vital document, but also for granting me permission to reference it. I have used it extensively to include comments from Lem that have never before been published. Most of the quotes attributed to him in the book are from his oral history. I also want to thank Mr. Kennedy for granting me unrestricted access to the Lem Billings Papers at the JFKL, much of which was placed in the library as recently as December 2003 and accessed here for the first time. It contains a treasure trove of information about the friendship between the president and Lem, and includes Lem's scrapbooks, which he scrupulously maintained till the day he died.

There also are hundreds of photographs in the collection, which constitute a priceless record of his friendship, not only with President Kennedy, but also with other members of the Kennedy family, as well as his own family. I very much appreciate the permission to use what seemed to me to be the most relevant and interesting photographs for this book. Lem did not keep a daily diary during JFK's presidency because he thought the president would not want him to—with one exception. Over a two-week period during the spring of 1961, in the aftermath of the Bay of Pigs fiasco and while the Laotian crisis was on the front burner, Lem did keep a daily record. This short diary, which was part of the Lem Billings Papers at the JFKL, provides a fascinating glimpse into JFK's thinking about both these events at this time. It has enriched the text immeasurably.

In writing this story, I adopted a journalistic approach. I have included only information I could substantiate either through documented evidence or through interviews with people who knew John F. Kennedy and/or Lem Billings. In important instances, I used more than one source to authenticate the material. But no matter how prodigious the research or how extensive the interviews, ascertaining the truth about something as complicated as a close attachment between two people is always difficult. We can find out what they did, but we cannot know precisely how they felt. There is an element of the unknowable for the two people involved, let alone for a writer such as myself who did not know them. In addition, over time, memories fade, documents disappear or become unavailable, and the past becomes increasingly difficult to reconstruct. I have tried as best as I could to render an accurate, truthful account of the friendship between Jack and Lem. Any errors I made in doing so are my own.

To all the people who knew John Kennedy and Lem Billings and who kindly devoted their time—in some cases, more than once—to talk to me about them and to answer my questions, I express my deepest gratitude. They included Ben Bradlee, Ted Sorensen, John Seigenthaler, Charlie Bartlett, Andy Williams, Letitia Baldrige, Larry Quirk, Francis McAdoo, Priscilla McMillan, Lucretia Billings Fisher, Sally Carpenter, Hugh Auchincloss III, Dick Donahue, Bill Elder, Michael Butler, Morris

Stroud, Sigrid Gassner-Roberts, Walter Smyth, Retha Gharzita, Donza-leigh Abernathy, Thales Vassilikiotis, Sidney Brinkley, Judy Donald, and Betty Beale. I am particularly indebted to Gore Vidal, who spoke with me numerous times about his memories of Jack and Lem and who was also most helpful in other ways. Finally, I would like to thank those people who talked to me on condition that they not be quoted by name, either in full or in part.

The hundreds of books and articles already published about John F. Kennedy are an indispensable beginning point for a writer embarking on a new JFK project. Numerous authors of Kennedy books offered their help and encouragement, including Laurence Leamer, Michael O'Brien, Nigel Hamilton, C. David Heymann, Joan Blair, Geoffrey Perret, Sally Bedell Smith, Robert Dallek, David Horowitz, and James Giglio. The insights of Ms. Blair, Mr. Heymann, and Mr. Horowitz, who were able to interview Lem before his death more than a quarter century ago, were particularly valuable in this regard. I also am grateful to Mr. Hamilton for making the large collection of materials used in his book on JFK available to authors and scholars at the Massachusetts Historical Society. David Michaelis, who knew Lem, wrote a wonderful chapter mostly about Jack and Lem in their younger days for his book *The Best of Friends*. Although not a source for my book, Mr. Michaelis neverthe-less provided thought-provoking perspectives.

I am indebted to my researcher, Mona Esquetini, a wonderful friend, without whom the book would not have been written. This was very much a collaborative effort. To put it simply, I did the writing and talked to people and Mona took charge of the research. It included scouring all the previous books written about JFK, identifying relevant files at various research centers such as the JFKL and the Massachusetts Historical Society, and locating people who knew Jack and Lem—no easy task in some cases. More important was Mona's encouragement throughout this project, especially during times of frustration and disappointment. During our long discussions about the material we accumulated, Mona's comments helped sharpen and focus my own insights and perceptions. Her dedication to completing the book was extraordinary. I am eternally in her debt.

Allan Goodrich, the chief archivist at the JFKL, was tremendously helpful in facilitating research for the book, ably assisted by Sharon Kelly and Stephen Plotkin. I am particularly grateful to Maryrose Grossman at the JFKL, who not only offered advice about the selection of photographs for the book but who also spent a great deal of time scanning them for publication. Kim Nusco at the Massachusetts Historical Society also worked hard to obtain all the materials I requested at that institution. The best manuscript reviewer ever in my opinion is Charla Hatton, whose ability to spot a needle in a haystack is amazing. Charla gave the book a thorough reading and spotted problems early on while I still had a chance to fix them. Thanks also to Guvany Guem for his unfailing support and reassurance throughout the three years it took to write the book. In addition, I would be remiss if I did not mention the many useful ideas and suggestions made by Donn Barrett, Rick Marshall, John Ward, Don Symmes, Al Conyers, and Estelle Baird.

I want to express my appreciation to my agent, Anne Devlin, who believed in this project from the beginning, not least because she shared my fascination with JFK. Anne streamlined the proposal and tirelessly pursued a quality publisher. My editors at Avalon, Don Weise and Lukas Volger, offered wise counsel at moments when it mattered. Their razorlike focus on the story of Jack and Lem improved the book immeasurably. Don, a senior editor, was in overall charge of the project and marshaled it to completion with superb skill and dedication. Last but not least, my profound thanks to my mother and father, who indulged my overriding passion for politics beginning at an early age when they probably thought I should be riding my bike or playing marbles.

Although I have lived all my adult life in the United States and have been a U.S. citizen for decades, I am conscious of the fact that the subtleties and nuances of a culture, especially one as large, complex, and diverse as ours, can sometimes escape even the most perceptive and sensitive of writers, especially one whose formative years were spent elsewhere. Too many nonnative-born authors, it seems to me, are tempted by the broad stroke and the overarching generalization in describing this vast country, a tendency I hope I avoided.

David Pitts
Washington, D.C., August 2006

APPENDICES

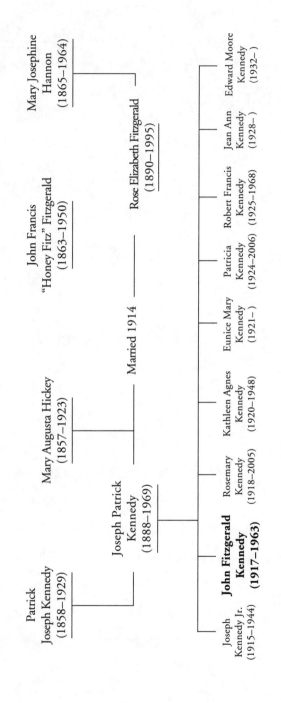

Kennedy Family Tree

Patrick Joseph Kennedy (1858–1929)

Mary Augusta Hickey (1857–1923)

John Francis "Honey Fitz" Fitzgerald (1863–1950)

Mary Josephine Hannon (1865–1964)

Joseph Patrick Kennedy (1888–1969)

Rose Elizabeth Fitzgerald (1890–1995)

Married 1914

Joseph Kennedy Jr. (1915–1944)

John Fitzgerald Kennedy (1917–1963)

Rosemary Kennedy (1918–2005)

Kathleen Agnes Kennedy (1920–1948)

Eunice Mary Kennedy (1921–)

Patricia Kennedy (1924–2006)

Robert Francis Kennedy (1925–1968)

Jean Ann Kennedy (1928–)

Edward Moore Kennedy (1932–)

Billings Family Tree

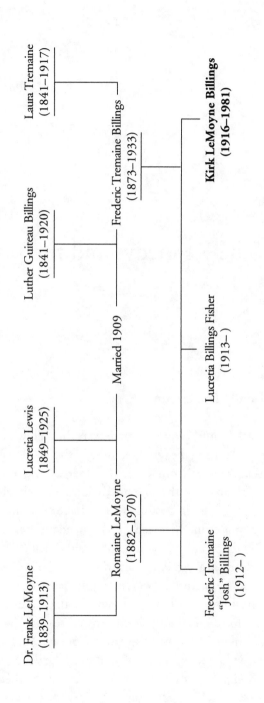

Dr. Frank LeMoyne
(1839–1913)

Lucretia Lewis
(1849–1925)

Luther Guiteau Billings
(1841–1920)

Laura Tremaine
(1841–1917)

Romaine LeMoyne
(1882–1970)

Married 1909

Frederic Tremaine Billings
(1873–1933)

Frederic Tremaine
"Josh" Billings
(1912–)

Lucretia Billings Fisher
(1913–)

**Kirk LeMoyne Billings
(1916–1981)**

The Kennedys and the Billingses

∾

Jack's Family Background

Both of Jack Kennedy's grandfathers were the children of immigrants driven from Ireland during the potato famine of the 1840s. On the maternal side, Thomas Fitzgerald from County Limerick and Rose Anna Cox from County Cavan were the parents of John Francis Fitzgerald (known as "Honey Fitz"), born in Boston in 1863. In 1889 he married Mary Josephine Hannon of Acton, Massachusetts, the daughter of Irish immigrants Michael Hannon and Mary Ann Fitzgerald. Their eldest daughter was Jack's mother, Rose Elizabeth Fitzgerald, born in 1890 in Boston.

On the Kennedy side of the family, Patrick Kennedy, a cooper, left his ancestral home in Dunganstown, County Wexford, and sailed from New Ross for the United States in the 1840s. In 1849 in East Boston he married Bridget Murphy, also from County Wexford. Nine years later she was a widow with four small children, the youngest of whom, Patrick Joseph Kennedy, would become Jack's grandfather. In 1867, Patrick Joseph ("P. J.") Kennedy married Mary Augusta Hickey, daughter of

James Hickey of Cork, Ireland, and Margaret M. Field, also of Ireland. Their son, and John F. Kennedy's father, Joseph Patrick Kennedy, was born in 1888 in East Boston.

The Fitzgeralds and Kennedys settled in Boston in search of the economic opportunity the United States offered. But they had to overcome the harsh discrimination prevalent against Irish Catholic immigrants at that time. The early Kennedys and Fitzgeralds worked as peddlers, coopers, and laborers; later they became clerks, tavern owners, and retailers. By the end of the nineteenth century, Patrick "P. J." Kennedy and John "Honey Fitz" Fitzgerald, the president's grandfathers, had become successful politicians. Honey Fitz served twice as mayor of Boston and as a member of the U.S. Congress. P. J. Kennedy served in both the Massachusetts House and Senate.

Joseph Patrick Kennedy Sr. was the architect of the Kennedy political dynasty. Famously ambitious, he graduated from Harvard and by age twenty-five was already president of a small bank. Later he moved into the investment banking, film production, and liquor businesses and became wealthy. He supported Democrat Franklin Delano Roosevelt in the 1932 election. In 1933, the new president selected Kennedy to be chairman of the Securities and Exchange Commission. In 1938, FDR selected Kennedy to be ambassador to Britain, the first Irish Catholic to hold that post. He died in 1969.

Jack's mother, Rose Fitzgerald Kennedy, was born in 1890, the eldest of six. A devout Catholic, she nonetheless longed to attend the secular Wellesley College, but her family intervened and sent her to Manhattanville College for the Sacred Heart in New York instead. Multilingual and skilled in the social graces, she wore the mantle of matriarch elegantly throughout her family's ascent to national political and social prominence. In 1984 she suffered the stroke that left her confined to a wheelchair until her death at age 104 in 1995.

Joseph P. Kennedy (1888–1969) and Rose Fitzgerald (1890–1995) were married in 1913 and had nine children:

- Joseph Patrick Kennedy Jr. (1915–1944). Died when his World War II bomber, heavily laden with high explosives, blew up over the English Channel on August 12, 1944.

- John Fitzgerald Kennedy (1917–1963). Thirty-fifth president of the United States, assassinated in Dallas on November 22, 1963.

- Rosemary Kennedy (1918–2005). Died January 7, 2005 at the age of eighty-six. Severely developmentally disabled, she had been institutionalized since 1941.

- Kathleen "Kick" Agnes Kennedy (1920–1948). Died in a plane crash on May 13, 1948.

- Eunice Mary Kennedy (1921–). Founder of Special Olympics for the mentally and physically challenged. She is married to Sargent Shriver, the first director of the Peace Corps.

- Patricia Kennedy (1924–2006). Died of pneumonia on September 17, 2006. She was the former wife of Peter Lawford, who died of alcoholism in 1984.

- Robert Francis Kennedy (1925–1968). U.S. senator and former U.S. attorney general. He was assassinated in Los Angeles on June 6, 1968. His widow, Ethel, never remarried.

- Jean Ann Kennedy (1928–). Former U.S. ambassador to Ireland. Her husband, Steve Smith, who managed Kennedy family finances, died of cancer in 1990.

- Edward "Teddy" Moore Kennedy (1932–). U.S. senator since 1962 and the sole surviving son. He is married to Victoria Reggie.

Lem's Family Background

The Billings side of the family can be traced back to Andrew Billings, who fought in the American Revolution. Lem's grandfather, Luther Guiteau Billings (1841–1920), joined the Union Army at sixteen and fought in the Civil War. He also went on to fight in the Spanish-American War and served as an admiral in World War I. He married Laura Elizabeth Tremaine (1841–1917). Their son, Lem's father, Frederic Tremaine Billings, was born in 1873. Educated at the U.S. Naval Academy and Yale University Medical School, he specialized in diseases of the heart and was the first doctor to bring the electrocardiograph machine west of the Allegheny Mountains.

The LeMoyne side of the family goes back to the landing of the *Mayflower*. His original American ancestor was the Puritan leader William Brewster. Lem was a direct descendant of George Washington's father and was related to both Abigail Adams and Abraham Lincoln. He shared an ancestor with Marie Antoinette and was also descended from the eighteenth-century French sculptor and court artist Jean-Baptist LeMoyne, for whom he was named. John Julius LeMoyne de Villiers, a doctor in the French Army and a French Royalist, fled to Gallipolis, Ohio, after the French Revolution, attracted by the promise of a land deal. A leader of the "French 500," he was given a land grant by President Washington. Later, the family resettled in Pennsylvania, not far from Pittsburgh. In the days before medical schools, LeMoyne tutored students in medicine at home. His only child, Francis Julius LeMoyne (1789–1879), took up what would become the family tradition of practicing medicine, but his interests were broader than medicine.

Francis Julius LeMoyne was also strongly committed to fighting for the rights of African Americans. He founded the Washington County Anti-Slavery Society and ran as a vice presidential candidate on the Abolitionist platform. The LeMoyne house became a stop on the Underground Railroad, a network of safe houses that helped slaves escape to the North. Francis LeMoyne also established what would become LeMoyne College to educate "freedmen of color" in Memphis, Tennessee. In 1968, LeMoyne and Owen colleges combined to become LeMoyne-Owen College, still a predominantly African American institution today. LeMoyne married Madeleine Romaine Bureau in 1823; they had eight children.

A son, Dr. Francis LeMoyne (1839–1913), who would become

Lem's grandfather, also followed a career in medicine and was an assistant surgeon in the Union Army during the Civil War. After the war, he became a pediatrician in Pittsburgh, where he realized his dream of building a hospital devoted solely to the care of sick children, Children's Hospital. He married Lucretia Lewis (1849–1925). Their daughter, Romaine, was Lem's mother.

Romaine LeMoyne (1882–1970) and Dr. Frederic Tremaine (Josh) Billings (1873–1933) were married in 1909. The marriage produced three children:

- Dr. Frederic Tremaine (also known as Josh) Billings Jr. (1912–). He is a retired physician in Nashville, Tennessee.

- Lucretia Billings Fisher (1913–). She is active with the Preservation Society in Baltimore, Maryland.

- Kirk LeMoyne Billings (1916–1981). Died on May 28, 1981. He was an advertising executive, inventor, and John F. Kennedy's best friend.

Timeline

∾

1916:   April 15, birth of Kirk LeMoyne Billings in Pitts-
        burgh, Pennsylvania.

1917:   May 29, birth of John F. Kennedy in Brookline,
        Massachusetts.

1933:   Jack and Lem meet at Choate.

1933:   Lem's father, Josh, dies.

1935:   Muckers incident at Choate.

1935:   Jack and Lem graduate from Choate.

1935:   Jack and Lem spend fall semester at Princeton. Lem
        continues there. Jack leaves because of illness at the
        end of the semester.

1936:   Jack spends much of spring and summer in Arizona
        and California convalescing.

1936:   Jack enrolls at Harvard in the fall.

1937:   Jack and Lem take summer European vacation.

1938:   Joe Kennedy Sr., Jack's father, becomes U.S. ambassador to Britain. Jack spends part of 1938 and 1939 in Europe.

1939:   Lem graduates from Princeton.

1940:   Jack graduates from Harvard University.

1941:   Jack, age twenty-four, is sworn in as an ensign in the navy.

1941:   Jack and Lem are together in Washington when they learn about the attack on Pearl Harbor on December 7.

1942:   Lem joins the Ambulance Corps. Sees action in North Africa.

1943:   Jack serves in the navy in the South Pacific.

1943:   Jack's PT boat 109 is rammed by a Japanese destroyer. Under his leadership, most of the crew is eventually rescued.

1944:   Lem receives a commission in the U.S. Naval Reserve and serves in the South Pacific.

1944:   Joseph Kennedy Jr. is killed while flying a mission over Europe.

1945:   Jack is discharged from the navy.

1946:   Lem is discharged from the navy.

1946:   Jack is elected to the House of Representatives, Eleventh Congressional District, at age twenty-nine. Lem works on campaign.

1946–48:   Lem attends Harvard Business School.

1948:   Kathleen ("Kick") Kennedy is killed in a plane crash.

1948–52:   Lem works at General Shoe, Nashville, Tennessee.

1952:   Lem lands job as VP with Emerson Drug Company, Baltimore. Invents '50s fad drink "Fizzies."

1952:   Jack defeats incumbent Henry Cabot Lodge Jr. to win election to the United States Senate. Lem celebrates victory with Jack in Hyannis.

1953:   Jack marries Jacqueline Bouvier. Lem attends wedding.

1957:   Caroline Bouvier Kennedy is born.

1958:   Lem moves to New York to become advertising executive with Lennen & Newell.

1960: Lem works for Jack in the Wisconsin and West Virginia primaries and helps gather delegates at the Democratic convention in Los Angeles. Jack wins the Democratic nomination for president and picks Lyndon Johnson as his running mate.

1960: John F. Kennedy Jr. is born.

1961: January 20. Jack takes the oath as president. Lem attends all the inauguration events.

1961: Lem goes with Jack on his first European trip as president.

1963: Lem visits Ireland, England, Germany, and Italy with Jack on the latter's final trip to Europe.

1963: Jack is assassinated in Dallas. Lem hears the news in New York.

1964: Robert F. Kennedy is elected to the U.S. Senate. Lem works on campaign.

1965: Lem goes with Jackie, John, and Caroline to event in Runnymede, England, to commemorate Jack's life.

1968: Robert F. Kennedy is assassinated while campaigning for president in Los Angeles. Lem flies down to Hickory Hill to be with Bobby and Ethel's children, and then to California.

1970: Lem's mother, Romaine Billings Fisher, dies at the age of eighty-eight.

1971: John F. Kennedy Center for the Performing Arts opens. Lem was instrumental in getting it built and named after Jack.

1981: Lem dies of a heart attack in New York.

Source Notes

∾

The following abbreviations are used:

JFKL—John F. Kennedy Library (located in Boston, Massachusetts)

MHS—Massachusetts Historical Society (also located in Boston)

LOH—LeMoyne Billings Oral History, closed without permission, JFKL

TBP—The Billings Papers, closed without permission, JFKL

TBC—The Billings Collection (a tribute to Lem by people who knew him, organized by Robert F. Kennedy Jr. and Sally F. Carpenter)

NHC—Nigel Hamilton Collection, MHS

Lem Billings's 815-page oral history, which was recorded in multiple sessions from 1964 to 1966, is closed at the JFKL. I appreciate Robert F. Kennedy Jr.'s granting me permission to read and quote (indicated below) from this document. The Billings Papers are also closed at the JFKL but were also accessed by the author with the kind consent of Mr. Kennedy. The TBP consists of dozens of boxes of documents and photographs, including the scrapbook that Lem kept during his 1937 trip to Europe with Jack (also cited below). This material was placed in the library as recently as 2003 and has never before been accessed by an author. I obtained Lem's FBI file, also referenced below, through a freedom of information request.

Much of the information in the earlier chapters of the book is based on letter and telegram exchanges between Jack and Lem. Some of the letters are open and can be read by researchers at the JFKL. Others are restricted. I want to thank Mr. Kennedy for allowing me to read and reference the latter. Nigel Hamilton, who wrote *JFK: Reckless Youth,* placed copies of Jack and Lem's correspondence, as well as other materials, in the MHS. I am grateful to him for being able to access that collection. Since it is clear from the chapter texts when a letter or telegram from either Jack or Lem is excerpted, there is no reference to the correspondence in these source notes.

Of the many books written about JFK over the years, I read and analyzed over a hundred, especially those that referenced Lem. The ones cited in my book are indicated in the source notes. In addition to written materials and interviews, I made use of my library of films and tapes relating to John F. Kennedy, including NBC's coverage of the 1956 Democratic convention, the 1960 Democratic convention, the 1960 presidential campaign, the 1961 inauguration, and the events of November 22–25, 1963, when the network's news division was on the air most of the time.

INTRODUCTION

xv　　"It's hard to describe it as just friendship," David Michaelis, *The Best of Friends: Profiles of Extraordinary Friendships* (New York: William Morrow, 1983), 175.

xvii　"Lem was President Kennedy's best friend," ibid., 189.

xiii　 As he walked through the lobby doors, ibid., 181.

xiv　 "I'm so sorry about the president," ibid., 182.

xiv　 Lem talked on the phone with Jack's sister Eunice, William Manchester, *The Death of a President* (New York: Harper & Row, 1967), 255.

xiv　 In Lem's datebook, Michaelis, *The Best of Friends,* 181.

CHAPTER ONE—THE TIES THAT BIND (CHOATE, 1933–35)

4　　From all accounts, author interviews with Billings family members, 2004–2006.

4　　Lem's "lifelong friendship," Teddy Kennedy, TBC, 67.

5　　"Forgoing cynicism," Ethel Kennedy, ibid., 31.

5　　"Jack had the best," LOH, 6.

5　　"Jack couldn't or wouldn't conform," Rose Fitzgerald Kennedy, *Times to Remember* (New York: Doubleday, 1974), 177.

6　　"Josh was nothing like," author interview with John Seigenthaler, May 4, 2006.

7　　Lem, too, "burned with curiosity," Robert F. Kennedy Jr., TBC, 29.

7　　"All my life," LOH, 423.

8   "Together, they really had everything," TBC.

8   One series of boys' books, author interview with Sally Carpenter, July 20, 2006.

9   "He talked a good deal," author interviews with Francis McAdoo, May 31, 2005 and June 2, 2006.

9   "He was affected by his father's death," author interview with Sally Carpenter, July 20, 2006.

11   "Jack was charismatic," author interviews with Gore Vidal, October 5, 2005, and July 21 and August 4, 2006.

11   "Lem was always an equal to Jack," Michaelis, *The Best of Friends*, 168.

11   "I certainly don't think," LOH, 105.

12   "[T]heir schoolboy banter," Seymour St. John, article in NHC at MHS.

12   "Of course, this infuriated the teacher," LOH, 9.

12   [T]he Muckers Club—There are many accounts of this in various prior JFK books. The most detailed accounts, however, are in Michaelis, *The Best of Friends*, 127, and Kennedy, *Times to Remember*, 180.

14   "He lacked the proper qualities," LOH, 74.

15   "If the Muckers Club would have been mine," Nigel Hamilton, *JFK: Reckless Youth* (New York: Random House, 1992), 127.

15   "Jack had to have a good talking-to," Rose Kennedy, CBS Interview with Harry Reasoner, CBS News Collector Series, *Great Figures in History*, John F. Kennedy (VHS, 1981).

15   "[T]hat Jack has established a reputation," Dr. Prescott Lecky, psychologist's report, NHC at MHS.

15   "Olive rushed out to the car," LOH, 86.

16   "Whenever he was home," ibid., 66.

17   "I remember we were driving along," ibid., 88.

17   Lem "remained Jack's lifelong close friend," Kennedy, *Times to Remember*, 182.

17   "I wouldn't say," LOH, 65.

18   "Almost all his life," Kennedy, *Times to Remember*, 85.

18   "I know that there are few simple answers," ibid., 85.

18   "Actually, he came very close to dying," LOH, 5.

19   "I seldom ever heard him complain," ibid., 41.

19   "Sometimes he found it hard to breathe," author interviews with Francis McAdoo, May 31, 2005 and June 2, 2006.

20   [L]ose their virginity, Geoffrey Perret, *Jack: A Life Like No Other* (New York: Random House, 2002), 37.

20   "I closed my eyes and masturbated," author interviews with Larry Quirk, July 15, 2004 and June 2, 2006.

20   "They had a similar," author interview with Sally Carpenter, July 20, 2006.

22   Boys who wanted sexual activity, author interview with Geoffrey Perret, June 15, 2006.

22   "Please don't write to me," letter (June 27, 1934) open, JFKL.

23   "I don't know," LOH, 6.

24   "Jack made a big difference in my life," Michaelis, *The Best of Friends,* 181.

24   [A]lways assumed Lem was gay, Michael O'Brien, *John F. Kennedy: A Biography* (New York: St. Martin's Griffin, 2006), 63.

25   "I liked Lem," author interviews with Charlie Bartlett, March 8, 2005 and June 8, 2006.

26   [S]ubtracted a year from his age, Michaelis, *The Best of Friends,* 141.

27   "I was at Choate," LOH, 7.

28   "These schools will not survive," Choate archives, Wallingford, CT.

28   [W]as coeducational, author visit to Choate, May 5, 2006. Interview with Judy Donald, archivist.

30   "He made it clear," LOH, 17.

30   "For me, the beginning with Lem," Teddy Kennedy, TBC, 67.

31   "They called it Mother's terrible summer," author interview with Sally Carpenter, July 20, 2006.

31   "I really got to know them well," LOH, 4.

32   "After a while, though," Kennedy, *Times to Remember,* 178.

32   "We were always thinking of ways to make sure," David Horowitz and Peter Collier, *The Kennedys: An American Drama* (New York: Warner, 1984), 436.

33   "His father would always assign a subject," Evelyn Lincoln, *My Twelve Years with John F. Kennedy* (reprint, Boulder: Black Pebbles Publishing, 2003), 97.

33   Joe "encouraged them to form their own ideas," LOH, 13.

33   "[H]e was very bright," Michaelis, *The Best of Friends,* 144.

33   "He has continued to be to this day," Kennedy, *Times to Remember,* 182.

34   Lem knew the words, Robert F. Kennedy Jr., TBC, 22.

34   Jack sang that haunting song, Kenny O'Donnell and Dave Powers, *Johnny, We Hardly Knew Ye: Memories of John Fitzgerald Kennedy* (New York: Little, Brown, 1972), 449.

36   "This is as good a time to tell you," letter to Lem from Joe Kennedy, Michaelis, *The Best of Friends,* 145.

37   "Oh, me, I'm wife number five," Perret, *Jack: A Life Like No Other,* 45.

CHAPTER TWO—REBELS WITH A CAUSE (COLLEGE, 1935–37)

39   "I believe Ambassador Kennedy," Rip Horton Oral History, June 1, 1964, interview conducted by Joseph Dolan, Justice Department.

40   "These boys are going to have a little money when they get older," Kennedy, *Times to Remember*, 170.

42   "He had never been secretive with me," LOH, 128.

44   He was sick most of the time, ibid., 45.

44   "We're puttin' on our top hats," *New York Times*, January 17, 1961. "Kennedy (c. 1935) Models Informal Formal Wear" [Special to the NYTs].

44   "It had the appearance of jaundice," LOH, 45.

47   "[T]he beginning of troubles with his back," Kennedy, *Times to Remember*, 215.

47   "I saw him an awful lot," LOH, 134.

50   Lem's Republicanism, author interview with John Seigenthaler, May 4, 2006.

CHAPTER THREE—TRIP OF A LIFETIME (1937)

Note: Both Jack and Lem kept diaries during their trip to Europe in 1937. The information in this chapter is largely taken from those documents and is so evident in the text. Their diary references are therefore not repeated below. Lem's diary is part of the TBP at the JFKL and can only be accessed with permission from Robert F. Kennedy Jr., which the author obtained. It is actually more of a scrapbook than a diary and contains scores of photographs and other mementos of the trip but fewer written entries than Jack's diary. Therefore, Lem's diary impressions of the visit are supplemented by comments from his oral history, which are cited below. Jack's 1937 diary is open at the JFKL.

52   "Though all American passports legibly state," Michaelis, *The Best of Friends*, 153.

53   "I really feel that this trip," Joseph P. Kennedy letter, TBC, 74.

53   "I borrowed the other half," LOH, 38.

54   "I went over with very little money," ibid., 37.

55   "He did enjoy seeing the cultural," ibid., 151.

57–58   "Jack Kennedy was intensely interested," ibid., 25.

60   "He [Jack] was tremendously inquisitive," ibid., 28.

62   "We ran into them on the beach," author interviews with Francis McAdoo, May 31, 2005 and June 2, 2006.

63   "We just had awful experiences," Hamilton, *JFK: Reckless Youth*, 193.

65   "There was a noticeable change in Jack Kennedy," LOH, 34.

66   "I remembered we listened," ibid., 158.

CHAPTER FOUR—THE RESTLESS YEARS (1938–41)

69   "It was a period," LOH, 166.

70   "Come on Lem, you know you're not the marrying kind," Horowitz and Collier, *The Kennedys: An American Drama*, 440.

71   "Of course, I continued to see Jack," LOH, 172.

72   "None of us are worrying too much about jobs," K. LeMoyne Billings letter to Kathleen Kennedy, April 30, 1939, LBP.

75   Jack, Joe Jr., and Kick, Kennedy, *Times to Remember,* 252.

75   "[W]hen we were on our way home," ibid., 252.

77   "Democracy is finished in Britain," Seymour Hersh, *The Dark Side of Camelot* (New York: Little, Brown, 1997), 80.

77   "It's my feeling," LOH, 168.

77   "This book is an attempt," 1940 radio interview, *Remembering Jack* (CD), edited by Vincent Touze and Christophe Loviny.

78   "I know why he went to Stanford," LOH, 183.

79   Jack talked to Chuck for hours, Laurence Leamer, *The Kennedy Men: 1901-63* (New York: William Morrow, 2001), 225.

80   "I've known many of the great Hollywood stars," Robert Stack, *Straight Shooting,* (New York: MacMillan, 1980), 72–73.

82   "He had a very nice apartment," LOH, 205.

Chapter Five—Courage under Fire (War, 1941–45)

83   "We found a game," LOH, 207.

86   "I hear the hotel clerk at the Sumter," FOIPA 1000949-000, 21.

86   The FBI reported, ibid., 2.

87   "After you hear someone call you a fairy," Gore Vidal, *Palimpsest: A Memoir* (New York: Penguin, 1995), 380.

90   "When he was all finished," LOH, 225.

93   "Ours was one of the bigger units," L. B. Cuddy, TBC, 79.

94   "October 24th, [the day after the second battle," The AFS at Alamein, L. B. Cuddy, *AFS News Bulletin,* vol. 1, no. 6, February 1943.

94   "We chased the German Army," L. B. Cuddy, TBC, 82.

99   "Lem got hold of some of the first lenses," author interview with Josh Billings Sr., April 7, 2004.

103   "When two brothers are growing up," LOH, 64.

Chapter Six—Turning Point (1945)

Note: Jack kept a diary at the UN conference in San Francisco and in Europe reporting on the British election and observing the devastation in Berlin. It was published for the first time in full in a book titled *Prelude to Leadership: The European Diary of John F. Kennedy, Summer 1945,* edited by Deirdre Henderson (Washington, D.C.: Regnery Publishing, 1995).

106   "When I think of how much this war," Henderson, ed., *Prelude to Leadership*, dedication page.

108   "Tonight it looks like Labor," Jack's diary, June 21, 1945.

110   "[T]he British as the worst colonizers," FOIPA, No. 1000949-000, reported conversation, February 23, 1943.

111   "All the centers of the big cities," Jack's diary, July 29, 1945.

111   "The devastation is complete," ibid., undated.

111–10 "The walls were chipped," ibid., undated.

112   "One or two of the women wore lipstick," ibid., undated.

112   "Jack told me that Eisenhower," LOH, 231.

113   "I was reluctant to begin law school," radio interview, *Remembering Jack* (CD), edited by Touze and Loviny.

115   "We don't want any losers around here," Kennedy, *Times to Remember*, 143.

116–17 "We wrote each other a lot," LOH.

CHAPTER SEVEN—SEEKING THE TORCH (1946–59)

120   "Jack and I would go to bed," Horowitz and Collier, *The Kennedys: An American Drama*, 129.

120   "He was never that interested in politics," author interview with Sally Carpenter, July 20, 2006.

120   "Every district that poor Lem," Rip Horton's Oral History, June 1, 1964, interview conducted by Joseph Dolan, Justice Department.

121   "Lem was a relaxation for the president," author interviews with Francis McAdoo, May 31, 2005 and June 2, 2006.

123   "It made him realize," Edward Klein, *All Too Human: The Love Story of Jack and Jackie Kennedy* (New York: Pocket Books, 1997), 96.

124   Lem's closeness to Jack "went too far," author interview with Billings family member on condition of anonymity.

125   "I wondered whether he was gay," ibid.

126   "[G]ood and efficient" worker, author interviews with Francis McAdoo, May 31, 2005 and June 2, 2006.

127   To his delight, it was a hit, "Advertising: Soft Drink Tablet," *New York Times*, April 5, 1957.

128   "Never in our conversations," Lester David, *Jacqueline Kennedy Onassis: A Portrait of Her Private Years* (New York: St. Martin's Press, 1995), 69.

128   "I can remember that a sort of officious little guy," LOH, 430.

129   "I will say that it was Moyne's," author interview with Lucretia Billings Fisher, June 13, 2006.

130   "Of course, he had it," LOH, 479.

132   "It was a very daring thing for him to do," ibid.

133   "By the time he was approaching his mid-thirties," Kennedy, *Times to Remember,* 346.

133   "And I could tell Jack was interested in her," author interview with Hugh Auchincloss III, May 15, 2006.

134   "Jackie was different from all the other girls," LOH.

134   "But don't get into any arguments with him," author interview with Hugh Auchincloss III, May 15, 2006.

135   "Jack was intrigued by Jackie," ibid.

135   "When Jackie and Jack had problems," LOH.

136   "I can remember we were going to Bobby's," ibid., 376.

136   "He had never been involved as a friend with girls," ibid., 384.

137   "I felt I should prepare her a little bit," ibid., 390.

137   She was not offended by Lem's warning, author interview with Hugh Auchincloss III, May 15, 2006.

138   "I only got married," author interview with Priscilla McMillan, June 2, 2005.

138–39   "I mean, I don't want to marry a girl who's traveled sexually," Klein, *All Too Human,* 83.

140   "The Senate's Gay Young Bachelor," O'Donnell and Powers, *Johnny, We Hardly Knew Ye,* 108.

140   "I don't think he was the kind of person," LOH, 386.

142   After the marriage, "she wasn't the same," author interviews with Charlie Bartlett, March 8, 2005 and June 8, 2006.

142   "While on one level," Klein, *All Too Human,* 183.

142   "He wasn't moody in any way," LOH, 186.

143   "She liked him, but she didn't like him," Sally Bedell Smith, *Grace and Power: The Private World of the Kennedy White House* (New York: Random House, 2004), 32.

144   "This beautiful set," LOH, 401.

145   "I saw him [Jack] writing the book," LOH, 462.

148   "Lem helped take care of him," author interviews with Francis McAdoo, May 31, 2005, and June 2, 2006.

150   "We haven't seen the last of Senator Kennedy," Chet Huntley, NBC news coverage of the 1956 Democratic convention.

150   "[A]nd of course he talked about nothing else but the convention," LOH, 495.

150   Jackie often found herself left, Anne Garside, *Camelot at Dawn: Jacqueline and John Kennedy in Georgetown, May 1954* (Baltimore: Johns Hopkins University Press, 2001), 38.

152   "'LeMoyne, you've got to understand here and now," LOH, 347.

153   "Weekends at the Cape were no longer," LOH, 505.

CHAPTER EIGHT—ROOM AT THE TOP (THE 1960 ELECTION)

157   "I told him I didn't see how," LOH, 512.

157   In addition, Jack also persuaded, author interviews with Francis McAdoo, May 31, 2005 and June 2, 2006.

158   "Lem was in Milwaukee and Madison," author interview with John Seigenthaler, May 4, 2006.

158   "I actually didn't even know where to start," LOH, 520.

159   "The problem is if you take a New York advertising executive," author interview with John Seigenthaler, May 4, 2006.

160   "In all fairness to myself," LOH, 517.

161   Jack "had never been too anxious to go into West Virginia," ibid., 546.

165   "Paul called and I told him about Lem," Gertrude Corbin, TBC, 102.

166   "Lem was very witty," author interview with John Seigenthaler, May 4, 2006.

168   Then at 7:19 A.M. eastern standard time, *NBC News* election coverage.

170   [T]old a story that is revealing, Paul Fay, *The Pleasure of His Company* (New York: Harper and Row, 1966), 119.

171   She recalls one Sunday morning, Evelyn Lincoln, *My Twelve Years with John F. Kennedy* (New York: David McKay, 1965), 217.

CHAPTER NINE—ONE FINE DAY (THE INAUGURATION, 1961)

176   He managed to deliver the first three lines, NBC News inauguration coverage.

177   [R]emarked on how cold the day was, ibid.

177   But Judy Donald, the current archivist at the school, author interview with Judy Donald, archivist, Choate, May 5, 2006.

179   "This is one of the most astounding parts," Michaelis, *The Best of Friends,* 173.

179   "Some people like to go on long walks alone," Michaelis, *The Best of Friends,* ibid., 174.

179   "He recognized that even as the people would reject a king," Bedell Smith, *Grace and Power,* 58.

180   "Why, with a telephone call like this, we can change the world," Arthur Schlesinger Jr., "Robert Kennedy, The Lost President," *Esquire,* August 15, 1978.

180   "I remember Eunice and I went in together," LOH, 700.

181   Lem stayed at Bobby's house, author interview with John Seigenthaler, May 4, 2006.

182   "Lem was at all the parties," author interviews with Francis McAdoo, May 31, 2005 and June 2, 2006.

182   Jackie gave him a chilly look, O'Donnell and Powers, *Johnny, We Hardly Knew Ye*, 286.

CHAPTER TEN—FIRST FRIEND (1961–63)

186   "Can you imagine," Michaelis, *The Best of Friends*, 172.

186   "[B]eing considered for an appointment to the Peace Corps," Lem's FBI file, initially classified secret, no page number.

186–87 "Needless to say," LOH, 711.

187   So he did take a small part-time position, *New York Times*, September 20, 1961. Washington, September 19 (Associated Press): Kennedy Names Friend.

187   There was a minor scandal of sorts, Associated Press report, March 24, 1962.

187   "Many people think," LOH.

188   "They both saw each other a lot," author interview with Lucretia Billings Fisher, June 13, 2006.

192   "[F]ast friends" going back to prep school, author interview with Ted Sorensen, April 12, 2006.

192   "Lem was in and out of the White House," Ralph G. Martin, *Seeds of Destruction* (New York: Putnam Publishing Group, 1995), 335.

192   Lem "just moved into his room," J. B. West, *Upstairs at the White House: My Life with the First Ladies* (New York: Coward, McCann & Geoghegan, 1973), 235.

192   "In all the books about Jack Kennedy," LOH.

193   "Well, I did stay there a lot," LOH, 706.

194   "He was always around," author interview with John Seigenthaler, May 4, 2006.

195   "[R]emembers Lem at many of the social events," author interview with Letitia Baldrige, March 27, 2006.

195   Lem "used to glare at me," Arthur Schlesinger Jr., NHC at MHS.

195   "[O]ften saw Lem there," author interview with Hugh Auchincloss III, May 15, 2006.

196   "Lem Billings entered Jack's life," Herbert S. Parmet, *Jack: The Struggles of John F. Kennedy* (New York: Dial Press, 1980), 302.

196   "Lem was great around the president," author interviews with Charlie Bartlett, March 8, 2005 and June 8, 2006.

197   "I suppose it's known that Lem was gay," author interview with Ben Bradlee, March 22, 2006.

197   The friend was Joe Alsop, there is a full account of Alsop's secret life, including the 1957 attempted blackmail by the KGB, in *Joe Alsop's Cold War: A Study of*

Journalistic Influence by Edwin M. Yoder Jr. (Chapel Hill: University of North Carolina Press, 1995).

197   But the story Susan told Jack, Barbara Leaming, *Mrs. Kennedy: The Missing History of the Kennedy Years* (New York: Free Press, 2001), 57.

199   "I think he [Jack] felt quite comfortable in the company of homosexuals," author interviews with Gore Vidal, October 5, 2005 and July 21 and August 4, 2006.

201   "Kennedy's most significant attachments," Hersh, *The Dark Side of Camelot*, 24.

202   "It can now be confirmed," author interview with unnamed source, August 4, 2006.

202   "Nobody read his press criticism," LOH, 119.

203   "I think that was the end of it," ibid., 123.

203   "Jack and Jackie were to be the guests," Leaming, *Mrs. Kennedy,* 57.

204   On one occasion, Indian Premier, ibid., 241.

205   "Lem returned from France boasting," Michaelis, *The Best of Friends,* 177.

207   "I just seem to be attracted to men like that," Carl Sferrazza Anthony, *The Kennedy White House: Family Life and Pictures, 1961–63* (New York: Touchstone, 2002), 97.

207   "The great thing about Jack Kennedy," author interviews with Charlie Bartlett, March 8, 2005 and June 8, 2006.

209   But she made an exception for Lem, West, *Upstairs at the White House,* 235.

209   "[H]as been a houseguest every weekend since I've been married," ibid., 235.

209   "The relationship between Jackie and Lem was complicated," author interview with Sally Carpenter, July 20, 2006.

209   "Lem, hello," the telephone call can be heard at jackandlem.com and also at the JFKL, Dictabelt 4B1, Cassette A.

210   "Jackie would usually go down Friday," LOH, 712.

211   "He was desperately unhappy about the result," LOH, 728.

216   "I knew about Cuba," Lem's diary, ibid., 132.

216   "Lem said he encouraged the president," author interview with Thales Vassilikiotis, August 28, 2006.

217   "He told me again that he probably wouldn't run in '64," LOH, 751.

218   "I probably spent more time with him," ibid., 126.

219   Lem "was devoted to Jack," author interviews with Charlie Bartlett, March 8, 2005 and June 8, 2006.

219   "He was very fed up with his mother," LOH, 793.

222   "Some of the most informal film," *JFK in Ireland* (VHS/DVD), Telefis Eireann.

CHAPTER ELEVEN—A TOUCH OF CLASS (1961–63)

225   "Let the skeptics snort about Camelot," Hugh Sidey, *Time* magazine, May 30, 1994.

226   "White House entertaining," author interview with Letitia Baldrige, March 27, 2006.

226   "The kind of things that were done," LOH, 423.

227   "Hey, how about me," Bedell Smith, *Grace and Power,* 253.

228   Lem "sometimes had one too many," author interview with Hugh Auchincloss III, May 15, 2006.

228   [R]iding on an elephant, C. David Heymann, *A Woman Named Jackie: An Intimate Biography of Jacqueline Bouvier Kennedy Onassis* (New York: Lyle Stuart, 1989), 214.

228   Jack's language was old navy talk, author interview with Ben Bradlee, March 22, 2006.

230   "[W]as very malicious," Christopher Andersen, *Jack and Jackie: Portrait of an American Marriage* (New York: Avon, 1997), 326.

230   "He came up to me and attacked me," author interviews with Gore Vidal, October 5, 2005 and July 21 and August 4, 2006.

231   "[T]he real reason for Gore's 'expulsion,'" George Plimpton, *Truman Capote: In Which Various Friends, Enemies, Acquaintances and Detractors Recall His Turbulent Career* (New York: Anchor, 1998), 379.

231   "Well, he knew that Jack and I had a relationship," author interviews with Gore Vidal, October 5, 2005, and July 21 and August 4, 2006.

232   "Jack was an invalid all the time," ibid.

232   "I've often wondered why," LOH, 374.

233   "[W]hales and socks," Andersen, *Jack and Jackie,* 281.

234   "Certainly, Jack and Jackie had their share of rumors," LOH, 708.

235   "You never saw him on crutches," ibid., 473.

236   "Their marriage never seemed more solid," Arthur Schlesinger Jr., "JFK Revisited," *Cigar Aficionado Online,* November/December 1998.

238   "I want to come," Manchester, *The Death of a President,* 63. There is a detailed account of Jack's final days in this book.

CHAPTER TWELVE—BLOOD AND TEARS (NOVEMBER 22–25, 1963)

240   "It nose-dived from 76 percent," Arthur Schlesinger Jr., "Robert Kennedy: The Lost President," *Esquire,* August 15, 1978.

240   "In 1963, by irreversibly insisting," Ted Sorensen, *The Kennedy Legacy* (New York: MacMillan, 1969), 225.

241   "The fact is," he said, "that same poll," JFK News Conference no. 61, September 12, 1963.

241   "[H]e wouldn't have won any of them," Guthman and Shulman, editors, *Robert Kennedy In His Own Words* (New York: Bantam, 1988), 76.

242   "[S]topped by the all-black college on impulse," Robert F. Kennedy Jr., TBC, 20.

242   "I don't think Lem had as much of a committed interest," author interview with John Seigenthaler, May 4, 2006.

244   Consumed by grief, Michaelis, *The Best of Friends,* 181.

244   "It was much harder for him than anybody." LOH.

245   "I talked to him that week," author interviews with Francis McAdoo, May 31, 2005 and June 2, 2006.

245   "Well, he could never get over it," author interview with Lucretia Billings Fisher, June 13, 2006.

245   "[W]as devastated," author interview with John Seigenthaler, May 4, 2006.

245   "I was always afraid of losing him," author interview with Sally Carpenter, July 20, 2006.

246   "It has all been shocking," David Brinkley, NBC news coverage of the assassination.

246   "There is no way of calculating," Frank McGee, ibid.

249   A month after the funeral, Teddy White, "For President Kennedy; An Epilogue," *Life* magazine, December 6, 1963.

249   "I don't think there is any consolation," *Look* magazine, November 17, 1964.

249   "I think that my biggest achievement," Jackie Kennedy to John Russell, "Portrait of a Friendship," *Time* magazine, May 30, 1994.

249   "[U]nbearable sorrow," Teddy Kennedy's eulogy to Jackie Kennedy, New York, May 23, 1994.

250   "In many ways, Lem thought of his life as being over," Michaelis, *The Best of Friends,* 182.

CHAPTER THIRTEEN—THE SEA CHANGE (1933 V. 1973)

253   The word *gay,* or even *homosexual,* author interview with Sidney Brinkley, gay rights historian, July 15, 2006. Sidney was also an early pioneer of gay rights for African Americans.

256   "[M]ore than twenty thousand gay men and women marched from Greenwich Village," Colin Spencer, *Homosexuality in History* (New York: Harcourt, 1996), 367.

257   It was probably first referenced in the United States in the 1880s, Spencer, *Homosexuality in History,* 10.

257   "[L]ook startlingly suggestive today," Charles Higham and Roy Moseley, *Cary Grant: The Lonely Heart* (Harcourt, 1989), 108.

258   "Listening to the telephone call today," telephone conversation between Lyndon Johnson and FBI Director J. Edgar Hoover, October 1964. "I guess you're going to have to teach me about this stuff," LBJ to Hoover.

258   "During World War II, an estimated," *Paragraph 175,* a documentary about repression of gays in Nazi Germany (DVD/VHS, 2000), directed by Rob Epstein and Jeffrey Friedman.

258–59 An estimated ten thousand to fifteen thousand gays, ibid.

259   "Paragraph 175 remained on the books," ibid.

260   "Many people at parties would ask me, 'Is it true about Rock Hudson?'" author interview with Doris Day, May 4, 1988.

260   [H]is agency had identified 406 "sexual deviates," Spencer, *Homosexuality in History,* 357.

262   "There is no such thing as a homosexual or heterosexual person," Gore Vidal, "Tennessee Williams: Someone to Laugh at the Squares With," *The New York Review of Books,* June 13, 1985.

264   "[N]ever talked to me about that," author interview with unnamed source.

265   "I didn't bring it up with him," author interview with Ben Bradlee, March 22, 2006.

266   "Lem was terribly confused," author interviews with Larry Quirk, July 15, 2004 and May 15, 2006.

266   "You could tell there was a strong friendship," ibid.

267   Lem "was very upset," ibid.

267   "[A]lso considers the rumors vicious," author interview with unnamed source.

268   "I don't know. He could have been," author question to Chris Lawford, book appearance, Borders, Santa Monica, October 6, 2005.

269   "Although there was a sexual element," author interviews with Larry Quirk, July 15, 2004 and May 15, 2006.

Chapter Fourteen—His Final Years (1963–81)

271   "[G]ave me an uncommon insight," Andrew Wyeth, TBC, 125.

272   "I grew up within a few blocks," John F. Kennedy Jr., ibid., 178.

274   "[W]ould ever have existed," Eunice Kennedy Shriver, TBC, 150.

277   "He didn't want to work under me in Cambridge," LOH.

278   "He was terrible," Horowitz and Collier, *The Kennedys,* 290.

278   "Stay out of this, Sarge," Anthony Shriver, TBC, 172.

280   She called the *New York Times,* "Mrs. John F. Kennedy Calls *Times* on Shooting," *New York Times,* June 5, 1968.

280   Ethel was surrounded by family, "Relatives Keep Vigil at the Hospital," *New York Times,* June 6, 1968.

281   "This became our refuge," Christopher Kennedy Lawford, *Symptoms of Withdrawal: A Memoir of Snapshots and Redemption* (New York: William Morrow, 2005), 100.

282   "I saw my aunt Ethel," ibid., 104.

283   "We shall honor him not with useless mourning," Kennedy, *Times to Remember,* 478.

283   "He was ripped apart," author interview with John Seigenthaler, May 4, 2006.

283   "Lem just couldn't get over," author interviews with Francis McAdoo, May 31, 2005 and June 2, 2006.

283   "I just don't think," author interview with John Seigenthaler, May 4, 2006.

284   "I hate this country," Jackie Kennedy, Horowitz and Collier, *The Kennedys,* 331.

284   "Lem and I were always friends," Bobby Kennedy Jr., TBC, 19.

285   "Ethel wanted various friends to help out," author interview with John Seigenthaler, May 4, 2006.

285   "[H]ad always been a person of low self-esteem," author interviews with Larry Quirk, July 15, 2004 and May 15, 2006.

285–86 "He helped Bobby a great deal," author interview with Andy Williams, August 16, 2006.

286   "He went there a lot and I went there a lot. We became quite good friends," ibid.

288   "He saw the ridiculousness of the human condition," Ethel Kennedy, TBC, 31.

288   "Lem was the most fun person," Bobby Kennedy Jr., ibid., 19.

288   "Not all of it was giddy of course," Peter Kaplan, ibid., 15.

288   "The stories he told and the examples he set," Bobby Kennedy Jr., ibid., 269.

289   "Lem was Jack Kennedy's best friend," Lawford, *Symptoms of Withdrawal,* 54.

290   "The day he told me this," ibid., 55.

290   "His love for our parents' generation," ibid., 101.

290   "I spent many years competing for Lem's attention," ibid., 101.

291   "I think it was hard on him," author interview with Lucretia Billings Fisher, June 13, 2006.

291   "He was really close to our mother," ibid.

291   "They both had a great time together," author interview with Sally Carpenter, July 20, 2006.

291   "[H]is eyes filled with tears," Ethel Kennedy, TBC, 31.

291   He would often talk about his mother, author interviews with Sigrid Gassner-Roberts, August 11 and 17, 2006.

292   "Lem and I developed a very good understanding," ibid.

292   "[T]he person he talked most about was John Kennedy," ibid.

293   "I would say he was," ibid.

296   "[B]ecame addicted to drugs," author interviews with Larry Quirk, July 15, 2004 and May 15, 2006.

296   Bobby "got a lot of magnetism from Lem's fixation," Lawford, *Symptoms of With-drawal,* 101.

298   "My god, why does he have to do it," Horowitz and Collier, *The Kennedys,* 401.

299   "Jackie was more cautious," author interviews with Larry Quirk, July 15, 2004 and May 15, 2006.

300   "We were kindred spirits," author interview with Donzaleigh Abernathy, August 27, 2006.

301   "I remember him as a very funny guy," author interview with Morris Stroud, June 6, 2006.

302   "He had grown out of touch," Horowitz and Collier, *The Kennedys,* 402.

302   "Sometimes he was the same old Lem," author interviews with Francis McAdoo, May 31, 2005 and June 2, 2006.

302   "He had times when he was in a bad mood," author interviews with Sigrid Gassner-Roberts, August 11 and 17, 2006.

303   "[T]o patch things up," author interview with Retha Gharzita, August 20, 2006.

304   Jack was the only person whom Lem had truly loved, author interviews with Larry Quirk, July 15, 2004 and May 15, 2006.

305   "He had just come back from Timmy Shriver's graduation," Jeff Ruhe, TBC, 189.

306   "So many grown-ups lose their sense of play," Jackie Kennedy, TBC, 209.

306   "It says a lot about their relationship," author interview with Retha Gharzita, August 20, 2006.

306   "He felt pain for every one of us," eulogy for Lem by Bobby Kennedy Jr., May 30, 1981, TBC, 269.

306–7 "I'm sure he's already organizing," Eunice Kennedy Shriver, ibid., 150.

Bibliography

∽

Alsop, Joseph, and Adam Platt. *I've Seen the Best of It.* New York: W. W. Norton & Co., 1992.

Andersen, Christopher. *Jack and Jackie: Portrait of an American Marriage.* New York: Avon, 1997.

Anthony, Carl Sferrazza. *The Kennedy White House: Family Life and Pictures, 1961–63.* New York: Touchstone, 2002.

Baldrige, Letitia, with Rene Verdon. *In the Kennedy Style: Magical Evenings in the Kennedy White House.* New York: Doubleday, 1998.

Blair, Joan, and Clay Blair Jr. *The Search for JFK.* New York: Putnam, 1976.

Bradlee, Benjamin C. *A Good Life.* New York: Simon and Schuster, 1995.

———. *Conversations with Kennedy.* New York: Norton, 1975.

Branch, Taylor. *Parting the Waters: America in the King Years 1954–63.* New York: Touchstone, 1988.

Clark, Thurston. *Ask Not: The Inauguration of John F. Kennedy and the Speech That Changed America.* New York: Henry Holt and Co., 2004.

Collier, Peter, and David Horowitz. *The Kennedys: An American Drama.* New York: Warner, 1984.

Cooper, Ilene. *Jack: The Early Years of John F. Kennedy.* New York: Dutton Juvenile, 2003.

Dallek, Robert. *An Unfinished Life: John F. Kennedy, 1917–1963.* New York: Little, Brown and Company, 2003.

David, Lester. *Jacqueline Kennedy Onassis: A Portrait of Her Private Years.* New York: St. Martin's Press, 1995.

Davis, John. *The Bouviers: Portrait of an American Family.* New York: Farrar, Strauss, 1969.

Fay, Paul B. Jr. *The Pleasure of His Company.* New York: Harper and Row, 1966.

Gailbraith, John Kenneth. *A Life in Our Time.* Boston: Houghton Mifflin, 1981.

Garside, Anne. *Camelot at Dawn: Jacqueline and John Kennedy in Georgetown, May 1954.* Baltimore: John Hopkins University Press, 2001.

Giglio, James. *The Presidency of John F. Kennedy.* Lawrence: University of Kansas Press, 1991.

Goodwin, Doris Kearns. *The Fitzgeralds and the Kennedys: An American Saga.* New York: Simon and Schuster, 1987.

Guthman, Edwin O., and Jeffrey Shulman. *Robert Kennedy in His Own Words.* New York: Bantam, 1988.

Hamilton, Nigel. *Reckless Youth.* New York: Random House, 1992.

Harrison, Barbara, and Daniel Terris. *A Twilight Struggle: The Life of John Fitzgerald Kennedy.* New York: Harper Collins, 1992.

Henderson, Deirdre. *Prelude to Leadership: The European Diary of John F. Kennedy.* Washington, D.C.: Regnery, 1995.

Hersh, Seymour. *The Dark Side of Camelot.* New York: Little, Brown, 1997.

Heymann, C. David. *A Woman Named Jackie: An Intimate Biography of Jacqueline Bouvier Kennedy Onassis.* New York: Lyle Stuart, 1989.

Higham, Charles, and Roy Moseley. *Cary Grant: The Lonely Heart.* New York: Harcourt, 1989.

Kennedy, John F. *Why England Slept.* New York: Wilfred Funk, 1940.

———. *As We Remember Joe.* Cambridge, MA: privately printed at the university press, 1945.

———. *Profiles in Courage.* New York: Harper, 1955.

Kennedy, Joseph P. *I'm for Roosevelt.* New York: Reynal and Hitchcock, 1936.

Kennedy, Rose. *Times to Remember.* New York: Doubleday, 1974.

Klein, Edward. *All Too Human: The Love Story of Jack and Jackie Kennedy.* New York: Pocket Books, 1997.

Lambert, Gavin. *Natalie Wood: A Life.* New York: Knopf, 2004.

Lawford, Christopher Kennedy. *Symptoms of Withdrawal: A Memoir of Snapshots and Redemption.* New York: William Morrow, 2005.

Lawford, Patricia Seaton. *The Peter Lawford Story.* New York: Carroll & Graf, 1988.

Leamer, Laurence. *The Kennedy Men: 1901–63.* New York: William Morrow, 2001.

————. *The Kennedy Women.* New York: Villard, 1994.

Leaming, Barbara. *Mrs. Kennedy: The Missing History of the Kennedy Years.* New York: Free Press, 2001.

Levy, Shawn. *Rat Pack Confidential.* New York: Doubleday, 1988.

Lincoln, Evelyn. *My Twelve Years with John F. Kennedy.* Boulder: Black Pebbles Publishing, 2003.

————. *My Twelve Years with John F. Kennedy.* New York: David McKay, 1965.

Loviny, Christopher, and Vincent Touze. *Jack: Remembering Jack.* San Francisco: Seuil Chronicle Books, 2003.

Manchester, William. *The Death of a President.* New York: Harper & Rowe, 1967.

Martin, Ralph. *A Hero for Our Time.* New York: Ballantine, 1984.

————. *Seeds of Destruction: Joe Kennedy and His Sons.* New York: Putnam Publishing Group, 1995.

Michaelis, David. *The Best of Friends.* New York: William Morrow, 1983.

Nichols, Jack. *The Gay Agenda: Talking Back to the Fundamentalists.* Amherst: Prometheus Books, 1996.

O'Brien, Michael. *John F. Kennedy: A Biography.* New York: St. Martin's Griffin, 2006.

O'Donnell, Kenny, and David Powers with Joe McCarthy. *Johnny We Hardly Knew Ye: Memories of John Fitzgerald Kennedy.* New York: Little, Brown, 1972.

Oppenheimer, Jerry. *The Other Mrs. Kennedy: Ethel Skakel Kennedy: An American Drama of Power, Privilege, and Politics.* New York: St. Martin's Press, 1994.

Parmet, Herbert S. *Jack: The Presidency of John F. Kennedy.* New York: Dial Press, 1980.

Perret, Geoffrey. *Jack: A Life Like No Other.* New York: Random House, 2002.

Plimpton, George. *Truman Capote: In Which Various Friends, Enemies, Acquaintances and Detractors Recall His Turbulent Career.* New York: Anchor, 1998.

Reeves, Richard. *President Kennedy: Profile of Power.* New York: Simon and Schuster, 1993.

Renehan, Edward. *The Kennedys at War 1937–1945.* New York: Doubleday, 2002.

Salinger, Pierre. *With Kennedy.* New York: Doubleday, 1966.

Schlesinger, Arthur Jr. *A Thousand Days: John F. Kennedy in the White House.* New York: Houghton Mifflin Co., 1965.

Sinatra, Tina, and Jeff Coplon. *My Father's Daughter.* New York: Simon and Schuster 2000.

Smith, Sally Bedell. *Grace and Power: The Private World of the Kennedy White House.* New York: Random House, 2004.

Sorensen, Theodore. *Let the Word Go Forth.* New York: Dell, 1998.

————. *The Kennedy Legacy.* New York: MacMillan, 1969.

Spencer, Colin. *Homosexuality in History.* New York: Harcourt, 1996.

Spoto, Donald. *Jacqueline Bouvier Kennedy Onassis: A Life.* New York: St. Martin's Press, 2000.

Tierney, Gene. *Self Portrait.* New York: Berkeley Books, 1979.

Vidal, Gore. *Palimpsest: A Memoir.* New York: Penguin, 1995.

Waldron, Lamar, and Thom Hartmann. *Ultimate Sacrifice: John and Robert Kennedy, the Plan for a Coup in Cuba, and The Murder of JFK.* New York: Carroll & Graf, 2005.

West, J. B. *Upstairs at the White House: My Life with the First Ladies.* New York: Coward, McCann & Geoghegan, 1973.

White, Theodore H. *The Making of the President 1960.* New York: Atheneum, 1961.

Wyden, Peter. *Bay Of Pigs: The Untold Story.* New York: Simon and Schuster, 1979.

Yoder, Edwin Jr. *Joe Alsop's Cold War: A Study of Journalistic Influence.* Chapel Hill: University of North Carolina Press, 1955.

Index

∾